Science for a Polite Society

SCIENCE
for a
POLITE
SOCIETY

Gender, Culture, and the Demonstration of Enlightenment

Geoffrey V. Sutton

WestviewPress
A Division of HarperCollinsPublishers

Published in 1995 in the United States of America by Westview Press, Inc., 5500 Central Avenue, Boulder, Colorado 80301-2877, and in the United Kingdom by Westview Press, 12 Hid's Copse Road, Cumnor Hill, Oxford OX2 9JJ

Library of Congress Cataloging-in-Publication Data
Sutton, Geoffrey V.
Science for a polite society : gender, culture, and the
     demonstration of enlightenment / Geoffrey V. Sutton.
         p.   cm.
     Includes bibliographical references and index.
     ISBN 0-8133-1575-1. — ISBN 0-8133-1576-X (pbk.)
     1. Science—History—17th century.   2. Science—History—18th
century.   3. Science—Philosophy—History—17th century.
4. Science—Philosophy—History—18th century.   I. Title.
Q125.S982   1995
509.4′09032—dc20   95-20157
                                                                             CIP

The paper used in this publication meets the requirements of the American National Standard for Permanence of Paper for Printed Library Materials Z39.48-1984.

10   9   8   7   6   5   4   3   2   1

Contents

Figures

Preface

This project has taken longer than most first books by academic authors, since I have never been subjected to a tenure review. I certainly hope that the length of time it has required, and the circumstances surrounding its composition, have made it a more mature work than it would otherwise have been; I know that I owe thanks to a more diverse group of readers, critics, and sources of encouragement than would have been the case had my career demonstrated conventional academic success.

The early chapters are drawn from dissertation research. I was fortunate to spend my graduate years in the Program in History and Philosophy of Science and the Department of History at Princeton University. My fellow students provided an intellectual cohort and social circle that demonstrates that youth is not always wasted on the young. JoAnn Morse remains my closest intellectual companion and my most helpful critic. Ted Porter, Larry Owens, Peter Dear, Renato Pasta, Monica Green, and Jim Secord were contemporaries there, and we shared what seems still to have been a superb education. John Servos was a young enough member of the faculty to join our circle. Senior professors permanent and visiting whose names will lend dignity to this preface include Thomas Kuhn, Charles Gillispie, Anthony Grafton, Michael Mahoney, Robert Fox, Michael Mulkay, Robert Darnton, and Lawrence Stone. None of them should be held responsible for anything that follows—indeed many may disagree with much that I say—but all contributed in important ways to my development as a historian.

The vicissitudes of the academic market provided me with a post-doctoral fellowship at the Bakken Library and the University of Minnesota. Roger Stuewer engineered the position—a feat much more difficult and unusual in history of science departments a dozen years ago than now. Leonard Wilson and John Eyler were kind enough to provide me with an office and an intellectual community in the university's Department of History of Medicine. Fred Fellows and Karen Johnson provided stimulating conversation about a more technical style of history of physics than I had been accustomed to. The Bakken was a delightful place to work; its incomparable museum collection and thorough eighteenth-century electrical library provided the sources for the latter half of this book. Elizabeth Ihrig and Albert Kuhfeld were wonderfully cooperative staff and also very kind to me personally during my three years as their most persistent patron. The Bakken also provided a constant stream of interesting visiting scholars, including Lisa Rosner, Willem Hackmann, and I. Bernard Cohen. I benefited tremendously from their expertise.

The postdoc having proven no more useful in terms of gainful employment than a Ph.D., I found my way to another, very different, sort of community. For the past decade I have worked in the Physics Department at Macalester College, running the laboratories and demonstrations for the first-year physics courses. My colleagues, especially Sung Kyu Kim and Ray Mikkelson, have been incredibly generous; they have tolerated the vast, peculiar gaps in my training and taught me a great deal about the practice of science education and science. Without their support and encouragement I would never have embarked on this project.

Macalester's program in Gender Studies sponsored a number of courses in the history of science, which allowed me to keep my hand in the field and to remember how much I like it. I was invited to join an informal faculty writing group, run primarily by Michal McCall and Karen Warren, and including Roxane Gudeman, Diane Glancy, and Ruthanne Kurth-Schai, and to show them what have become two of the chapters that follow. I thank them especially, and Ted Porter and I. Bernard Cohen, for encouraging me to write this book without the usual inducements and support offered college faculty. I hope that they will find it worthy of their urgings. Ted Porter and Peter Dear both read near-complete drafts and offered advice and encouragement. Westview Press likewise decided to take a chance on an unconventional author and extended every courtesy.

Finally, I must thank my family. My sons, Joshua and Jonah, have tolerated a father whose work has been extended too much. JoAnn Morse has not only provided constant encouragement; she has read and criticized more drafts of more chapters than either of us likes to think about. She is constant proof that our educations were not wasted, even though neither of us managed to find a professorial job. Her intellect is livelier than those of most academics, and she has found that embracing the challenge of life in business does not exclude her from the life of the mind. By all rights she ought to be a coauthor of this book.

Geoffrey V. Sutton

Science for a Polite Society

1

The Introduction, in which the Author offers two tales of the Scientific Revolution

My INTEREST IN THE SCIENTIFIC REVOLUTION began with a fascination with its science. What follows offers an explanation for the growth of the new science of the seventeenth and eighteenth centuries. It is not a technical history, strictly speaking, of the physics and astronomy and chemistry developed by students of nature. Instead, it is a cultural history of the birth of the new science in seventeenth- and eighteenth-century France. It will concern itself with the women and men who practiced what they usually called "natural philosophy" and "natural history," and with the literary and cultural reflections of the new science in the mirror of polite society. Much of the material taken up in this cultural history has generally been viewed as the puff pieces surrounding science rather than science itself. Yet the story is ultimately and fundamentally about the science of the scientific revolution, and it will not recoil from technical niceties when they are necessary. To follow certain aspects of the intellectual development of astronomy and physics and chemistry is no more than the ladies or the gentlemen of the courts of Louis XIV and Louis XV expected of themselves, and it carries many rewards. Not the least of these is the inherent interest of the material.

The aim of the study is to show that the French adopted science as the basis for their Enlightenment because of their very personal fascination with the philosophy of nature and the history of its creatures. Theirs was not a spectator's respect for the accomplishments of others, a conviction that someone or some group had discovered

1

profound but arcane truths about the world. (The notion that such discoveries might have had such an effect on that culture is at any rate rather naïve.) Long before anyone could justify the truth of her or his opinions about the natural world, the ladies and gentlemen of France embraced the new science. Indeed, on several important occasions they had to change their minds about the physical construction of the worlds they examined. Their faith in natural philosophy survived even the rejection of the particular philosophies they had accepted. It is this larger faith in natural philosophy, a widely based movement in elite culture, that I hope to present in what follows. The particular philosophies are but the details required to tell the larger tale.

This approach might seem to put some cultural cart before some technical horse. The outcome of the cultural history will nonetheless offer an interpretation of the scientific revolution in all its technical glory. The thesis that accompanies this story is that the cultural institutions within which the new science emerged provided not only the context but also the direction for the development of the new natural philosophy of the seventeenth and eighteenth centuries. Conversely, opposition to various new aspects of physical theory, which is often attributed to the philosophical and cultural prejudices of the French, depended quite reasonably on technical objections, especially to the new science from Britain.

There has long been a standard story, itself in part a product of the French Enlightenment, about the development of science in the seventeenth and eighteenth centuries.[1] According to that story, the birth of the new science represented the discovery of immutable truths about nature. This intellectual odyssey began with the astronomical system of Nicholas Copernicus, who produced a mathematical model for the motion of the planets around the stationary sun. The theory appeared in 1543 in his book *De Revolutionibus,* "On the Revolutions of the Heavenly Bodies," which suggested the name of the "Scientific Revolution" to describe the developments that followed. The Copernican solar system revived the technical pursuit of a Platonic belief that the heavens are essentially mathematical and perfect but rejected the ancient notion that the earth was the center of the world. This parochial prejudice, embraced as a central item of dogma by the Catholic church, caused the Copernican system to remain a bit of abstruse mathematical science.

Half a century and more later, the story continues, four scientists more or less simultaneously discovered the basis for a new science. Three of them embraced the Copernican hypothesis; all four saw their work as an alternative to the cumbersome Christianized Aristotelian worldview that dominated the teaching of the schools. The courage and genius of these early-seventeenth-century thinkers transformed the obscure musings of the solitary Polish cleric into the basis for a new, modern worldview.

The oldest of the new generation of scientific revolutionaries was Galileo Galilei. He turned the newly invented telescope to the heavens and saw in the phases of Venus and the moons of Jupiter irrefutable proof of the truth of the heliocentric hypothesis. Galileo was so struck by this truth that he stared down the Inquisition for the right to proclaim it, although he suffered dire consequences for his courage. Embracing the same Platonic notion of a mathematically perfect universe that had inspired Copernicus, Galileo derived the laws that govern falling bodies in an abstract world freed from the complicating factors of friction and air resistance.

Johannes Kepler, Galileo's younger contemporary, found his evidence for the correctness of heliocentrism in the theory itself. He took on the challenge of perfecting the Copernican system. Armed with data on planetary positions collected fanatically by the Danish astronomer Tycho Brahe, Kepler formulated three laws of planetary motion. These described planetary paths around the sun shaped like ellipses rather than the complicated combinations of perfect circular motion embraced by Copernicus. Kepler's love of calculation allowed him to discover that the square of the time required for each planet to revolve around the sun bears a constant ratio to the cube of the planet's distance from the sun, and that the area of the elliptical sector swept out by a planet is directly proportional to the time required to move along the chord that bounds the sector—that is to say, the closer a planet is to the sun, the faster it moves.

René Descartes, also a heliocentrist of Kepler's generation and the third of our four revolutionaries, developed a new style of mathematics—analytic geometry—which differed markedly from the geometrical style practiced by Copernicus and Kepler. Cartesian mathematics proved extremely conducive to the development of physical theory. Descartes himself applied that algebraic system most successfully to the study of light, achieving a veritable revolution in the science of optics, which enabled algebraists to perfect the design of lenses for use in instruments like telescopes and microscopes. More important still, Descartes's algebra provided the basis for a quantitative approach to magnitude in general, which allow the mathematization of a broad range of natural phenomena.

Fourth in this generation, the British Lord Chancellor Francis Bacon formulated an empirical method for the study of science that set out a method for the systematic scientific investigation. Bacon's contribution came in the organization of the scientific enterprise rather than insights of technical genius like those of his contemporaries. He explained how scientists of more modest talent, engaging in collaborative efforts, could sift exhaustively through the materials of the world to discover their wonders and secrets.

Beginning with the generation after this group of early-seventeenth-century thinkers, progress in science became continuous and unified. A large school of experimentalists, most notably Robert Boyle, discovered and catalogued a huge collection of facts about the world. In the process of this great enterprise they invented the air pump and demonstrated the truth of Galileo's predictions about motion in the absence of air resistance. A number of gifted mathematicians (Christiaan Huygens is usually cited as the strongest) used Cartesian algebra to develop Galileo's rules of motion to embrace nearly all of the motion of bodies in the laboratory and in everyday life. This knowledge produced a myriad of useful devices, including the pendulum clock, convincing everyone of the truth of the theoretical systems that allowed their development. Huygens and his contemporaries also developed ever more powerful telescopes to provide more material and confirmation for mathematical astronomy, and microscopes to open the world of the invisibly small to a similar scrutiny. They participated in the foundation of permanent scientific institutions, most notably the Royal Society of London and the Académie Royale des Sciences in Paris. These institutions established a permanent and verifiable record of Baconian investigation and mathematical theory alike.

Finally, in the last decades of the seventeenth century "the incomparable Sir Isaac Newton" produced a brilliant mathematical synthesis of the work of the midcentury scientific community. His *Mathematical Principles of Natural Philosophy,* known by its Latin short title, the *Principia,* provided three laws of motion that applied not only to bodies on the surface of the earth but also to planets in the heavens. Newton used his mathematical description of the causes of motion to derive the terrestrial mechanics that described phenomena like collisions and falling bodies, already understood by the practitioners of Descartes's mathematics. Newton's laws of motion, coupled with his law of universal gravitation, could be manipulated to explain the celestial mechanics described by Kepler's laws of planetary motion. Furthermore, Newton's understanding of the underlying forces that produced these laws allowed the required if barely discernible mathematical corrections to Kepler's laws. In principle, Newtonian theory provided the basis for an understanding of planetary motion so complete it survived intact until the twentieth century and has required only the subtlest of correction, provided by no less a thinker than Albert Einstein.

According to the standard story, the eighteenth century consolidated the advances of the seventeenth. A host of mathematically adept practitioners worked out the details of Newton's theories and applied them to problems both celestial and terrestrial. Organized, systematic investigation of the stuff of the world continued on a massive scale. The most successful avenue of inquiry produced the new phenomena of electricity, and a theoretical framework provided by the mathematical sciences allowed the reduction of these phenomena first to qualitative and then to quantitative laws by the end of the century. A similar process was brought to bear on phenomena related to heat—Bacon's own favorite problem. The ensuing researches spawned a revolution in chemistry that followed the one in electricity and produced a self-consciously methodical science based on the rhetoric and precepts of the Enlightenment.

With the triumph of science came a sort of intellectual prestige that made it a model of what rationality should be. The Enlightenment of the eighteenth century took scientific thought as the basis for human progress. Enlightened thinkers believed that the application of the methods and techniques of scientific theory could reform political and economic thought, just as the applied fruits of scientific physics and chemistry could improve the human condition. The revolution in science was transformed into a scientific revolution in the organization of all human activity.

The story is of course told with much greater subtlety than this description of it allows. It has been long acknowledged, for example, that the various contributors to the scientific revolution did not always agree with one another. The most famous individual arguments came between Isaac Newton and Gottfried Wilhelm Leibniz, the two inventors of the mathematical calculus. Their disagreement ranged from questions of notation and formulation of mathematical theory through differences on technical points in physics—most notably questions involving quantities now characterized as momentum and energy—to full-scale philosophical rejection of each other's most basic notions of how to practice science. A more general division between French Cartesians, British Newtonians, and German Leibnizians involved whole schools of scientific thinkers. The most embarrassing point for those who wished to see a uniform march toward the truth came when the Cartesians rejected Newton's law of universal gravitation and the Leibnizians rejected his laws of motion in the last decade of the seventeenth century—rejections that continued through the first quarter of the eighteenth.

Reconciling problems of this sort led to a bit of a revolution in the scholarship that concerns itself with science studies, generally associated with Thomas Kuhn's *The Structure of Scientific Revolutions.*[2] Most of those who study scientific change seriously now acknowledge that scientists are as intellectually conservative as any other scholars and that change takes time measured in decades and generations and often fails to touch individuals brought up in the old ways. The virtues of progress and right thinking, the notions that the truth will out and demonstrably false theories will wither, have largely been transferred from the individual scientist (with the exception of the occasional towering genius) to the long-term collective wisdom of the scientific community.

More recently, and in intellectual terms more daringly, historians of science have come to acknowledge that the development of new theories is neither so rational nor so systematic as the old, standard story seemed to indicate. Kepler held views distinctly mystical; these shrouded his work in a style of presentation that the modern reader finds nearly impenetrable. (Indeed it has become something of a cliché in the literature of science to say that Newton's greatest achievement was discovering Kepler's three laws buried in the vast and confused Latin tomes that contained them.) Newton, too, had strong and well-documented mystical beliefs and hoped to direct his scientific efforts to ends distinctly alchemical. The medical and chemical and chemical and mathematical traditions of the sixteenth and seventeenth centuries are filled with mysticism and unscientific spirituality. All these things, it is clear, contributed to the growth of what became modern science.

In addition to this increasing sophistication and subtlety about the technical development of science, there is a growing literature concerning the social context and institutional support for science in early modern Europe. Scholars have turned their attention both to the internal constitution of the community of practitioners and to the patronage and promotion of scientific practice by the state and the social elites. Although, with a few brave exceptions, this scholarship remains notably silent about the relations between the social and the intellectual aspects of scientific practice, accounts of the scientific revolution no longer ignore the fact that science is a social activity.

Despite tremendous changes in the historiography of science, several crucial elements of the old, standard story remain essentially unchanged. Histories of science, influenced by sometime ties to the philosophy of science, have tended to use arguments about what science was or might have been to explain what science is, or might be, or should be. The answers to the appropriate questions are practically literary conventions: Science is objective; it proceeds methodically; it is quantitative and disinterested. Physical theory produces exclusive, correct descriptions of the physical world. Although the contemplation of nature occasionally inspires its own peculiar brand of creativity, that creativity is not artistic or literary. Science, in the shorthand of the academy, is hard rather than soft and masculine rather than feminine, as its practitioners and aficionados are male rather than female. Above all, scientific advances are (ultimately) accepted because they are true, and their truth is self-evident to all who understand the arguments. Even the harshest critics of science and scientific practice have largely accepted these characterizations, occasionally painting them as deficiencies rather than advantages, but assuming that they characterize the essence of science.

I shall not pronounce upon what science is or what it should be. Yet I will venture to say what science was in France in the seventeenth and eighteenth centuries. In its essentials, the new science began as a literary pursuit, allowing great latitude in discourse about nature. It offered a source of polite conversation for dabblers as well as a discipline for the serious; it was a more callow pursuit than the scholarly fields of philology and metaphysics; it appealed to feminine culture; women frequently were devotees of the study of nature and contributed significantly to the development of natural philosophy.

The new science matured in a number of ways during the eighteenth century. Above all, it attracted adherents because it provided a source of amusement and spectacle. The demonstration-lecture, replete with explosions and splashes and sparks, became the primary locus for the exposition of the truth of science and by extension for the demonstration of Enlightenment. It was in this locus, I suggest, that the great experimental advances of the eighteenth century found their driving force, and that the philosophes found their faith in the progressive nature of the scientific method.

I hope that what follows will show that these gentler attributes of natural philosophy in seventeenth- and eighteenth-century Paris proved crucial to the way in which the field entered into the intellectual world. The glorification of the scientist as socially inept, whether out of deviousness or good intentions, is a more recent invention. If the secrets of nature were apples of gold, the natural philosopher needed still to present them in vessels of silver in order to enchant the courtiers of Louis XIV's France. Within that polite society, nothing could have been more gauche or more certain to alienate than persistent insistence upon the truth. In the event, when socially maladroit experts did stand upon their authority, they invariably suffered ostracism.

Moreover, insistence on the truth of any scientific cosmology that was accepted through the first third of the eighteenth century would have had little demonstrable basis in fact. Within the context of the traditional account of the history of science, acceptance of the new science of the seventeenth and eighteenth centuries hardly required explanation. Instead, explanations have been offered to account for rejection of science by an intellectual world with minds apparently closed. Like Galileo, most historians have taken the truth of the emerging science of the seventeenth century to be self-evident. The response to challenges to this view has always been to insist (rarely with Galileo's wit or with his arrogance) upon the truth of the scientists' position. A more careful examination of the seventeenth-century evidence presents a decidedly different picture. Justification for true opinions about matters scientific came more slowly than those who believe in the importance of those opinions find comfortable.

Only in retrospect did the famous quantitative achievements of the seventeenth century verify the claims of their authors even to save the phenomena. Johannes Kepler's three laws of planetary motion turned out, it is true, to describe the paths of the wandering stars with astounding precision. Yet there were detectable departures between even Kepler's theory and the observed behavior of the heavens, although these were smaller than for any previous theory. They were large enough, nonetheless, that seventeenth-century astronomers were by no means unanimous in their acceptance of Kepler's laws. No reasonable reader could be convinced of the truth of Kepler's laws by studying the huge Latin tomes that articulated them, and no one managed to extend Kepler's convoluted reasoning to improve upon the agreement betweeen those laws and observations.

Kepler's work instead served as a point of departure. Contrary to the popular mythology, astronomers before Newton did perform their calculations of planetary positions on the basis of elliptical orbits. Indeed, a few consciously and effectively departed from the safe haven offered by the theory of elliptical orbits, attempting as Newton did to improve its agreement with the phenomena. The story of the development of astronomy apart from the great Newtonian revolution between the middle of the seventeenth century and the middle of the eighteenth remains largely untold. The lively community that practiced the craft did not simply perform blind Keplerian calculations and await the coming of Newton; they believed that they, like students of terrestrial mechanics, moved ever closer to complete solutions along other avenues. It was, at any rate, Kepler's work and that of other empirical astronomers, unaided by Newtonian theory, that produced all tables of planetary position until well into the eighteenth century. The law of universal gravitation, to be sure, appeared as a tantalizing bit of theory. Yet its only major seventeenth-century prediction—concerning the shape of the earth—appeared to be wrong. Given this unpropitious beginning, no one but Newton pursued the theory through the incredibly difficult mathematical work required to make precise predictions of planetary motions.

Evidence for these highly technical claims will appear quite naturally in the course of this cultural account of the scientific revolution. For the present, however, suffice it to observe that justification of true opinions about the physical world did not come in time to explain the acceptance of science as an exemplar for intellectual activity during the early and enthusiastic years of the Enlightenment. Indeed, opinions both false and fleeting served in many cases to convince the Parisian elite of the importance, and even of the truth, of science. What requires explanation, then, is not why some early modern Europeans rejected the new science; that is easy enough to understand. Instead, we must find some reason why others, notably the literary elite in Paris in the mid–seventeenth century, decided to embrace natural philosophy as an example of a new intellectual order suitable to replace the centuries-old Aristotelianism of the schools. Only after an essentially universal acceptance among thinking people did the technical community produce a science that lived up to even the most modest Enlightenment claims—that natural philosophers could describe nature accurately and predict the paths of the most circumscribed motions with confidence.

What this study will offer is an answer to the question why, or at least how, the social elite in Paris came to accept science as both valid and interesting. Along the way, the character of that science will necessarily emerge. As we consider the natural history and natural philosophy of Louis XIV's Paris, we must be prepared to find something rather different from a modern scientific school. French science at the time is usually characterized as Cartesian, and in some sense that is true. Yet we must not look, in Kuhn's terms, for a Cartesian paradigm—a model series of questions and answers that any Cartesian scientist would have mastered as a rite of passage into the Cartesian school. Instead we must accept the term as it was used in common language in the eighteenth century. To be Cartesian in this context was simply to be clever, perhaps to set things in order, and always to exercise a peculiarly French genius. Descartes, to be sure, was Cartesian in this sense. So also, in the parlance of the late seventeenth century, was Puss in Boots—first introduced in published form at that time. Both the philosopher and the cat of folklore found their way into the literature of salon culture through the vehicle of the brothers Perrault. Charles Perrault, author of the collection of fairy tales that established the canonical Puss in Boots, provided in his *contes* a world every bit as clever as did Claude Perrault when he wrote an essay on the Cartesian theory of gravity. Equally important for the acceptance of the new science, Claude's essay on gravity offered the same elegance, *politesse,* and ineffable Frenchness as did Charles's fairy tales. The two cultural forms were equally definitive of and derivative from the Golden Age of the Sun King, Louis XIV's France.

This is not to say that the Cartesian natural philosopher could say just anything. It is rather to assert that defining or detecting what is Cartesian about Claude Perrault's science is a subtle thing, akin to defining or detecting what is French about Charles Perrault's fairy tales. Certain characteristics of the Cartesian physical world are fairly constant: It was a mechanical world; it was filled with tiny particles called "subtle matters" whose shapes and sizes and motions could be expressed with exquisite precision; these particles bumped and swirled and pushed one another and equally precisely defined particles of visible and sensible matter. These characteristics came to be called the Cartesian "system," a name as vague as "paradigm" in our own time and place. Apart from its broad outlines, there were few rules for the Cartesian philosopher; explanation within this framework was a creative art.

The creative art of Cartesian explanation within the context of the system bore tremendous fruit. On the one hand, it allowed even the casual amateur to understand her world; it provided a system in which the dilettante could phrase his description of the quickly expanding natural history of wonders and curiosities. On the other hand, it provided a theoretical framework for the development of detailed mathematical models. The first and clearest example of the significance of such a framework came in an analysis by Huygens of the swirling of the subtle matters that cause bodies to weigh down toward the center of the earth. Combined with Galileo's mathematical description of falling bodies, this analysis led to the formulation of mathematical rules governing the motion of bodies moving along circular paths. These rules were correct and have survived quite independent of the system that spawned them; their discovery and its publication as it occurred cannot be imagined outside of the intellectual and cultural context of Cartesian science.

The particulars of the Cartesian system were not, however, rigid or uniformly mathematical. It has been quite properly observed that for most of the interesting phenomena in natural history during the early years of the eighteenth century, explanations offered by French Cartesians and British Newtonians seem essentially interchangeable. The terminology is different—British thinkers developed an early aversion to Frenchified "subtle matters"—and to the aficionado there is a certain Cartesian cleverness in the French texts that contrasts with a sort of homespun simplicity peculiar to the stolid British householder. It is in the cultural as well as the philosophical niceties of the two schools that we must look to locate the distinctions between the natural philosophies emerging on opposite sides of the channel; to find a pair of paradigms that differentiates the two is a quixotic task at best.

To the modern philosopher of science unmoved by a sociological disposition, the sins of the Cartesians far exceed the failure to implement a paradigm. The cleverest explanations in the system were never verifiable; the whole point of the invocation of subtle matters to explain natural phenomena is that these materials manifest themselves only indirectly through matters so "gross" as to be sensible, literally accessible to the senses. More careful reflection on verifiability produces an even more stringent demand: A theory must be falsifiable. That is to say, a theory must make predictions that result in observable phenomena. The predictions, to be sure, lend credence to the theory if they prove accurate; they must also be able to disconfirm the theory if they prove inaccurate. This is a criterion rather more general than the old notion of the crucial experiment, already current in the eighteenth century, which would choose between two theories that predicted different results. The doctrine of falsifiability calls for the abandonment of a theory despite the lack of any alternative should a prediction prove false. Although working scientists in fact rarely concede that their theories have been utterly falsified, the criterion seems to be a good one to employ in the judgment of theories in their early stages—the "paradigm formation" period so crucial to the analysis of the scientific revolution.

The modern philosopher's stringent theoretical test must seem to miss the point of philosophical practice in Louis XIV's Paris. Falsifiability would have denied precisely the Cartesian cleverness that the French brought to bear on matters scientific and otherwise. In fact, the system had a built-in deniability. A notion on which all Cartesians seemed to agree was that there are an infinite number of ways in which plausible subtle matters might manipulate the gross stuff of the world to produce any given outcome. According to Descartes himself, the role of experiment was to determine which of these ways might in fact operate in the world we inhabit.

The rather casual Cartesian approach to the contingency of opinions about the physical world might at first seem to fly in the face not only of modern ideas about physical theory but also of seventeenth-century thought. For Kepler and Newton, to be sure, the laws of nature provided a window into the mind of God; anomalies in physical theory represented fundamental error, probably indicating deficiencies in the soul as well as in the intellect of the scientist. For the Cartesians, however, the manipulation of subtle matters within the broadest outlines sketched above seemed more an exercise in cleverness. In the same way that participants in the culture that produced Molière's farces dismissed the political philosophy of the British as overly serious boorishness, they found Newton's deep distrust of hypotheses and his delving into the ontology of causality a bit embarrassing—more so for him than for them. Yet his ruminations and criticisms hardly presented a serious objection to the successes of a system that had beat him to the formulation of the laws of centrifugal force. Indeed, the Cartesians were the ones who described the shape of the earth as the best early-eighteenth-century measurements found it. In short, the soundness of the basic approach using subtle matters did not seem in doubt. It was in the details that the Cartesian philosophy allowed its practitioners latitude.

As Perrault's Puss in Boots could bring to bear an understanding of human behavior to find just the right, "Cartesian," solution out of a multitude of possibilities to produce the most satisfying outcome for his master, so the adept natural philosopher could puzzle out just the right solution from a range of plausible ones—all the more satisfying if a bit surprising—to explain the behavior of the stuff of the world. An anomaly in this scheme meant simply that nature had tricked the philosopher and usually demanded nothing more than a little twist in the tale. Nothing could be more French, more Cartesian, in the event of an anomaly than to apply such a twist in order to, as they would say, *tromper le trompeur*—to trick the trickster—and save the phenomena with a new subtle matter or a new, invisible hook or hole in the stuff of the gross world. An elegant presentation, both verbally and mathematically, counted for a great deal in natural philosophy, as in all things in Paris and Versailles.

The success and power of this broadly Cartesian system persisted in France through the middle of the eighteenth century. The locus for the growth of the system of subtle matters changed slowly. Clever manipulation of the gross and subtle stuff of the world passed from the verbal to the physical realm. During the eighteenth century, amateurs of science observed and acquired increasingly sophisticated philosophical apparatus capable of controlling the motion and the effects of the materials posited in their discussions. Technical mastery over the surprising secrets of nature proceeded from the manipulation of the barometer and colliding balls (already well in hand by the middle part of the seventeenth century) through the air pump and chemical explosions (developed for public display by the turn of the century) to the most elaborate and energetic electrical machines employed before the emergence of high-energy physics in the twentieth century. The effects of these machines—which by the end of the eighteenth century produced sparks more than a foot long, accompanied by crackling sounds and even secondary explosions sufficient to blow the roofs off toy houses and model churches—seem more worthy of Dr. Frankenstein than of Puss in Boots. It is difficult to imagine the effect they must have produced in a society that illuminated its evenings with tallow candles.

Yet until the end of the old regime, the participants, the patter, and the pleasures evoked in the great lecture halls and demonstration theaters of Paris remained thoroughly charming, elegant, and clever. The science of entertainment, the philosophy of shocks and sparks: These rather than the elegance of Newton's description of the motions of the planets convinced the eighteenth century of the power of the new philosophy to describe and especially to control nature. The huge majority of the philosophes who did not themselves participate in the mid-century elucidation of gravitational theory (like the vast majority of modern believers in the truth and the rationality of science) adopted their respectful attitude out of wonder at nature in the lecture hall rather than out of understanding of the dance of the planets. My aim in what follows is to make plausible the wonder of nature in the literary salon, in the demonstration theater, and on the amateur's table top. It must have produced a fascination so engaging as to make a whole society change its mind about what is interesting and valid and true, for the age of the Enlightenment certainly believed that science was all those things.

PART ONE
Science in the Reign of Louis XIII

2

Pawning off the New Science: Theophraste Renaudot and the Conferences of the Bureau d'adresse

BEFORE LAUNCHING INTO THE SCIENCE of the scientific revolution, it is probably worthwhile to examine the status quo ante. What did people think about their physical surroundings before the scientific revolution taught them to think scientifically? How did people make sense of the stuff of the world, its changes, growth, and decay? What did they believe about the heavens and about the place of the earth in the heavens? Painting this world picture is a tall order, more suited to the talents of the anthropologist, perhaps, than of the historian. There were layers and levels of belief and understanding, of course, and there were disagreements, contradictions, and plain confusion in discourse about nature.

The only thing that we may assert with confidence is that the world inhabited by the peoples of the early seventeenth century was very different from our own and was shared with beings and powers that have for the most part ceased to operate in the twentieth. The significance of those powers, especially the spiritual ones, can be lost in a historiography that concentrates on issues of the political powers of the Church. Galileo's self-consciously public difficulties (largely brought on by his insistence that his own intellectual authority outweighed all other considerations) obscure the very real operation of spiritual and symbolic substances. Human understanding suffered challenges from the miracle of the transformation of dirty rocks ripped by miners from the bowels of the earth into copper, from the transformation of copper into gold attempted by alchemists, and from

the transformation of bread and wine into the body and blood of
Christ. A range of saints and angels and of demons and devils and
demiurges intervened in the world; the elements of the mass or, more
impressively, the relics of patron saints when they were available always had the best place in the parades and processions so central to
the life of towns and cities well into the eighteenth century. The reality of these entities in the minds of most Western European women
and men, more than the doctrinal opinions of the Church, set the context in which the new science would evolve.

Lest we push these powers from the physical world into the familiar cloister of communion, we should recall that a less quaint and decidedly uglier manifestation of spiritual powers operated as well. The
late sixteenth and early seventeenth century represented the height of
the witch craze. Thousands of women and hundreds of men were
burned at the stake, convicted of dealing with the devil and causing
him to intervene in the world, of raining pestilence and storms and
famines through his agency upon the decent peoples of Europe. These
persecutions were by no means the rantings of an outraged and outrageous peasantry. The greatest legal minds in all Europe believed fer-
vently in the necessity of the trials and executions; both Jean Bodin
and Francis Bacon wrote of the dangers of witches. It is not some extreme ideology of the Church that we must understand to account for
the development of science and impediments to it, the famous stories
of Galileo's trial and his viewing of the instruments of torture
notwithstanding. Instead, it is the world in which men in positions of
authority believed that even dispossessed old women, perhaps especially dispossessed old women, could trade their souls for plagues and
droughts. It was a world filled with signs and portents, a world that
most of us can no longer imagine.

The intellectual foundation for the great philosophical and legal
minds like those of Bodin and Bacon came from the apparently un-
holy alliance between the Church and the philosophy of Aristotle.
Known best as Peripateticism, after the alleged habit that the Philosopher had of wandering about the groves of his academy, the Lyceum,
as he lectured, the great medieval edifice of Aristotelian philosophy
allied itself with the Church through the educational system and dog-
matic cosmology. Aristotle had been interpreted and abridged and
Christianized so thoroughly that students of the original Greek texts,

reintroduced in the sixteenth century, might not have recognized them. Even as late as the beginning of the seventeenth century, the Schoolmen—those who learned their Aristotle in the great universities of Christendom—ruled the academic world with what must sometimes appear a schoolboy's naïveté. Modernity had not penetrated the groves of academe when Louis XIII acceded to the throne in 1628. The purposes of a liberal education were no clearer in the early seventeenth century than in the late twentieth, and the effects it had on those subjected to it were no more predictable.

Natural History and Natural Philosophy at the Bureau d'adresse

The lessons offered by late Renaissance practitioners produced an easily recognizable style of discourse. This curious admixture of classical and Christian learning is perhaps better understood by example than by analysis. A peculiar and remarkable source, the *Conferences* on questions philosophical and scientific held at a strange institution called the Bureau d'adresse and transcribed by Theophraste Renaudot, himself a sort of strange institution in Louis XIII's France, provides us with a window into that discourse and the world it created. It also offers a window into the operations of the physical world perceived by what must have passed for the educated public on the eve of the scientific revolution.

For Renaudot (1586–1653), popular science was but one source of amusement, administrative responsibility, editorial practice, and income. Renaudot began his career as a physician in the province of Louis's chief minister, Cardinal Richelieu. In 1618, Richelieu offered Renaudot the post of commissioner general for the poor—effectively the director of public welfare in France. Renaudot established the Bureau d'adresse as an employment agency. Since it was obvious that the unemployed needed interim support while the *bureau* was doing its job, the commissioner-general began to offer short-term loans and pawnbroking services; the latter inevitably led to the sale of unredeemed goods. Advertising brochures, which Renaudot also published for himself, bragged that at the *bureau* one might "sell, buy, rent, exchange, let, borrow, learn, or teach" practically whatever one wanted.[1] The *bureau* offered, among other things,

Academies and individuals to instruct the nobility, Advice on the regulation and relief of the poor, Anatomies and dissections, Animals of all sorts [including, on one occasion, a dromedary], Antiques, . . . Bachelor's and other degrees, Baths, Bankers, Boats, Benefices, Books, . . . Companions for traveling, Consultation in medicine and [business] affairs, Courses in theology, medicine, law, philosophy, and the humanities, . . . Soldier's enlistment, . . . Tapestries, . . . Vocations for religious and other orders, and the conditions for entrance, Wine.[2]

Renaudot proved a sufficiently effective and compliant ally of the crown that the government granted him a monopoly for periodical news publications, despite the competition and protest of a duly licensed printer. Renaudot offered in return unlimited and unabashed royal propaganda in the *Gazette,* the first weekly newspaper in France. The Bureau d'adresse offered a medical clinic (free to the poor on Tuesdays), referrals, an apothecary shop, and a mail-order diagnostic service based on an intricate illustrated pamphlet of symptoms, also printed on the premises.

In addition to the thousands of goods and services to which Renaudot attended, the *bureau* came to host a weekly "*Conference.*" The meetings continued from about 1632 until the deaths of Louis XIII and his minister in 1642. Among the offices set aside for employment interviews, the chemical furnaces of the apothecaries, the examining rooms, printing presses, and warehouse space for hocked merchandise of all descriptions—indeed, in the very room where these items would be auctioned off unless redeemed by their owners—a hundred or so people met to discuss topics of interest. Every Monday, year in and year out, a diverse collection of listeners came; the *Conferences* were open to the public. Religion Renaudot quite sensibly made taboo, although the taboo was honored mostly in the breach; slander and politics were discouraged with little more success. Otherwise the field was as open as an intellectually inclined doctor, lawyer, noble, teacher, or merchant might desire.[3] Men of all stripes, and conceivably some women, attended the meetings.[4]

The presses of the *Gazette* lay idle most of the week, and a staff of at least twenty printers stood at the ready. An experienced editor and condenser, Renaudot began to record the substance of the discussions at the *Conferences* and to print this record during the slack period of the week. For almost ten years, the colporteurs who came around to buy the *Gazette* picked up the new sheets too and hawked the reports of the *Conferences* on the streets of Paris. The little pamphlets sold very well. Renaudot continued to print complete sets for fifteen years after the meetings themselves came to an end. These reprints, like the originals, were piecemeal jobs, set in odd moments. Blocks of pages carried running heads in different typefaces. The type was often worn, the typography sloppy, and the paper cheap (though even cheap paper from the seventeenth century has survived quite well for a third of a millennium). Tables of contents more than once reported the wrong pages; perhaps these were copied without editing from one printing to the next. Pirates and translators added to the circulation. In all, at least twenty editions of selected or collected *Conferences* succeeded the original pamphlets.[5]

Renaudot managed to peddle his wares to something more than the elite. The *Conferences* represented, as much as anything could, a popular literature for the "cultured classes."[6] One step above the "*bibliotheque bleu*" (the cheapest of printed materials, such as fables and almanacs, bound in little blue covers more suited for wrapping fish than books), Renaudot's quirky periodical nonetheless remained within the range of the middling sorts. And, it seems, it told the cultured classes what they wanted to hear. These published reports must stand as the best evidence for popular science in their time and place. If historians of science have dismissed the content of the *Conferences* as amateurish and confused, it is nonetheless in their pages that one can learn what effect the great revolution in science going on around Renaudot's contemporaries had on the larger thinking community.

When Renaudot determined to publish the proceedings of the *Conferences,* he did it up as a special occasion. He hoped that his record of the discussion would offer something like a universal treatise, systematically organized by a careful ordering of the questions, which would be informed and discussed by the collective wisdom of the participants:

> All were seated in the great hall of the *Bureau:* it was reported that the resolution of the last *Conference* had been henceforth to print the material which might be proposed, and the opinions upon them which might merit attention; and thus to speak of the most beautiful things which are found in the sciences, in order. [The *Conference* determined] that it

would today treat of what method must be followed, and that it would begin the practice of this method with the most general of things, which is Being.[7]

A scholar concerned with late Renaissance learning could hardly have hoped for a more topical question than the one that Renaudot set, to which we shall return. Moreover, for fully two months, Renaudot directed a systematic inquiry into the great epistemic and scientific bases of his intellectual world: "On Method," "On Being," "On Principles," "On the End of All Things," "On Causes in General," "On First Matter," "On Fire," "On Air, Water, and Earth." From the reports of these *Conferences,* it is possible to piece together the intellectual and physical worlds inhabited by the cultured classes during the early reign of Louis XIII.

One striking aspect of the discussions at the Bureau d'adresse is the relative importance of scientific topics. About a third of the questions considered dealt with natural history, medicine, natural philosophy, astronomy, and the like. Only a dozen or so of the questions dealt with what might be characterized as "the new science"—problems that directly confronted the reality of the Copernican system or inquiries that invited discussions of Galileo's mechanics or the rapidly evolving field of optics. The participants, in short, exhibited an interest in the natural world quite independent of that generated by the ostensible revolution in its study going on around them. The old, Christianized Aristotelian view of the world, along with elements of Renaissance Platonism, provided a perfectly adequate framework for their extensive discussions.

The conversations on the Aristotelian elements during the second month of the published *Conferences* presented the best chance for the auditor or the reader to discover the standard Peripatetic description of nature entertained by the schools. The story as it was told ran something like this. We live among a confused mixture of the four elements. On the whole, earth, which is cold and dry and the heaviest of the elements, tends toward the center until it encounters other earth, when it comes to rest. Our Earth—the place we all live, which got a bit confused with the element in the heat of the argument[8]—is not, however, a perfect sphere, for there is no perfection in things terrestrial. High and low spots mar the surface, so the tendency of elemental earth to move toward the center must produce constant change and motion. Around this cold, dry core there is a cold, wet layer of water, which likewise moves downward until it encounters either earth or more water. Above this comes the natural place of air, the first hot element, humid like water, and naturally light. Fire, hot and dry, comes next in the scheme, the most upwardly mobile element— although exactly where it exists and how far it extends were matters of debate.

According to Aristotle, of course, all four elements are sublunar; beyond the terrestrial realm all is perfect and immutable. The Christianized Peripatetic cosmology of the schools connected this immutability with the perfection of God's creation—it didn't need changing. Yet the first speaker on fire contended (most unconventionally) that the element in fact does not reside below the sphere of the moon.[9] We do have a good bit of heat from various sources, but they needn't be conjoined with fire. If there were fire below the lunar sphere, it would produce "refraction or parallax" and cause the stars to appear in places different from where they do, as a coin in a vessel of water appears displaced. The fact that astronomers can predict eclipses, according to this novel bit of reasoning, should serve to demonstrate the fallacy of that eventuality. The only things that could possibly make anyone believe that there is elementary fire on earth, according to this speaker, are the "fires" that burn here. Yet these pitiful images are but mere accidents (speaking in terms of Aristotle's categories), and accidents (from that same perspective) can't be elements.

A second speaker went even further in the same vein, declaring that fire is not an element at all.[10] The "fire" on earth cannot mix with substances; any time we see it, it tears substances asunder. According to Aristotle, that which cannot mix with a substance cannot be a substance and therefore not an element. Furthermore, the argument that fire exists beyond the moon is no good to us, for we certainly cannot go out there and find it. All the heat on the earth comes either from the sun or from animals, two perfectly natural sources of heat independent of ordinary fire. The third speaker went on in a similar Peripatetic manner, invoking the logic and categories to construct a sort of late-scholastic variation on Aristotle's elemental theme. The argument, however, took a different turn, claiming that fire has no elemental effect on water. To be sure, it can warm water, which is by nature cold, but it does not change the essence of water. Moreover, the very mixing it seems to do—conjoining its heat with the coldness of water to produce warm water—shows that fire (which is hot and dry) is not an element, since it combines with its opposite, water (which is cold and wet).

The conference's next speaker objected strenuously.[11] Fire, this modern Peripatetic proclaimed, is an element. So it was judged by Aristotle, Plato, Empedocles, and Pythagoras. Yet this champion of orthodoxy proceeded to turn the world upside down. Instead of placing fire farthest from the center of the terrestrial realm, as Aristotle had done, the modern put its natural place below the ground, a position deduced from the eruptions of volcanoes. Another voice rose to support the elementary nature of fire, above the ground as well as below.[12] Indeed, the speaker asserted, it can even move comfortably into the heavens, past the moon, and to the regions of Mercury and Venus. For of what but fire are comets composed, which astronomers "for reasons of optics" place in those elevated regions?

This all gave the curious, unschooled auditor no little to ponder. Accidents, substances, elements, refractions, and eclipses: These were the things of learned discourse. The application of this discourse to the question at hand does seem a bit perverse. It was Aristotle's texts that suggested the elementary nature of fire, as of earth, air, and water, whereas a scholastic insistence on precision tore the elemental nature of fire to shreds. The speakers were more concerned with Aristotle's logic than with his reflections on nature. It was never made clear just how this firelike accident on earth that had been spuriously dignified with the appellation of substance in fact worked, or just what positive alternative there might be to the common opinion that fire is an element. The very domination of Peripatetic logic and analysis rendered Aristotle's own description of the physical world suspect at best.

The last of the participants made this abundantly clear. The lone participant able to claim with any justification to support "the common opinion"—that is, orthodox school Aristotelianism—reminded the assembly that fire cannot enter the heavens, since the heavens are perfect and unchanging.[13] Nor can it derive from the rays of the sun, which are neither substantial nor ignited. Rather, fire is one of the terrestrial elements. Most of it sits in a relatively hot and dry form just under the sphere of the moon. Tucked safely up there, elementary fire presents no danger of burning the earth, since the air is by nature humid, protecting us from the qualities of fire.

The discussion of the elements presents a rich and archetypical example of the intellectual milieu of the Bureau d'adresse. It is undeniable that the speakers who put forth their ideas brought with them the scholastic Aristotle they had learned in school, and that practically all discussion of both nature and logic was cast in its terms. Yet a liberal education proved spectacularly unsuccessful at communicating either an accurate or a uniform picture of Western thought to students who experienced that education. Everyone, to be sure, learned the names of the great thinkers (there were only a few of those to keep track of at any rate) and appropriate academic jargon. It was the application of this vocabulary and the system of thought that it represented to even the most straightforward and thoroughly discussed problems that proved a rather more difficult matter.

Aristotle on the elements is neither obscure nor particularly subtle. The speakers, excepting the last one, did not explore the fundamental properties of fire—its heat, its dryness, and its levity. They did not inhabit the consistent and comfortable world of the medieval Schoolmen. Instead, they saw a world so full of a number of things that it was hard to keep track of how it all fit together. Volcanoes—hardly a matter of first-hand experience to most Parisians—could play a role in the construction of the world so important as to render meaningless the everyday observation that fire as it burns things moves upward and lifts smoke and glowing embers with it. (In a world lit by candles and heated by wood, this phenomenon really was encountered everyday.) Comets were, for Aristotle, events like the weather, taking place in the upper reaches of the sublunary realm, the natural place of fire. That this theory was clearly stated and universally adopted may be gleaned from the word "meteorology," which still describes the science of weather, centuries after meteors and shooting stars and comets were cast out of its competence. Indeed, comets were openly alleged at the Bureau d'adresse to inhabit the heavens and even to violate the perfection and immutability of the superlunary world, to carry into that perfect place the most violent earthly agent of change. Yet no one at the *bureau* raised the specter of the Inquisition to defend the orthodoxy; the auditors seemed not so much scandalized as bemused at the confused introduction of modernity into the confused background of Aristotle.

The discussions at the *bureau* of course drew upon the composite understanding of all those who came to the sessions and felt moved to speak. In one sense, this makes the proceedings an inappropriate source for a simple worldview, since it lacked the coherence a single speaker might have brought to each subject. Yet this fractured picture in fact reflects Renaissance pedagogy rather more clearly than twentieth-century expectations might lead one to believe. Individual speakers ranged rather widely in their pursuit of sources. In this they emulated the greatest minds of the late sixteenth and early seventeenth centuries. One cannot read that last generation of unfamiliar intellectuals, Joseph Scaliger or Girolamo Cardano or Pierre Gassendi, as simple narrative text; they offer long quotations and constant references to works both important and obscure that communicate great learning but not necessarily a great deal of evidence for their arguments. To understand this style, it is necessary to consider the most mundane aspect of early-seventeenth-century learning. The "notebook" method, in one variation or another, found a place in practically every work on pedagogy in the sixteenth century. The idea was to extract knowledge from the books one reads and to classify and catalog it for future use. In Juan Luis Vives's formulation:

> Make a book of blank leaves of a proper size. Divide it into certain topics, so to say, into nests. In one, jot down the names of subjects of daily converse: the mind, the body, our occupations, games, clothes, divisions of time, dwellings, foods; in another, idioms or *formulae docendi;* in another, *sententiae;* in another, matters which seem worthy of note to teach thyself.[14]

Despite the persistence of a few true believers in the use of color-coded index cards, the influence of the notebook method on late Renaissance scholarship is hard to imagine in our own technological century. The expense of books, the difficulty of travel, and the isolation and poverty of even the great early modern libraries all significantly retarded the transition from the culture of the manuscript to the culture of the book. The Latin mass and the Lord's prayer imbued words and phrases with a significance and a mysticism that rendered the notebook method all the more important. The modern assumption that a work has a thesis and that a competent reader reads for that thesis was simply not something that university students in the early modern period learned. Instead, they learned that every issue, no matter how obscure, had been addressed by a mind greater than one's own, and that the educated person could quote the words generated by the greater mind verbatim. The contribution of the liberally educated modern would be to show how those words supported one's opinions. It is in light of this notebook method, this early modern pedagogical technology, that we must understand the world described in the *Conferences*. Only in its context do we have any chance of understanding what Renaudot's speakers meant when they addressed the philosophical problem of method.

This is not to say that the late Renaissance was not awash in high philosophical method. Half a dozen speakers took up the question during the inaugural hour Renaudot assigned to it. Three of them agreed on the major points, adhering to classic School philosophy. The first speaker offered a solid if stolid definition. Method, according to the formula recorded in countless notebooks, consisted in composition and resolution. Composition pertains to the contemplative disciplines and precedes the parts of a thing; resolution pertains to the practical disciplines and addresses the parts of a thing. The tool of this method is definition, which is subservient to both the parts. A second speaker for this method found the sketch a bit too condensed and proceeded to elaborate certain particulars. Begin first with the object under investigation; distinguish its usage. Then (and only then) comes the time for definition. Assign principles and causes, deduce the properties of a thing. This done, the time is right for resolution: Discuss the uses and causes of a thing. The last of the Aristotelian speakers, after an interruption in the Schoolmen's discourse by advocates of other schemes, provided a variation on the theme. There is no need, he said, to go beyond the bounds of "ordinary philosophy" in the quest for a proper method. The first speaker had got it right, although he might more propitiously have employed the terms "invention and disposition of doctrine" for his divisions. Invention provides the place to proceed from the particular to the general. If (following an example from Aristotle's *Posterior Analytics*) the earth's being interposed between the sun and the moon causes one lunar eclipse, the methodical thinker forms the universal conclusion that lunar eclipses infallibly arise from this configuration. Following this invention, disposition proceeds like resolution in the first speaker's scheme.

Even the unschooled auditor could come away from these short speeches with some idea of the philosophy taught in the schools and with a good bit of the jargon associated with learned discourse. It is not at all clear that those setting out to read the published *Conferences* from cover to cover would learn enough method from these speeches to apply it, but certainly the introduction to the terms would have proven useful. If the Aristotelian world appeared a bit fractured, that impression was accurate. Nevertheless, it was flexible and pliable enough to accommodate a wide variety of opinion. Internal consistency and universal agreement did not count for as much as a vague connection to ancient wisdom and to university training.

The Aristotelians did not so dominate the intellectual world that no other method found its way into the discussion. The second speaker, for example, offered a self-proclaimed "cabalist" philosophy. Again the message came in a sort of catechism. Go first, the cabal directed, to "the archetypical world of the divine Idea; descend thence to the world of intellect or intelligence, and finish with the elements, which are physics." This condensed, neo-Platonic epistemology served as a proper, if outnumbered, counterweight to the digested synthesis of Aristotle.

The next speaker was prepared to provide a rather more extensive summary of yet a third method—that of Raymond Lull. Not content with mere epitomes, the Lullian launched a full-scale disquisition on all thirteen points of the master's method. The first element assigned six attributes to each of the letters of the alphabet from *b* to *k*—a transcendent, a comparison, a question, a substance, a virtue, and a vice. The letter *b*, for example, took goodness, difference, whether, God, justice, and avarice. (The uses and application of these categories would, we must assume, become clear in the course of the lesson.) Droning on through the attributes assigned to the letter *c*, even the devoted Lullian sensed the need to abridge and left the letters *d* through *k* as an exercise for the auditor. The second of the thirteen parts of Lull's method revolved around four figures; the third, the orator hastily added (apparently in the midst of some commotion), around definitions. Like presenters of long and complicated papers in works-in-progress sessions in academic meetings today, the Lullian detected the need to condense rather late in his allotted time. Instructions ceased rather abruptly, leaving fully ten steps "which I might deduce more amply for you, except that they would require at least a whole *Conference*. The method is so great that Lull promised to his disciples that through its application they might respond pertinently, to the point, to all questions which might be proposed to them."[15] As it turned out, the speaker did not spoil things for his school; the *bureau* did devote a *Conference* to Lull some four years later.[16]

Such was the intellectual world on the seedier side of the contemplative life during the ministry of Richelieu. Several points are worth remarking. For our purposes, the most important is the level of scientific literacy among Renaudot's patrons. The explanation of lunar eclipses sprang immediately to mind as an example of sound method; cabalist and Peripatetic thinkers alike found in physics the fundament of rigorous thought. In more general terms, the debate was lively and pluralistic. A scholastic Aristotelianism—what passed then as the exclusive foundation of Western thought—made the most frequent appearance, but neo-Platonism, Lullian logic, and even Montaigne's militant modernism found a place in the discussions at the Bureau d'adresse that was not open to them in the universities. The eclecticism of late humanism came alive in Renaudot's great auction hall. The guardians of Western civilization reacted to new ideas not so much with the desperate viciousness of inquisitors as with a sort of bemused recitation of the canon and a patient explanation of how it could account for anything the newer philosophies sought to introduce. The scientific revolution, according to these defenders of the status quo, would hardly need to happen; the learning of the universities already encompassed anything worthwhile it might produce.

Platonic and modern and Lullian philosophies nonetheless made their way quite frequently into the discussions that followed these admonitions on method. The table of contents of the *Conferences* presents a collection of topics appropriate to the peculiar eclecticism that surrounded Renaudot. Science played a prominent part but by no means dominated. The logical, ordered succession of topics considered during the first two months of published discussion gave way to a disordered jumble of problems considered one after another, with no connection among them. Occasionally a short series of topics would emerge with some coherence, as when the five senses were considered in order,[17] but the discussion reflected no more coherence than that of fire. An irregular participant might have heard or even contributed to discourse on the following topics:

> Whether it is easier to resist the voluptuous than the ugly. Why is no one content with his station? Which is more noble, man or woman? Means of obtaining nobility. On Comets. Whether it is more important to speak well than to write well. On light. On Chastity. What is the soul? Whether peasants have reason to kill themselves. On Hermaphrodites. Whether it is expedient for women to be learned. On Volcanoes. Which is the most excusable of human passions? Whether music causes more ill than good. Which came first, the chicken or the egg? Whether nature contributes more to poets than to orators. Whether when two bodies of different weights fall, one falls more quickly than the other, and why? Is the *Conference* the most instructive method of teaching? [And, at about the time of the death of Richelieu,] is it more expedient to remain neutral in a civil war or to take sides?

The scientific topics, after the first two months' attempt at coherence, ranged just as widely and randomly.[18]

The view of the physical world that emerged from the later discussions proved even more eclectic than those that had constructed the Peripatetic world from earth, air, fire, and water. Three discussions, for example, addressed the growth of minerals:

> Minerals encompass metals, stones, and all sorts of fossils. We will discuss the causes by which they grow. For everyone agrees that they grow, excepting those who believe that God created them at the beginning of the earth, or that they contain the germ of some other production, which occurred at the time of the creation. But anyone who has left a stone in water for a long time, and found it augmented, will convince them with this experiment.[19]

Only in the case of precious stones did Aristotle offer much help. Such stones are clear, since they have the diaphanous qualities of water—rather like the observation that opiates put people to sleep because of their soporific qualities. Earth gives the stones their hard quality. The combination of earth and water, both by nature cold, assures that they are very cold indeed, although one speaker ventured that they contain small amounts of air and fire as well.

Even speakers from some opposing schools cast their arguments in appropriate logical terms. One who believed in "a certain rocky sugar that takes the place of a seed" sought to explain its action in terms of the good Aristotelian categories of a material cause and both a nearer and a further efficient cause. The "sugar" provides the material cause; if it is coarse, it produces ordinary rocks; if it is pure and subtle, precious stone. It transforms itself and everything else—wood, fruits, fish, animal carcasses, and all else that petrifies "in certain waters"—into hard, rocky stuff. The further efficient cause required to effect this transformation is heat, which separates unlike things and unites like. The nearer efficient cause is cold, which condenses. This peculiar hybrid of modern materials and ancient causes actually provided the clearest explanation of the growth of minerals offered in the *Conference*.

Other schemes dealt more familiarly than the Aristotelian with questions of elemental composition. Alchemists had long maintained that metals consist of mercury, which causes their ductility and sheen; and of sulfur, which also serves as the principle of combustion. In the sixteenth century, Paracelsus had stirred in salt to lend hardness and codified the three principles of matter. These principles, more amenable to metallurgical theories and certain medical practices than earth, air, fire, and water, represented an uneasy and ill-defined complement to the traditional elements; indeed many texts referred inconsistently to both systems. The one Paracelsian who spoke up during the discussion of precious stones stayed clearly within the framework of the school. Not the elements earth and water, but the single Paracelsian principle salt, gives precious stones their hard and clear qualities. This principle is joined with volatile spirits, and in the joining, the two lose their natural acrimony and become stable. Those stones that are colored acquire their tints through concoction or calcination—chemical operations rather than vague categorical or causal classes. No mere partisan content to recite the formulas of his master, the Paracelsian offered up an observation from natural history to refute the association with cold and water: Most precious stones, he claimed, come from hot rather than cold regions. Just as the Aristotelianism of the schools filtered down to the *bureau*, the Paracelsian principles of the apothecaries and renegade physicians bubbled up.

In a discussion of the question "From Whence Comes the Salt of the Sea,"[20] the Paracelsian notion that salt is the principle of life provided the most coherent explanation of the way that the salt of the earth gets to the sea—a proposition that everyone seemed to embrace. Salt, according to the Paracelsian, binds the soul to the body, and when the body dies the salt remains, ready to be washed to the ocean. Even the most notably Aristotelian interlocutor who brought up the final causes for the salt of the sea—to make it better suited to float boats and fishes, to prevent the sea from boiling in the heat of the sun—acknowledged that "chemistry shows" that nearly all bodies contain salt.

For the visitor who learned about science at the Bureau d'adresse or from the published *Conferences,* the various opinions and systems must have appeared as equal alternatives to be mixed and matched in any fashion that produced a plausible explanation for the phenomenon under discussion. Acute observations and sound arguments came from both the mainstream of Aristotelian thought and schools like the disciples of Paracelsus, generally characterized as a sort of fringe group inspired as much by a mystical spirituality as by any analytic framework. Confusion and circularity likewise were found in arguments from speakers of all persuasions. It is not the quality of the arguments so much as their style that lent a certain coherence and consistency to this late Renaissance potpourri of philosophy. Philosophical analysis appeared as a series of facts, recited as it were from the appropriate notebooks and the "nests" within them. Peripatetics and Platonists and Paracelsians understood one another perfectly well, and the fundamental disagreements among their notions of the true constitution of the world did not inhibit their conversation. Their common world was one understood by an accumulation of relevant information, connected to the question at hand through a logic that drew its vocabulary from Aristotle. Yet it was not a world, even for the professed Aristotelians, that depended in any fundamental way on the theoretical connections between qualities like hot and cold or wet and dry, elements that instantiated these qualities, and the causes that produced change. Aristotle's own *Physics* was simply not terribly relevant to the analysis of the physical world. The breakdown of the Aristotelian view of the world thus did not come as a simple consequence of technical developments outside the realm of Peripatetic philosophy. Instead the comfortable medieval world crumbled from within and came to look more and more like the alternative philosophies that competed with it, as those philosophies frequently came to look more and more like the Peripateticism of the time.

Science and Orthodoxy at the Bureau d'adresse

The locus classicus for debates between the old philosophy and the new science came in astronomy. In this field, as in the natural history of minerals and the nature of fire, a dominant Aristotelian view traded facts with competing Platonic and modern schools. The earliest astronomical topic taken up by the *bureau* aimed at the heart of the controversy: "On the Motion or Rest of the Earth."[21] The inaugural speaker emphasized the serious nature of the question and the near miss the canon had had with misguided novelty. Copernicus's claim that the earth moves, in print for nearly a century, had lost its novelty; common sense had again prevailed. Tycho Brahe "and most philosophers" had returned to the "common opinion" of Aristotle and Ptolemy: The earth rests at the center of the world. This arrangement presents a most pleasing symmetry. All the fixed stars appear the same size, which must indicate that they are the same distance from the earth; the earth must therefore (by geometrical definition) be at the center. The zodiac, the sun, and the moon likewise spin in a perfectly balanced fashion about the earth. The great weight of the terrestrial globe could rest nowhere else but the center. If greater reasons be sought, the skeptic need only consider the consequences of the alternative. (The logical analysis here gives the lie to anyone who might contend that Galileo's Simplicio is but a straw man.) The earth's motion must be either straight or circular. Gravity provides the only natural straight motion, and gravity drives bodies toward the center. Were the earth to move in a circle, it would be completely unstable. If a rock were hurled into the air on a moving earth, it would no more fall back to its launching point than would a rock thrown from a moving ship. A cannon fired toward the east could not send its charge as far as one aimed toward the west. Clouds would not float serenely in the air; horrendous winds would blow, cities would fall to ruin, and animals would suffocate.

A second speaker pointed out that in addition to these excellent arguments, the Bible quite explicitly refers in several places to the motion of the sun about a stationary earth. How else could the word of God correctly describe the sun as rising and setting? Faith thus conformed with reason.[22]

One Copernican, at least, remained unconvinced.[23] Orpheus, Thales, Aristarchus, and Philolaus, perfectly respectable ancient authorities, had all maintained the motion of the earth. Copernicus had completed the explanation: The sun is at the center of the universe, and the earth moves with the other planets about it, rotating all the while. Proofs the Copernican had in abundance. The sun is the most noble of all the bodies in the heavens; is not the center the most noble place? As the heart is at the center of the man, the source of heat and life, so is the sun the source of heat and life for the universe; it ought therefore to occupy the central position. Rest is more admirable than motion; the sun is more noble than the earth; therefore the sun rests and the earth moves. It is more reasonable to suppose that the earth seeks out a path around the sun in order to obtain its heat and light, than that the sun seeks out a path to provide these for the earth. And, finally, concerning all the fuss about motion, it is true that Copernicus would have the earth move five leagues in a minute. Yet the geocentrists wish to move eight great spheres forty million leagues in the same amount of time!

Such were the arguments concerning the great world systems. Aside from the simple points about the speed of the motion of the earth or the heavenly spheres, no one presented an argument from mathematical astronomy. No one claimed to save the phenomena, to predict the dates of the equinoxes or eclipses or Easter, on the basis of one system or the other. What was at stake was cosmology, and what the speakers argued were the simplest and most commonly cited consequences of the new or the old cosmology. The only clear areas of disagreement came in the battle between ancient authorities and in the relations between science and religion. Questions of terrestrial and celestial physics could clearly come to the support of either side, as could evidence from simplicity or aesthetics. Like many of the arguments in Galileo's *Dialogue Concerning the Two Chief World Systems,* Renaudot's Copernican made the heliocentric position more like that of the Aristotelians, assigning nobility to the sun and servility to the earth. The argument raised at the Bureau d'adresse did not pit the predictions of Copernicus's *De revolutionibus* against those of Ptolemy's *Almagest*, but the cosmology of Orpheus against that of Aristotle.

The student of the heavens had a great deal to think about in the wake of this discussion. So, it turned out, did Renaudot. Scarcely a month after he put on sale the pamphlet describing the debate about the Copernican system, news reached Paris that the Church had condemned Galileo's *Dialogue Concerning the Two Chief World Systems* as heretical; its author had abjured the work.[24] In a special edition of the *Gazette*, Renaudot published the text of the condemnation and likewise abjured his own publication on the question; just to be sure, he promised that such conversations would in the future be banned at the *bureau*.[25]

After the condemnation, Renaudot did avoid the capital question of the motion of the earth. Only that question had invoked the full wrath of the Church, only that did Galileo have to abjure, curse, and do penance for. A number of other issues nonetheless rankled. Renaudot's resolve to avoid discussion of the forbidden question did not, it seems, cover these other potentially explosive astronomical problems. Scarcely six months after Renaudot's retraction of opinions supporting the motion of the earth, the *bureau* turned its attention to comets.[26] Previously, in the discussion of fire one speaker had suggested that those wondrous bodies reside above the moon. When the *bureau* took up the phenomenon explicitly, there was little to distinguish the attitudes and heterodoxy from that displayed in the discussion of the motion of the earth. The opening speech, ostensibly embracing the orthodox position maintained by Aristotle, presented a properly Gallican disregard for the niceties of Christian cosmology:

The tricks of our senses make it difficult to know comets. Just as there are true colors, and others that are merely apparent, so it is with lights. Who would not say from afar that glistening glass, certain rotting wood, some fishes' scales, and cats' eyes are true fire? Not even leaving the heavens, who would not believe, without astronomical reasoning, that the Moon and the other [wandering] stars shine with a true light? Yet experience makes us see the contrary on earth, as reason makes us understand in the heavens. At any rate, concerning doubtful things it is better to embrace the common opinion: I range myself among those who expect that comets are warm, dry exhalations burned in the highest region of the air, if the heavens are solid, and among the celestial orbs if they are liquid. This exhalation resembles the oily smoke of a torch just extinguished, which serves as the pasture for the fire which the reflection of the sun or the violence of motion ignites. It presents the shape in which this matter is disposed to burn, and appears to us until it is consumed if it is inflamed in a suitable manner.[27]

The next speaker pointed out the heterodoxy contained in this tentative embrace of orthodoxy: Comets cannot burn in heavens, since the heavens are immutable. Yet it is also true that fires in the sublunary regions burn out quickly, whereas a comet in 1618 had shined both bright and long. "I judge," the speaker concluded, "that it is easier to say what a comet is not than to say what it is."

This admonition had no particular effect. A third speaker produced a legitimate variation on the orthodox view. Comets are exhalations from the earth in the upper reaches of the sublunary realm, but their persistent light results from the reflection of the sun's rays rather than terrestrial fire. Although the explanation departed from the "common opinion," it did so without upsetting any cosmological apple carts. Expectations of reasonable adherence to a Catholic view of the world at the *bureau* nonetheless quickly vanished. The fourth speaker asserted that comets are planets that have long been invisible because of their great distance from the earth, and that their paths have brought them near enough to be seen for the first time. Those in the Church who feared that heterodox views about the heavens might open the floodgates of unconventional belief could have found no better example than the discussion of comets at the *bureau*. The speaker claimed that God had made them visible at particular times for a purpose. A fifth interlocutor hastened to proclaim that comets are not natural; they are extraordinary phenomena that presage strange things, particularly in religion. Another chorused that they are signs, "celestial hieroglyphs," and that their size indicates their vehemence. People would be well served, this reader of glyphs concluded, to take notice of them.

A final speaker attempted to introduce some semblance of philosophical analysis into this discussion. Perhaps, according to the new science, comets are not signs from God of impending punishment. Perhaps they are instead the causes of truly natural disasters. Perhaps the plagues, wars, seditions, ardent fevers, and other maladies that follow the appearance of comets are effects of the inflammation and drying of the air, which act on our bodies and our souls. Thus did modern science answer early modern superstition. (Explanations of phenomena both questionable and outrageous would become a sort of hallmark of the community of natural philosophers during the seventeenth century, and requests for such explanations occasionally served as the source of philosopher baiting.)

Nor did the discussion of comets end Renaudot's excursions into illicit astronomy. A few years later, the *bureau* again took up a question that had brought Galileo much grief with the Church. The Italian had announced in his *Letters on Sunspots* in 1613 that the surface of the sun is marred with tiny spots. In the work he had suggested his Copernican leanings and declared the mutability and imperfection of the heavens. The pamphlet in fact produced his first official brush with the Church; critics claimed that Galileo's teachings might lead to heretical views. In December 1635, Renaudot's assembly set the topic "On the Spots on the Moon and the Sun"[28] and proved those critics right.

The first speaker boldly declared that nothing in the universe is perfect, since even the sun and the moon have spots. The moon's were explained by the Pythagoreans and by "some excellent mathematicians of the last century," who recognized that the nearby planet must have surface features like those on the earth. Indeed modern observers (according to the rather optimistic account) had examined these "inequalities" with telescopes. Instantiating the worst fears of the priests, the speech jumped to the claim that the moon must be peopled. Like the earth, it is solid and cold. It has hard, reflective parts made of material like rocks and wood that appear bright from our great distance. Other parts that are wet, that is to say, they are diaphanous and transparent, reflect less light, and appear dark. If an earthling could be carried to the moon, our earth would look like the moon's moon. Following in the footsteps of Galileo, the speaker declared that his argument was not contrary to faith but strengthened faith, since it showed the great power of God in the creation of more creatures. (The commentary did not touch upon the souls of those creatures, their participation in salvation, or any other theological issue; those, we must presume, were the responsibility of the religious authorities.) This discoverer of brave new worlds went on to suggest that the planets of planets—the little moons of Saturn and Jupiter and even the spots of the sun—are made of the same substance as the earth. The solar system might contain a veritable plurality of worlds.

Without comment on the larger question of the peopling of the solar system, a more sober student of Galileo made a small technical point drawn from the condemned *Dialogue Concerning the Two Chief World Systems.* Polished places, like the water on the surface of the earth, would appear dark, as they reflect light off in straight lines, most of it away from the earth. Rough places, although less reflective, disperse light in all directions and appear like large patches of light to distant observers. A third speaker agreed and argued that both the sun and moon must be uneven, although the "defect of our eyes" does not allow us to observe the changes in altitude.

The last advocate of modernity allowed an entrée for a more orthodox position. A champion of the official explanation suggested that the spots ostensibly observed on the sun and moon are more likely spots in people's eyes. A thinly veiled reference to the telescope suggested that any spots that really do appear do so because of a source rather closer to the eye than the heavens. The moon's surface is simply composed of areas of different reflectivity—without any necessity that this is caused by such imaginary things as oceans on the moon.

This contention found an answer. In an impressive display of experimental skill and extended reasoning, a final speaker developed the most successful scientific argument ever witnessed at the *bureau.* One needn't employ a telescope to detect sunspots: In a darkened room with a single small hole to admit a ray of sunlight, one can see the blemishes quite clearly on a white piece of paper that intercepts that ray. Nor are the spots likely to develop from any intermediate source, as one can follow their progress together across the face of the sun from day to day; an atmospheric disturbance on earth would hardly follow the heavens in such a particular and obliging manner. In response to the first speaker came the observation that over the long run these spots form and dissipate. They must therefore result from some activity on the surface of the sun rather than from permanent little satellites nearby.

Thus did Copernicus and Galileo have their unpredictable influence at the Bureau d'adresse, an influence rather different from that of the technical mathematics of planetary astronomy. The heliocentric hypothesis spawned a plethora of new ideas, bandied about among Aristotelian elements, Paracelsian principles, and all the rest. Renaudot's *Conferences* on science, like everything else associated with him, proved a collection of the new and the old, the orthodox and the heterodox and the outrageous. Natural philosophy at the *bureau* was nothing else if not eclectic. Not only did half a dozen styles of natural philosophy vie for the attention of the auditors, but many individual speakers displayed a serious internal tension between a given natural philosophy and the formulation of arguments in support of that philosophy. Paracelsians invoked Peripatetic principles of growth, even as the Philosopher's categories rendered his elements untenable. No clear fundamental principles grounded reflections about nature, for no one agreed in any precise way about fundamentals. The words for the elements and the principles nonetheless survived and were used by the speakers to address the various, disjoint problems that nature presents.

The great conflict so frequently portrayed between Church and science, between stultified authority and ingenious reasoning, simply did not show itself at the *bureau*. This is perhaps just as well for science, because the reasoning of the moderns frequently suffered by comparison to the recitation of ancient wisdom. Indeed, the Gallican church never had any substantial difficulties with the pronouncements of natural philosophers. Anonymous speakers quoted through the agency of the influential Renaudot could blaspheme with impunity, it seems; the Church never felt particularly challenged or threatened. French Catholicism simply ignored the overly zealous pronouncements of the interpreters of the new natural philosophy.

The Comparative Case of Literature

The battle between ancient and modern learning came in a rather different context in France: Literature, rather than science, provided the field of conflict. Far from the rambunctious bustle of the Bureau d'adresse and the frantic hustle of Theophraste Renaudot, another institution—the Académie française—and another creature of the Paris of Louis XIII—Jean Chapelain[29]—provide a much clearer insight into the ways in which French culture dealt with the failure of the medieval, Christianized, Aristotelian view of the world and the challenge offered to it by self-consciously modern thinkers.

Chapelain (1595–1674) represents the archetypical, indeed the prototypical, French academic politician. Like Renaudot, he started his career as a medical student, but upon the death of his father, Chapelain turned to the world of learning. For nearly twenty years he served as a tutor in the household of the Marquis de La Trousse, where he had access to an excellent library. He gained a tremendous reputation as a student of ancient and medieval texts and as a wit and poet. He would win pensions from a whole series of patrons who hoped to ease his burdens to allow the production of the great epic poem he always claimed to be at work on. The first was the Duc de Longueville, who awarded him the considerable income of 2,000 livres a year; he would entice further stipends from Richelieu and his successor, Mazarin, and indeed from Louis XIV himself.

Chapelain did not depend on his written output for his primary reputation. Despite the success of an early preface, when the first books of the long-announced epic finally appeared in the 1660s, the work proved a terrible failure; indeed, the vast majority of the poem would be published only as a scholarly curiosity some two centuries later. Instead, Chapelain rode the crest of a great cultural movement that culminated in the glorious early reign of Louis XIV and that dominated French literary politics through the end of the old regime. He became the lion of the literary salons, which dictated the course of social and cultural life in Paris during the seventeenth and eighteenth centuries.

The greatest of salons met in the apartments of the Marquise de Rambouillet (1588–1665).[30] Catherine de Vivionne, Italian by birth, was married to the Marquis de Rambouillet at the age of twelve, in 1600. Related to Marie de Médici, the queen of France, and married to a powerful noble, the marquise immediately took an important place in the court. She already had acquired the Italian Renaissance sensibilities of civility and literary taste, and she spoke perfect Spanish and Italian as well as French. The young woman was justly horrified by the barbarism of a court filled with coarse military men dueling and brawling and sharing bawdy stories. With the birth of a daughter in 1607, she removed herself from the court and began extensive renovations of the family home. She banished the staircase—formerly the center of the great hall of any respectable *hôtel*—to a corner and introduced a curve into this architectural edifice, setting a style that would soon come to dominate Parisian architecture. She introduced walls and screens and alcoves, breaking the vast expanse of the traditional hall into intimate little rooms. Her own chamber, in which she received guests from her daybed, she decorated in blue velvet, countering the uniform taste of tan walls. Every Thursday from about 1617 until 1665 she opened her apartments to guests. It is little exaggeration to claim that the Hôtel de Rambouillet and its mistress civilized the French court. She required of her visitors gallantry, wit, and elevated speech. Richelieu himself called on the charming hostess, and an invitation to her home—and especially into the famous blue room—came to carry more social cachet than any other.

Chapelain had found his way to the Hôtel de Rambouillet by about 1620. In its confines he learned to turn his erudition into a witty classicism, for on Thursday afternoons pedantry stood next to coarse language as symbols of boorishness. Chapelain followed the fashions of the rondeau and the riddle, always informing his conversation with his learning but never allowing it to become overbearing. He managed, setting the tone for Parisian style, to combine technical facility with charm and *politesse*.

Perhaps the most significant boost to Chapelain's career as a creature and creator of the new civility came in about 1629 when he took up with a circle of nine literati who met weekly, generally at the home of the writer and royal secretary Valentin Conrart. They took to calling themselves the "*académie*," reflecting their concern with ancient learning.[31] A few years later the circle expanded to include about a dozen, including François Le Mêtel de Boisrobert. Boisrobert also made his reputation as a wit and came into the confidence of Cardinal Richelieu, whom he amused with clever repartee. He convinced the cardinal to initiate the practice of granting pensions to literary figures; the cardinal-minister suggested himself as a patron for the *académie*. Richelieu politely pointed out that any continuing gathering of more than five people required royal permission, and the circle reluctantly agreed to accept his ministerial patronage.

Chapelain took the largest part in drafting the regulations for the organization, which would be called the "Académie française."[32] Like the ground rules for the *bureau,* the rules for the *académie* forbade the discussion of religion; acknowledging that complete abstinence from the topic was impossible, the members were admonished to submit always to the laws of the Church when the topic came up. Political and moral questions were to be addressed only in accordance with the authority of the prince and his laws; slander was not to pass from the pens of the members. Otherwise, however, Chapelain's design represented the antithesis of Renaudot's gathering. Membership in the society he limited to forty; meetings he closed to anyone but the members. Elaborate election procedures required the dropping of white or black balls into an urn; the count of white balls for acceptance of a new member had to exceed that of black balls by at least four. Similarly, a member could be cast out if the count of black balls exceeded that of white by four—should such a ballot be required by the turpitude of one of the members.

Chapelain inserted his own pet projects immediately after the rules concerning governance: a great dictionary of the French language, a grammar, and treatises on rhetoric and poetics. Yet the main business of the *académie* would be the consideration of new literary works. Each member should take a turn reading aloud work in progress, and the assembled group would offer criticism and suggestions. Other authors could submit their efforts as well, and the *académie* would judge them by committee or en masse. It was Chapelain's hope, in short, that the organization would gain control over the language by setting standards and exerting literary influence—a rather more formal process than the weekly meetings at the Hôtel de Rambouillet, but one using the same standards and techniques. Yet Richelieu had grander schemes in mind. The final series of regulations governed the granting of academic approbation. Members of the *académie,* and others as well, could submit work to the secretary for official approval. Academicians could suggest alterations to make the work acceptable, and only when such alterations met their expectations would they grant their approbation.

Richelieu's aims clearly included control of publication in France. The vehicle of the *académie* appeared to many to be a method of wresting the right to grant publishing permits from the parlement into his personal sphere. Conrart, secretary to the king as well as academician, drew up letters patent for His Majesty to sign. He began with the compulsory, flowery preamble: "As soon as God had called Us to the conduct of this State, it was our aim not only to remedy the disorders which the civil wars, by which it has so long been afflicted, had introduced, but also to enrich it with all the adornments befitting the most illustrious and most ancient of all the Monarchies today in the world."[33]

The first adornment, fitting the style set in the Hôtel de Rambouillet, came in the use of language. The letters, dated January 1635, went on to give Richelieu sweeping powers to form the *académie.* The keeper of the seals, impressing the king's Great Seal, took an interest in the body and asked if he could be included in its membership, a wish that was granted without election. His inclusion, along with the established role of Conrart, meant that the Académie française, although officially under the private sponsorship of Richelieu, took on a decidedly royal flavor. The Parlement of Paris indeed refused for two and a half years to register the letters patent. Only under extreme royal pressure did the letters finally get official registration in July 1637, the date that is usually given as the official foundation of the Académie française.

The time soon came to test the organization's mettle. In 1636, Pierre Corneille had presented *The Cid,* one of the truly great landmarks in French drama. Its premiere fell neatly at the midpoint of the *Conferences* at the Bureau d'adresse—about the time when Renaudot's guests took on the question of the origins of metals and precious stones. The work provided more popular dialogue than the *Conferences* in the seventeenth century, and it has proved substantially more lasting.[34] To say that Corneille's play evoked controversy is to indulge in understatement. The play launched the literary equivalent of war.[35] It served as a test case for the authority of the *académie* and for the behavior of the theater in Paris. *The Cid* was as impolitic as it was popular. To begin with, it portrayed valiant Spaniards with a highly developed sense of honor, boldly defeating the evil Moors. France at the time had its own war with Spain; Richelieu for one did not wish to see his enemy so praised; the cardinal-minister understood, perhaps more acutely than any of his contemporaries, the power of propaganda. The same posture that led him to protect Renaudot's compliant but legally tenuous *Gazette* and the Académie française forced Richelieu to object to *The Cid.*[36]

Far more infuriating to the cardinal than the overt political difficulties of the play, although a rather more subtle issue, was the world that Corneille portrayed in his play. High-born nobles turned to their swords to settle points of honor. France was too close to this grim notion of nobility for romanticism: Barely a decade before the premiere, Richelieu himself had promulgated a strict decree against dueling, the first such edict to produce any noticeable behavioral effects.[37] The cardinal could not tolerate the elevation of this slaughter, which threatened to destroy the noble blood of France. His own patronage of the Hôtel de Rambouillet and his support of its literary coterie came largely as an attempt to provide positive role models for the male nobility as an alternative to sexual innuendo, self-destructive violence, and weapons.

Nor could Corneille hope for any individual protection from the minister. The two had naturally met in the tiny world of the French cultural elite. Richelieu in fact had a lively interest in the theater, and for a time he even worked closely with Corneille. The relationship did not turn out well. The minister had hired Corneille along with four other aspiring dramatists to compose plays. The patron provided the characters, the plot, the general tenor of the pieces, blocking out a single act for each of the five poets. They had but to scribble the verses. Corneille, it seems, took it upon himself to do more. He changed his act. Richelieu, miffed at this insubordination and clear lack of taste and talent, fired the writer. Corneille retreated to the provinces; *The Cid* represented his triumphal return to the capital. It was hardly a propitious time for Corneille to seek the protection of the state.[38] (In a great turn of irony, Richelieu, seeking expert reaction, would show "his" plays to Chapelain; Chapelain shared them with the *académie* and returned such a searing critique that Richelieu tore up the letter and scattered its pieces.[39])

Yet none of the potential areas of conflict actually inspired official interference. The most negative reaction surfaced in another quarter. Georges de Scudéry published a set of "Observations on *The Cid*" in which he claimed: "(1) that the subject is entirely worthless; (2) that it affronts the Principal Rule of Dramatic Poetry; (3) that it lacks judgment in its [characters'] conduct; (4) that there are many bad verses; and (5) that almost everything beautiful in it is stolen."[40] The first and fourth are matters of taste; both contemporaries and posterity have disagreed. The last is a point of fact, and Scudéry's claim does not hold up.[41] The second and third accusations, concerning the rules of dramatic poetry and the moral fiber and conduct of the characters, offer more interesting historical material.

Corneille's play was completely modern. Indeed, *The Cid* is the oldest play in French literature to enjoy continuing regular performances. In a formal sense, it rejected the ancient dramatic forms and proscriptions. Corneille took his model not from an ancient author but from a contemporary Spanish work; the characters displayed modern virtues and vices rather than the conventional devices of ancient tragedians. Corneille offered no classic hero brought down by a flaw linked to his virtues. Scudéry expected a strong moral exemplar rather than a psychological portrait of vacillation and weakness. The novelty of the play offended him.

Aristotle clearly governed more in the intellectual realm than the borders between the place of fire and the immutable heavens; he presented something like an ancient constitution for learning. Any moderately educated individual looked to the Philosopher for guidance in all fields of learning. Scudéry—no scribbling crank—effectively filed charges against Corneille's violations of Aristotelian doctrine. The course of this surprisingly formal trial may inform the extent of the jurisdiction of Aristotelian learning in Richelieu's France.

Like orthodoxy in science, Aristotelianism in literature came in a digested, concentrated formula. Three unities, schoolmasters told their pupils, constituted the rules for good dramatic literature. Unity of action governed plot. Unity of place dictated the scenes. And third, Aristotle prescribed unity of time—the tragedian had but twenty-four hours in which to unfold his tight-knit plot. Corneille's play challenged these rules with a multiplicity of multiplicities. Characters wandered in and out; invading Moors appeared conveniently as fodder for the martial prowess of the protagonist without a bit of inspiration from the hero. Subplots cropped up, and little resolutions dotted the play. Even if the members of the audience could keep it all straight—a task they manifestly managed—Scudéry found the whole plot messy and ununified. As for unity of place, the settings changed: Enough said, according to Scudéry. Corneille did manage to get it all into one day, but the sequence lacked plausibility—of poetic necessity, the hero won the daughter of the king he had vanquished on the very day of her father's death.

Scudéry submitted his brief, the "Observations on *The Cid*," to the fledgling Académie française. The time had come to set a precedent concerning the power and authority of Richelieu's lettered judges. The legal problems proved significant. Under the regulations finally registered by the Parlement of Paris, the *académie* could not consider a work that the author did not submit. Corneille did not offer up his play, but Scudéry's "Observations" did not make sense without Corneille's *The Cid*. Chapelain's circle found itself in a quandary.

At this juncture, Richelieu took an interest. Through an intermediary he advised the poet in no uncertain terms to authorize the *académie* to pass judgment. Corneille at first declined as humbly as he could. The precedent would not, he suggested, be a good one. If the *académie* considered *The Cid*, then any hack writer who suffered at the hand of a critic would feel compelled to appeal to the important body—to take up its valuable time—in a vain and selfish attempt to save face. But Richelieu was not impressed by even this groveling response. He sent word that it would please him if Corneille would submit the play. The poet responded curtly that the *académie* could do as it wished with his work; the cardinal promptly informed the body that he had received the proper authorization. It fell to Chapelain, Richelieu's closest ally in the literary circle, to draft a report on the matter of *The Cid*.

Chapelain, a well-respected critic and a consummate politician, took a middle course whenever he could find one. He judged *The Cid* and Scudéry's "Observations" together, avoiding his own critical opinion of the play as a whole. Chapelain phrased his justification as diplomatically as possible: "Since we are examining [Scudéry's] examinations, we cannot fail to follow some roads which he has followed without giving him reason to complain that we have changed the spirit of his cause, or to say that we take another route in order to make his false."[42] The original title expressed this aim: *The Sentiments of the Académie française Concerning the Observations Made on the Tragi-Comedy of the Cid.*

The review nonetheless required that Chapelain speak of several important issues—and Richelieu required that he speak directly. At bottom, Scudéry accused Corneille of the arrogance of the "moderns": His attack came from the "ancient" quarter. On the authority of the author alone, *The Cid* broke the rules of dramatic poetry revered since time immemorial. The *académie* had to take a stand. Even in this dispute Chapelain, with his vision of classicism, steered as best he could between the opposing factions. He depended on his erudition, his command of both ancient and modern works, which far excelled the school texts on poetics and the barbarized Aristotle they presented.[43] Corneille did, he acknowledged, break the letter of the Aristotelian law cited by Scudéry. Yet in this the poet could defend himself with three sorts of arguments. First, Aristotle presented a more complex theory of poetry than Scudéry acknowledged; a learned student of the Philosopher could cite the subtleties necessary to explain Corneille's compliance. Chapelain scolded: "This error of Scudéry is common with some commentators on this Philosopher . . . they have not considered what Aristotle's meaning was."[44] Second, the ancients themselves often broke (or bent) Aristotle's rules—even great ancients like Virgil, Tacitus, Aeschylus, Euripides, and Seneca.[45] Finally, Aristotle himself wrote, not from some nebulous position of authority, but from his own reason. The modern could reason, too; he could invent as well as imitate.[46] The proof of the play is in the watching. In the watching, the play turned out to work.

> With all this we conclude that although according to Aristotle's doctrine the subject of *The Cid* is deficient, the denouement is not praiseworthy, it is filled with unnecessary episodes, propriety is not always entirely observed, nor the proper "disposition of theater," and it has many base or impure phrases in its verses; nonetheless the naïveté and the impetuous passions, the elevation and delicacy of several thoughts, and that inexplicable agreement which mixes among all the faults gives it a remarkable advantage over the common poems which have appeared in the French scene up to the present.[47]

Corneille, in short, had composed a great, modern tragicomedy. In this new style of classicism, modernity triumphed over the scholastic orthodoxy of the schools. According to Chapelain, *The Cid* earned Corneille a place among the great writers, ancient as well as modern. The poet met his classical predecessors on their own creative ground, bending the rules of poetic theory as skillfully and masterfully as they had done. The very novelty of the play transcended the whole debate over dramatic form—it rendered the argument between the ancients and the moderns superfluous.

So, at any rate, Chapelain reckoned. But Chapelain alone, even the entire *académie,* could not simply express an opinion. The critics too had their critic, one who had to be satisfied before the *Sentiments of the Académie* could appear to the public. They sent the manuscript to Richelieu. He made his notes and sent it back, demanding "more flowers and ornamentation" in the preamble, an example here, a clarification there; in short, the cardinal wanted a work "more worthy of the *académie.*" The *académie* revised by committee. (Chapelain was not awfully good, despite his apprenticeship at the Hôtel de Rambouillet, at ornaments.) Properly flowered by another academician, the *Sentiments* went back to the cardinal-minister; again he returned it for correction and improvement. Even after the pamphlet finally went to the printer, Richelieu stopped the presses for a few last-minute changes.[48] Somewhere in the referee process, there occurred a signal alternation in the conclusion. Someone struck the phrase "according to Aristotle's doctrine" in the paragraph quoted above. The meaning of the passage changed significantly, stating simply that "we conclude that the subject of *The Cid* is deficient." The academicians now spoke as ancients, not for them. And they spoke more harshly. The title of their reflections dropped any reference to Scudéry's "Observations": The printed version was simply *The Sentiments of the Académie française on the Tragicomedy of The Cid.* Richelieu had his vengeance on Corneille, and Chapelain served as his instrument.

The quarrel about *The Cid* nonetheless had a rather different flavor from that of the quarrel between Galileo and the Inquisition—a French flavor more likely to inform the acceptance of the new science in Paris than the Italian episode so often offered up as the standard for the relations between science and authority in early modern Europe. There are of course a number of parallels between the two stories. In each case, the discomfiture of the authorities came not so much from the positive innovations of the appropriate prophet of modernity as from the self-consciously heterodox consequences that advocates drew quite publicly from those innovations. It was Galileo's claim that the Church erred in doctrine and Corneille's praise of Spanish martial virtues that had drawn the ire of the authorities—not questions of mathematical astronomy or poetic theory. The innovations of modernity suffered from the effects of the defense of these larger doctrinal or political goals rather than from the primary attack of reflexively reactionary ideologues.

Yet the consequences of the alleged transgression proved rather less significant in the French case. The public failure to win unsolicited approbation by the Académie française is punishment different in kind from the display of the instruments of torture, abjuration of one's work, and house arrest, no matter how congenial the household. At the hands of Chapelain and in the style of the Hôtel de Rambouillet, the rebuff could be pulled off quite gently. The success of Chapelain's diplomacy may be judged by the fact that both Corneille and Scudéry won election to the Académie française after Richelieu's death and became reconciled to each other

The affair of *The Cid* makes a fitting companion piece for the *Conferences* of the Bureau d'adresse in the analysis of the state of the new natural philosophy in Paris during the reign of Louis XIII. In a society equipped with the printing press, the ideas of Copernicus and Galileo and the Paracelsians were common coin, although in a culture still dominated by the notebook and the disputation, Copernicus, Galileo, and the Paracelsians seemed more suppliers of facts than proponents of grand world systems. Richelieu's France, calming itself after decades of civil war and near barbarism, had more pressing sources of irritation than disquisitions on the cause of the appearance of the moon or arguments concerning the relative nobility of the earth and the sun. In contrast to the cities of Italy after whose culture the Marquise de Rambouillet fashioned her salon, Paris had to learn the lessons of gentility and civility. The contexts in which the new learning arose—the *bureau*, the theater, and the *académie*—all enjoyed significant royal (or ministerial) patronage and protection. The tiny intellectual and literary elite likewise enjoyed the support of the crown, which had no strong, entrenched intellectual bureaucracy of its own. The Gallican church felt no particular obligation to follow the lead of Rome and, at any rate, found no pressing challenge to its authority in the rambling discussions at the Bureau d'adresse.

Innovations in natural philosophy simply did not play a very important role in Louis XIII's France. Despite the explosion in scientific theory and the intellectual excitement it generated among a few cognoscenti, neither the educational system nor the culture of Paris in the 1620s and 1630s supported any serious understanding of the work of Copernicus or Galileo or the Paracelsians. Instead, the new science provided a pastiche of facts and ideas and speculations to be copied into notebooks and recited like the phrases in *Bartlett's Familiar Quotations.* Sources and evidence and arguments for these signs of learning were optional at best, and the new science presented no coherent alternative even to the decaying Aristotelianism of the schools. What was new and exciting in the Paris self-consciously constructed by Cardinal Richelieu and his advisers was literature, architecture, and the culture of the salon. It was in those realms, rather than in science, that French intellectual life grew and changed. The circles around the salons solidified sufficiently during the Richelieu years that any innovation in the life of the mind would have to enter into society through their sufferance rather than through either the universities or the *bureau.*

3

Of Black Sheep, False Suns, and Systematic Thought: René Descartes and His World

It was into the confused intellectual and cultural milieu in the Paris of Louis XIII that René Descartes would move as a young adult. Always counted as part of the canon of great thinkers—or of dead white European males, as some would have it—Descartes surely merited his academic reputation. Yet this towering intellect, in contrast to the equally canonical Kant, was not a predictable, staid professorial sort. There was very little conventional about him. With Jean Chapelain, he believed that he could by dint of his own intellect and experience address the questions that the ancients had addressed and that he might legitimately arrive at a different conclusion than they had reached. Yet Cartesian modernity was a very different thing from Chapelain's respectful collegiality with the ancients. As we shall see, Descartes developed an entirely new way of looking at the physical and the philosophical world. His impact was so significant that it has become habitual to attribute to him a whole school of philosophy that has developed over the three centuries and more since his death; such is danger of studying a canonical author. The present chapter will offer a view of Descartes that in many ways departs from the received account. To a certain extent such an approach is justified by the fact that a received account exists; there is little danger that the quirks in this story will cause a serious misapprehension of the life and work of Descartes throughout the learned world. Yet the interpretation that I set forth in this chapter is more historical than any of the received accounts—it takes Descartes's life and time more seriously, and the schools that have at various times called themselves Cartesian less seriously, than that of most scholars who write on the subject. For the present purposes, this search for the historical Descartes is more important than the philosophical discussion that his seminal works unquestionably raised.

A biographical sketch of the philosopher as black sheep

René Descartes's early life is not terribly well documented, although that fact has not inhibited his biographers.[1] The bare facts have been clearly established: He was born in 1596, the second son and third child of a minor provincial noble in Poitou. He entered a Jesuit school at La Flèche a few months after it opened in 1604. Beyond those clerical records, however, little about his early life can be stated with certainty. It is claimed that the school turned out to be a good one (a claim based as much as anything on the fact that it produced Descartes), although if this was true, it was largely a matter of chance. It seems likely that René's father, widowed and remarried, wanted mostly to remove the boy from his household. The curriculum at La Flèche is no better known than that at any other boys' school.[2] Latin literature and ancient history and philosophy surely surfaced, but the specific works deemed appropriate by the learned fathers remain a matter of conjecture—of which there is no shortage. Selected books of Aristotle (in Latin translation or summary and with extensive commentary) could not have been avoided, although the question of which books and which commentaries is one that has no documentable answer despite herculean efforts to produce one. Nor, probably, could Descartes have missed the first few books of Euclid's *Elements* in some edition or summary. Yet texts abounded, and the Jesuits adopted no canon sufficiently rigid to ensure any very uniform cultural literacy among their students. What guidelines there were changed quite frequently, and instructions to follow the guidelines came with sufficient urgency to assure the historian that they were routinely ignored. One of the few facts solidly known about the school is that Galileo's announcement of his discovery of the Medicean satellites revolving around Jupiter in 1611 received favorable notice there; at that early date the Jesuits had little reason to distrust the Italian scientist.[3] Retrospective accounts point to this open-mindedness in matters of natural philosophy at about the time Descartes left the school as a formative influence; they also refer to Descartes's mathematical precocity, but evidence for either claim is totally lacking.

Descartes left La Flèche at the age of fifteen and probably spent a year or two at the family home. A younger son, he could scarcely aspire to join his father at the Parlement of Rennes—especially since the second marriage had produced a new heir. The eldest sons from both marriages would need to have parliamentary positions bought for them. Our philosopher was destined to the life of the provincial cadet, a younger brother in a society based on the concept of primogeniture. His fate was better only than that of a daughter or a member of the third estate; those majorities of the population in early modern Europe counted for nothing but childbearing and labor.

To establish a patina of education in preparation for this dubious career, René Descartes purchased a baccalaureate at Poitiers in 1616 and a licentiate in law the very next day. It is unlikely that his education had progressed in any formal way after he left La Flèche. Although some nineteenth- and twentieth-century biographers report that he actually spent some time near his alma mater, that precaution would hardly have been necessary: Degrees in the liberal arts and in law were commodities, and unlike the similarly traded positions in the parlement, there was no limit to their supply. The curriculum at Poitiers is at any rate even more obscure than that at La Flèche; the only academic advantage to have been gained by study there would have been to provide future biographers with further fields for cultivating speculative sources of influence. The standard seventeenth-century account, cognizant of the relaxed interpretation of residency requirements, placed Descartes instead in Paris from the time he left his father's house.[4] No matter what experiences might have followed his exposure to the Jesuits, Descartes spent a few of his late adolescent years in the capital, accompanied by a valet—precious little supervision, some thought, for a lad in such a perilous place. The inevitable rumors of gambling and debauchery have been circulated about our philosopher, as about all young men in Henri IV's Paris; there was perhaps little else to do, but again no solid evidence backs up the allegations.[5]

When Descartes was twenty-two, it was time for him to take up a career. His father, aiming for the military, sent him to Holland in 1618 as a soldier in the retinue of Maurice of Nassau. The Dutch prince had a reputation as the most brilliant military man in Europe; the secession of the Low Countries from the Spanish empire had provided him with a good deal of up-to-date experience in warfare. Although the prince's adamant Protestant stance served as a minor political irritation in Gallican France, his wars were waged against Spain—admittedly Catholic, but an archenemy nonetheless. A French provincial cadet could scarcely have found a better master to train him for military service under Louis XIII. Provided with weapons and a reasonable stipend from this father, Descartes had as good a start as a younger son of middling means might have hoped for.[6] Yet he saw no military action in Holland; he joined the Dutch forces during a fragile truce with Spain, and soldiering occupied very little of his time. To pass the days, he dabbled in natural philosophy and mathematics, most frequently with a friend named Isaac Beeckman. Beeckman's notebooks, which survived and have been published, provide yet another source of hints about the education of René Descartes, but no solid evidence to determine just who it was that the French soldier had been reading.[7]

The military arenas in which Descartes gained experience are better documented than the intellectual ones. His collaboration with Beeckman was ruined by a substantial peace between Holland and Spain. The Thirty Years' War beckoned gentleman volunteers, so Descartes made his roundabout way to Bavaria. Again he failed to accomplish his ostensible goal of gaining military experience, although for once his intellectual activities present more grounds for study than for speculation. It was in Germany that Descartes found himself cooped up in an overheated barracks and dreamt his famous dreams, generally taken as the first turning point in his philosophical career and signaling his total rejection of Aristotelian thought.[8] At that point, he would later claim, he came to realize that he could believe nothing that he did not apprehend as clearly and distinctly as he grasped mathematical quantities and relations. Those enamored of psychohistory have found the stories of the dreams, lost long before anyone practiced psychohistory, extremely important.

Whatever significance the dreams may have had, Descartes began work on his *Rules for the Direction of the Mind* during the sojourn in Germany.[9] Just the early drafts of this unfinished work have produced sufficient grist for innumerable philosophers' mills over the course of several centuries. According to the traditional academic wisdom, Descartes had already initiated modern philosophy and launched the most brilliant career in early modern thought. Yet the young military apprentice behaved as though he saw things differently. He did not neglect his profession; Descartes's first published work, dating from this period and now lost (and unreconstructed), was a fencing manual. As late as 1690 a biographer observed that the skeptic need only read that first published work to realize its author's competence in the military arts.[10] The contemporaneous philosophical manuscripts, by contrast, remained unpublished during their author's lifetime; they appeared only because of the historical interest generated by his later philosophical texts.

In the early 1620s the Cartesian apprenticeship should have given way to a stable livelihood in the military or civil administration. The way was appropriately prepared: The pension from his father continued, and in 1623 Descartes received an inheritance of three small properties from his mother's estate, which brought him a fortune of some 30,000 livres.[11] Had all gone according to family plans, René would have used his capital to purchase a modest position and settle down to the life of a gentle soldier or bureaucrat. Indeed, within a few years, a relative managed to produce an offer of gainful employment: For 50,000 livres, Descartes could have had the office of lieutenant-general of Châtelleraut. A friend agreed to lend the difference between Descartes's assets and the purchase price at no interest. Descartes, in an extraordinary move, declined. He gave as an excuse the peculiar argument that he was not qualified for the position, a claim scarcely credible as an independent reason for rejecting an office in France in the old regime. From that point on, his career departed from the standard pattern for a younger brother from the provinces.

Like his contemporary Jean Chapelain, Descartes settled in Paris. The philosopher arrived on what he intended to be a permanent basis in about 1625. Descartes moved, as did Chapelain, in the more philosophically inclined of the polite and erudite communities of the capital. He knew a few of the circle who would later join the Académie française, most notably J. L. Guez de Balzac, and mixed frequently with the natural philosophers around Marin Mersenne, a friar in the mendicant order known as the Minims. Descartes's relations with the scientific community were regular and stimulating. He took up with Claude Mydorge, a character in the history of science even more obscure than Beeckman, and the pair began a collaborative effort in natural philosophy.[12] Only the sketchiest details of their work remain; what is clear is that they came to understand the sine law governing the refraction of light—the mathematical rule that controls the bending of optical rays as they move from one material to another. (This is the phenomenon, for example, that causes an oar to appear bent at the point where it enters the water.) With this work, Descartes gained the reputation of being one of the leading scientific thinkers in Paris.

Although distinction in natural philosophy did not imply the sort of social success that Chapelain had managed to achieve in literary circles, Descartes did make his way into society. His position is illustrated by a stock anecdote offered about these Parisian years.[13] In 1628, the papal nuncio entertained a group of "beaux esprits"—a phrase also used to describe those who attended the gatherings at the Bureau d'adresse, perhaps too glibly translated as "free spirits." They listened attentively to a chemist, one M. de Chandoux, who attacked the Peripatetic teachings of the schools. Only Descartes reserved his praises. No less a personage than Cardinal Bérulle, the founder of the Congregation of the Oratory, asked why. The failed soldier proved diffident but eventually voiced his reservations: Although Chandoux had quite effectively criticized Aristotelian dogma, he had put no positive philosophy in its place. To demonstrate the ease with which one might carry out the destructive program, Descartes played a little parlor game. He asked the assembly for some truth, some indisputable fact agreed to by all; and for a falsehood, a claim universally rejected. Through skillful argument, he convinced the assembly of a chain of reasoning that led to the refutation of the truth and the affirmation of the falsehood. At Chandoux's expense, Descartes became the intellectual darling of the assembly. Early biographers excused this Cartesian cruelty by noting that the chemist Chandoux would later suffer the consequences of a bit of practical alchemy when he was caught counterfeiting gold coins. Descartes managed, in good Parisian fashion, to *"tromper le trompeur"*—to trick the trickster.

Bérulle, according to the story, found the display so brilliant that a few days later he urged Descartes to devote his life to the articulation of his philosophy. Such a suggestion from this quarter could scarcely have counted for less than an explicit offer of patronage: Bérulle was a powerful man. Descartes at last had an alternative to the military and the bureaucracy, an honorable way of life in the social world of France in the old regime. He could have moved among the great, his refusal to buy an office rectified by a workable intellectual career. Patronage would not only have improved Descartes's material position—although money was never a problem for him[14]—but it would also have provided him with immense prestige. Bérulle's endorsement represented a feather in his cap, a ribbon on his gown; in Chapelain's Paris, such embellishments counted for more than money.

Descartes declined the offer, once again snatching failure from the jaws of conventional success. He disliked the notoriety his discourse had brought him and the social demands imposed on a young intellectual like Chapelain. The constant expectations of wit, of amusing performances like the one played out at Chandoux's expense, would have consumed too much of his time and creative energies. Again he took a road less traveled by in Louis XIII's France. Descartes quite suddenly left his Parisian triumph to return to the anonymity of a Frenchman in the Low Countries, this time "living nobly" without occupation, enjoying the fruits of his estates.

From 1629 on, excepting three short trips to France and the last few months of his life in Sweden, Descartes lived in Holland. Rarely spending more than a few years in a given city or town, the shy intellectual preferred to rent a solitary house in one place or another and to disappear before old friends figured out just where he was. Generally he left behind only an address, and mail would be forwarded to him. This is not to say that Descartes was a recluse or a totally isolated thinker. A gentleman in a foreign country scarcely needed to feel himself a stranger in a strange land. Descartes passed his time dining with prominent local families, playing tennis, supporting a small retinue of servants (indeed fathering a daughter by one of them), and occasionally matriculating in a university. Once in a great while he permitted friends from France to call on him. Descartes initiated several direct lines of communication with powerful political characters away from the Parisian scene. Most significant of these, perhaps, were continuing intellectual relations with Elizabeth of Bohemia, to whom he would dedicate his *Principles of Philosophy*, and with Christina, later queen of Sweden, in whose court Descartes would spend his last months.

Free to indulge his interests, Descartes lived an idiosyncratic life. Almost everyday during his first Dutch winter he spent his afternoons at the butcher's, studying anatomy during the slaughter and conveying home organs of interest.[15] A bit odd even for a philosophical foreigner in Holland, such behavior would have been unthinkable in Chapelain's Paris. This empirical research, rarely mentioned in intellectual biographies, would lead to significant discoveries both in the optics of the eye and in the role of the heart in the circulation of the blood. Descartes's handling of eyes from freshly killed animals, for example, required considerable dexterity.[16] It is difficult to imagine a protégé of Cardinal Bérulle's pursuing such interests.

The peculiarity of his habits did not, however, prevent him from entering into what the postmodernists might now call simply "the discourse," intellectual intercourse with his peers. Descartes maintained a voluminous correspondence with the intellectual world, disseminated to and informed by a network of philosophers both natural and metaphysical, loosely organized by Marin Mersenne, in whose personal circle Descartes had moved in Paris. The Dutch setting simply served to avoid the hustle-bustle of the French capital and the constant intellectual and social demands imposed by an immediate community of scholars and thinkers and their patrons. In his leisure, he thought and read and wrote and performed scientific experiments.

The opportunity to engage the intellectual community presented itself in a significant way shortly after Descartes's arrival in Holland in 1629. He addressed a problem that Mersenne was circulating in philosophical circles. Observers in Rome had reported seeing "false suns"—an optical oddity in which for a time five suns apparently lit the cloudy sky. Though the phenomenon was well attested, no one understood how it happened. The assembled multitude at Renaudot's Bureau d'adresse took up the issue at one of its *Conferences*, though without any notable success.[17] Interested amateurs sent word to Descartes, hoping for an explanation. Descartes responded through Mersenne, opining that his earlier optical researches on refraction, coupled with new ideas about meteorology, would easily account for the phenomenon. Mersenne asked to see the solution as soon as it was formulated and agreed to publish it in Paris. The exchange initiated an eight-year saga in which Descartes offered up increasingly ambitious projects, only to put Mersenne off every time he asked to see results.[18]

Having to his own satisfaction addressed the initial problem of the false suns, Descartes first proposed to compose a little treatise on meteorological optics.[19] He seemingly paired this with another treatise he was contemplating, on physiological questions, about which he felt sufficiently tentative that he informed his correspondents that he might burn the manuscript once he finished it.[20] Each draft, as it neared completion, suggested a new direction; the essay grew in scope and bulk. At the next step, he wrote:

> I undertook to do no more than expose quite amply what I conceived the nature of light to be. Then I took occasion to add something about the sun and fixed stars because almost all light proceeds from them; and about the planets, comets, and earth, because they reflect it; and in particular all bodies on earth, because they are either colored or transparent or luminous; and finally about man, since he is the observer of light.[21]

Not until mid-1633 could Descartes finally inform Mersenne that *The World*, a pair of treatises, *On Light* and *On Man*, was finished. Even then he promised only that a fair copy would arrive in Paris before the end of the year.[22]

Descartes's behavior represents a striking departure not only from the social norms of Louis XIII's Paris but from the style of the European scientific community as well. Nature had presented a puzzle, and Descartes claimed privately that he had solved it. The community accepted the puzzle as a sort of a prize problem; Mersenne, the obvious conduit for the dissemination of a solution, stood ready to transmit it. Such an opportunity would have made as great a splash in the international philosophical community as dispatching Chandoux had in Paris. Descartes, however, chose to wait until he could put his answer in context. He hoped to phrase the explanation of false suns in an appropriate new terminology and to offer parallel explanations for other phenomena—to construct nothing less than a coherent account of the weather. For years he withheld his explanation because of his peculiar desire for completeness.

In the event, Mersenne would not receive the promised explanation even after his three-year wait. Reports of Galileo's condemnation reached Descartes in November 1633, a few weeks before the newshound Renaudot found out about it in Paris. Descartes had considered the motion of the earth in *The World,* taking the same side as Galileo. Suddenly the book seemed an unpropitious beginning for an intellectual dedicated to the avoidance of conflict and notoriety. Unlike Renaudot, Descartes had not yet published on the question and therefore was spared the indignity of offering a retraction. He took the simplest course and suppressed his book. An apology to Mersenne argued that

> all of the things I explain in my *Treatise,* among which was included also this opinion of the motion of the earth, depend so fully one on the other, that it is enough to know that one is false, to be convinced that all the reasons which I used are without force; and while I think they are founded on very certain and very clear demonstrations, I do not want at all for anyone to hold them contrary to the Church.[23]

For a time the author suffered a total loss of nerve, bewailing the decision of the Church and nearly, he once again claimed, burning his papers.[24]

The Cartesian System; or,
a lengthy explanation of false suns

As time passed, Descartes decided that not every bit of his natural philosophy must remain incomprehensible without all the rest. By 1635 he had resolved to publish an intermediate version of his researches—less than the treatise he had promised Mersenne, but a complete explanation of the false suns and the theory required to understand it. He suggested a pair of essays on optics and meteorology.[25] In reworking the material into its new form, his earlier work in mathematics seemed a natural companion piece and a necessary tool for the optics, so he prepared a redaction of his geometry. Still he found that the collection failed to produce the kind of solidity and conviction provided by the suppressed *World,* so the author prepared a fourth piece by way of preface and to make excuses for the missing integrity of the system set forth in the larger work. This essay he entitled a *Discourse on Method.* The collection, presented in French rather than the more conventional academic Latin, appeared in 1637. Descartes would later say that he had chosen the vernacular in order to enable women to read his ideas.[26]

Finally, at the age of forty-one, Descartes launched a career. After a lengthy preliminary discussion, the *Discourse on Method* arrived at the starting point, that whatever Descartes might doubt, he could not doubt his own existence. The phrase that made this claim, originally published in French, is usually offered in Latin translation as *cogito, ergo sum,* or more cryptically as "the *cogito,*" which perhaps lends it more philosophical dignity than the statement "I think, therefore I am" and certainly reads better than "the I think." The *Discourse* proceeded to invent the so-called mind-body problem in philosophy, seriously probing the connections between the physical world and mental perception or analysis of that world. By far the best known of the essays of 1637, the *Discourse* is probably the most widely read of all Descartes's writings. This introductory afterthought to the theory of false suns remains one of the seminal works of Western thought.

As an example of the application of his method, Descartes offered his proof of the circulation of the blood. Descartes had developed this theory independent of William Harvey's contemporaneous work, although the Cartesian formulation came a bit later and without such convincing experimental demonstrations. Descartes had planned to present it in the essay *On Man,* which would have appeared as the second part of *The World.* Although it did not fit into the three essays that followed the *Discourse,* Descartes apparently hoped to publish at least a sketch of his own theory, perhaps to establish a simultaneous claim to Harvey's articulation of the principle.

The other essays offered to help the reader understand the *Meteorology* fared equally well. The *Geometry* standardized and expanded the principles of symbolic algebra and presented the new mathematical field of analytic geometry. Descartes's success in his attempt to provide a uniform symbolic system may be inferred from the fact that the conventions of notation he introduced (the use of the letters a, b, c . . . for known quantities and . . . x, y, z for unknowns) have remained commonplaces in mathematical discourse. As to the substance of analytic geometry, it serves as the basis for many branches of modern mathematics and is generally cast in terms of a coordinate system still called Cartesian. This new style of geometrical reasoning championed analysis as an alternative to construction for the examination of spatial relations and provided the basis for methods of tangents, which would lead, two generations later, to the development of the differential calculus. Descartes did rather better with his New Math than the reformers of the post-Sputnik era did with theirs.

The third essay, the *Optics,* presented the first publication of the sine law of refraction that Descartes had worked out with Mydorge in Paris a decade earlier. Moreover, in the *Optics* Descartes applied this law to the mathematical theory of lenses—an enterprise that has proceeded on the same basis ever since. The essay also duplicated the significant passages on the relations between the anatomy of the eye, the physics of light, and the physiology of vision, which had been prepared for the essay *On Man.* Again, the essay remade the field it addressed.

The collection that Descartes prepared to set the stage for his explanation of the appearance of false suns was not a bad start for a career in philosophy both natural and metaphysical. Although prolonged gestation for these works rules out any awards for an annus mirabilis, the first three essays compete with Einstein's three papers of 1905 for being the most brilliant hat trick in the history of science. The *Meteorology,* by contrast, does not arouse much enthusiasm among modern students of either philosophy or the weather.[27] Indeed, it contains very little in the way of bold new discoveries. Yet it was the *Meteorology* that spoke to Descartes's original promise to Mersenne and that came as the culmination of the series of essays that preceded it. Descartes would later explain, "In the *Meteorology* I hoped that [readers] would recognize the difference between the philosophy I cultivate and that taught in the schools where the same matters are treated."[28] Above all, the essay on weather offered a solution to the puzzle of the false suns; it was also a lesson in systematic thought.

Appropriate to that end, the *Meteorology* was the most pedagogically successful of the essays. The *Geometry* addressed a mathematically adept audience; it could succeed by holding out tantalizing goals and leaving them as an exercise to the reader. (Descartes used a more elaborate circumlocution, saying, "I am wearied by so much writing."[29]) The *Optics* likewise had a natural audience of technical readers and offered a formidable mathematical task for the uninitiated. The more general audience to which the *Meteorology* addressed itself expected a less formal tone. The gentlemen and commoners who bought the weekly sheets of *Conferences* from Renaudot's Bureau d'adresse needed an inviting essay if they were to learn the lessons Descartes had to offer. Descartes understood this pedagogical requirement and met it in the work that at last fulfilled his promise to explain the riddle of the false suns.

Straightforward and qualitative, the introductory passage offered a glimpse of Descartes's suppressed world, at first sight not so very different from that encountered in the *Conferences* of Renaudot:

> I shall speak in this first discussion of the nature of terrestrial bodies in general, so that in the next one I may better explain the nature of vapors and evaporations. Then, because these vapors rising up from the sea sometimes form salt on its surface, I shall take the opportunity to pause a little and describe salt, and to see if in it we can ascertain the forms of these bodies that the philosophers hold to be composed of a perfect mixture of the elements, as well as those of meteors which they say are composed of the elements in an imperfect mixture. After that, propelling the vapors through the air, I shall examine the origin of the winds; and making them gather together in certain places, I shall describe the nature of clouds. And by causing these clouds to dissolve, I shall say what causes rain, hail, and snow—nor shall I neglect snow whose particles have the shape of very perfectly proportioned, small, six-pointed stars (although this was observed by the ancients, it is nevertheless one of the rarest marvels of nature). Nor shall I neglect storms, thunder, lightning, and the various fires that are kindled in the air, or the lights that may be seen there. But in particular, I shall try to portray the rainbow correctly, and to explain its colors in such a way that we can understand the nature of all those which may be found in other objects. To this I shall add the cause of the colors we commonly see in the clouds in the circles which surround the stars, and finally the cause of the suns, or moons, several of which sometimes appear together.[30]

Descartes planned to do nothing less than present a complete natural history and natural philosophy of the weather, by way of preface to his explanation of the appearance of false suns. Such a plan touched closer to home for the sort of readers who had gotten their introduction to natural philosophy from Renaudot than did the other three essays published with the *Meteorology*. The *Conferences,* for example, had not only considered the problem of the false suns in 1629; over the years more than two dozen questions addressed directly in Descartes's essay had been debated at the Bureau d'adresse: "What is the nature of earth, air, fire, and water?"; "Why is the sea salty?"; "On the rainbow"; "On the causes of vapors." Each of these problems, drawn from the tables of contents of the *Conferences,* occupies the larger part of one of the ten discourses of the *Meteorology.* The essay set out to beat the contemporary Parisian Aristotelians at their own game.

In two crucial ways, however, Descartes departed completely from the style of his contemporaries. First, he did not cite authorities ancient or modern. Although he would occasionally mention Aristotle or Paracelsus in his writings, Descartes's references remained general and served merely to point out that the new Cartesian system explained what these earlier efforts had attempted to explain, but did it better. The contrast with the speeches at the Bureau d'adresse, or with other, vaster products of the notebook method, represents a complete departure—a radical rejection of the canon and all that was dear to the academic world. To the modern reader, accustomed to the self-confidence of the scientist, Descartes's writings offer little in matters of scholarship that is striking. When they were composed, however, this manner of exposition was nothing short of revolutionary. Indeed, the most empirical of the British experimentalists of the late seventeenth century rarely placed as much trust in their own ability to describe the phenomena as Descartes did in his essays; even in their rejection of ancient authority they tried always to offer as the best evidence for their claims the testimony of people of quality who observed the experiments with them.

The second, equally revolutionary departure from the norms of the time came in the way in which Descartes built his argument on a consistent picture of the world. Again the sort of progressive description employed in the *Meteorology,* building from one step to the next and referring back to earlier conclusions, seems so natural in arguments verbal as well as mathematical as to pass as quite ordinary to the modern scholar. Yet in an intellectual world dominated by the notebook method, sustained developments tended to exhaust readers. The skills required to follow the niceties of an analytical chain of reasoning are different from those employed to retain the details of a series of citations of authorities. The art of memory as it was self-consciously practiced in the late Renaissance favored the latter skill over the former.

These difficulties for early modern readers did not present a great impediment to the mathematical and mechanical arguments of the *Geometry* and the *Optics*. Yet the sustained discussion of the *Meteorology* came in almost exclusively verbal forms and began with the familiar Peripatetic problems taken up at Renaudot's *bureau*—a description of the structure of matter. An unwary educated man (with or without an educated boy to copy out the good parts) might well have mistaken the early sections of the *Meteorology* for standard, if not canonical, fare. Descartes pointed out that in *The World* he had offered a careful explanation for his assumptions drawn from first principles, but that the framework of the essay required that he merely assert his beliefs: "I assume, first, that water, earth, and air, and all other such bodies that surround us are composed of many small parts of various shapes and sizes, which are never so well arranged, nor so exactly joined together, that there do not remain spaces among them."[31] Gross matter consists of two sorts: "one long, smooth, like little eels," and another whose parts "have very irregular shapes, so that they need be only slightly intertwined to become hooked and bound to each other."[32] The first of these form water, a mass of little particles slipping over one another, easily separated and moved by more solid stuff. The branching material, by contrast, can be packed quite tightly, intertwining and very difficult to separate, to form earth and other solid substances. Once this branching material is untangled, however, its pieces lie loose and springy upon one another and form air—light, compressible, easily separated, and essentially empty.

All this matter, Descartes contended, is made of the same fundamental stuff. One can but say it is extended, without assigning any other properties to the substance itself. Earth, air, and water vary only in the shape and relative position of their material constituents; "they differ among themselves only as pebbles of many different shapes would differ, had they been cut from the same rock."[33] Indeed the same bit of matter might change from one "element" or "principle" to another; a piece might break off the branching stuff of the earth or the air to form a particle of water. (The exposition here was quite sketchy;

explicit discussion of the formation of the straight or branching forms of matter remained unpublished in the manuscript of *The World*.)

The *Meteorology* presented a new interpretation of the natural world. Aristotle's four elements had no special place in the first three discourses, which addressed Descartes's theory of matter. Indeed, like some of the speakers at the Bureau d'adresse, Descartes explicitly rejected the notion of elemental fire. The spaces among the little "eels" and "branches" of gross matter, he said, contain a still finer matter, a smooth and regular fluid that transmits light; for an explanation of its diaphanous properties he referred the reader to the *Optics*. This "second matter," interspersed through the gross stuff of the physical world, played another role as well. Its parts, very fine and mobile, constantly bump around, shaking each other and the coarser stuff that surrounds them. It is this motion in the fine second matter, Descartes contended, that we perceive as heat. The sun moves and shakes the second matter and causes most of the agitation of its particles and therefore most of the light and heat on the earth. Yet some bodies, for example, ice and marble, are so rigid and compact that the second matter cannot enter into their pores in sufficient quantity to move the coarser stuff; these bodies feel cold to the touch.

Descartes proceeded to build his system: Even dense, cold bodies nonetheless contain little pores and apparent vacuities. Descartes referred to these spaces by the wonderful name of interstices. The system denied that they were truly empty. To fill them there was a "first matter," still finer than the "second," incomparably small and without any noticeable power to agitate the coarse stuff of the phenomenal world that surrounds it. These three matters—the first, the subtlest material that filtered into crevices too small for any other; the second, the medium of heat and light; and the third, the ultimate particles of gross matter—would suffice to construct the entire physical world.

The *Meteorology* would not yet build this world in public. Descartes had only to explicate those parts required to understand his explanation of the false suns. Although he said nothing that contradicted the description in *The World*, he rarely strayed beyond what was essential to his immediate purpose. The entire system by implication stood behind his explanations, and Descartes hoped that readers would perceive the system and its coherence. His purpose in the essays was to illustrate the power and diversity of his understanding of nature. The best way to accomplish that end was to turn the system to the familiar, to draw out its competence to deal with real questions.[34] The problem of the false suns provided such an example.

In applying the lessons of his world to the weather, Descartes clearly had to begin with an account of water—the most active substance in the meteorological realm. The discussion of water began by considering the effect of the motion of the second matter, the matter of heat, on the minuscule "eels" of the third matter. Constant agitation must certainly bend the pliable rods, allow them to slide over one another, and render them easily separable. Water in its normal state thus allows harder bodies to divide or shape it and flows easily over itself in a container. Yet if the agitation of the second matter is lessened, even slender rods of the third matter would come to rest on one another. Without agitation to allow them to flex and move and fill the little spaces left between the other bits, they require more space, and the heap of the third matter expands slightly:

> This is the reason they come to a stop, haphazardly joined to and lying upon one another, thus forming a hard body, namely ice. Thus you can picture the same difference between water and ice as between a group of eels—either alive or dead—floating in a fishing boat full of holes through which the water of a river flows, agitating the eels; and a group of these same eels, quite dry and rigid with cold on the shore.[35]

The river in the analogy corresponds to the second matter in the mechanical explanation, the stuff of heat and light; the eels correspond to the third matter, the microscopic stuff of real water.

Only after both the theoretical discussion of the mechanical motions and the large-scale analogy did Descartes turn to the phenomena of the world of experience. His observations exhibit the experimental philosopher's acute and accurate sense for the isolation of the phenomena in question:

> We can see this by experiment, if we fill a beaker—or some other container having a rather long, straight neck—with hot water, and expose it to freezing cold air; for the water level will go down visibly, little by little until the water reaches a certain degree of coldness, after which it will gradually swell and rise, until it is completely frozen. Thus the

same cold which will have condensed or shrunk it in the beginning will rarify it afterwards.[36]

This experiment certainly captured what was crucial about the relations between the temperature and the volume of water near its freezing point.

Descartes offered similar series of explanations over and over again in the *Meteorology*. First came a mechanical examination of the motions of the three matters. The smooth, agitated parts of the second matter bounced around in prescribed ways, always consistent with their shape and subtlety. The third matter, the smallest bits of the gross stuff of the world, always reacted gently or briskly, urged to motion or left to rest by the changing agitation of the second. The terms of this discussion remained abstract and technical, variants on motion, shape, and arrangement. Descartes next fixed the technical explanation in the reader's mind with an analogy, a picture from the everyday world of real experience. The analogy might change from one situation to another: In the passage just considered a river represented the second matter; in the *Optics*, the motion of the second matter frequently found an analogy in the motion of a tennis ball. At this analogical level, Descartes's explanations resembled those of his contemporaries at the Bureau d'adresse. One never knew just what might come next or how seriously to take it. The *Meteorology* and the other essays always made it clear, however, that these were merely heuristic aids; although water particles are in some sense like eels, the essential description derived from the initial discussion of the three matters. Only after the illumination of the technical, mechanical discussion by an analogy from common experience did Descartes proceed to the description of an experiment or of an observation from the phenomenal world. In this step, he strove for precision, for an observation as simple as possible to isolate the phenomenon under consideration. Most of the examples from the *Meteorology* are deceptively elementary: the use of a long-necked beaker to amplify the expansive properties of water hardly bespeaks brilliant laboratory technique. Yet its very simplicity inspires confidence; Descartes clearly singled out the phenomenon at hand.

Using this reiterative style, Descartes explained those aspects of his world that would eventually be required to understand the appearance of the multiple suns. Proceeding systematically, he next accounted for the evaporation of water. First came the mechanical analysis aided by an analogy from common experience: The slightest and most flexible bits of the third matter, floating in a surging sea of the second, become separated from their neighbors, "not because of some particular inclination they have to rise upward, nor because the sun itself has some force which attracts them, but solely because they cannot find any other place in which it is as easy for them to continue their movement, just as the dust of a plain arises when it is merely pushed and agitated by the feet of some passerby."[37] As experimental evidence for his explanation, Descartes offered the fact that vapors rise up from heated waters. The explanation deftly turned aside the Aristotelian idea that evaporation is due to the natural tendency of fire to rise, but without making any explicit reference to the Schoolmen's Philosopher or any serious disruption to his own argument. Descartes was conscious of his intellectual competition but was neither obsessed nor intimidated by it.

Proceeding with the analysis, Descartes turned to the behavior of the vapor once it escaped the liquid. Agitated bits of water, the little eel-shaped particles of the third matter, spin rapidly and fill large spaces. Switching analogies as the situation demanded, Descartes represented the third matter as a toy popular at the time. A string passing through a hole in a stick would fly out and make a spinning circle when the stick was rotated between moving hands, filling the space around it and driving out any light objects in its path (see Figure 3.1). Likewise, the vapors arising from water whirl about, agitating the second matter and driving away other bits of vapor to fill an ever larger volume (see Figure 3.2). As their expedition continues, the bits of the matter of water may collide or congregate or may wear out their strength on the second matter, drooping like the string after the stick has stopped spinning. They may swim through the space around them still as ice. By the end of the second discourse, the system could account for mists, clouds of ice or water, humidity, and half a dozen other sorts of atmospheric moisture. Each corresponded to an alternative path for the various bits of the third matter as it spun away from the evaporating water.

With the aid of these graphical illustrations and home-spun analogies, the least philosophical reader could have reeled off an explanation

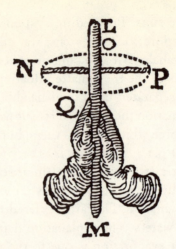

Figure 3.1 A seventeenth-century children's toy with a spinning cord describing a circle, used to show how the long, thin, flexible particles of water can spin rapidly, occupying large amounts of space as water vapor. Reproduced from René Descartes, Opera Omnia *(Amsterdam, 1685), in which the figure is slightly different from the original,* Meteorology, *figure 2. Courtesy of the Bakken Library, Minneapolis, Minn.*

for the action of the second and third matters without any considerable thought. The interplay between text and figures, between gross phenomena and the mechanisms that drove them, between mechanism and analogy, cemented the appropriate pictures in the mind. Just as he had done with the *Optics* and the *Geometry,* Descartes homed in on his audience; the audience for the *Meteorology* came from the Bureau d'adresse. That is not to say that the author "dumbed down" his exposition. The work presented more than a simplistic, decorated picture of nature. Descartes did not merely produce a careful mechanical description of his bits of matter; he used their properties and their motions as a consistent form of explanation. Because of the thoroughgoing, systematic nature of his text, Descartes did not have to mount a rhetorical attack on Aristotle. His system, his three matters and their motions, rendered the Peripatetic elements of earth, air, fire, and water superfluous, irrelevant, and imprecise. The rebuttal of the teachings of the schools remained implicit: To the schooled reader, the contrast was clear; to the unschooled, the explanation remained positive and without polemic.

Figure 3.2 Illustration of water particles in various forms: as liquid, at A near the bottom of the illustration; as vapor, at B above the surface; and condensing at C, D, and E. Note the use of a circle bisected by its diameter—reminiscent of the toy in Figure 3.1—to represent the evaporated third matter of water. Reproduced from René Descartes, Opera Omnia *(Amsterdam, 1685), in which the figure is slightly different from the original,* Meteorology, *figure 1. Courtesy of the Bakken Library, Minneapolis, Minn.*

Before the introductory system of matter came to an end, Descartes implicitly struck a similar insider's blow at the Paracelsian principles. The lightest and most flexible bits of the matter of water, it had already been observed, represented those most likely to evaporate. At the other end of the scale, there are relatively stout and sturdy particles, still straight and fairly slender but impervious to the normal pummeling of the second matter. In the presence of the more flexible particles, with which they are normally associated, they float at random, lending but little weight to the water by their greater bulk. Yet when the lighter bits are evaporated out of the water, these heavy ones remain behind and lie rigid on one another even at normal temperatures. These particles, congealing like ice, constitute salt. Descartes offered both a theoretical explanation and experimental evidence for his conclusions. As the agitation of heated seawater increases, it throws the salt particles up with the lighter bits of vapor. The air and the second matter cannot, however, sustain the greater weight of the heavy salt particles, so these fall back on the surface of the evaporating water. As enough of these particles collect, solid and unshielded by the flexible particles, which evaporate and leave the pot, the stouter bits begin to rest upon one another, forming little pieces that at first look like ice. Detailed illustrations accompanied Descartes's precise description of how they begin to collect, form a film, and crystallize; he was certainly no stranger to the chemical workshop. Only by great heat could he cause this salt to melt; the second matter must batter the stiff particles with a tremendous violence to bend and move them.

The description of the salinity of the sea, which followed the theoretical explanation of salty matter, presented a stark contrast to the opinions on the subject offered at the Bureau d'adresse. Within the Cartesian system the seas are naturally salty, since salt is but a coarse form of water—one hardly needed recourse to Paracelsian principles to explain it. Further, great bodies of water remain salty, since salt cannot evaporate along with the more flexible parts of the water. Moreover, since the stout particles cannot escape the sea, they do not enter the rain cycle, and the waters of streams and rivers are therefore fresh. Ships float higher in the seas because saltwater is heavier than inland waters diluted by rain; this too follows directly from an analysis of the shape and disposition of the particles that make up the various sorts of waters. The evaporative process by which salt is harvested from the sea is but an application of the action of the second matter on the third and involves no mysterious transformation of Aristotelian elements or Paracelsian principles. The exposition tarried to investigate the other properties of salt in terms of the stout particles that form it. The difficulty in bending the littlest bits of salt causes them to prick the tongue, giving the characteristic taste of salted foods. Moreover, when these particles become lodged in salted meats, they act as a stabilizing force, fixing the shapes of the pores and calming the motion of the second matter around them. This rigidity prevents, or at least slows, the random motion that leads to decay—a motion encouraged by the presence of the more flexible rods of ordinary water, which promote putrefaction.

So the systematic web spun out. The first three discourses of the *Meteorology* offer a discursive but not rambling account of the mechanical aspects of the Cartesian world. They are inviting in their simplicity and their completeness. Descartes, still a long way from his explanation of the false suns, did not simply produce a mechanism when he needed an explanation; he exhaustively pursued the mechanical possibilities of particles of water and second matter. The discussion of salt, for example, hardly followed the meteorological framework of the text; it nonetheless derived quite logically from the mechanical analysis of the third matter required to get at the behavior of water and its vapors, crucial to meteorology.

The next four discourses, "Of Winds," "Of Clouds," "Of Snow, Rain, and Hail," and "Of Storms, Lightning, and Other Storms That Blaze in the Air," set out to put the matter of water into the context of the weather. The mode of argument of necessity changed a bit. Whereas the first three discourses had determined how the second and third matters conspired to produce certain phenomena in the world around us, the next series sketched out how these phenomena could operate to produce a large-scale effect. The requisite properties of waters and vapors had been rigorously developed; Descartes did not need to repeat the derivations each time he invoked one of those properties.

For the winds he offered several causes. The most constant, easterly winds result from the heat of the sun as it moves from east to west, dilating the air with its warmth. Descartes also alluded to another reason, "the explanation of which cannot be conveniently derived except by explaining the entire fabric of the universe, which I do not intend to do here."[38] The suppressed explanation was the rotation of the earth; the specter of Galileo's condemnation was still much on his mind. Yet other explanations followed as well: Late in the afternoon, westerlies spring up as the sun warms the western air; equatorial heat helps dilate the air and drives warm breezes north or at other times straight up, making room for cold, northern breezes blowing to the south. The ebb and flow of the tides, the motion of the rivers, any large-scale motion at all, it seems, might have its effect. Here the *Meteorology* presented the stuff of Renaudot's *Conferences* or, more significantly, of Galileo's extravagant explanation of the tides in the *Dialogues Concerning the Two Chief World Systems*.

More important than any of these gross causes, however, and totally unrelated to daily and seasonal regularities, is the fact that vapors and exhalations must drive the air before them. (The mechanism presented in the first three discourses, the spinning bits of the third matter of water flailing anything near them, lent familiarity and plausibility to this cause.) Descartes offered the analogy of the aeolipile, a hollow copper ball with a bit of water in the bottom and a hole in the side. The illustration that accompanied his text (see Figure 3.3) used the symbol of a circle bisected by its diameter—reminiscent of the illustration of the toy with a spinning cord filling a circular space and the diagram of the motion of vapors that followed—to represent the evaporated third matter of water spinning in the cavity, driving the

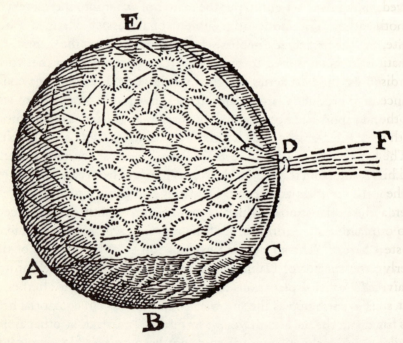

Figure 3.3 The aeolipile, a hollow copper ball with water in the bottom and a hole in the side, used to produce artificial breezes. Note the use of a circle bisected by its diameter—reminiscent of the illustration of the toy in Figure 3.1—to represent the evaporated third matter of water. Reproduced from René Descartes, Opera Omnia *(Amsterdam, 1685), in which the figure is slightly different from the original,* Meteorology, *figure 8. Courtesy of the Bakken Library, Minneapolis, Minn.*

wispy air particles before it.[39] When water is heated, vapors arise from the water and send a little wind out through the hole, like steam from a teapot. More than anything, the illustration tied the discourse on winds to that on vapors. Like the texts, the illustrations moved with a minimum of fuss between abstract representation of the three matters and pictures of phenomenal world.

On and on the discourse went, describing how the winds might drive the clouds, or the clouds the winds; how a southerly breeze might melt a cloud of ice, or a northerly blast freeze one of water. The details of putative cloud and mist formation occasionally became tremendously elaborate. Descartes took special care in the explanation of snowflakes, presenting a detailed description of their formation complete with references to the dates of the snowfalls he had observed. This exacting natural history he punctuated with an involved hypothesis for the action of the third matter required to produce the white, six-pointed marvels. Similar circumstances, with only slight variations, could instead produce hail. The section closed with a rousing discussion of storms: Descartes wrote knowingly of thunderclaps induced by huge, hard clouds running amok and colliding with one another and, when punctured by the crosses atop steeples, spewing forth lightning (see Figure 3.4).

The world Descartes inhabited was mechanical, almost crudely so, and his boldness in explaining phenomena in those terms must appear to the modern reader as Leibniz would characterize it two generations later: a pretty novel of physics. Yet the stories of rigid clouds banging into one another and showering out lightning sparks like flint struck by steel appear childish and primitive rather than the products of an overly romantic imagination. We see in Descartes's theories of storms a naïve first attempt to produce a mechanical explanation. If we know that such an explanation must be more complex and sophisticated, this fact can but offer evidence for the success of the Cartesian project. We do not question the proposition that an explanation of storms is properly mechanical. Contemporary mechanism simply presents a system at once more abstract and infinitely more complicated.

The mildly indulgent discussion of thunderstorms completed, Descartes returned to the problems of meteorological optics that had initiated his researches eight years before. He began with a thorough mathematical theory of rainbows, which like the theory of lenses in

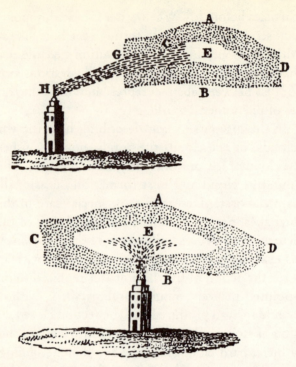

Figure 3.4 Two views of lightning streaming from a torn thundercloud to-ward a steeple. Reproduced from René Descartes, Opera Omnia *(Amsterdam, 1685), in which the figures are slightly different from the originals,* Meteorol-ogy, *figures 17 and 18. Courtesy of the Bakken Library, Minneapolis, Minn.*

the *Optics* offered an essentially complete explanation. Not until the tenth and final discourse, however, did Descartes turn to the question of the false suns, which had inspired the work. Imbedded in the *Mete-orology,* following on the heels of the most impressive mathematical explanations in the history of meteorology, it may have seemed plau-sible. Alone it would have been difficult to swallow—more worthy, perhaps, of the discussion at the Bureau d'adresse than the fount of modern philosophy. The rare phenomenon required a rare cloud (see Figure 3.5), formed by a combination of the north and south winds:

> I assume that these two winds encounter, or form, a cloud made of
> pieces of snow; and this cloud is so extensive in depth and width, that
> the winds cannot pass one above and one below, or else between the
> two of them, as they usually do. Instead, they are forced to take their

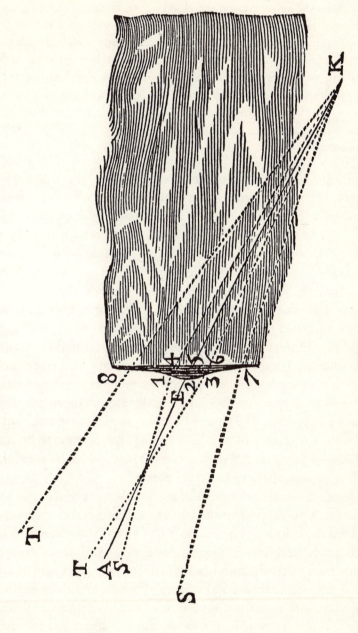

Figure 3.5 Illustration of a cloud of ice forming a lens. Reproduced from René Descartes, Opera Omnia (Amsterdam, 1685), in which the figure is slightly different from the original, Meteorology, figure 28. Courtesy of the Bakken Library, Minneapolis, Minn.

course around it. By this means, not only do the winds make the cloud round, but also, because the wind coming from the south is warm, it slightly melts the snow around the cloud's circumference; and because this snow is immediately refrozen—by the cold north wind as well as by the proximity of the interior snow, which is not yet melted—it can form, as it were, a large ring of ice which is completely continuous and transparent, whose surface will not fail to be quite polished, for the winds which round it off are very uniform. And in addition, this ice is thicker on one side . . . , which I assume to be exposed to the warm wind and sun, than on the other side, . . . where the snow was not able to melt quite so easily.[40]

Suddenly the elaborate discussion of the middle of the *Meteorology* fell into place. The northern and the southern winds; the formation of raindrops, snowflakes, and ice; the elaborate paths of the wind and the great rigidity of the clouds: They all conspired to create a magnificent lens of ice, suspended on a breeze. Its shape, mirabile dictu, produced several images of the sun (see Figure 3.6). Five had appeared in Rome in 1629, setting the *Meteorology* in motion. Descartes presented a picture replete with five suns and a rainbow. The king of Poland, not to be outdone, reported that he had seen six images in 1625.[41] Such regal results did not impress the philosopher. Descartes assured his readers that a cloud could form capable of adding a seventh image above the sixth or, with a proper combination of warming zephyrs and bitter blasts, "up to twelve of them"—in practically any arrangement about the sun one might wish. The chance of seeing such a thing would have been a bit like the chance of monkeys typing Shakespeare, to be sure, but the Cartesian system did provide an explanation in the event that some prince or some pauper might witness it.

The passage describing the cause of multiple suns served as the conclusion not only to the *Meteorology* but to the four essays together. It provides the best key in the essays of 1637 to understanding the Cartesian world as Descartes's near contemporaries understood it. This is not to say that the mind-body problem, the invention of analytic geometry, the mathematical science of optics, and the identification of matter with extension should not serve as fundamental roots of civilization as we know it. However, those abstract and recondite contributions to Western thought did go over the heads of the likes of Theophraste Renaudot and Jean Chapelain and most of the other genuine Western thinkers who lived in Louis XIII's Paris. Moreover,

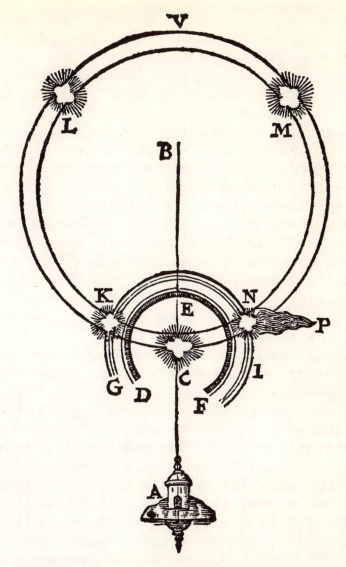

Figure 3.6 False suns refracted through the cloud illustrated in Figure 3.5. Reproduced from René Descartes, Opera Omnia *(Amsterdam, 1685), in which the figure is slightly different from the original,* Meteorology, *figure 29. Courtesy of the Bakken Library, Minneapolis, Minn.*

they did not produce any short-term reaction in the academic establishment. Aristotelians in the schools largely ignored the essays—especially the first three, which contained the foundations of modern philosophy, mathematics, and mathematical physics—for they had no need of a scientific revolution. It was the explanation of the false suns, of the nature of water and salt and fire, of the rainbow, that spoke to the Parisian circles considered in the first chapter. Moreover, it was the Cartesian system, the pretty novel of physics, that won converts to the new philosophy in the generations that first had the chance to read the Cartesian corpus.

No matter what interest posterity might have eventually discovered in the essays, they got off to a slow start. Descartes ordered a press run of about two hundred copies of what might be described as a self-published work.[42] An unbound advance copy went to Mersenne to clear the French censors—a process required of all books, whether or not they appeared at the author's expense. After the official publication allowed by that clearance, Descartes sent out a few dozen copies to appropriate readers: Three went to his old school at La Flèche; several to Mersenne for members of his circle; more to Italy (where the bookseller refused to handle them because of theological suspicions); a pair to Louis XIII and Richelieu. Descartes maintained the first-time academic author's dream of a second edition and made bold to refer to it in the essays: "I beg all those who have some objections to my writings, send them to my book dealer, and when I am informed of them, I shall try to append my replies to them at the same time; and by this means the reader, seeing them together, will more easily judge the truth."[43]

Several replies were indeed forthcoming, and Descartes set out to produce a pair of new works to elaborate his ideas. The first one, the *Meditations on the First Philosophy*, took up the theological and metaphysical points raised in the *Discourse on Method*—the method itself and the proof of the existence of God and the external world. His efforts reversed the accessible strategy of the essays entirely. The *Meditations*, written in Latin, were rigorously developed and tremendously difficult to read. Descartes offered no particular help to the incautious reader. Nor did he release his work to an unsuspecting public, awaiting whatever response it might be moved to give. He sent a manuscript copy to Mersenne and through him to Antoine Arnauld, a leading French theologian; to Pierre Gassendi; and, among the English, to Thomas Hobbes—a pretty good group of referees. All four offered criticisms, and Descartes prepared careful responses to their difficulties. Not until this entire exercise had transpired did the manuscript, along with the objections and responses, see print in 1641.

A similar project in natural philosophy proceeded apace, and in 1644 Descartes published the *Principles of Philosophy.* The *Principles* fulfilled the promise of the long-suppressed *World,* building a complete picture of the physical universe. The reception of this work in France proved a sufficiently important matter that Descartes actually made a short visit to Paris to promote the work. He adopted another uncharacteristic political ploy to further the readership of the *Principles,* dedicating the work to Elizabeth of Hanover, who he said had the commanding and penetrating understanding of his philosophy required to master it. Although such obeisance to royalty was of course conventional and need represent nothing more than political puffery, Descartes's extensive correspondence with Elizabeth makes the dedicatory compliments plausible.

The *Principles* offered two long parts devoted to metaphysical disquisition before it built the physical world in its Cartesian completeness. Squeamishness over the condemnation of Galileo's contentious challenge of Catholic cosmology had faded as the intellectual world continued its study of nature with no further intervention from the Church. Descartes at last could speak his mind. The most significant departure from the earlier essays came in Part 3 of the new work, on the "Visible World." Here Descartes finally discussed his thoughts on the construction of the heavens, including a gingerly endorsement of the Copernican theory. The section provided nothing less than a natural history of the whole universe.[44]

After God created the universe, Descartes began, it consisted of confused, agitated bits of matter.[45] As things settled down (and God gracefully withdrew), the world began to take its present shape, following the laws of motion. The restless agitation of the undifferentiated bits of matter started to organize into huge spheres of motion, each more or less independent of the others except at the edges, where they encountered one another. The random agitation within each of these became more and more coherent, turning in great vortices; these regular, stable whirlpools set the pattern for heavenly motion followed ever since.

The circulating matter of the universe bumped and clumped and ground itself up to form the three sorts of matter originally described in *The World.* The first—extremely fine and subtle—was the shavings and chips worn away from the larger bits by the friction of motion. The second—smooth, round, mobile, and uniform—occupied most space, lubricated in its motion by the first. Yet in some places large chunks of matter congregated and, pressed together by the incessant pummeling of the other two, formed the third, larger sort of matter, which makes up the stuff of the gross world.

As the confused amalgam of the two subtle matters circulated around the vortex, the first—the smallest bits with the least "determination" to follow a straight line toward the edge of the whirlpools—tended to move toward the center to form the sun or the stars. This central reservoir of the first matter in each of the great whirlpools is the only place that the extremely fine stuff can act to much effect. Without the inhibiting presence of the larger particles of the second matter, the tiny bits of the first move about in frenzied commotion, battering each other at tremendous speed. So great is their fury, in fact, that they send out continual ripples through the second matter that fills the vortex—ripples that we perceive as light and heat. The great wells of first matter make up the sun and the stars "fixed" in the heavens and provide a continual source of agitation for the entire world. Unlike the fires on earth, they require no fuel for their activity; they send out vibrations through the vortex by their very nature.

The evolution of the huge whirlpools produced more subtle interactions. Here and there, bits of the second matter clumped together, forming the third, grosser sort. If some of the bits congregated on the surface of the central well of first matter, they made sunspots, wandering dark clouds across the face of the star. If the process continued until a solid crust obscured the entire surface of a star, that star became a comet. A small, cometary body, with its attendant whirling vortex of second matter, might be captured in the vortex of a larger star. Circulating in the huge whirlpool, these captured comets settled in as planets; their own captured comets could follow them as moons.[46] Comets that formed near the outer edges of the great stellar vortices might slip from one sphere of influence to another (see Figure 3.7). As they wander through the heavens they remain as comets, lighting the sky near one vortex under the agitation of its central first matter for a time until they are captured by yet another star's whirlpool to disappear from the realm and the sight of the temporary host. This too Descartes illustrated with a series of figures sufficiently striking that one or another of them has decorated most accounts of his cosmology from the time of its publication on.

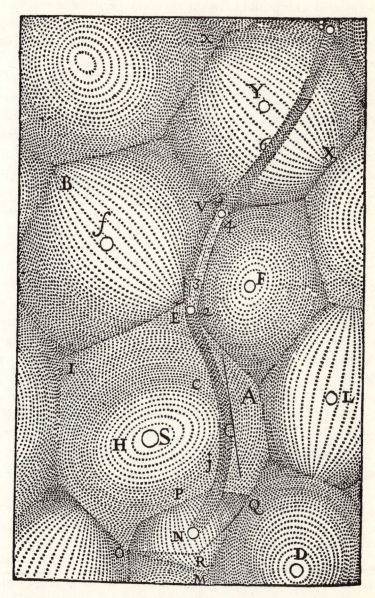

Figure 3.7 The path of a comet among the celestial whirlpools surrounding stars. Reproduced from René Descartes, Principia philosophia *(Amsterdam, 1685), p. 64. Courtesy of the Bakken Library, Minneapolis, Minn.*

Thus the third part of the *Principles* provided the celestial system, the portion of *The World* that Descartes had prudently omitted from the essays of 1637, suppressing it because of the condemnation of Galileo. It also offered a clear link between the natural history of the heavens and that of the terrestrial sphere: The seamless web of philosophy promised to Mersenne as an explanation of the false suns fifteen years earlier found its place in the exposition published in 1644. The fourth part of the work went on to present a complete natural history of the development of our own planet, accompanied by a philosophical commentary on just how its evolution occurred. Descartes began his discussion of the terrestrial realm with a detailed history of our planetary vortex. Much of this history it shared in general terms with the other planets. The whirlpool effect of the vortex of fast-moving second matter drives the large, immobile chunks of the third matter inward, causing the apparent "gravity," or weight, of solid objects. The transmission of coherent agitation through the little balls that form the whirlpool causes light, already treated in the *Optics;* the local, random pummeling of the third matter causes the effects of the motion we perceive as heat, of which the discussion of freezing and melting and evaporating in the *Meteorology* provides only one example.

Descartes provided a more careful explanation of our particular cometary star, based on peculiarities observable only at close range. The pressure of the moon, transmitted through the swirling second matter, drives the water of the oceans up and down in tides.[47] The crust of third matter is but a thin coating on our earth; it cracks and buckles under the strain of floating on the little star within. These reactions to stress produce the uneven geological surface of the earth, a phenomenon that Descartes illustrated with a figure (see Figure 3.8) offering utterly fantastic detail.[48] He explained how vapors escaping from the bowels of the planet through the resulting fissures cause earthquakes and volcanoes.[49] Geological and climatic changes followed straightforwardly from uniform and continuous physical causes. (Had the continental drift theory been put forward a few decades before it was, the precursor-hunting generation of historians of science between the world wars would have found geological plates and volcanic island chains in the Cartesian system more plainly even than they found quantum mechanics in the Lucretian swerves of the ancient atomists.)

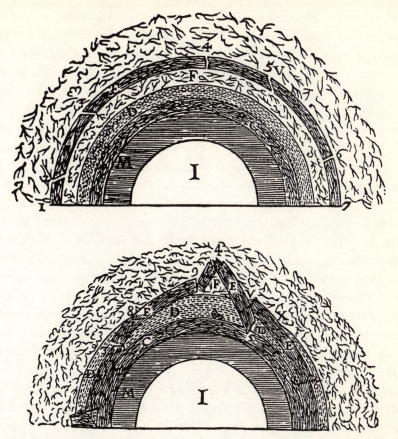

Figure 3.8 Illustration showing how mountains are formed when the crust of the earth buckles. Reproduced from René Descartes, Principia philosophia *(Amsterdam, 1685), p. 155. Courtesy of the Bakken Library, Minneapolis, Minn.*

The whole of the fourth part of the *Principles* relentlessly pursued the behavior of the three matters as they floated and bumped along in the terrestrial vortex. Subterranean formation provided the key to the qualities of most of the stuff of the world as well as to its weather. The interior of the earth, according to Descartes's scheme, is nearly completely filled with chunks of the third matter. The chunks are sufficiently large in the micromechanical scale of the three matters that they cannot be driven any closer together. In the pores and interstices that survived the accretion of the earth are found little bits of the first and second matter, for a vacuum is impossible: All extension implies matter that occupies it. In the tiny passages, with their rigid walls, even the extremely subtle bits of the first two matters lie nearly at rest, constantly forced more firmly into the interstices of the earth by the agitation of the surrounding vortex. As the pressure increases, their agitation can cease altogether, so the matters congeal, forming new chunks of the third matter conformable to the spaces among the stable, solid core. This process (a precursor, perhaps, of injection-molding as well as of the formation of diamonds) creates the stuff of the earth.

The finest pores create the common materials Descartes had described in the *Meteorology*—the wispy, branching stuff of the air and oils, the pliable rods of water, and the thicker rods of salt. More substantial pores, however, produce more complex and compact materials. One species grows as it slides through the larger passages, driven by the constant agitation of the subtle matters and smoothed by contact with the solid walls of the passages that contain it. These strong, smooth pieces resemble water, except that they are heavier than even the stoutest, saltiest parts of water. They form the matter of quicksilver: Large, smooth pieces slip easily over one another but fit so closely together that they block the path of the second matter in the whirlpool around the earth almost completely, so they transmit no light and they weigh down toward the center of the vortex with great gravity.

The investigation of the earth continued in like detail for a dozen other sorts of matter: In some places, brittle particles form to constitute "corrosive sugars" and acids;[50] in others, flexible branching bits more compact than air but more pliable than earth form oils and fatty substances. The three principles of the Paracelsians in fact follow quite readily from the Cartesian system, and its author was quick to point out that fact:

> I have thus explained three sorts of bodies which seem to bear a strong resemblance to those that the chemists habitually take for their principles, and that they call salt, sulfur, and mercury: Since one can take the corrosive sugars for their salt, the little branches that compose oily matter for their sulfur, and the quicksilver for their mercury. And my opinion is that the true cause that makes metal grow in mines is that the cor-

rosive sugars flow here and there among the layer C [that is, the crust of the earth] in such a manner that they detach certain of their parts from others, which afterwards find themselves enveloped and as it were cloaked by the little branches of the oily material, and are easily pushed from [the crust] C toward [the surface layer] E by the little pieces of quicksilver, as it is agitated and rarified by heat.[51]

Descartes lamented only that he hadn't the facilities to do all the experiments required to verify his reasoning.[52] He went on to describe the conditions he imagined might be required to produce suitable mixtures of the three principles and suggested that areas at the foot of mountains, butting up against a plain, offered the most likely spot to find newly formed metals—needless to say, a prediction that agreed with the usual location of mining sites at the time.

To drive home the superiority of his system even further, Descartes explicitly compared it to the Aristotelian corpus, without naming his adversary:

Up to this point, I have tried to explain the nature and all the principal properties of air, water, earth, and fire—since these are the bodies which are found most generally throughout the sublunary sphere which we inhabit—that are called the four elements. But there is still another body, namely the magnet, that one might say has a greater extension than any of the other four, since the whole mass of the earth is a magnet, and we know of no place where its virtue does not operate.[53]

The prolonged discussion that followed played a role similar to that of the false suns in the *Meteorology*. By itself, the Cartesian system of magnetism might have presented nothing more than an elaborate exercise in romantic imagination. Yet it drew extensively on what had preceded it. As the theory of the false suns tied together the constitution of water and air, the causes of winds, and the explanation of thunder and rainbows, so the explanation of magnetism depended upon and lent credence to the motions of the three matters, the natural history of the formation of acids and sulfurs and metals, and the spatial arrangement of the pores and interstices of the third matter pressed inside the earth.

To explain all the properties of magnets, Descartes needed but one more type of passage to mold the subtle matters. He described a class of pores shaped like long corkscrews, passing from one pole of the earth to the other. As bits of the first and second matters become clogged and compressed in these, they congeal to form bits of the third matter conformable to their shape. As the little "screws" suffer even more pummeling, they bore through the pores, creating ever more perfectly shaped spiral paths. When the screws emerge from one or the other of the poles, they break into short pieces and are swept confusedly around the terrestrial vortex until they find their way to the other pole, where they may enter the appropriate interstices in the crust to repeat their circulating journey. This continuous stream provides the source of magnetic orientation from south to north and north to south. The *Principles* illustrated this theory with a woodcut the modern student of magnetism would immediately identify as field lines (see Figure 3.9). In short, the Cartesian system of magnetism provided an account of the phenomena that the Francocentric world could count as the equal of William Gilbert's *De Magnete*.

Not quite so rare as observations of false suns, magnets nonetheless represented quite a novelty in the seventeenth century. Strongly magnetized lodestones commanded a handsome price; kings and princes were more likely to enjoy their antics than peasants working outside in the rain. The fragile and ugly black rocks were frequently mounted in beautiful little boxes made of precious metals and worked by skilled jewelers, enhancing their mystique. Descartes's extended discussion of the magnet, like the extended explanation of the false suns in the *Meteorology*, represented a self-conscious tour de force explaining a rare and exotic phenomenon. With that explanation, he concluded the fourth book of the *Principles*, which dealt with the construction of the earth, as he had concluded the *Meteorology* with his description of the false suns. Like the explanations of the false suns, that of magnetic phenomena made sense only within the larger system that preceded it.

The *Principles* thus completed the project in what we might identify as physical science intended when Descartes finished his manuscript of *The World* in 1633. There is of course a great deal more in the work than the present account offers and a great many other interpretations of what it means. A new analysis of any scrap of Cartesian jottings must be above all an exercise in hubris, and an analysis of the *Principles* as an essay on magnets (and of the *Discourse* and accompanying

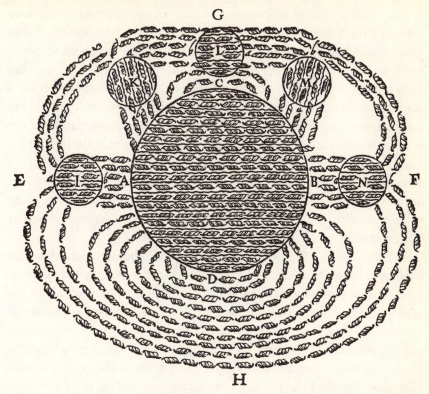

Figure 3.9 The magnetic configuration of the earth. The poles are shown at the left and right; the screw-shaped magnetic particles are shown both inside and outside the earth. Above the earth, magnets align themselves with the stream of magnetic particles; below, the map of the path is reminiscent of field lines. Reproduced from René Descartes, Principia philosophia *(Amsterdam, 1685), p. 196. Courtesy of the Bakken Library, Minneapolis, Minn.*

essays as an essay on false suns) must present one of the more peculiar spectacles in this genre. Let me hasten to agree that this analysis does not offer any great insight into the foundations of Western thought or modern philosophy. It is instead uninformed blundering through a field sown with great ideas, perhaps tromping on shoots destined to flower and admiring only the few weeds already sprouted. But it is blundering with a purpose; it intentionally avoids the opportunity to be informed by the centuries of scholarship devoted to pursuing problems raised substantially or in passing in Descartes's writings.

The spirit of the *Principles* would inform the Cartesian school of natural philosophy for nearly a century after its appearance; that much should be noncontroversial. What is offered here is an idiosyncratic reading, a twentieth-century reading to be sure, but one that might help a twentieth-century audience to understand how a denizen of Renaudot's Bureau d'adresse might have dealt with these books before anyone knew for sure that they would one day form the basis of a modernity that remained a twinkle in the collective philosophical eye of the Rationalists. It is a reading that follows Descartes's directions, one guided by the idea that only in understanding the broad sweep of the argument might we understand its parts, a reading willing to sacrifice a whole series of beautiful little insights into details for the sake of providing a coherent interpretation.

To finish the biographical story already begun before I delved into its intellectual complications, the *Principles* won for Descartes immediate recognition as an important author. A veritable Cartesian school began to flourish in Paris. The Duc de Lioncourt translated the text of the *Meditations* into French, and Claude Clerselier prepared the objections and responses that Descartes had appended to the work for inclusion in the translation. Descartes reviewed and revised their efforts, and Clerselier financed the publication of the *Meditations* in 1647.[54] The abbé Picot produced a companion piece, a French translation of the *Principles,* which Clerselier revised. Descartes read, commented on, improved, and altered this French edition—making it more valuable to the scholar than the Latin edition, which preceded it. Clerselier published the translation in the same year as his translation of the *Meditations.*[55]

Conventional success loomed. Offers of patronage again beckoned Descartes to Paris. Clerselier's circle managed to wangle a pension of 3,000 livres out of the minister Cardinal Mazarin. This sum, equal to the income that Descartes enjoyed from his own estates, lured the philosopher back to France in 1648.[56] Descartes passed a short time there, but his aversion to success quickly overcame his enjoyment of it. He took the opportunity of the turbulence surrounding the Fronde to flee the popularity bestowed upon him, and to return to Holland. Yet the importance of patronage and the prestige of court came to have a stronger hold on the peripatetic philosopher. In fall 1649 he accepted an offer from Queen Christina of Sweden, moving to her court to take up an active role as her personal philosopher. As the story goes, Descartes had risen late all his life. Nonetheless, he roused himself in time to meet with the queen at five each morning, convenient for a philosophically inclined monarch if not for an academic philosopher. Between the rigors of the climate and the severity of his regimen, Descartes took ill and died in early 1650.[57] It was perhaps just as well that he had avoided patrons and appointments for over twenty years, preparing his writings in private.

The death of Descartes ends only one part of his story. Immediate hagiography and the disposition of relics we will leave for another chapter. The philosophical part goes on and on. At his movable doorstep we must place responsibility for the transition from Renaissance to modern thought. The remainder of this chapter will struggle with the long-range consequences of that problem, before turning (in Chapter 4) to the immediate reception of the Cartesian corpus in a period that historians have taken to calling "early modern"—a period itself poised between the Renaissance and the modern world.

Descartes, aware of the novelty of his approach and the difficulties it would cause for readers, prepared an extensive preface to the French translation of the *Principles* that appeared in 1647. The most important passage for the present purpose suggests a plan of attack, a sort of owner's guide to the Cartesian system:

> I should also have added a word of advice regarding the manner of reading this work, which is, that I should wish the reader at first go over the whole of it, as he would a romance, without greatly straining his attention, or tarrying at the difficulties he may perhaps meet with, and that afterwards, if they seem to him to merit a more careful examination, and he feels a desire to know their causes, he may read it a second time, in order to observe the connection of my reasonings; but that he must not then give it up in despair, although he may not everywhere sufficiently discover the connection of the proof, or understand all the reasonings—it being only necessary to mark with a pen the places where the difficulties occur, and continue reading without interruption to the end; then, if he does not grudge to take up the book a third time, I am confident that he will find in a fresh perusal the solution of most of the difficulties he will have marked before; and that, if any remain, their solution will in the end be found in another reading.[58]

Variations on this theme remain the guiding pedagogical principle behind most instruction in mathematics and physics even today. Algebra, the calculus, elementary physics and chemistry; all are taught again and again to students in high school and college, out of different books to be sure and perhaps in increasingly subtle detail, but with an undeniably repetitive flavor. Instructors offer what Latin teachers used to call "paradigms" when that word meant nothing more than correct examples. Yet as much as we may like to pretend that our pedagogical brilliance will convince our students of each theorem we present and each physical law we demonstrate, and that our examples will immediately clarify the application of the laws, the inexperienced must come first to learn not a single step or a particular detail, but the way mathematicians or physicists or chemists approach their subjects. Only in the context of these arcane systems of belief do the individual points make any sense. Descartes understood this pedagogical fact.

The Cartesian advice that prefaced the *Principles*—"Cartesian" in the eighteenth-century French ordinary-language sense of "clever" and "ordered" as well as in the literal meaning of the term—turned Renaissance pedagogy on its head. The notebook method suggested marking useful, instructive, or (above all) quotable passages; in its more aristocratic formulations it left even the transcription of these verbal nuggets to a scribe, removing them forever from their context. Descartes by contrast urged his readers to read the *Principles* whole and indeed to mark only those lines that gave trouble—lines of little use for future citation. Even with these passages, the solution to difficulties came not with commentary or directed contemplation; Descartes assured his students that elucidation would derive only from another perusal of the whole text. The system was all. Education for Descartes, as for no one before him, was what remains when we have forgotten where we learned it.

Pedagogy seems a peculiar place to locate the crux of Cartesian modernity; to do so would surely overstate the case. Nevertheless, the notion of system—be it philosophical, physical, mathematical, or biological—grounded all Descartes's work. It introduced a search for consistency altogether novel in late Renaissance discussion of method. Moreover, this conception of consistency is at odds with our own ideas about the internal coherence of a rigorous theory. The parts of the Cartesian system needed not so much to fit together as to find a secure place in the whole. Thus, once the system was grasped, inconsistencies among the various parts did not produce the sort of cognitive dissonance in Descartes or his readers that it would in philosophers of the nineteenth and twentieth centuries. Instead, Descartes acknowledged what he saw as very real but minor difficulties and omissions; for example: "I have not described in my *Principles* all the motions of each planet, but I have supposed in general all those that the observers have found and I have attempted to explain the causes."[59] On his own testimony, these gaps and inconsistencies pointed to the personal frailties of his own intellect. (The philosophical branch of modern Cartesian studies seems lately to have been unwilling to acknowledge such infirmities, taking the comments as ironic self-depreciation. Yet they had a serious pedagogical as well as rhetorical purpose.) Descartes argued that only through a better understanding of the system, a more complete grasp of the whole, could the philosopher figure out the last details. This required a reasoned consideration of the world tempered by experience both mental and physical.

This way of thinking, this ontology, this willful belief that we must understand the mental and physical worlds above all as a system—such was the essence of Cartesianism for the first hundred years or so of its existence. The "spirit of systems" would become, appropriately, the aspect of Cartesian thought that Enlightened critics attacked a century and more after the death of its founder. This book is about the rise and fall of Cartesianism during the seventeenth and eighteenth centuries; it is fundamentally about the Cartesian system. The epistemology and metaphysics that seem today to be those aspects of Western thought properly initiated by Descartes, although they are undeniably there, did not attract the attention of the vast majority of those who considered themselves Cartesians. The story told here is therefore about, not the place of Cartesianism in Western thought, but its place in French culture during the early modernity that transpired between the ascension of Louis XIV and the French Revolution.

Reflections on the mind-body problem

In the three and a half centuries intervening between the appearance of the *Principles* and the present, Cartesian studies have taken on a life of their own—indeed, each generation has produced a new Cartesian school, providing its founder with significantly more than nine philosophical lives. This is as it should be, and I have no desire to venture into the modern Cartesian quagmire. Yet a few cautionary tales need telling, more to separate the texts of Descartes from the discourse they have engendered than as corrective to that discourse. Like the Marxist and Freudian passages in *Don Quixote,* Descartes's opinions on post-Kantian philosophy of mind or nineteenth-century mechanism must have flowed from some other pen than that of the original author.

The philosophical problem most frequently associated with Descartes is the distinction between the mind and the body. This distinction is certainly there to be discovered. Moreover, the mind-body problem is interesting independent of what Descartes thought about it. It is one of the cornerstones of Western philosophy, and the formulation of solutions different from the Cartesian one has occupied and interested Western philosophers ever since. It forms the first step in the classic progression of early modern philosophy from Descartes through Locke and Hume to Kant, a series of problems and solutions that seem so natural to those trained to have modern minds that one can scarcely imagine getting through a semester that begins with Descartes without reaching the *Prolegomena to Any Future Metaphysics.*

For our purposes, as distinct from those of the analytic philosopher, it is important to recognize that Descartes did present a solution explaining the communication between our mental and physical selves, between the *res cogitans,* whose existence we cannot doubt, and the *res extensa,* whose toes we sometimes sense we stub. Appropriate to the spirit of systems, the connection came in terms of physiology. Like much of the physical system that Descartes described in the essays of 1637 and in the *Principles,* the physiology began in an identifiable way in the manuscript of *The World.* That work had contained a long essay *On Man.* Descartes returned to this material after the publication of the *Principles;* he composed a *Description of the Human Body* in about 1648, although he prepared nothing for the press. It was in *On Man,* finally published posthumously with the *Description* in 1664, that Descartes left his most extensive discussion of the relations between the mind and the body.

Thoroughly convinced of the mechanical nature of his world, Descartes assumed that the connection between the mind and the body must have a definable mechanism. With an enthusiasm and naïveté reminiscent of his explanation of the false suns, Descartes confidently located this connection in the pineal gland. There, he asserted (to the metaphorical roll of thunder produced by colliding clouds of ice), the soul senses the motion of animal spirits conducted thence by the nerves. Moreover, the soul can change the course of the vital particles that travel away from it through the nerves without disturbing their "quantity of motion." It is through this mechanism that the mental world interacts with the physical. Like the explanations of false suns and magnetism, this linkage between the mind and the body seems a bit contrived when considered on its own merits. Yet like the others, the secret of the pineal gland played a unifying role in the Cartesian system, at once gaining credence from all the details on which it depended and lending coherence to them. In short, Descartes found the solution to the mind-body problem in his system. Nor did the place of the pineal gland and the brain represent a young philosopher's passing fancy. The theory found brief recapitulation in the responses to objections to the *Meditations* and again in the *Principles*. Descartes, to be sure, made distinctions between those sorts of ideas retained in the mind and those impressions etched in the brain, but the basic physiological relations between the *res cogitans* and the *res extensa* expressed in the early 1630s continued to inform his mature philosophical writings.

This opens a new Pandora's box, especially in light of twentieth-century philosophy, in the form of the question of mechanism. To be sure, the *Principles* presented a mechanical system. Like the mind-body distinction, mechanism has been embraced and attacked by thinkers and dogmatists both naïve and sophisticated ever since Descartes and seems likely to continue to engage advocates and detractors as long as Western thought remains a discernible intellectual or historical trend. Mechanism has become, in our own time and place, something of a political hot potato, particularly in feminist critiques that see it as opposed to the sort of holism with which women have traditionally approached the world.[60] (This formulation of course crassly overstates and generalizes the valid and subtle reasoning that has been offered, but such is the danger of one-sentence summaries.) The feminist critics of "Cartesian" mechanism in fact speak appropriately to modern "Cartesian" philosophy. As a matter of taste, for me at least, the analysis offered by feminism seems infinitely preferable to positivism.

Having tromped into this field where angels fear to tread, and recognizing that Descartes embraced a mechanism charming only for its naïveté, I find myself compelled to offer a bit of explanation to extricate the seventeenth-century system from what must seem in our own time a potentially insensitive as well as an intellectually implausible position. The reconciliation of naïve mechanism with Descartes's post-Renaissance pedagogy of system is certainly not philosophical. One must appeal again to the frailty of the Cartesian mind. The world is full of a number of things, and the mind cannot grasp them all at once. When push inevitably came to shove between mechanism and system, between proofs in the mathematical style and ontology, it was the system that won out. Indeed, the very basis of Descartes's mechanism came couched in terms that rendered it subservient to the larger picture sketched out in this chapter.

The crux of the mechanical system is usually located in a passage in Part 2 of the *Principles* that sets out three "laws of nature" and six "rules of impact," a passage left out of the standard English translation and therefore referred to only glibly by most recent philosophical literature in the United States. It is probably worthwhile to consider the argument in some detail.[61] The series of rules of motion suggested that the "quantity of motion," the mathematical product of the bulk of an object and its speed, remains constant unless the object is pushed by another object. In a move that has been ridiculed and dismissed by aficionados of mathematical physics ever since, Descartes asserted that whereas this *quantity* of motion must be conserved in the absence of other physical pushing, the *direction* of motion may change without such an external influence. Fully incarnating the evils of mechanistic rationalism, Descartes closed his explanation of the rules by noting that "the demonstrations of all these are so certain that although experience often seems to make us take the contrary to be the case, nevertheless we are obliged to put more faith in our reason than in our senses."[62] The action of the two rationally controlled bodies thus seemed in Descartes's world to defy common sense. Even more so, then, they must trample on the sensibilities of those who embrace common sense as a touchstone for all thought and behavior.

Descartes was not so naïve as to miss the thrust of this putative criticism. He acknowledged that the rules do in fact fly in the face of experience and that

> the reason for that is obvious: these laws presuppose that the two bodies B and C are perfectly hard and separated from all others in such a manner that there are not any around them that can aid or block their movements; and we do not see such conditions in the world. That is why, before a judgement can be made whether they are observed or not, it does not suffice to know how two bodies, such as B and C, can act on one another; but beyond that, it is necessary to consider how all the other bodies which surround them can augment or diminish their action.[63]

It is hard to imagine a more politically correct acknowledgment of the failure of simple-minded mechanism or a more inclusive response to it. The system, Descartes's vision of the world taken as an interrelated whole, outweighed the intricate reasoning with which he derived rules of motion.

It is thus in terms of Descartes's own instructions for reading his work, rather than those of his teachers or the practices of his modern critics, that we should approach his texts to understand their impact on science in the seventeenth and eighteenth centuries. This should be something of a relief to those who don't particularly like, or aren't particularly good at, the technical details of science. What is required to catch on to the Cartesian system is a willing suspension of disbelief rather than a command of mathematical physics. The question of whether one or another seventeenth- or eighteenth-century Cartesian "got it" is more a judgment about how thoroughly she absorbed the system than whether the details of her explanation agreed with some axiomatic mathematical or physical theory. It is a judgment that can be made without the intervention of experts, a judgment that must often fly in the face of experts who judge one position or another absurd because it disagrees with the way, in some abstract sense, the world really works. The feminist with literary or historical sensibilities brings as much relevant expertise to bear on the science offered in the *Principles* as does the mathematical physicist; she will probably bring it with less hubris. The question of what Descartes really meant I shall leave to those who see themselves as arbiters of the truth and consistency of other people's thoughts—a role that many philosophers still believe they can and should play. What his generation and the next found in his works is a matter of historical inquiry.

As that historical inquiry into the reception of Descartes's work proceeds, it is probably at least as important to bear in mind the tone of the *Meteorology* as it is to keep track of its details. The early generations of Cartesians delighted, as Descartes had done, in contemplating rare and complex natural phenomena. They tried always to be clever in their explanations of these things and indeed often offered explanations too clever by half. Such exercises in speculation—during the Enlightenment they were dismissed as speculations infected with the spirit of systems—contrast strongly with the learned pedantry spawned by the notebook method and displayed to equal excess at the Bureau d'adresse. The difference was not so much in how any particular phenomenon might be explained—Renaudot's patrons never managed anything more baroque than Descartes's explanation of the false suns—but in the way that Cartesian explanations fitted into the system.

PART TWO

Science in the Reign of Louis XIV

4

A Science for a Polite Society: the Crown as the second most Philosophical Hat in Paris

Science and the literary salon, as they emerged from the reign of Louis XIII in the late 1640s, constituted antagonistic if minor social forms. The salon served as a center for *politesse* and *honnêteté*, accomplishments in French culture scarcely echoed by the yeoman virtues of their English cognates. Natural philosophy by contrast was practiced in a context of political free thought that bordered on radicalism, of social misalliance carried to the point of scandal, and of the contemplation and manipulation of machinery and materials suited only for the lower reaches of the third estate. It brought to mind neither *politesse* nor *honnêteté*. After the death of Richelieu and the failure of the Bureau d'adresse, that kind of raucous gathering came to a halt. With the rise of the literary salons cultivated by Mazarin and his lieutenants, the style of natural inquiry practiced under Louis XIII faded from the Parisian scene, if not from memory. Descartes, to be sure, found his circle of admirers during his infrequent visits to Paris, but it was a circle of intellectuals bordering on the egg-headed. In the reconciliation of natural philosophy and elite culture under Louis XIV, it was philosophy that was adapted to conform to social norms. On the eve of Louis XIV's assumption of personal rule, science remained suspect in those few places where it impinged at all upon the fringes of elite society.

Polite culture in Mazarin's France revolved around literature, from poetic theory to the lightest of prose. A highly mannered form of behavior associated with the word *"précieuse"* (precious) reached its height during the Fronde; it continued to dominate society throughout Louis XIV's minority and remained important for literary forms even after Mazarin's death in 1661. The *Cyrus* novels of Madeleine de Scudéry and her weekly salons formed the center of this cultural movement in the late 1650s; Molière's first Parisian success, the *Précieuses ridicules,* in 1659, took "Sappho's Saturdays" (as Scudéry's meetings were called) for a model. Molière's farce had but one reference to the workings of nature: The young ladies hoped to "fill the void" of their hall with charming suitors. This Aristotelian reference aside, the playwright's caricatures of the social elite concerned themselves with verse and dance and music and wit but not with natural philosophy.

The precious pursuit of natural philosophy

Molière's farcical portrayal represented a sort of affectionate if condescending acceptance of the *précieuses* in the newly dominant literary elite. It succeeded a more seriously critical analysis of the fashion in elite society. We may take in contrast a work that had appeared just the year after, in 1660. *Le Dictionnaire des précieuses,* by Antoine Baudeau de Somaize,[1] an obscure gentleman who counted himself one of their circle, contains not only a glossary of the new terms and orthography spawned by Mlle de Scudéry and her guests but also a list (which Somaize claimed to be complete) of the ladies and gentlemen who called at the salons of the elite. Nowhere did the general discussion bring up the practice or the content of any of the scientific fields that had enjoyed such extensive development in the first half of the seventeenth century. Natural philosophy neither provided nor required any new terms in the *Dictionnaire,* despite the work's exhaustive collection of neologisms. Among the three hundred or so individuals Somaize counted worthy of notice, only fourteen practiced natural philosophy or mathematics conspicuously enough that he remarked on the habit.[2]

All the more extensive comments on science in Somaize's little biographies indicated or implied some oddity on the part of the amateur natural philosopher. Mlle de Chetaignaires, for example, studied

> above all chemistry (she has a furnace in her house for this purpose) and works perpetually to discover the philosophers' stone. I do not know

how it happens, but I am told on good authority that she sometimes takes up novels, and that she shows such an interest when she puts herself to it that she reads as many in a month as others do in a year. . . . Her library is composed solely of books on chemistry, which she has always in her hands.[3]

Other ladies and gentlemen, to be sure, displayed more catholic tastes in the sciences; nonetheless, even a wide variety of intellectual pursuits could not make Somaize sympathetic to the practice. He said of Mme de Guédreville, for example:

She has this quality which is peculiar to herself—or at least which she shares with few others—of learning philosophy. She has a master who comes to teach it to her, as [she has a master] also for mathematics, for white magic, for chiromancy, philosophy, law, and the languages of Italy and Spain; for each she has someone different to instruct her—so much so that she spends the greatest part of her time at these different studies.[4]

In short, although Somaize did have to admit that a few of his subjects studied natural philosophy, he did not consider that study an appealing habit.

The *Dictionnaire* indicted inquiry into the secrets of nature on two counts. It portrayed the activity on the one hand as mysterious and occult and on the other as socially degrading. The philosophers' stone, white magic, and chiromancy appeared as necessary adjuncts to chemistry and natural philosophy. Curiosity about such matters struck Somaize as unwholesome; in less polite contexts the stronger charges of impiety and rebelliousness were leveled as well. Moreover, strange masters were welcomed in grand households; ladies melted and melded the stuff of nature in hot, smelly furnaces; philosophy occupied and consumed the student, encouraging compulsive and antisocial behavior. Much of the social elite shared Somaize's perception of the pastime of their philosophically inclined colleagues.

In the years after the Fronde, certainly by the early 1660s when the *Dictionnaire* appeared, both aspects of the critique were dated. The study of nature was neither so mystical nor so vulgar as Somaize suggested. The impression of the philosophical enterprise he offered reflected the scientific practice of the previous generation. An insider's view of science in polite society around the time Louis XIV assumed personal rule reveals a completely different style of natural philosophy than that which Somaize portrayed.

During the winter of 1660–1661, the first social season after the *Dictionnaire* appeared, Christiaan Huygens, a young natural philosopher officially if tenuously connected with a Dutch diplomatic mission, visited Paris. Well born, well spoken, and largely at leisure, Huygens moved comfortably in the circles Somaize described. He became, for example, a frequent companion of the *Dictionnaire*'s Mme de Guédreville and her husband not only at a number of scientific entertainments but also at the theater (where he saw the *Précieuses ridicules* in its first run), the ballet, and the opera. Huygens's philosophical activities ran the gamut from the most informal contacts and encounters to the most exclusive and serious scientific circles in Paris. He was equally comfortable with the light conversational style of the salons and the language of mathematics, with the science of mechanics and mechanical contrivances, with musical instruments and the theory of harmonics. The young man kept a journal of his day-to-day activities; its brief descriptions offer our most extensive and consistent insight into the milieu and character of science in polite society around the time Louis XIV assumed personal rule.[5]

Huygens's interests, and those of his hosts and hostesses, embraced a range of activities nearly as wide as those retrospectively offered as possible sources for the growth of early modern science. Mme de Guédreville arranged a tour of the stage set for the opera *Jason,* equipment that produced a stage deus quite literally ex machina. (Huygens's understanding of the backstage workings in no way decreased his enjoyment of the scene, which he described with great glee.[6]) On other occasions he called on clock makers and mechanics, mathematicians and natural philosophers, and the owners and suppliers of physical cabinets. Yet such private interviews do not accurately reflect the activities available to Somaize's philosophically curious ladies and gentlemen. Huygens and the Guédrevilles met more frequently at formally constituted philosophical gatherings; if not all of them were open to the public, social credentials and the slightest interest would produce manifold invitations.

On Wednesday afternoons there were the demonstrations of Jacques Rohault, scientific entertainments where women occupied the first row of an audience that Huygens described as quite numerous.[7] The main attractions of Rohault's Wednesdays were his demonstrations; at each meeting, a philosophical object or instrument served as the centerpiece. His cabinet included one of the finest lodestones in Europe, Huygens noted, and it was used to great effect. Moreover Rohault had the beginnings of an impressive array of glassware with which he explored the Torricellian vacuum in the top of the barometer and the elevation of water in a capillary tube—the latter a phenomenon Rohault himself first discovered and described.[8] The most impressive display, however, demonstrated the Torricellian vacuum. The lecturer did not simply bring out his mercury barometer. Instead, he affixed a glass bulb to the end of an iron pipe over thirty feet long, and filled the huge vessel with water (see Figure 4.1). This apparatus he held inverted, its mouth in a small bowl. The assembled multitude trooped upstairs to the highest rooms in his apartment, from which Rohault triumphantly displayed the bulb atop its tower, transparent and empty of water. A trip back downstairs showed the bottom of the pipe still sitting in a bowl of placid water, well below the brim. The laws of nature had saved the philosophy master a tremendous job of mopping up.[9]

Rohault was a showman and an entertainer: In his laboratory, nature delighted by its surprising behavior. Yet despite Somaize's impressions, the audience heard no Faustian schemes for perverting natural processes. To be sure they enjoyed the wonders of nature as they might an elaborately staged play, but Rohault always explained his effects and exposed the props and mechanisms that nature used to set his stage. Unlike the gentlemen amateurs at the Royal Society of London who performed similar investigations, Rohault offered Cartesian theories: Screw-shaped particles circulate through the magnet and when they encounter the screw-shaped passages in other magnets (or the deformed passages in iron), they push these passages together to produce the apparent attraction of magnets for other magnets and for iron. The weight of the air supports water in a barometric pipe or mercury in a barometric tube; when the column of liquid outweighs the air, its level sinks until equilibrium is reached. Rohault accounted for meniscus—the shape assumed by the free, top surface of water near the side of a vessel—by the motion of a subtle matter swirling up or down the side of the vessel; the elevation of water in a capillary

Figure 4.1 A large water barometer mounted outside a building (upper right), similar to the instrument Rohault used in his lectures. Reproduced from Otto von Guericke, Experimenta Nova *(Amsterdam, 1672), figure 10. Courtesy of the Bakken Library, Minneapolis, Minn.*

tube he explained by the decrease of the weight of the air in the tube caused by that swirling.[10]

These philosophical discourses served primarily as patter for the experiments and demonstrations, which above all offered a diverting way to pass an afternoon. But insofar as the lectures had a lesson, it lay in the rational description of nature. Parisian science throughout the age of Louis XIV would display this concern to illuminate rather than to mystify the workings of the world. Somaize was out-of-date as soon as his *Dictionnaire* was published. It was to Descartes that Rohault and his audience would look for their new, scientific approach to explanation; the system he introduced in the *Meteorology* came into fashion with the light literary style of the *précieuses.*

Rohault's was the most overtly entertaining and the least analytic of the Parisian scientific circles Huygens visited. Philosophically inclined ladies and gentlemen more frequently confronted the everyday fundamentals of nature, common experience that required no illustration and certainly no apparatus. For example, the visiting Dutchman joined Mme de Guédreville in a strictly intellectual salon she hosted.[11] With her friend Mme de Bonneveau, she offered her own philosophical academy—Somaize's comments notwithstanding, Mme de Guédreville shared her instructors quite freely. Nor were her speakers hired masters like Rohault; rather, she invited people of quality who addressed their friends, their spouses, and their peers. The hints of social misalliance in the *Dictionnaire des précieuses* were hardly justified.

At each of the five weekly sessions Huygens attended, a different philosophical gentleman addressed the assembly. Mme de Guédreville's friends had no need of the props Rohault employed; they confronted nature in the manner of the literary salons, with words. All the speakers embraced the new Cartesian philosophy, the whirling gross and subtle matters directed by mechanical laws. The curious ladies and gentlemen in the audience heard an explanation one week for the phenomenon of rarefaction; on another occasion they learned how the subtle matter transmits light.[12] Astronomy came in for discussion twice; each time the speaker used Cartesian vortices to account for the nature of the heavens. The stars and planets float in these celestial whirlpools, tracing their courses according to precise laws. Mme de Guédreville's husband in fact argued that the great heavenly eddies offer a clear explanation for the correctness of the Copernican hypothesis.[13]

All this might have appeared dry stuff to Somaize, but it was by no means mystical. The philosophical ladies and gentlemen at the academy manifestly delighted in the discussion. They displayed a comfortable familiarity with a style of science most intellectuals of Galileo's generation had been unable to assimilate, and with arguments and factual claims that their learned predecessors had rejected out of hand on the grounds of theological authority. Vociferous eighteenth-century critics of this scientific style indeed argued that the Cartesians ignored the very real ambiguities and caprices of nature, explaining in overly simple terms the wonders of a universe more mysterious than the machine described at the ladies' philosophical circle. Somaize not only missed the mark with his images of chiromancy and white magic; he shot wild. Mme de Guédreville was a woman totally up-to-date in her philosophizing about nature.

Her attitude was by no means out of character. The social elite portrayed in the *Dictionnaire des précieuses* had never rejected the intellectually up-to-date or even the risqué, so long as it did not offer political complications. This elite supported the literary theories that the "moderns" ranged against the rigid rules of the "ancients" on the battlefields of the Académie française and the salons. The new orthography that occupied a large place in Somaize's *Dictionnaire* represented an attack on tradition in the name of a more rational phonetic scheme. The young ladies Molière portrayed in his *Précieuses ridicules* tormented their uncle and guardian as much for his old-fashioned ideas as for his outmoded language. Cartesian natural philosophy and Copernican heliocentrism presented philosophical parallels, modernisms not a priori incompatible with the intellectual habits of the social elite.

Only a few things were a priori incompatible with the social elite. One was impropriety; another was pedantry. Huygens repeatedly noted both of these great impediments to sociability among the philosophically inclined. The most serious circle he visited, the academy of Henri-Louis de Montmor, consistently bored and occasionally shocked him. Indeed from time to time it had the same effect on its host. Montmor belonged to an established family with impeccable social credentials; he owned positions as councillor to the Parlement of Paris and as *maître de requêtes* in the royal bureaucracy—connections to both old and new power. An income on the princely order of

100,000 livres a year allowed him to spend lavishly to support men and equipment of science. Montmor was urbane and cultivated, a longtime member of the Académie française, a guest at the proper literary salons, and, as Huygens discovered, a charming host at dinner. His forte was Latin epigrams—just the stuff for polite society.[14]

Despite the best efforts of its patron, the Montmor academy frequently exceeded the bounds of polite conversation. Huygens wrote to his family that the "philosophical gentlemen" who gathered at Montmor's had "the patience to listen to pedants for hours on end."[15] Advocates of one brand or another of the new science argued with "a marvelous and ridiculous vehemence."[16] But Huygens did not witness the worst of their behavior. Montmor, the most philosophical of gentlemen, had been obliged to disinvite the mathematician Giles Personne de Roberval from the weekly assembly: The man was simply a rude guest.[17]

Herein lay the greatest difficulty for the acceptance of science in polite society around the time that Louis XIV assumed personal rule. Not only did natural philosophers suffer from a largely dated reputation as odd, secretive, and antisocial; they tended in fact to be pedantic and rude. That they displayed their pedantry in a completely public context hardly furthered the cause of the new philosophy in Parisian culture. Seemingly incapable of letting any matter pass incorrectly stated, they insisted on their own erudition—a strategy considered in extremely poor taste among those who moved in the circle described by the *Dictionnaire*. Even Huygens, a dedicated student of nature who quite happily tolerated the elementary lessons at Rohault's and sat quietly through the lectures at the Guédreville and Bonneveau academy, found the Montmorians boorish and boring.

Yet the situation was not hopeless. Huygens himself had been the center of a polite philosophical exchange with a proper gentleman, seen as more pleasant by the denizens of the salons at the two earliest documented meetings of the Montmor academy. It provides a perfect example of how a denizen of the literary salons could turn science to the service of elite culture. The gentleman in question was Jean Chapelain, whom we have already met as the founder of the Académie française. Chapelain put in frequent appearances in all of the prestigious salons, and for that matter was present in Somaize's *Dictionnaire*—although the latter nowhere mentioned Chapelain's philosophical activities. From the beginning, Chapelain attended Montmor's academy. In March 1658 he heard Roberval read a theory to explain the strange, noncircular shape of Saturn.[18] The mathematician suggested that storms raging on the equator of the planet send out huge, opaque clouds, which appear as appendages growing from and shrinking to its surface. In his boorish way, Roberval hinted broadly that the young Huygens, who had recently published an anagram for his own explanation of the phenomenon, had stolen his theory of the storms.

Chapelain could barely contain himself. He had befriended the young Dutch philosopher during Huygens's first visit to Paris and was privy to the alternative hypothesis he had devised. Huygens had constructed a large telescope that produced a sufficiently clear image for him to recognize that Saturn was surrounded by a ring that slowly changed its orientation. Shortly after this observation, Huygens had become a Cartesian scientist, transforming the *Principles* into the source of a system. The picture of a huge ring floating about a planet made sense in a world filled with vortices. The third matter, the stuff of earth and planetary crusts, simply found its place in the proper stratum of the second matter—the gravitational material circulating about the planet. The ring was the natural consequence of the Cartesian construction of the solar system; Huygens took it both as evidence for and confirmation of the vortex theory and shared his view with Chapelain in a letter.

Chapelain dashed off an effusive note to Huygens, begging permission to read the letter containing the disclosure.[19] As soon as Huygens consented, the Montmorians readied themselves for a proper afternoon's entertainment: Invitations went out to persons of quality who were not members, and Chapelain conspired with his host to produce the greatest possible effect. He planted questions in the audience, arranged a casual suggestion that Huygens's pamphlet containing the anagram concerning Saturn's appearance be read, and made sure that someone else had a copy on hand to comply with this request.[20]

The philosophical matinee was a smashing success. The impromptu introduction went exactly as planned: Huygens's pamphlet containing the anagram established his priority and technical competence. Chapelain disclosed the meaning of the anagram, elegant in its simplicity and almost epigrammatic in precision: Saturn "is encircled by a thin, flat ring, nowhere touching, inclined to the ecliptic." Even Roberval, consigned to the back of the room among all those persons of quality, had to recognize the intelligence of this alternative to his solution.[21] Nor did the entertainment end there. The reading concluded with a comment that Huygens had made in the private epistle to Chapelain:

> This is my system, which is without a doubt most pleasing and which will give new material for the speculation of Philosophers. At least it seems of no little importance to those who know that Saturn is a body whose diameter is eight to ten times that of the earth, and who do not find it impossible that there are creatures who gaze on this planet from a closer [vantage point] than we can do.[22]

Here we find a bit of science for polite society.

Huygens, to be sure, had composed his epistle for the benefit of a dilettantish gentleman. Indeed his French champion suffered a mild disappointment when the young astronomer sent him a copy of the thick pamphlet, the *Systema Saturnium,* prepared later to explain his discovery to working astronomers.[23] Chapelain had hoped for something more along the lines of Kepler's *Dream*—an account of an imaginary voyage to the moon. Instead he received a work replete with mathematical details and devoid of further "speculation of philosophers." Huygens clearly distinguished this technical explanation from the account appropriate for the likes of Chapelain.[24] The letter read to the Montmorians nonetheless had provided a certain delightful style of philosophizing for a particular audience, and it succeeded marvelously. Even the strictly qualitative statement it contained broke new ground, difficult ground, as Roberval's failed attempt to solve the problem clearly indicated. That a gentleman spoke of Saturn's ring with charm and style did not strip the theory of either its novelty or its significance; the mathematical details could in fact have easily been left to Roberval.

Huygens did not restrict his speculation to issues of extraterrestrial observers. In the *Systema Saturnium,* he observed that Descartes's theory of planetary motion provided a convenient model for explaining the remarkable ring. Saturn, like all the other planets, must swim in a celestial vortex. Saturn's moons, located outside the ring, indicated that the Saturnian vortex extended past the marvelous decoration. Thus the ring would naturally float in the circular vortex.[25] Indeed, Huygens went on from this conclusion to contemplate the way in which the circulating celestial matter must push the ring and moons, and—like Newton a generation later—concluded that the same mechanism must be responsible for free fall on earth. Within a few months, he worked out privately the rules that must govern circular motion (now known as the laws of centrifugal force). These rules in fact constitute one of the great quantitative contributions of the Cartesian school of mathematical physics.[26]

The victory scored at Montmor's was a coup not only for Huygens and Chapelain but for science itself. Chapelain's charm emerged unscathed from the philosophical lists: His prompt action in response to a rival theory, his careful orchestration of the meeting, his handpicked audience, and his implicit snub of Roberval for once lent science a character thoroughly *précieuse*. As in literary matters, Chapelain wore his erudition lightly and without the slightest taint of pedantry. He avenged a boorish attack, not only protecting the reputation of a young genius wrongfully scorned, but also displaying his polite demeanor and his sense of wonder and of humor.

For Somaize, that Chapelain spent his Tuesday afternoons at Montmor's was less than the least of his literary exploits; even the matter of Saturn's ring did not merit notice in the *Dictionnaire des précieuses*. Yet the episode indicates the possibilities for science in the society described by the *Dictionnaire*. Nature delighted not with its mysteries but with its workings. Somaize's talk of chiromancy, white magic, and the philosophers' stone reflected the general unfamiliarity of natural philosophy in elite culture more than it did the practice of science in that culture, for what science there was seemed to Huygens quite up-to-date. Chapelain showed that that science could be cast in terms of *politesse* and *honnêteté*, that it could take on a properly French flavor without compromising the science. The lessons learned at Rohault's Wednesdays, the Guédreville and Bonneveau academy, and Montmor's circle offered perfectly suitable topics for conversation in polite society, if only they were properly phrased and presented. What was required was not a French natural philosophy but a French style of philosophizing.

The style made its way into polite culture. When Molière presented the *Bourgeois gentilhomme* in 1670, he provided his protagonist with masters not only of music, dance, and fencing but also of philosophy. The first three instructed their arriviste charge in courtly arts generally associated with the world of Louis XIV. The philosophy master, however, represents a less familiar aspect of Parisian culture in the age of the Sun King. Even within the play the role was a bit controversial:

PHILOSOPHY MASTER: And what of philosophy, then? I find all three of you impertinent, speaking before me with this arrogance and impudently dignifying with the name "science" things one ought not even honor with the name "art," and which can but be counted as the miserable trades of gladiator, songbird, and jiggler.
FENCING MASTER: Out, philosopher of dogs!
MUSIC MASTER: Out, scoundrel pedant!
DANCING MASTER: Out, boorish prig!

(2.1.5)

Despite their bickering and general inanity, however, the eager bourgeois of the stage—like the court and elite society of Paris—paid all the masters richly to teach him what they could.

Molière had a particular philosophy master in mind when he wrote the *Bourgeois gentilhomme*. It was his friend and fellow entertainer Jacques Rohault. The two had met as young men struggling to make careers of their respective talents; both had succeeded brilliantly.[27] By 1670, Rohault was cutting so striking a figure in Paris that Molière tried to bamboozle out of him the hat in which he lectured—"a *chapeau* which had such a singular shape it had no equal"—to adorn his character in the premiere. When Rohault discovered the plot and preserved the dignity of his headpiece, Molière was defeated: He knew that no search could produce "as philosophical a hat as that of his friend."[28]

Since the opening of the *Précieuses ridicules* a decade earlier, the little band of philosophical conspirators portrayed by Somaize had blossomed into a fad worthy of the ribaldry of Molière. Notions of the scientific amateur as socially maladroit and awkward had faded sufficiently that Rohault could affect flamboyant haberdashery to achieve an image of amiable eccentricity at his Wednesday lectures. The occasionally bizarre behavior of the philosopher now invited a playful caricature by one of the most perceptive observers of Parisian society. Molière's affectionate poke at a popular figure in that society is a far cry from the disdainful notice given masters of the various aspects of philosophy by Somaize a decade earlier.

The study of nature in general had become more visible and more accessible during Colbert's ministry. The philosophical matinee was no longer the only regular source of scientific intercourse. Beginning in early 1665, the *Journal des sçavans* appeared (with more or less regularity) every week, and later every fortnight, for sale at the printer or at a growing number of distribution points.[29] The curious student had but to call for the printed sheet, folded and stabbed, thus readable even before proper binding, in order to learn of the newest advances in the world of the intellect. (Those in the provinces or foreign countries could obtain the periodical for the going price plus the postage for a single letter; the one-sheet format had its commercial advantages.)

As promised by its title, the French periodical covered all fields of learning. Science and medicine shared the largest place with religion, but literature, poetry, antiquities, history, law, and politics appeared quite regularly. By subscribing to the *Journal,* the would-be *savante* could supply herself admirably with the necessaries of polite learning. The bulk of the *Journal*'s contents consisted of book reviews prepared by anonymous experts and done over into a conversational style by the editor. He borrowed quite freely and openly from other printed sources, especially the *Philosophical Transactions* of the Royal Society of London.[30]

In matters of natural history and philosophy, however, the *Journal* was frequently more original. The periodical indeed maintained its clearest French ambiance in its scientific coverage. Many such reports had the pleasant air of a literary salon. Indeed, preparations for the press involved a philosophical meeting on the weekly schedule so popular in the social circles of the capital:

Those who would bring [the editor] their books, their machines, their discoveries, letters from their friends, or indeed any other curiosity which they want to be known to the public, are asked to choose for this purpose each Thursday, after dinner, when they will always find him

without fail. They can further have the pleasure of being able themselves to remark on the beauties of all those works of interest which are
assembled at his offices on that day.[31]

Various curious contributors availed themselves of this opportunity,
coming along always with a new device, a solution to a pleasant mathematical problem (or a tricky one to solve), an observation, a query, or
a comment.

Those who were not fortunate enough to live in Paris could participate in this philosophical intercourse through the mails. Leibniz, for
example, communicated a marvel on behalf of his patron, the Duke of
Hanover. The duke had been most taken by a report of a monstrous
birth that he had read in the *Journal* a few weeks earlier and thought
that he might share a similar oddity. He had in his possession the portrait of a most peculiar goat, one with an extraordinary coiffure. Although the duke had not actually seen the goat, he had it on good authority that the rendering did the animal justice. Leibniz dutifully
enclosed the portrait for the entertainment of the editor and his readers. On the page there appeared a woodcut of the animal adorned
with the long, curly locks so de rigueur in the seventeenth century
(see Figure 4.2). Leibniz, playing the part of court philosopher, did his
best to produce a "physical cause" for the striking appearance of this
beast.[32]

Philosophical amateurs did not need the acumen of a young Leibniz or the prestige of a Duke of Hanover to participate in the scientific
exchanges carried out in the *Journal des sçavans*. Snippets of natural
philosophy, details of natural history, and successful or promising
medical techniques, which were presented by characters obscure even
according to the standards of seventeenth-century science, filled the
pages of the French publication, as they did those of the *Philosophical
Transactions*. Nor did the *Journal* exhibit the sort of editorial restraint
one might have expected from the publishing industry under Colbert:
perpetual-motion machines described in credulous detail and even illustrated with elaborate engravings, devices to make fountains spurt
without any motive power, and geometrical constructions for the tri-
section of the angle took their places among learned disquisitions and
reviews of the most adept scientists of the day. Natural philosophy in
the *Journal* amused, as it did in Rohault's lecture hall.

Figure 4.2 Illustration of a goat with a seventeenth-century coiffure, sent by Leibniz. Journal des sçavans *5 (1677), no. 14, p. 205. Courtesy of the University of Minnesota Libraries.*

Molière's model philosopher was not the only alternative to the *Journal* for philosophical amusement. If Rohault's style, or his Wednesdays, did not suit, the curious Parisian could turn to other expositions of the natural world. Around the time the *Bourgeois gentilhomme* opened, half a dozen demonstration-lecturers competed with its prototype. After obtaining the *Journal* on Monday morning, the eager student could choose whatever day or philosophical style she fancied for her lessons. On Tuesdays, after the demise of Montmor's academy, M. de Brache sponsored a lecture followed by philosophical discussion. M. Marion conducted a scientific and intellectual salon on Thursdays, when the *Journal* collected objects and items to report the next week. On Fridays M. de Launay offered an alternative exposition of Descartes's philosophy. For those who did not call on Mlle de Scudéry on Saturdays, there was M. de Fontenay's exposition of Gassendi's atomism. Louis Delaforge offered lectures on Cartesian biology. The Prince of Condé sponsored both the academy of Pierre Michon, the abbé Bourdelot; and courses by the chemist Nicolas Lémery, where "even the ladies, swept along by fashion," observed the operation of furnaces and retorts and vials.[33] The scorn Somaize had directed at Mlle de Chetaignaires in the *Dictionnaire des précieuses* for her discreet, private study of chemistry had evaporated. The ladies of polite society could now join apothecaries in public lecture halls to receive instruction in the same subject. The enthusiasm that filled the pages of the *Journal des sçavans* and the lecture halls of philosophers each week represented a veritable cultural movement.

Science as *gloire* in the court of the Sun King

It was in the context of this growing enthusiasm for natural philosophy that Colbert brought together a coterie of philosophers to form an Académie royale des sciences.[34] The crown was no less anxious than Molière's bourgeois to remain absolutely au courant in all cultural affairs; naturally, Louis XIV, as the greatest patron in the kingdom, determined to sponsor his own scientific gathering. Like other household expenditures, the funds allocated to the royal philosophers were intended to buy Louis *gloire*.

Jean Chapelain, the most *précieux* of the Montmorians and a member of the "Little Academy," which advised Colbert on cultural matters, played the greatest part in the conception of the Académie royale des science, as he had with respect to the Académie française during the ministry of Richelieu. Acting as Colbert's agent, in June 1665 Chapelain negotiated an invitation for Huygens to become the first and leading member of a new philosophical company in the royal household. Yet these initial efforts were not as *colbertiste* in their details as in their inspiration. When the young man inquired about the conditions of his appointment and the nature of the organization he was about to head, Chapelain could but send assurances of the minister's good faith. These sufficed to draw Huygens to Louis's capital the next spring, and Chapelain proved as good as his word: Until Colbert's death the Dutch Protestant philosopher received an annual pension of 6,000 livres and elegant apartments for his personal use.[35] The promised organization, too, began to take shape. Shortly after his arrival in Paris during June 1666, Huygens was joined by half a dozen gentlemen concerned chiefly with "mechanical and chemical experiments," and they set about "framing a philosophical society."[36]

The appearance of grandeur of the enterprise must be tempered by the circumstances of membership of the local recruits. The philosophical gentlemen of Paris did not enter into the king's service as Huygens had done; they were not domiciled in royal apartments, and the modest gratuities they received were not offered as compensation for services rendered. Instead they met in the household of the king, as they had all done at Montmor's or some other philosophical salon, at the invitation of the host, but on their own time. The king's new philosophers maintained their original professions, posts, or offices even after their academic appointments.[37] Moreover, Chapelain and the Little Academy developed no scientific agenda, and the mission of Colbert's band of philosophers remained vague for the remainder of the year. Huygens showed little more initiative than his patrons; with Adrien Auzout, the foremost telescopic astronomer in France, he initiated a program of celestial observations in July, but few other activities transpired during the summer and fall.[38] Only the presence of the Dutch philosopher in the royal household contributed significantly to Louis's philosophical *gloire*. There is no evidence that the envisaged society even met with any regularity or direction.

It was indeed Auzout, rather than the expensively courted Huygens, who had presented the most recent public display of royal academic science. Early in 1666, the *Journal des sçavans* published Auzout's reflections on a work by the Italian astronomer Guiseppi Campani that described observations of Saturn and Jupiter.[39] (Regular readers of the periodical could count themselves initiates in this debate, for a notice of Campani's book had already appeared in an earlier number.[40]) Auzout felt compelled to respond to the optical extravagance of his Italian rival. Campani's claims struck the Frenchman like the musings of those who, "as Descartes had hoped, and as Hooke does not despair, imagine seeing men on the moon."[41]

In the next number, the *Journal* reviewed Auzout's ensuing debate with Robert Hooke, curator of experiments at the Royal Society of London.[42] Although telescopic design had its place in the discussion, the editor noted that the "principal question" in the argument between the philosophers revolved around Hooke's claim in the *Micrographia* that his telescopes might be refined to the point where they could spot animals on the moon. Auzout, too, strayed beyond the bounds of the mathematics of optical resolution. He discounted Hooke's extravagant claims on the basis of simple, logical deductions from common knowledge. Where on the moon, he asked, does the white of winter give way to the green of spring or the yellow of autumn? Where, if there be builders, are the buildings? With a final rhetorical flourish he let fall the mocking comment that even if we could sight an object the size of a building, it would be quite another matter to spot one the size of a man.

Questions surrounding extraterrestrial life did play an important role in contemporaneous scientific discussion. That Auzout addressed the problem in the context of an optical debate was within the realm of ordinary scientific discourse. Yet the timing of his polemics underlines the complexity of creating an institution likely to produce scientific *gloire* for the French crown. It was Huygens who had suggested to the Montmorians that extraterrestrial observers might wonder at the marvels of Saturn's ring, providing an occasion for Chapelain's first successful foray into philosophical *politesse.* Yet Huygens's first astronomical colleague in the king's household took Campani's description of the same heavenly body as an occasion to lash out against such philosophical speculations.

The irony of the situation did not go unnoticed. When in 1672 Molière returned to the subject of his *Précieuses ridicules* with a new play called the *Femmes savantes,* the caricatures of polite society in Colbert's Paris were quite prepared to discuss natural philosophy. Indeed the little band of intellectual ladies organized itself into a proper academy of science:

ARMANDE: I am waiting to see our assembly open
   and to bring us attention by some discovery.
TRISSOTIN: We are anxiously waiting your clear insight.
   For you, nature holds few secrets.
PHILAMANTE: For my part, without flattering myself, I've already
   made one:
   I've seen clearly men on the moon.
BÉLISE: I've never yet seen men, I don't believe,
   but I've seen steeples just as I see you.

(3.2)

For Molière, the comings and goings and doings of the king's scientists were no more private or secret or authoritative than the musings of a flamboyant philosophy master. To be sure, the playwright did not show any particular disdain for the academicians; his jab was no more vicious than the one he had aimed at his friend Rohault. Yet royal scientific rhetoric, like philosophical headgear, was part of public culture and fair game for public amusement.

The original band of astronomers, mechanicians, and chemists around Huygens did not, in fact, form a society much more cohesive than that of Molière's farce. Chapelain's philosophical protégés, like Montmor's guests, each continued to pursue individual interests without any unified program. There is no evidence that they had any notions of creating scientific *gloire* as novel or as memorable as Rohault's hat in its own popular realm. What distinction Huygens and his colleagues brought to the crown by the force of their expertise did not arouse the admiration or envy of the mass of readers of the *Journal des sçavans* or auditors of popular lectures. Rather, the academicians were perceived as just another band of philosophers, engaged in respectable pursuits, to be sure, but hardly more dignified than Rohault and by no means an elite organization.

The crown took steps aimed at making a more public splash with its philosophical salon. Chapelain was not the only cultural adviser that Colbert listened to. Charles Perrault (who would later compose the fairy tales) also served in the Little Academy that made recommendations to the minister. His brother Claude was a physician to fashionable circles as well as an occasional royal architect. Some time during fall 1666, Claude Perrault (along with the first and second physicians to the king) signed on to add natural history to the competence of the royal household, influence to the family Perrault, and more direct connections between the king's scientists and elite culture.[43] The motives for the inclusion of this new scientific competence were mixed. Although neither of the king's physicians played an active role in the organization,[44] Claude Perrault not only took up naturalizing but also won the commission for designing the Royal Observatory. As an architectural project, the edifice succeeded brilliantly; the stairway is still counted one of the finest in all of Paris. As quarters for a scientific society, however, it left much to be desired. When the Italian astronomer Jean-Dominique Cassini was called in as a consultant to equip the half-finished building with observational instruments, he felt compelled to combine the top two stories in order to allow sufficient space for the large quadrants and telescopes required in a major astronomical installation. Over Perrault's strenuous objections he had his way and then assumed control of the facility that remained a virtual Cassini fief for four generations. Redesigned and equipped for astronomical purposes, the Royal Observatory could not accommodate the rest of the king's philosophers.[45]

Whatever the motivations for recruiting its members, the expanded organization first convened in December 1666. The group resolved to assemble each Tuesday to consider questions of natural history and on Saturdays for mathematical discussion. In the style of the literary salons, all the king's philosophers were invited to participate in both meetings. To Huygens fell the leadership of the philosophical and chemical side of the organization; Claude Perrault took charge of natural history. This organizational assembly was later chosen as the official date of the foundation of the Académie royale des sciences; regular meetings began in January 1667, although no charter was granted for a half-century.[46]

It was Claude Perrault who set himself most promptly to the task of defining and creating scientific *gloire*. His talents proved better suited to naturalizing than to the design of the Royal Observatory. He suggested long-term projects for the study of plants and animals, and supervised the latter personally.[47] By June 1667, the academicians under his direction had produced the first installment of what came to be called *Mémoires pour servir à l'histoire naturelle des animaux*, or the *Histoire des animaux*. The little pamphlet contained descriptions and engravings of a lion and a thresher shark dissected by the king's assembled philosophers.[48] Additional *mémoires*, reprints, and collections of the *Histoire des animaux* appeared irregularly for over sixty years; the success of the publications repaid royal patronage in full.[49]

The second installment of the series, first published in 1669 and reprinted in an expanded version in the early 1670s, represented the greatest foray of the *académie* into polite society. A vogue for travel to exotic places had led some gallant to Egypt, from whence he sent appropriate gifts to the gentle denizens of Parisian salons. Madeleine de Scudéry, the hostess of the most prestigious gathering, received two chameleons; Claude Perrault, a regular visitor at "Sappho's Saturdays," accepted a third chameleon on behalf of the *académie*. The scientific investigation he launched was a joint venture of Mlle de Scudéry's salon and the king's philosophical company. The hostess to the *précieuses* did not suffer in the least in comparison with the *académie*. Thanks to an elaborate heated cage, both of her chameleons survived a winter in Paris; one of them lasted through four. The specimen entrusted to the *académie*, by contrast, perished at the first frost. Even the final demise of her pets, which evoked proper elegies in her salon (perhaps the most *précieuses* of verses ever penned), could not quell her attachment to the remarkable lizards. Mlle de Scudéry carefully preserved the skeletons of her little prizes and would bring them out for the philosophically curious a quarter-century later.

Perrault followed the lead of his hostess in the pursuit of his academic researches.[50] The charming investigation with which he assisted resulted in a literary as well as a natural history of the chameleon:

> There is scarcely any animal more famous than the chameleon. The changes of color, and the peculiar manner of nourishment attributed to it, have through the ages given it great admiration, and exercised those who apply themselves to the understanding of nature. These marvels that students of science [*physique*] have recounted concerning the poor animal have served in ethics [*morale*] and rhetoric to represent the lazy compliance of courtiers and flatterers, and the vanity in which their silly and simple souls wallow. Its very name in Tertullian is the cause for serious meditation on false appearances.[51]

Mlle de Scudéry and her entire salon joined Perrault in the philosophical investigation of those attributes. Upon the death of the academic beast, the group concluded its naturalizing with an anatomical study.

Perrault's refutations of literary canards associated with the chameleon, and later of those concerning the salamander and the pelican, have frequently been cited as evidence for the scientific spirit of the seventeenth century and its celebration of observation over superstition. The *Histoire des animaux* is praised particularly as a work of comparative anatomy. Mlle de Scudéry's role in this project, if mentioned at all, was long reduced to that of an auxiliary dilettante. The conclusions drawn in Perrault's essay, however, suggest a rather different interpretation of both his own attitude and the reaction it might have evoked in his friend Mlle de Scudéry:

Now to hear it said, as Plutarch remarked, that flatterers lack candor, that vain and ambitious souls feed themselves on nothing, it is not necessary that real chameleons take all colors, . . . or that they take nourishment only from the wind. One can find many other subjects on which to moralize with greater truth: The chameleon, who is without ears, and practically without movement in most of its body, has a quickness of tongue from which nothing can escape, and eyes that can see everything at once.[52]

Even while the *académie* approved the morals of the old tales despite their technical inaccuracy, it produced new lessons suitable for Mlle de Scudéry's salon. Just as the romantic and colorful beast of the myth presented a metaphorical adversary to *politesse* and *honnêteté,* so the real subject of the *Histoire des animaux* provided a proper cautionary note for the ladies and gentlemen who helped to study it. A number of stories, in nature as in literature, proved susceptible to similar morals.

One more-recent account does give Mlle de Scudéry's work rather larger play and indeed examines the essay on the chameleon that she wrote a few years after Perrault published the official academic record.[53] In this account, hers is presented as a completely feminine interest, a reaction against the analytical anatomizing of the men in the royal circle. This analysis, too, seems to accept the standard story about Perrault's work. To be sure, Mlle de Scudéry's sensibilities proved more romantic and more positive about the little animal; she claimed, for example, that her male lizard could hear her call its name and that the female refused to eat flies. Yet this assertion of feminine, if not feminist, interest on the part of the lady of the salon implicitly accepts the view that Perrault's anatomizing was a manly act of cold science. It ignores the way in which the science of the *académie,* too, partook of the culture of the salon, remarking in passing about the moralizing of Plutarch and touching lightly on the weaknesses of flatterers. Like Chapelain dispatching Roberval at the Montmor academy, Perrault fired his precious verbal shots at his own competitors from the fastness of the king's library. His, like Rohault's and Mlle de Scudéry's, was a science for polite society in Louis XIV's Paris.

Perrault did not reserve his moralizing for the salon or for publication; it was an integral part of his anatomizing. In the privacy of the *académie* he drew his lessons as well. When the Versailles menagerie proved fatal to four lions in 1670, the royal academicians arrived at the following conclusions about the king of beasts:

> The anatomy of two lions and two lionesses justifies the Koran, which says—in the Oriental manner, explaining everything by allegories or fables—that in the Ark, the cat was born of the sneeze of the lion. We found great conformity between these two sorts of animals, not only in the particular structures of the paws, the teeth, the eyes, and the tongue, but also in the internal parts. However, the cat has more brain, in proportion to its size, than the lion. . . . Thus it follows that the lion, while it gives every indication of genius, is at the same time so cruel; and that the cat, which always retains a well of ferocity—in which it resembles the lion—has infinitely less of it. We found that in all the lions we dissected the pineal gland was very small, which some take as a mark of courage and boldness; perhaps also the extraordinary size of the heart and the capacity of its ventricles contribute to this.[54]

The allegorical style of the Orient found a striking consonance with the Western obsession for philosophical speculation. Ethical reflections were no less a part of natural history for Perrault than they had been for Plutarch.

If their success may be measured by their growth, the volumes of the *Histoire des animaux* fared brilliantly.[55] The quarto pamphlets of 1667 and 1669 gave way in the 1670s to lavish elephant folios. The early descriptions had been accompanied by plates depicting the animals in the wild, with insets containing the most interesting anatomical features. In the elephant folios, anatomical diagrams appeared in separate engravings, with full sheets devoted to the natural historical illustrations of the studied beasts. The plates introduced devices of portraiture; settings were transformed from natural to formal; the general tone of the art conformed increasingly to the tastes of polite society. Behind the tortoise, for example, stood a Greek pavilion (see Figure 4.3), reiterating in its dome the shape of the animal's shell.

The image of the early *académie* was most self-consciously portrayed in an engraving by Leclerc, which appeared as the frontispiece of the new edition of the *Histoire des animaux*.[56] The king stands with his minister in the *académie*'s precincts, flanked by the philosophical gentlemen who gather in his household (see Figure 4.4). Scattered about are the mathematical instruments and curiosities of natural his-

Figure 4.3 A tortoise. Note the buildings, especially the Greek-style pavilion, in the background. Reproduced from Mémoires pour servir à l'histoire naturelle des animaux, published by the Académie royale des sciences (Paris, 1671). Courtesy of the University of Minnesota Libraries.

Figure 4.4 Frontispiece of the 1671 volume of the Histoire des Animaux, *depicting the king, his minister, and the philosophical gentlemen of the* académie. *Reproduced from* Mémoires pour servir à l'histoire naturelle des animaux, *published by the Académie royale des sciences (Paris, 1671). Courtesy of the University of Minnesota Libraries.*

tory he provides for their researches; derricks perch atop the nearly completed Royal Observatory designed to house the philosophical assembly. The royal patron gazes with magnanimous approbation upon all that he has wrought.

The scene captures a certain image of the *académie* that has survived until the present day. According to that image, the vast resources of the crown allowed Colbert to assemble a remarkable group of academicians from all over Europe. The Royal Observatory and precision instruments embody the generosity of the king and symbolize the mathematical aspects of the science to be pursued by the *académie*. Leclerc's iconography is interpreted as evidence that the court philosophers, by their very participation in such abstruse exercises, gratified the attentive minister and glorified the monarch.

More generally, the grand image of the *académie* has come to characterize late-seventeenth-century French science as a whole. The voluntary fellowship of the Royal Society of London embraced the ramblings of gentlemen dilettanti alongside the ruminations of mathematical mechanicians and astronomers; by analogy the *académie* is often taken as the sole locus of natural philosophy in Paris. Abstruse mathematical papers, the best-known products of the first French academicians, exceeded the grasp of all but the most serious of the amateurs in the British organization; such work could have no place in the salons of Louis's capital. The exclusivity accorded academic research on this view of natural philosophy in France follows the monopolistic pattern characteristic of other royal academies established during the ministry of Colbert to encourage arts, letters, and learning.[57]

All this is a misreading of the propaganda. Louis XIV derived no smug satisfaction from patronage of the sciences; at the time the engravings were made, he had never called on an academic meeting. Like the jumble of instruments scattered about the room, his presence was a purely conventional artistic device. What the central figures of the royal household were after with their Académie royale des sciences was control of cultural affairs; the supporting characters in the background at the court—as in the frontispiece engraving—served rather to frame and decorate than to inform and entertain the king and his minister. Before Leclerc set out to construct an image for the royal philosophical institution, perceptions of natural philosophy had changed from the sinister and secretive connotations it had conjured up during the Minority. The *Dictionnaire des précieuses* was already (and, in its own terms, appropriately) out-of-date as a guide to the social elite, at least in questions of philosophical education. Leclerc's engraving, diametrically opposed to Somaize's sketches in prose, distorts the practice of science for clear purposes.

Such was scientific *gloire.* The philosophical company assembled by Charles Perrault and Jean Chapelain came to play a popular part in elite culture, as did the flamboyant Rohault. The cabalistic secrecy perceived by Somaize at the end of Mazarin's ministry gave way in Colbert's to an open investigation in the most prestigious salon of the day. Instead of the pedantic tinge portrayed in the *Dictionnaire des précieuses,* the science published by the *académie* displayed a refreshing, wholesome curiosity about the stuff of literary allusions. Far from erudite pedantry, the royal philosophical society showed an easy toleration of literary license and an indulgent delight in its half-truths. The *Histoire des animaux,* more than the formidable scientific reputations of the royal philosophers, justified the expense of maintaining the *académie.*

The accessibility and *politesse* of academic science was by no means confined to natural history. Perrault and his colleagues frequently brought the same disarming delight to the physical sciences. The literary and ethical excursions of the *Histoire des animaux* complemented its considerable anatomical merit; experimental demonstrations and philosophical speculations likewise grew out of many of the mechanical, chemical, and mathematical inquiries of the academicians. Such diversions were sometimes pleasant tangents, like Huygens's comments on Saturnian astronomers, but at other times they appeared as direct consequences of central philosophical problems. The results of the Saturday meetings devoted to these problems, like those of Tuesday's natural history presentations, appeared regularly in the public forums of the Parisian elite.

In 1670, Claude Perrault himself published three *Essais de physique.*[58] A full participant in the mechanical and chemical meetings of the *académie,* as well as those devoted to anatomizing, he had prepared the essays for academic discussion. Perrault's high visibility in elite culture, his decidedly amateur status in matters physical, and his early publication of the essays under his own name suggest that they should provide an entrée into the natural philosophy current in polite society in the later Colbert ministry. Positive reviews in the *Journal des sçavans* indicate that the essays did in fact receive favorable notice from the philosophically curious.[59]

All three essays clearly indicate Perrault's devotion to a mechanical philosophy in broad terms indistinguishable from the program pursued by such British contemporaries as Robert Boyle. Yet the French efforts were all self-consciously Cartesian. One essay presented a theory of weight and gravity composed for a discussion of the subject at the *académie* in 1669.[60] Perrault's contribution, which appeared in his collection of essays, represented a rather undistinguished variation on the Cartesian vortex theory. That theory maintained that a subtle matter swirling about the earth pushed outward, owing to centrifugal force; the gross matter, which does not participate in the swirling motion, finds itself pushed inward by the subtle matter seeking to move away from the center of the earth. The greatest difficulty with the vortex theory concerned the flow about the earth's axis of the celestial matter that caused gravity. Critics observed that such a flow must exert a horizontal pressure greater than the inward (downward) pressure of gravity. Perrault suggested a complex, ad hoc second vortex, spinning perpendicular to the first, a suggestion that he imagined removed this difficulty.

The Cartesian system, indeed, confronted the philosophical Parisian at every turn. The third of Perrault's *Essais de physique* offered an explanation of sound, which Perrault drew unabashedly from Huygens's theory of light.[61] At the time the wave theory was in an unpublished essay, which its author had presented to the academicians. Its mathematical details were missing in the derivative account of sound, for Perrault was no mathematician. Yet all the qualitative elements were there: Disturbances transmitted in straight lines through an elastic medium crossed one another without interference; at every given point on the wave front the medium behaved as a new wave center, allowing a sound to enter a window and fill a room; and so on. The phenomenon of pitch presented Perrault with some problems (as the phenomenon of color troubled Huygens), but in a general way the essay offered a clear and thorough qualitative summary of Huygens's wave theory.

The dry stuff of transmission did not exhaust Perrault's interest in sound. He followed the philosophical treatment with an aesthetical essay on harmonic theory and appended to that a history of ancient music. Both of these he included in his *Essais de physique,* as he had included his literary account of the chameleon in the *Histoire des animaux.* The boundaries of the new sciences were vague, to be sure, but it is clear that they were not technical. Rational reconstruction and critiques of ancient literature and arts, moral lessons drawn from natural history, "philosophical speculations" concerning people on the moon or on Saturn—all could take their proper place alongside the analysis of *physique experimentale,* anatomical investigations, optical devices, and astronomical calculations. On this there was broad agreement among Huygens, Perrault, Mlle de Scudéry, and the editors of the *Journal des sçavans.*[62] The Parisian social elite shared with the royal academicians a notion of what science was.

Huygens, too, prepared an essay for the debate on gravity; his effort modified the Cartesian vortex in a different way from Perrault's.[63] His gravorific ether did not fill the space around the earth. Rather, tiny particles traced individual circles about the planet at angles distributed randomly to the axis, so that together they exerted no horizontal pressure. Huygens described their motion in some mathematical detail, calculating the speed they must have to produce centrifugal acceleration sufficient to cause bodies to fall according to Galileo's law of acceleration. For the purposes of the discussion, Huygens also developed a striking demonstration experiment for his colleagues. In a cylindrical vessel filled with water, he dropped some bits of dense wax, which sank to the bottom of the vessel. He glued a glass top on his apparatus to prevent spilling and placed it on a rotating table. As he spun the vessel, the pieces of wax moved to the outside of its floor, carried there by centrifugal force. When Huygens suddenly stopped the table so that the water would continue to circulate in the stationary vessel, the pieces of wax spiraled into the middle of its floor, forming a little pile at the center. Similarly, Huygens claimed, the subtle matter spinning rapidly about the earth forces objects toward its center.[64]

This conceptually simple and visually striking demonstration was perfectly suited to the style of Jacques Rohault. Within about two years of the time Huygens presented the experiment to his colleagues at the *académie,* the man with the most philosophical hat in Paris was fitted out with a rotating table and a sealed vessel of water and dense wax.[65] His students saw the same demonstration that had been offered by the head of the physical section of the *académie*—and assimilated the most recent refinement to the system Rohault professed.

In the decade since Huygens had attended the lectures in the winter of 1660–1661, Rohault had changed his style of exposition as well as his manner of dress. He no longer simply displayed one phenomenon after another, explaining each with a Cartesian mechanism; instead, he presented a coherent Cartesian explanation of the world, carefully illustrated with the extensive cabinet he had been collecting since the 1650s. The lectures, in fact, contained a *System of the World,* as the title of the English translation would proclaim; Rohault taught Huygens's system. To be sure, the lectures presented a simplified, qualitative version, but they were absolutely up-to-date. It was that system the eager bourgeois would take, with memories of Rohault's hat, to Molière's comedies.

Of course, some of the work of the academicians was technical material inaccessible to the casual dilettante. The *Horologium oscillatorum* of 1673, Huygens's magnum opus, which was dedicated extravagantly to Louis XIV, presented mathematical mechanics comprehensible to only a handful of Huygens's colleagues. Unlike his theories of light and gravity (which appeared in all their mathematical detail in 1690), the difficult derivations and the mathematical laws governing centrifugal force could not be explained in qualitative terms by a Perrault or a Rohault. Yet the *Horologium oscillatorum* is hardly sufficient in itself to condemn an entire philosophical academy to technical inaccessibility.

More famous still is Huygens's publication in the *Journal des sçavans* in 1669 of the mathematical rules governing collision, among the classic problems of mathematical mechanics through much of the seventeenth century.[66] Far from being the result of Huygens's association with the *académie,* the publication of the rules derived from connections in Britain predating that institution by five years. Informed mechanicians in England had known as early as 1661 that Huygens, as well as a few British philosophers, could predict the course of collinear collision.[67] Henry Oldenburg, the secretary of the Royal Society and editor of the *Philosophical Transactions,* solicited these rules from Huygens, John Wallis, and Christopher Wren in 1668.[68] All three responded, but owing to the vicissitudes of the mails and the informality of the whole affair, Oldenburg published only the British solutions.[69] When Huygens saw a copy of the *Philosophical Transactions* without his solution, he hurried his version through the press in the *Journal des sçavans*. The misunderstanding was slight and quickly smoothed over,[70] but it left behind a published record that created an apparent institutional rivalry and simultaneity of discovery that never existed, a record that cast Huygens as a severely mathematical philosopher even in the public context of a popular periodical. The rules of collision looked even more out of place in the *Journal* than in the *Philosophical Transactions*.

More characteristic of the work of the *académie*, and of the public face that Huygens generally showed, was the spate of articles he published in the *Journal* in 1672. The first contribution came in February, when he presented an analysis of the new reflecting telescope invented by the young Englishman Isaac Newton.[71] Huygens played the part of elder statesman appropriate to the senior member of the Académie royale des sciences. Enthusiastic in his praise and precise in his description, he mentioned a few possibilities for minor improvements that demonstrated his competency without in any way detracting from the significance of the new instrument.

Next, in July, Huygens composed a long open letter to the *Journal,* concerning a phenomenon he had discovered earlier, and the explanation he had worked out to account for it.[72] The standard method for measuring the strength of the vacuum in a pneumatic pump employed a small water barometer inside the receiver. Huygens discovered that if he filled the tube with water that had been sitting in the evacuated pump for some time, the water would not descend in the tube, no matter how strong the vacuum in the receiver. Further investigation yielded several related phenomena and methods for defeating them. Siphons do not ordinarily operate in vacuo, yet by using water stored overnight in an evacuated receiver, Huygens could start a syphon. If mercury were stored three or four days at very low pressure and then used in a barometer, the experimenter could with care sustain a column seventy-five inches high, although the weight of the atmosphere ordinarily supports only about thirty inches. In each case, however, Huygens found it possible to interrupt the extraordinary phenomenon either by tapping the glass tube or by introducing a tiny bubble of air into it: Both the water and mercury barometers would drop suddenly to their expected levels, and the action of the siphon would abruptly cease.

The French king's first philosopher developed a thoroughly Cartesian explanation for all these phenomena. He suggested a new sort of subtle matter, grosser than the luminiferous ether, but much finer than the air. This stuff he believed could easily penetrate the pores of the air but traversed the more compact and convoluted interstices of solids and liquids only with difficulty. After it found its way through the glass of barometer or siphon tubes, it did not have sufficient agitation to enter the differently arranged pores of water or mercury. This new matter therefore affected his experiments in the same manner as did the atmosphere: It pressed down on the fluid in the barometer bowl and sustained the weight of a slightly higher column of water or mercury within the tube than did the ambient air.

By tapping the tube or introducing a bubble of air within it, the experimenter opened a vacuity into which the new matter could flow, despite its feeble agitation. Once this process began, more and more of the subtle matter could flow into the increasing Torricellian space above the barometric fluid. Its pressure therefore weighed down on the column inside the tube as well as on the reservoir in the bowl; the instrument quickly reached a new equilibrium, just as it does when the top of a normal barometer is broken. With a very perceptive connection of phenomena, Huygens suggested that the pressure of this same material is responsible for the fact that two plates of polished metal stick together, even within the evacuated receiver of a pneumatic pump. The pressure of Huygens's new matter forces the outside surfaces of the plates together; until they are detached far enough to allow particles of the stuff to flow between them, the new matter resists their separation, just as the pressure of the air holds together two half-spheres containing a vacuum between them.

A *Journal* subscriber of average intellect and learning would have easily assimilated the thrust of this argument. Had she been to Rohault's lectures, for instance, she would have been quite familiar with the course of gross and subtle matter in and around barometric tubes. Indeed, by the time Huygens's barometric experiments appeared in print, the popular philosophy master was employing an elaborate piece of glassware designed by Auzout to demonstrate the "barometer within a barometer."[73] Essentially the apparatus consisted of a large glass tube with a carp's bladder diaphragm covering its top. Inside the tube, near the end with the bladder, was a small barometer. The whole thing could be filled with mercury and then inverted, bladder up, into a bowl, as an ordinary barometer could.

Initially Rohault explained the apparatus in this configuration. The mercury fills about thirty inches of the large tube. In the Torricellian space above this tube, Rohault noted, there is only the luminiferous ether. The small barometer in the Torricellian space therefore experiences no pressure on the mercury in its bowl, so no mercury flows up into its tube. (This situation resembles that of an air pump with a barometer enclosed to measure the pressure, at a time when the pump is completely evacuated.) Rohault then pierced the diaphragm at the top of the large tube with a pin, letting air enter the large barometer a little at a time. This allowed the air pressure inside the top of the larger barometer to increase. Simultaneously the mercury level in the large tube falls as the air that enters it balances the pressure of the atmosphere, and the level of the mercury in the small inner barometer rises as the newly introduced air forces mercury up into its still evacuated tube. When the pin is removed completely, the mercury levels in the two barometers move immediately to the expected heights, just as Huygens's barometers equilibrated as soon as he tapped them. Molière's model philosophy master, in short, prepared his students to follow the experiments and theories of the king's first philosopher.[74]

Huygens was by no means alone in his frequent use of the *Journal* to announce his researches and discoveries. Quite regularly one or another of his colleagues at the *académie* submitted a report of ongoing philosophical activities. Beginning in 1668 the editor supplemented these individual offerings with notes drawn from the minutes of academic meetings. The royal band of philosophers, rather than being a closeted enclave of experts, proved almost as public in its activities as the Royal Society of London. Among reports of the unfortunate vogue for blood transfusions and of endless unworkable mechanical contraptions, "the company that meets in the king's library" put in regular appearances, always with some bit of scientific news.

All this information had its effect. The Parisian elite gained a certain philosophical literacy. Molière brought more than memories of Rohault's singular hat from the lecture hall to the theater. His estimation of the scientific sophistication of the ladies caricatured in the *Femmes savantes* in 1672 far exceeded that evident in the *Précieuses ridicules* at the close of the ministry of Mazarin. The particulars of Auzout's debates over men on the moon were not the only philosophical tidbits informing the humor of the production conceived around the time Huygens published his account of the new barometric subtle matter. Just before the ladies of the play formed their scientific assembly, for example, Molière offered this exchange:

TRISSOTIN: I am attached, for its order, to Peripateticism.
PHILAMANTE: For its abstractions, I like Platonism.
ARMANDE: Epicurus pleases me; his teachings are so powerful.
BÉLISE: I can accommodate little bodies well enough,
   but to suffer the void seems difficult to me.
   my taste instead is for subtle matter.
TRISSOTIN: Descartes on magnets makes sense to me.
ARMANDE: I like his vortices.
PHILAMANTE: I, his wandering worlds.

(3.2)

Scientific content, like the academic form they would affect for their debate about men on the moon, came naturally to the ladies of the new salons.

The passage indicates that the playwright followed natural philosophy with some sensitivity and that he expected his audience to do the same. The *femmes savantes,* denied the university education that still trained their brothers in a humanized Aristotle, looked to Platonism, atomism, and Cartesianism—the avant-garde philosophies of the popular lecturers. The erudite pedant Trissotin initially embraced the outmoded Peripateticism of the schools. Yet as soon as he heard Bélise express an interest in Cartesianism, Trissotin adopted its most systematic aspect. (On the stage, as in society, the persuasion of charm played as great a role as that of argument.) Molière's humor depended on the scientific knowledge of his audience: The Aristotelian's acceptance of the rotating bits of Cartesian subtle matter represented to initiates a reversal of monumental proportions.

The scene reflected reality. The ladies of the Bonneveau and Guédreville academy had infected their contemporaries with scientific curiosity and bombarded them with the fashionable systems of the day.

Mlle de Scudéry, for example, knew enough about Cartesian biology to know she didn't like it; without the slightest application on her part, she learned of the theory of the animal machine.[75] The salon of Mme de La Salbière, the most prestigious in the generation following the early phase of the movement of the *précieuses,* put an even greater emphasis on science. Indeed, the *Femmes savants* reflected the ambiance chez Salbière in the same way the *Précieuses ridicules* had captured the excesses of "Sappho's Saturdays" a dozen years earlier.

Mme de La Salbière kept herself unusually well informed in matters scientific and directed her considerable influence frequently to the popularization of the new philosophies of the seventeenth century. It was because of her urging that Bernier composed his *Abrégé de la philosophie de Gassendi,* which did much to rescue atomism from the convoluted learning of its great champion. The philosophical hostess likewise urged La Fontaine to prepare a redaction in verse of Descartes, although without success. Her own studies did not require such dilution. Mme de Salbière understood both Greek and Latin, and she read philosophical as well as literary texts. When her curiosity turned to astronomy, she called on the Royal Observatory. The popular hostess even managed to tame—or to tolerate—Roberval sufficiently to study mathematics with the exiled Montmorian turned royal academician. She and the guests at her salon, like the learned ladies of Molière's stage, could distinguish one brand of philosophy from the next.[76]

If the *politesse* of the salon struck a mortal blow to Peripatetic physics, in questions of cosmology, Aristotelianism was already dead. Quite on his own initiative, for example, the excitable Trissotin exclaimed:

TRISSOTIN: I come to announce important news.
   Madame, while sleeping, we have made a great escape.
   A world near us has passed by.
   It fell right across our vortex,
   And if it had encountered our earth on its path,
   We would have been shattered to pieces like glass.

(4.2)

Cartesian astronomy had penetrated even the scholastic erudition of Molière's pedant. The Ptolemaic system; the medieval distinction between immutable perfection in the heavens and corruption on earth;

the cosmological controversies of the early seventeenth century in which Copernicanism was deemed heretical in Italy and scandalous in France: These obstacles to the new astronomy had simply evaporated in Colbert's capital.

In this the dialogue of the *Femmes savantes* paralleled that of Auzout at the Académie royale des sciences. His first review of Campani in the *Journal des sçavans* had contained a forthright passage describing the French position:

> [Auzout] says that Campani's observations on Saturn and Jupiter, and those which he himself has made, tend to confirm the Copernican systems, which he claims many *sçavans* would affirm except that the Decree of the Inquisition of Rome condemned it. Nevertheless he maintains that this Decree need not prevent them from doing so, since it is only provisional, and does not absolutely condemn the doctrine. Further, he shows that it agrees with the principles of religion no less than those of philosophy.[77]

In good Gallican fashion, Auzout showed no particular hostility toward the Church in Rome. Rather, he ignored papal decrees insofar as possible, reconciled his position in a superficial sense with broad Catholic doctrine, and interpreted particulars as he saw fit. He reserved his disdain for Campani, who slavishly followed the strictest interpretation of the most excessive judgment of the Inquisition. The debate concerned, not religious freedom, but scientific curiosity. To apply the arbitrary admonitions of overly delicate doctrinal sensibilities to Saturn's ring, Jupiter's moon, or the wintry visage of our own satellite was to ignore the wonders of the heavens. Such an attitude more resembled the pedantry and boorishness of bickering Montmorians than the new style of science in Colbert's Paris.

Auzout's argument articulated the attitude implicit in Trissotin's speech and in the position of the curious among the Parisian elite. Naturalizing had become fashionable; nature alone set limits on its creatures. The new science allowed freedom not only from the bonds of scholastic learning but also from the boundaries of the senses. Novelty in natural philosophy had entered into the universe of routine discourse.

The causes for such a fashion present a difficult historical problem. There was nothing particularly French about the subjects of natural history and natural philosophy practiced by the royal academicians and their collaborators in polite society. The tiny audience for rigorous mathematical treatises of the sort Huygens occasionally published had always been international. Descriptions of plants and animals filled the pages of the *Philosophical Transactions*, as they did Parisian publications; Perrault's physical essays found their counterpart, to pick one example, in Hooke's *Micrographia*;[78] Boyle repeated Huygens's barometric experiments as soon as he heard of them.[79] As in England, the scientific community made its peace with a benign official church and rather successfully avoided entanglements with more controversial religious groups. Auzout's Gallicanism, like twentieth-century Anglicanism, did not so much address theology as avoid it.

Several aspects of natural inquiry nonetheless made it compatible with society in the age of Louis XIV. What was archetypically French about the science considered here was the style of entertainment it offered. Descartes's subtle matters, Auzout's rhetoric, and Rohault's hat captured the imagination of the greatest comedian of the French stage. Perrault could naturalize in the most prestigious literary salon of Paris; his hostess preserved the skeletons as well as the elegies of the anatomized chameleons as long as she lived. Fashionable ladies and gentlemen marched up and down the stairs in Rohault's apartments and filled out the complement of apothecaries among Lémery's furnaces and retorts. In all this, French science differed from British.

Perhaps most important for the acceptance of science in Parisian society was the attraction that natural history and philosophy held for women. Throughout the seventeenth century courtly ladies had controlled cultural life in Paris; only by their sufferance could a new form win a place in the world of the social elite in Colbert's Paris. Taught outside the traditional institutions of learning, the new science provided a source of study and entertainment at once accessible to and worthy of consideration by the important feminine elite. It provided a suitable topic for light conversation, a basis for entertaining speculation, and a subject for an afternoon's diversion in the lecture hall. For those with intellectual ambitions—and such women clearly populated the salons of Colbert's France—more substantial inquiry rewarded private efforts with the same satisfactions ordinarily attributed as a matter of course to men who had tested their rationality on nature. In short, science engaged the ladies of Paris, as it did the gentlemen of London's Royal Society.

Other social conveniences as well surrounded the new science. For a time, natural philosophy offered a neutral ground for intercourse between old and new wealth and power. If the bourgeois gentleman had little hope of equaling the nobility in fencing or dance, he could learn quickly enough to speak of nature in appropriately gentle terms. Although the field of speculating and moralizing was open and attractive, it did not come with overtones that favored its development and interpretation by one element or another of the uneasily mixed elite dominated by the Sun King. Insofar as natural philosophy had religious implications, it was quite acceptable to the crown. On the one hand, it offered proper Gallican resistance to the primacy of Rome; on the other, it presented no strident theology to rival the authority of the state.

The new fashion also enjoyed purely practical advantages. Scientific entertainment, unlike music, dance, and the stage, remained largely free from royal regulation. The king endorsed the validity of natural inquiry as a cultural form by inviting the philosophical band to meet in his library, but he granted the Académie royale des sciences no monopoly on the public practice of philosophizing. The great noble households could and did sponsor philosophical demonstrations, lectures, and entertainments of their own; even the least of the city's hosts and hostesses could assemble little scientific academies. In the age of *colbertisme*, access to free and legal assembly represented a very real virtue.

The relative importance of these and other factors in the acceptance of science in France is impossible to determine. It is certain, however, that the process borrowed nothing from the Protestant religion and liberal politics so frequently associated with the scientific revolution in England. Nor was the style or administration of the Académie royale des sciences an elite, regulated, and technically detailed—that is to say, a *colbertiste*—rival to the free association of British gentlemen that banded into the Royal Society of London. The philosophical company that met in the king's library was designed to contribute to Louis's *gloire*, but to a *gloire* intended for amateur consumption. It was the philosopher's *honnêteté*, the naturalist's *politesse*, that brought science into elite society during the ministry of Colbert. This cultural aspect of natural inquiry, more than any simple technical development, represents what was French about the consolidation of the new science in the third quarter of the seventeenth century.

5

A Pretty Novel of Physics, in which Cogito, ergo sum *meets* l'État, c'est moi

As Louis XIV GREW OLDER and more secure in his personal rule, the direction of his government changed in a number of ways. The court moved from Paris to Versailles, where elaborate social conventions largely replaced politics. Colbert's death in 1683 marked the end of any restraint in fiscal matters; lavish expenditures on the royal household and unsuccessful foreign adventures drained the treasury despite tremendous increases in taxation. Revocation of the Edict of Nantes in 1685 drove the Protestants from the kingdom or into hiding. The tone of Colbert's capital gave way to that of Louis's court, and the minister's cultural administration degenerated into a hollow glorification of the king. Absolutism became a way of life in France; political thought and action could operate only within the framework of the monarchy.

Science followed the larger cultural pattern. Just as the *politesse* of natural history and philosophy had contributed to *colbertiste gloire*, so in the latter part of the reign of Louis XIV the Cartesian system came to bolster the new political and religious orthodoxy. A few self-conscious adjustments were required and supplied, especially by those of Descartes's disciples afflicted with a metaphysical disposition. On the whole, however, accommodation with Louis XIV and his state proved a more subtle matter. The connection between natural and political philosophy has always been more metaphorical than theoretical. It was in the metaphorical arena that natural philosophy demonstrated the greatest flexibility, and the Cartesian system came increasingly to offer polite assistance to Versailles.

The greatest detriment to philosophical activity in Paris came with the exclusion of foreigners, owing either to their religious beliefs or to the nearly continual state of war, which excluded them as enemies. The Académie royale des sciences lost its leading light when the Calvinist Christiaan Huygens was excluded from the kingdom. Paris had achieved the status of the leading philosophical center of Europe during the Colbert years; all promising young mathematicians and natural philosophers spent time in Louis's capital. There had been no particular need for hometown heroes, since brilliant foreigners could light the Sun King's capital as well as Parisians.

The changes in Louis XIV's style of patronage proved a double-edged sword for the little band of natural historians and philosophers who gathered in his household. The Académie royale des sciences would gain a formal charter, a permanent home, and perquisites of membership, which offered all the benefits of an old regime sinecure. However, the institution increasingly adopted an orthodoxy as rigid as the absolutist political system in which it operated. A great deal of interesting inquiry into nature continued to emerge from the king's library, to be sure, and the academicians maintained a technically competent core. Yet innovation in matters of fundamental import—the mathematical mechanics and grand cosmological innovations at which Huygens excelled, the charmingly creative naturalizing of Perrault—moved away from Paris. At its best the *académie* represented a sort of competent, diligent, polite bureaucracy of natural philosophy and natural history. At its worst, it operated almost as a hereditary office of censor. Above all, it was transformed from a small but active circle intimately placed in the king's library to a largely independent body that reported its doings to the Parisian elite through the literary form of the periodical.

A Science for the Sun King

The strongest example of this archetypical French institution appears in the person of Bernard Bouvier de Fontenelle, himself an archetypical French institution during the first half of the eighteenth century. Fontenelle would move in the circles that succeeded the *précieuses*, playing the part of a well-connected gentleman who parlayed his associations and a profusely productive pen into a host of cultural pensions. It is Fontenelle's fate always to fall between glorious accounts of the golden age of *colbertisme* on the one hand and the High Enlightenment on the other. His talent pales by comparison to Molière's and Voltaire's, the eponymous giants of those ages. Yet the formal recognition that Fontenelle achieved is unexcelled in the academic history of France. More properly a successor to Jean Chapelain than to Molière, he won the triple crown of membership in the Académie française, the Académie royale des sciences, and the Academy des inscriptions et belles lettres—the renamed successor to Colbert's Little Academy. Only one other person (the even more obscure, late-eighteenth-century astronomer-turned-politician Jean Sylvain Bailly) would repeat that success.

Fontenelle was born in Rouen in 1647.[1] In his youth he frequently traveled to Paris. As a nephew of the poets Pierre and Thomas Corneille, Fontenelle's family connections won him easy introductions into the fashionable literary salons, most notably that of Mme de La Salbière. Anxious to make some noise in the world, the literary provincial had first tried his hand at his familial *métier*. A play called *The Comet*—a more extended and pedantic treatment of the astronomical phenomenon than Molière had offered in the *Femmes savantes*—failed to win any particular following. Yet the basic formula, a literary treatment of the more exciting aspects of the new natural philosophy, still appealed to Fontenelle. A novel called the *Conversations on the Plurality of Worlds* applied the same sort of philosophical twist to the genre of light romantic dialogue. Published in 1686, the *Conversations* provides an eloquent connection between the French style of philosophizing and the social style of Versailles.

Fontenelle's novel proved immediately and persistently successful. It was to be the most popular work in the literature of science during the reign of Louis XIV and well into that of Louis XV. The philosophical colloquies that it reported transpired between the voice of the author and that of an imaginary marquise during several summer evenings spent in the lady's country garden. The *Conversations* did provide a bit of painless literary instruction in natural philosophy for those who had not called on Rohault and his colleagues in the business of philosophical demonstration, or the pleasing reward of recognition for those who had. Yet in a very real sense its primary purpose was to entertain.

The meaning of philosophical entertainment offered by a clever young man for the benefit of a young gentlewoman had changed subtly with the ossification of politics and society under the aging Louis XIV. Fontenelle's excursion into the *politesse* of science was a product of the milieu of the salons and the philosophical curiosity of its denizens. His role bore no resemblance to that of Rohault, dashing about in the most philosophical hat in Paris and producing natural historical spectacle. Fontenelle partook in the culture of the salon; he did not sell his services to it. Were he forced into a Molière farce, the part of Trissotin might have been a better social fit than that of philosophy master, although Fontenelle's virtues and vices would have been a bit different from those of the imaginary pedant. He needed no conversion to the Cartesian view of the world, for his explanations were already thoroughly grounded in subtle matter; to suffer the void seemed to him implausible even without the urgings of a learned lady. Like Armande and Philamante, Fontenelle liked both the vortices and the wandering worlds of Descartes.

Some social conventions nonetheless had changed fundamentally. The fawning Trissotin's flexibility in matters of orthodoxy reflected a fact of salon life in the age of Colbert: Women maintained polite control. This control Fontenelle's *Conversations* wrested to the side of the gentleman. He did not, to be sure, insist upon his correctness, as the boorish Roberval had done at the *hôtel* of Montmor; Fontenelle would never have been ejected from anyone's salon for rudeness. Nonetheless, throughout the dialogue the voice of the philosophical gentleman maintained firm control of the facts. The Cartesian view of the world came in his work to represent a new orthodoxy, one that adopted the language and manners of the *précieuses,* but abandoned their radical acceptance of the role of women in polite culture. Silver tongues had replaced swords as the weapon of choice in refined circles, and the men of Louis's court were quick to assert their power over this new arsenal.

Fontenelle was a master of the new style of philosophizing; his prose requires no apology. The *Conversations* displays a certain flair for illustration and a grasp of the dramatic as well as a light and pleasant style. Fontenelle's genius lay primarily in his ability to fix a notion in the reader's imagination through a clever literary device. The conformity among the philosophical, social, and political orthodoxies embodied in the work likewise operated at a polite, metaphorical level; arguments came from style rather than logic. The dangers implicit in heterodoxy were the ostracism braved by the *bourgeois gentilhomme,* not the tools of the Inquisition.

The emerging literary party in the latter part of the reign of the Sun King adopted not only the language and mannerisms of the *précieuses;* even the bold, innovative topics that Molière had found so ridiculous took their place in the new courtly order represented in the *Conversations.* The first evening's discussion, for example, concerned the general Copernican constitution of the heavens. No longer a risqué theory, much less a dangerous opinion, by the mid-1680s Fontenelle's explanation of the heavens had ceased to be even a little naughty. Nor did it require any apologetic preamble. Before launching into anything more technical, the philosophical gentleman explained in general terms how the magnificent nocturnal scene is staged each evening. His was a gentler metaphor than that of Descartes.

Picture for yourself all the sages at an opera; the Pythagoreans, the Platonists, and the Aristotelians, and all those people whose names at this time make so much noise in the world; suppose that they saw the flight of Phaeton who, in appearance, is raised by the winds; that they cannot discover the cords; and that they know not how the machinery behind the curtain is disposed. The one of them says, "It is a certain secret virtue that raises Phaeton"; another, "Phaeton is composed of certain members which cause him to ascend." A third: "Phaeton has a certain friendship for the top of the theater, and that he is not easy but when he is there." Another: "That Phaeton was not made for flying, but he loves better to fly than to permit the top of the theater to be void," and a hundred other reveries—which astonishes me, that all antiquity hath not lost its reputation. At length, Descartes and some other moderns are come who say, "Phaeton ascends because he is drawn by cords, and weights heavier than him descend."[2]

Like Mme de Guédreville and her young friend Christiaan Huygens at the opera *Jason,* Fontenelle clearly delighted in theatrical applications of the new, mechanical philosophy and expected his readers to do so as well. More than that, his metaphor mixed stagecraft with the Cartesian system in a literal way. All the world was for Fontenelle a stage, and the subtle matters its cords and counterweights. Nature, like the theater, presented an appearance that should above all amuse and edify. In each case the appearances—characters in a play or the gross objects of nature—presented a world not quite real. The visible objects—actors ascending toward the heavens or the ordinary third matter of everyday experience—in fact reflected hidden stage management, which could be analyzed only in terms of the physical laws that govern motion. Recognition of these dual realities by no means diminished the pleasure that the onlooker might derive from them. To the contrary, Fontenelle moved in a highly mannered society where a nouveau riche bourgeois might try to transform himself into a gentleman by hiring the services of masters of dance and music in order not to make a fool of himself at the opera. In that society, an understanding of the way things are staged was a prerequisite to comfortable enjoyment of social amenities.

The theater of the heavens presented an appropriate first scene in this tour of cultural enlightenment, as Fontenelle turned from his introductory pleasantries to specific workings of nature. His knowledgeable gentlemanly voice set out the vortex theory, in which the planets and their satellites float about in placid whirlpools of celestial ether. Descartes's explanation of the Copernican system offered a natural starting point for the relatively technical part of the *Conversations*. It cast the heliocentric theory in terms that, like the language of the *précieuses*, had progressed in the polite world from the avant-garde to the au courant. Fontenelle would himself occupy this moderate position during the imaginary colloquies, as he would occupy it throughout his career. He adopted without any great argument positions that, if they were still officially taboo even in the latter years of the reign of the Sun King, no longer aroused passions. This echo of the great noises made by the *précieuses* never developed even as far as the little acts of defiance of orthodoxy so common in the *colbertiste* salons. For Fontenelle, natural philosophy could coexist peacefully with the political philosophy famously and appropriately summed up by the declaration "*l'état, c'est moi*"—an expression that loses all its Frenchness when translated into the usual English "I am the State." Louis XIV in fact found at least an unconscious metaphorical connection with Copernicanism when he adopted the title of the "Sun King," the center of a court and capital that whirled about him.

Fontenelle's presentation of the heliocentric and monarchical view of the physical world consisted mostly of an exposition of the most fundamental stage trick required by the Copernican system. It is an effect so convincing that we all believe that the entire expanse of the universe revolves around our own little planet. The conversation explained how in fact the earth spins on its own axis in the great vortex of subtle matter that fills the space around it with a motion so smooth that it gives the impression that the heavens rotate about the earth. To correct this mistaken perception, Fontenelle conducted the marquise in imagination to a stationary point in space—a quiet backstage corner of the solar system just far enough away to ride in the solar rather than the terrestrial vortex. From there, the two French subjects observed the gentle circulation of the surface of their planet. This thought experiment allowed more than a dry exercise in physics; it inspired a sort of *National Geographic* tour of the countries of the earth. Fontenelle and the marquise commented on the customs and morals of each society that passed beneath them: the serious Englishmen, thinking only of politics; "the Iroquois, who are eating some prisoners of war"; Japanese women, dedicated solely to their husbands, "the greatest brutes of the world"; and so on, until the return of France and their descent to a new reality.[3]

This interlude speaks volumes about Fontenelle's notions of natural philosophy and its place in the larger intellectual world. To be sure, the discussion conveyed a sense of the rotation of the earth from west to east. It did so in a manner at once more pleasant for his audience and more memorable than any dry didactic exposition, fixing the direction with a march of cultures. At the same time, it tied the new natural philosophy to the political and social world in which Fontenelle moved. A nascent ethnography, Francocentric and Eurocentric, drew credence from and lent credence to the newly hegemonic Copernican system. The Europeans, who (on their own account) had discovered the new worlds of America and the heavens, looked on both as territories more proper for conquest than analysis. These brave new worlds represented domains that Fontenelle and his compatriots hoped to subject to laws both natural and civil based on the European model.

In this, as in many other ways, the *Conversations* serves to illuminate the beginnings of the Enlightenment. Knowledge of nature became an exemplar for knowledge in general. Science provided a framework for intellectual discussions of all sorts. No matter that the connection between the rotation of the earth, the politics of the English, and the wildly exaggerated stereotypes of peoples and cultures foreign to Fontenelle's own little world had no intellectual basis. The new natural philosophy somehow subsumed politics and ethnography; the new natural philosopher could speak about whatever he chose, with an authority based on the success of his science.

Fontenelle's voice and that of his marquise were never so heavy-handed as interpretations of their conversation must seem. The majority of their light instruction touched upon recurring themes in salon science, matters of less moment but greater conventional amusement than the motion of the earth. Fontenelle began the second evening's conversation with the claim that the moon must be peopled. His variation on this theme had a tone less strident than the debate carried out in the *Journal des sçavans,* but it took the question more seriously than the sarcasm of the *Femmes savantes.* The resulting dialogue embraced the possibility of the plurality of worlds but resembled a parlor game rather than a scientific discussion even in a *colbertiste* salon. The marquise, like the king's philosophers, at first politely rejected the idea as absurd. Fontenelle, quicker with a quip than Hooke had been, took the offensive. If the moon is like the earth, he demanded, why should it not be peopled? And in what, he asked, does it differ from the earth? His fair companion suggested, one after another, the standard distinctions offered by the likes of Auzout (omitting any discussion of the eternally wintry visage of the moon); her guest dispelled them with scientific explanations.

Fontenelle clearly intended to accomplish an agreeable inversion where the less knowledgeable partner participated in the conversation with her questions and repaid her tutor with the attention and kind remarks that one might extend to a clever student. The author perhaps learned this lesson in Mme de La Salbière's salon; it allowed him to recite snippets of information about the world without the pedantic qualities imposed by systematic organization. Yet only the willing suspension of disbelief expected of the readers of romances permitted even this bit of control to the imaginary marquise. Fontenelle of course fed her the lines that allowed him to tell the story he wished to tell. Within his context, unlike the practice in the salons, she was nearly always wrong and he was always right. The conduct of the *pré-cieuses* that their critics had always found most galling derived from the ways in which women took control—control of the salons, control of the language, control of their own romantic involvements, and control of the topics of acceptable conversation. Control of all these things Fontenelle took back as he instructed the young lady in her garden. The transition from the generation of the *précieuses* to the Enlightenment constituted a backward step for the intellectual role of women in the social world of Paris.

Those situations in which even a modicum of control could be extended to the marquise were artfully placed in the dialogue. The literary structure of the *Conversations* proved as carefully constructed as the scientific explanation was casual. Once habitability was established for the moon, for example, the philosophical gentleman could colonize the planets as well. His relatively rigorous defense of the existence of lunar inhabitants against the strongest skepticism of the marquise allowed Fontenelle a certain literary license in his excursions elsewhere in the solar system. Never again would the young lady offer objection after objection to her philosophy master's tale. Less detailed knowledge of the appearance of the earth's more distant neighbors required philosophical speculation in place of the telescopic observations available for the initial discussion of the moon; the marquise, allowed at least to have a reasonable philosophical intuition, could join in with her tutor.

It was in the speculative voyages to the other planets, too, that the *Conversations* exhibited most of their moralizing. The feminine mind seemed to Fontenelle appropriate for that purpose. To be sure, whatever definite information the gentleman's voice could articulate he exploited to the fullest. As the interlocutors took their imaginations to Venus, for example, they had but one sure fact: That planet is closer to the sun than our own. Although the precise figures Fontenelle supplied were out-of-date, he got across the crucial point that Venus must receive considerably more light and heat than does the earth.[4] The marquise, convinced of this simple truth, volunteered a description of the inhabitants of such a warm place: "They must resemble the Moors of Grenada, a little black people, burned by the sun, full of spirit and fire, always amorous, loving of music, every day inventing festivals, dances, and tourneys."[5] Fontenelle again took polite charge: He disagreed in that they must be hotter and wilder still: "Our Moors of Grenada could not be any more like them than the inhabitants of Lapland and Greenland for their cold and stupidity."[6]

When the marquise realized that Mercury is even closer to the sun than is Venus, it was too much for her tenderhearted temperament. In desperation she suggested, "Let's give Mercury long and abundant rains to refresh him, as are supposed to fall in hot countries for four months at a time."[7] Fontenelle, with his seemingly endless knowledge of the world, had a less prosaic solution, worthy of the editor of the *Journal des sçavans.* He told of a region in China where "exhalations of saltpeter" so cooled even tropical regions that the rivers froze in July and August. Were Mercury a little planet of saltpeter, he reasoned, the sun would rouse up such exhalations as to cool even the great heat it caused in its nearest neighbor.[8] Again Fontenelle's own character echoed the sensibilities of the young lady he tutored, and again the charming gentleman was allowed to do her one better.

The conversation continued in the same vein. Their sojourn near the hot, inner planets finished, the travelers set out for the planets and peoples beyond the earth. The climatic fate of the inhabitants of the outer planets would, of course, reverse the earlier situation. They must suffer a lack of heat and light, owing to their great separation from the sun. Yet nature's munificence could provide them, too, with some relief. With a sense of showmanship worthy of Jacques Rohault, Fontenelle suggested that Mars might come equipped with great phosphorescent mountains to illuminate his dark face.[9] The strange glowing phosphors, like many rarities of the chemists, remained as close to natural magic as to philosophy, but Fontenelle appropriated them quite comfortably for the convenience of his Martian colonists. His eager student's wishes once more found fulfillment through his knowledge of natural history.

It appears that Fontenelle supplied nature with a munificence sufficient for any benevolent creator. Yet unlike contemporary philosophers in the Cartesian tradition, notably Gottfried Wilhelm Leibniz and Nicolas Malebranche, Fontenelle did not attribute his ameliorating wonders to God. Nature provided a certain relief from suffering for the inhabitants of Mercury or Mars, as it did for the inhabitants of Africa and the Americas, but it was nonetheless the lot of all those others to suffer. Fontenelle did not offer this as a theological claim, a

Gallican version of the Calvinist argument that some are elect and some are damned; it came merely as a literary touch. That this is more or less the best of all possible worlds even for those unfortunate enough not to be of the European gentry seemed obvious to the interlocutors, but the meaning of that implicit claim was different from the philosophical issue that caused such theological agonizing in Leibniz. For Fontenelle it was a social observation.

Without recourse to an active Cartesian god, the philosophical speculations that placed saltpeter on Mercury or phosphorous on Mars might have seemed overly arbitrary, were there not some evidence for similar benevolence elsewhere in the solar system. Saturn presented such evidence without any speculative additions. The great planet came equipped with the broad ring Huygens had discovered, now perfectly visible through fairly ordinary telescopes and known to everyone who conversed at all about the heavens. This appendage was perfectly suited to reflect the sun's light during long Saturnian nights, an appliance more magnificent even than phosphorescent mountains.[10] Fontenelle made almost as great a splash with this discovery as Chapelain had done at the Montmor academy, saving his explanations of the happy effects of natural history on other planets from dismissal for lack of evidence.

Against the torturous existences on far-off planets that required such extraordinary relief Fontenelle finally offered the example of our own little planet. The earth occupies a perfect mean between the overheating of the inner planets and the frigid darkness of the outer ones, just as Europe found itself happily situated between the tropical haunts of the half-mad Moors and the icy climes of the dull Lapps. The philosophical *politesse* of the *Conversations* surely represents an extension of the lessons Perrault had drawn from his naturalizing. Fontenelle mixed astronomical theory and geographical exotica to delight and amuse his charming companion. He employed the same sort of light erudition so masterfully demonstrated by Chapelain and Perrault. Curiosities and snippets of natural history, immensely exaggerated and transplanted arbitrarily, served to mitigate the plight of planetary inhabitants who might find them useful.

Despite the cooling effects of exhalations of saltpeter or the illumination provided by mountains of phosphorous with which nature provided her creatures, Fontenelle's marquise expressed her thanks for living on earth, in the temperate zone. This sentiment certainly followed in the tradition of Perrault's moralizing. The habits of the terribly foreign creatures of other planets—or other continents— evoked curiosity and amusement, even at times a sort of colonial compassion. Yet they rarely produced more than a flicker of genuine recognition or self-identification. Those the devotees of exploration real or imagined reserved for Europe and things European. Fontenelle indeed took matters a bit further in providing the following fortuitous reassurance to his companion: "If you believe me, madame, you should be thankful that you are young and not old; young and pretty, not young and plain; a pretty young French lady and not a pretty young Italian."[11] This message of the *Conversations* depended on no metaphor, no clever literary device.

The French style of moralizing, if not of philosophizing, had begun to change. Fontenelle's was not the same Paris as that of Chapelain or Molière. On several occasions an element of natural law, which had never intruded into Perrault's elaborate anatomizing, found its way into the *Conversations*. Insofar as he could account for the appearances with theory, Fontenelle tended to draw morals as necessary consequences of science rather than as merely amusing or cautionary lessons. The Cartesian vortex theory stood at the center of this stronger style of moralizing; its capacity to order the world spread beyond (or below) the astronomical realm. The moral for Fontenelle was inherent in science itself, not in the student of that science.

The political moral of the grand system of the sun and planets discussed in the first evening's conversation returned as Fontenelle considered its miniature manifestation on the edge of the solar vortex. The world, Fontenelle reminded his marquise as they embarked for Jupiter, is filled with a celestial matter.[12] Its particles bump and jostle one another, creating a chaotic fluid that rotates around the sun and carries the planets with it. The revolution of each planet on its own axis corresponds to a disturbance in the surrounding celestial matter, an eddy that moves around the local center even while the whole mass flows about the sun. These localized vortices capture any small bodies that find themselves within one of them, just as the solar vortex captured the planets. Our own moon fell under the influence of the terrestrial vortex; Jupiter, which Fontenelle reckoned ninety times as large as the earth, captured four little planets that happened to swim near him. Indeed, the philosophical gentleman observed, had we been nearer to the large planet, his vortex would have captured the earth, and we would have been but a satellite.

Fontenelle's gentle companion, who had known for only three days that the earth circles the sun, found this revelation most alarming. The Cartesian philosophy that had so far inspired a feeling of security and self-satisfaction abruptly threatened the world order. Aggressive whirlpools inverted the pleasing metaphor. Like Trissotin's raging comet in the *Femmes savantes,* nature had taken on an ugly aspect. Yet Fontenelle allayed the fears of his hostess. Just as oil floats on water, he explained, so the celestial matter varies in density and forms layers around the sun. Each planet swims at the proper distance determined by its own weight. Far from being threatening, the world is very well regulated. With a light literary hand, Fontenelle left it to his imaginary marquise to draw the consequence: "I can conceive that these different gravities will very well regulate the several ranks [of the planets]; I wish to God there were something similar amongst us to regulate ours, which would fix people in those spheres of life that are natural to them."[13] Nor were the specifics of this regulatory metaphor left to the imagination or the taste of the reader. When the marquise learned of Jupiter's satellites, she decided those little planets should obey their natural master: "I could wish, then . . . that the inhabitants of these four moons were like colonies belonging to Jupiter: that they had received from him, if it were possible, their laws and customs also, and that consequently they rendered him some sort of homage, and regarded the great planet with respect."[14] Such were the consequences of natural law in the latter years of the reign of the Sun King.

The political situation in France, and the political implications of science, had changed radically in the quarter-century between Chapelain's recruitment of Huygens to the Académie royale des sciences and the publication of the *Conversations.* The dashing young king who hoped to lure examples of all high culture in Paris, including even as minor a social form as the new philosophy at first represented, had matured into an absolute monarch. After the death of Colbert, Louis tolerated no one with dissenting opinions, no matter how talented the dissenter might be in his or her chosen field and no matter how far that field might be from the area of dissent. By the same token, natural philosophy had changed its political face. Previously a perfectly safe field, encouraged precisely because it had no political implications, the new science took on a metaphorical meaning consonant with the absolutist politics of Paris. The commingling of philosophies natural and political, a hallmark of Enlightenment thought, appears without question in Fontenelle's famous novel.

This literary introduction to natural philosophy represented a change from the conversational and experimental style that the *précieuses* had practiced in the previous generation. Rationality was for Fontenelle, as it would be for the vast majority of the philosophes, above all a verbal form. The very success of the likes of Rohault allowed the experience of natural philosophy to become primarily vicarious, encountered in the theater and the novel as well as the apartments of cognoscenti. Indeed many in Fontenelle's generation experienced natural philosophy above all as a literary venture, a delight of the mind unsullied by experience through the body. The *Conversations* completed a trend in the making for half a century. Discussion at Renaudot's Bureau d'adresse spawned published (and republished) volumes of *Conferences,* introducing readers to the real philosophical conversations they reported. The *Journal des sçavans* later invited contributors to bring their oddities and contributions to the offices of the editor for the purpose of publication, constructing a philosophical discourse for a literary audience. Molière used his plays to portray philosophical scenes in part invented, in part reflecting the real experiences of his audience and friends, in part based on the published accounts of philosophical activity. Fontenelle took the process one step further, inventing a purely literary version of the philosophical conversation for the amusement of a polite readership. Natural philosophy had long before joined literature as a subject of polite conversation; with Fontenelle it became a discourse constructed as a literary exercise.

Part and parcel of this new literary natural philosophy was the metaphorical connection to political philosophy. Fontenelle, like Chapelain two generations earlier, would flourish as a creature of the royal household; his personal advocacy of an absolutist Cartesianism is hardly surprising. The culture of the salon likewise provided a fertile field for the cultivation of patronage. The particulars of the political arguments in the *Conversations* are therefore the ones we might expect, once the interdependence of nature and government was established to Fontenelle's satisfaction. Yet there was no notable tradition in the Cartesian corpus or the Parisian school around Clerselier, Rohault, or the early Académie royale des sciences that intimated a political as opposed to a moral dimension to science. This was an innovation of the later, absolutist reign of Louis XIV, not of the era of Colbert.

Dutch Reformed Cartesian Liberalism, with notes on deconstruction and other things

The generic connection between natural and political philosophy did not escape notice, nor did the particulars of Cartesian philosophy and absolutist politics. One response in kind came from Christiaan Huygens. Huygens had withdrawn to Holland for reasons of health shortly before Colbert died, and when he applied for permission to return to Paris, it was refused. His royal stipend came to an end, and during the decade preceding his death in 1695, he lived at his Dutch estate at Zulichem on a relatively modest patrimony. Apparently serious about his Protestantism and manifestly embittered at his treatment by the institution in which he had pursued his philosophical calling, Huygens receded from the center of the European scientific scene. His departure diminished the centrality of Paris. From his Dutch retreat, like Descartes before him, he maintained an active correspondence with the philosophical and mathematical elite. Tidying up his affairs, in 1690 he published treatises on light and gravity, which dated in their essentials from his years at the *académie* in Paris. Until his death he remained an "important philosopher." Yet little productive new work emanated from the exile in his homeland. Huygens had truly operated as a creature of the *colbertiste* academy and found himself adrift when removed from it. Apart from the early pamphlets on Saturn's ring, his philosophical oeuvre was entirely Parisian—even the associated studies of centrifugal force had appeared only years after they were completed, in an academic publication dedicated to the king.

During the last years of his life, however, Huygens took up the philosophical cudgels. He composed a novel of his own, *The Celestial Worlds Discovered*,[15] which presented a portrait of the solar system very different from the one drawn in Fontenelle's *Conversations*. Huygens mentioned several earlier works in the genre but found them all wanting. "Nor," he added, "has the ingenious French author of the Dialogues about the *Plurality of Worlds* carried the business any farther."[16] Shortly before his death Christiaan passed the manuscript on to his brother Constantijn, who prepared it for the printers.[17] Constantijn too died before the book could be published; it appeared only in 1698 in Christiaan's Latin and an English translation.

The Celestial Worlds began with a somewhat less literary treatment of the same problem as Fontenelle had chosen to begin the *Conversations on the Plurality of Worlds:*

> A man that is of Copernicus' opinion that this earth of ours is a planet, carried around and enlightened by the sun like the rest of them, cannot but sometimes have a fancy that it's not improbable that the rest of the planets have their dress and furniture, and nay their inhabitants too, as well as this earth of ours: especially if he considers the later discoveries made since Copernicus' time of the attendants of Jupiter and Saturn, and the plains and hilly countries of the moon, which are an argument of a relation and kin between our earth and them, as well as a proof of the truth of that system.[18]

Metaphorical kinship quickly produced real live relations; Huygens agreed with Fontenelle that the planets must have their plants and animals. Bending the story only slightly, the Dutch response suggested that these creatures "deserve as well to be provided for by their Creator as ours do."[19] It was in the manner that Huygens would have the Creator provide that he differed from Fontenelle. Following good Dutch Reformed tradition, he excused the creatures of his planetary worlds from the tribulations to which Fontenelle had subjected them.

Huygens in fact proved truer to Descartes than the supposed Cartesian ideologue Fontenelle. The obeisance to Copernicus dispensed with, the Dutch novelist turned to a pattern reminiscent of Descartes's approach in the *Meteorology*. The first requirement of life, he observed, is water. In granting this necessity to his planetary creatures, Huygens showed more providential care than his French predecessor had done.

For this water of ours, in Jupiter or Saturn, would be frozen up instantly by reason of the vast distance of the sun. Every planet therefore must have its waters of such a temper as to be proportioned to its heat: Jupiter's and Saturn's must be of such a nature as not to be liable to frost; and Venus's and Mercury's of such, as not to be easily evaporated by the sun. But in all of them, for a continual supply of moisture, whatever water is drawn up by the heat of the sun into vapors must necessarily return back thither.[20]

Huygens proceeded through the other wants of plants and animals with the same benevolence; the lands he created resembled, not Lapland and Bedlam, but Eden. Certain inhabitants of the other planets he endowed with reason, that each might have "some such rational creature . . . which is the head and sovereign of the rest,"[21] as people are the head and sovereign of the earth. (Huygens did not dictate the sort of political sovereignty that Fontenelle had indicated but merely the God-given place of humans in the world.)

To the rational planetary creatures Huygens granted an upright stance "for the more convenient and easy contemplation of the stars" and eyes positioned high in the body to facilitate sight and to remove the "most uncomely parts out of sight as 'twere."[22] (Huygens's modesty reconciled the Cartesian system to the severe morality of Calvinism as thoroughly as Malebranche's metaphysics of occasional causes reconciled Cartesian mechanism with Catholic theology.) For these creatures, parts of the body of God's creation, Huygens also provided a rational soul, a society, and its pleasures. In his implicit critique of Fontenelle's condemnation of all but the French gentry to suffer, we see a decidedly liberal view of the world—appropriate, perhaps, to a Dutch diplomat's son and brother in the aftermath of the Glorious Revolution, a Protestant expelled by the revocation of the Edict of Nantes from Gallican France.

Rational beings blessed with all the organs of sensation must, Huygens reasoned, take up the sciences—for what sets rational beings apart from beasts is "the contemplation of the works of God, and the study of nature, and the improving [of] those sciences which may bring us some knowledge."[23] Indeed, Huygens granted a superiority to certain planetarians in the field closest to his own heart:

If amazement and fear at the eclipses of the moon and sun gave their first occasion to the study of astronomy, and they say it did, then it's almost impossible that Jupiter and Saturn should be without it; the argument being of much greater force in them, by reason of the daily eclipses of their moons, and the frequent ones of the sun to their inhabitants. So that if a person disinterested in his judgement, and equally ignorant of the affairs of all the planets, were to give his opinion in the matter, I don't doubt he would give the cause for astronomy to those two planets rather than us.[24]

Again we see classical Protestant liberalism—this time the invented anthropology of the British Empiricists—informing Huygens's Cartesian account of planetary society. In contrast to the literary world of Fontenelle's planetarians and his philosophical gentry, with their devotion to the divine right of kings, the narrative voice in *The Celestial Worlds* attributed the progress of research into nature to essentially utilitarian motives. Indeed, continuing in the same logical (and ideological) vein, Huygens suggested further that such an interest in astronomy would of course cause the development of mathematics, of writing, of navigation, and so on.

Nor did Huygens condemn the other inhabitants of the solar system to sterile utility alone. Like his own life, those of the planetary philosophers would include pleasures aesthetic as well as intellectual. Music they must have, "for the laws of music are unchangeable, fixed by nature, and therefore the same reason holds valid for their music, as we even now proposed for their geometry. For why, supposing other nations and creatures endued with reason and sense as well as we have, should they not reap the pleasures arising from these senses as well as we too?"[25]

Huygens launched into the wonderful consonance between mathematics and harmonics; he explained concord and discord, the tone, the semitone, and the comma; he granted our planetary cousins musical theory and instruments as different from our own "as formerly among the Dorians, Phrygians, and Lydians," discussed by Perrault in his essay on ancient harmony, "and in our own time among the French, Italians, and Persians."[26] Yet all would be sophisticated, highly developed, and pleasing. The laws of nature set boundaries for development, but Huygens inhabited a world in which he assumed that the spirits of all rational beings would soar toward those boundaries.

When Huygens drew his moral, it was completely opposed to Fontenelle's. Only after he had developed his description of the worlds of the other planets did he reflect upon them with Fontenelle's innocence. Huygens at last proposed a voyage to observe the planetarians with whom we share the solar system:

> We have allowed that they may have rational creatures among them, and geometricians, and musicians: we have proved that they live in societies, and have hands and feet, are guarded with Houses and Walls; yet if a man was but carried there by some powerful genius, some Pegasus, I don't doubt it would be a pretty sight, pretty beyond all imagination, to see the odd ways, and the unusual manner of their setting about anything, and their strange methods of living.[27]

Instead of a subject of ridicule and pity, Huygens saw in his putative plurality of worlds a source of delightful enlightenment. It was to the planetarians, not his interlocutor, that Huygens looked to find a pretty sight.

At this juncture it is probably worthwhile to pause and make explicit the moral of the present account of these discourses on the plurality of worlds. The natural philosopher Christiaan Huygens and the writer Bernard de Fontenelle had a great deal in common. Political interpretations of natural philosophy were, like the thoughts of conservatives in our own time, in the air. That philosophical miasma infected the British and Dutch scenes as well as the Parisian. Like discoveries of facts on the cutting edge of science, enunciations of political implications of natural philosophy poured forth from pens both liberal and absolutist. They appeared with something near enough to simultaneity to indicate that the community as a whole, rather than its members as individuals, had sought the goal. One needn't find any particular filiation of ideas to believe this assertion.

Fontenelle's *Conversations* represents the archetypical voices of the Paris of the latter part of the reign of Louis XIV; for that, more evidence will follow. Yet Huygens's response also presents a picture of thoughts in the air. John Locke's sojourn in the Low Countries as an exile from absolutism's last stand in England resonated with the

politics of the *Celestial Worlds.* During that period, Locke both visited with Huygens (himself exiled from absolutist France) and completed the final draft of the *Essay Concerning Human Understanding.*
Indeed in the *Essay's* "Epistle to the Reader," Locke named "the
Great Huygensius" along with "the incomparable Mr. Newton" as
the philosophical "masters" of his age. It had been their accomplishment to rescue philosophy from its prior state when "it was thought
unfit, or uncapable to be brought into well-bred Company, and polite
Conversation."[28] Locke's work made Huygens's and Newton's natural philosophy the exemplar of all human understanding and concluded that understanding based on such a foundation would lead to a
liberal philosophy.

Huygens was among those who made philosophy fit for polite, liberal conversation in a double sense. Like Newton, he set the analysis
of nature on the proper course. He also initiated the spate of well-
bred Parisian speculation into the plurality of worlds with his comments on the ring of Saturn in his letter to the darling of the *précieuses,*
Jean Chapelain. Huygens took no particular offense either at the
genre practiced by Fontenelle or at Locke's *Essay.* The Dutch gentleman had moved, as had both Locke and Fontenelle, in elite Parisian
circles; his response to the younger author's philosophical novel in the
political world of the liberal *Essay* was to produce a liberal philosophical novel of his own. Quite simply, natural philosophy had become a
part of the literary world, a subject of polite conversation in *le monde,*
appropriate for metaphorical reflection on political philosophy. It
stood as a model of rationality, an anchor of the self-conscious
modernity adopted by the au courant from the time of the *précieuses*
on. A person of parts could compose an example of the genre, and
Huygens was a person of parts.

This pair of Cartesian fictions present a rationalist mind very much
like the mind of the Enlightenment. Nature and nature's laws set the
parameters within which human society as well as the physical world
could operate. God has fitted our bodies to our surroundings and to
our needs. Mathematical rules and natural harmony dictate aesthetic
judgments; simple ratios must soothe the savage beast. Sliding as easily as the philosophes of the next generation would from derivation to
metaphor, these writers found also in the laws of nature a cause and a
pattern for government, for social structure, and for human relations.

That part of the agenda of the Enlightenment was well launched in both France and Holland before the dawn of the eighteenth century.

Huygens's liberal rebuttal of Fontenelle's absolutist contribution produced the contradictions that allow us to critique the discourse as soon as we detect it. On the one hand, the discourse and not merely a soliloquy within it connected nature to politics; on the other, the same (Cartesian) meaning that "nature" shared among various voices in the discourse found connections to diametrically opposed political philosophies within the same discourse. One must acknowledge, with the deconstructionists, that nature bore no inherent political or social message outside the discourse and that attempts to use natural philosophy to defend a political message were contrived and conventional. (The political opposition, in contrast, must have some meaning beyond its connotations within the discourse—surely the distinction between absolutism and liberalism matters.) Yet within the discourse all parties not only agreed on the meaning of Cartesian natural philosophy but also agreed that Cartesian natural philosophy did bear political meaning. Disagreement involved only the nature of that political meaning, also a question clearly addressed by the discourse.

All this is perhaps a bit heavy-handed and would not need belaboring, were it not for the canonical reading of the philosophy of the Enlightenment in which scholars still take seriously the philosophes' claim that Newton's truth did set them free, in the process turning them into liberals. That eighteenth-century writers might have produced those claims is no more or less surprising than that Huygens offered the same liberal hope for Cartesian truths or that Fontenelle made similar absolutist claims. Yet thinkers of our own age who still believe in natural right and who moreover feel compelled to ground that right in Newtonian physics are in a different situation. To mix metaphors across the centuries, they must risk the intellectual injuries sustained by those who choose to inhabit a structure ripe for deconstruction. They still speak with voices interjected into this eighteenth-century discourse, rather than commenting on it—a decidedly anachronistic approach for any but the most unreflective students of Western thought.

The young, provincial author of the *Conversations on the Plurality of Worlds* had no reason to fear such a fate. To the contrary, his work became the height of intellectual fashion. In 1687, the year after the

initial publication, Fontenelle was able to add a further evening's conversation to the work, already in need of a second edition. This was
followed in rapid succession by three more printings within the next
three years. Before its author's death in 1757 the *Conversations* had
gone through more than fifty printings, making it the best-selling
work of the age in scientific literature.[29] (Huygens's *Celestial Worlds*
enjoyed a more modest success, with three English, one French, and
two Latin editions in the same period.[30]) Significantly, Fontenelle's
work bridged the generations between the *précieuses* and the High
Enlightenment. From time to time Fontenelle updated his text with
more-current calculations of planetary sizes and orbits, but the bulk
of the work was not altered during the half-century and more that its
author continued to see it through the press. Despite its Cartesian
explanations and its absolutist stance, the conversation between the
curious lady and her philosophical guest remained an appropriate introduction to the study of nature well into the careers of such
philosophes as d'Alembert and Voltaire.

The Sun King strikes back

If *The Celestial Worlds Discovered* served as a sort of afterword to
Huygens's brilliant academic career in Paris, the *Conversations on the
Plurality of Worlds* represented a preface to that of Fontenelle. About
the time he prepared the second edition of his novel, Fontenelle
moved permanently to the capital. The Académie royale des sciences
was reorganized in 1699, receiving new letters patent and more official status than Colbert had provided. Because of the literary talents
that had already won him appointment to the Académie française and
because of his success as a popularizer, Fontenelle was called to take
up a new position as the "perpetual secretary" of the Académie royale
des sciences. Fontenelle's tremendous influence on the philosophical
community was due in part to his astounding longevity: It seemed as
though he might actually fulfill the promise of his official title. In his
early forties and by all accounts frail when he took up the post at the
close of the seventeenth century, Fontenelle produced an annual *Histoire* and a collection of *Mémoires* for each year from 1699 to 1742. In
the middle years of his secretariat he went back through the records of
the *académie* and prepared ten volumes of *mémoires* and commentary

on the foundation and work of the body during the three decades before he joined it.[31] Thus the official record of fully the first three-quarters of a century of the organization flowed from the prolific pen of the author of the *Conversations on the Plurality of Worlds.* The grand old man of philosophical literature finally died in 1757, a few months shy of his hundredth birthday.

The literary, absolutist Cartesianism that Fontenelle articulated in his novel would succumb, before its author, to a series of influences at first largely external to his philosophical community. The birth of the new physics of Sir Isaac Newton in England would eventually cause a reappraisal of the Cartesianism accepted as so certain in the Paris of Louis XIV. A new, demonstrative vogue of Enlightenment science would come to share the stage with the literary style of the age of the Sun King and to dominate it. Even before the end of Fontenelle's career in the royal household, the beginnings of a liberalism that would in France erupt as a revolution challenged the absolutism in which he found such security. Yet all these developments proved, at least in France, to belong to the reign of Louis XV rather than Louis XIV. We shall turn, in successive chapters, to the challenges offered to Cartesian natural philosophy by the experimental science canonically associated with British Empiricism, by the new British astronomy, and by British liberalism. The comfortable political and physical world inhabited by Fontenelle and by the real and imagined ladies and gentlemen of his generation nonetheless had its moment, as historians so knowingly characterize the beliefs of half-century epochs. The remainder of this chapter will follow the development of his comfortable world, explained quite ably and examined with glee in his secretarial voice, through the end of the reign of Louis XIV. The king, nearly as remarkable for his longevity as his last philosophical secretary, died in 1715.

It is appropriate to use Fontenelle's academic publications to get to know his world, for his editorial work both introduced and appraised science for the Parisian elite. It is likewise appropriate to put aside academic periodicals as the primary source for an understanding of French science after the decade ending in 1720, for Fontenelle had reached the end of a normal working life twenty years before his retirement. The world did change in his later years in ways that he never really understood; developments that would occur in his old age, during the reign of Louis XV, must be seen through other eyes.

Fontenelle initiated the new periodical publications of the reformed Académie royale des sciences with great vigor and confidence. The *Histoire* and *Mémoires* for each year came bound together. A number of reports of record appeared each year, institutionalizing such information as temperature, rainfall, tidal statistics, and routine astronomical observations. The bulk of the *Mémoires* presented the ongoing research of the *académie*—papers that form a miscellany nearly as eclectic as the contemporary *Journal des sçavans*. Occasionally Fontenelle included correspondence addressed to members. What tied all this material together was the introductory *Histoire*, Fontenelle's own work. In it he offered some comment on most of the articles that followed. The perpetual secretary took considerable liberties, often introducing even the statistical articles with extensive elementary discussions of the Cartesian system—references nowhere to be found in the *Mémoires* he ostensibly described. Tables of tides, for example, frequently inspired Fontenelle to recount Descartes's theory that tides are caused by the pressure of the moon transmitted through the terrestrial vortex to the oceans.[32] Owing in part to this editorial presumption, the periodicals of the *académie* presented a coherent view of the world, which was otherwise not evident in contemporary philosophical discussion.

Necessarily more current in questions of natural philosophy than Jean Chapelain had been and technically more adept, at least as a reader, Fontenelle laid claim to no more creative philosophizing than his academic predecessor. He would remain a literary popularizer. The *Mémoires* and more especially the *Histoires* of the *académie* continued the project Fontenelle had begun in the *Conversations*. The imaginary marquise had learned of wonders of nature, like shining phosphors and cooling sulfurs; in the *Histoires* her real models found enlightenment about the newest enchanting discoveries in the natural history of stuff animate and inanimate. The very organization of the *Histoires* invited the casual student's perusal. Each volume began with an account of what Fontenelle called *la physique générale*—a miscellany dominated by curiosities and controversies in the international experimental community. This was followed by discussions of anatomy—replete with accounts of freak births and sports of nature—and chemistry. The mathematical sciences—astronomy, geometry, algebra, analysis, and mechanics—came last and in Fontenelle's treatment rarely taxed the reader with technical details.

Like the contemporaneous British *Philosophical Transactions* of the Royal Society of London, the *Histoires* and *Mémoires* of the Académie royale des sciences in Paris now appear among the early numbers of the oldest and most distinguished continuing periodicals in the world. Both the British and the French publications would eventually take their places among the most erudite and stuffy journals of record in the scientific community. Yet this development was not the work of Fontenelle, no more than it was the work of his contemporaries who served as secretaries of the Royal Society of London. Whereas the British journal continued in the genre of the *Journal des sçavans,* Fontenelle's publications became something like a serialized version of his *Conversations on the Plurality of Worlds.*

Indeed Fontenelle occasionally published materials that would have elicited chuckles even from readers of the more clearly popular publications. The 1715 number of the *Histoire* is notable for an article in which the *académie*'s official publication resembled the proceedings of the *Conferences* of Renaudot's bureau d'adresse or the more woolly efforts of the *Journal des sçavans.* The story, presented here in its entirety, would undoubtedly have stirred the memory of a longterm regular reader of the *Journal:*

Without a guarantor such as Mr. Leibniz, an eye witness, we would not dare to report that at Zeits there is a dog who speaks. It is the dog of a peasant, of one of the most common sorts, and of average size. A young child heard it produce several sounds which the child believed resembled German words, and on that basis got it in his head to teach the dog to speak. The master, who had nothing better to do, begrudged neither time nor energy, and the disciple had a disposition so happy it would be difficult to reproduce in another. Finally at the end of some years the dog could pronounce about thirty words. Included in this number are *Thé, Caffé, Chocolat, Assemblé,* French words which have passed into German as they were. It should be remarked that the dog was fully three years old when it was put to school. It speaks only as an echo— that is to say, after its master has pronounced a word—and it seems that it repeats only with effort, despite itself, although no one has ever mistreated it. Once again, Mr. Leibniz has heard and seen it.[33]

Leibniz, usually known for his metaphysics, his mathematics, his mechanics, or occasionally even his role as a diplomat, appeared in the *Histoire* as he had thirty years earlier in the *Journal des sçavans,* as a purveyor of dog and goat shows.

Despite the occasional howler, Fontenelle's great gift as editor of the *académie*'s publications came not in his collection of wonders but rather in his ability to express the most technical aspects of academic work in the sort of conversational tone that induced the merely curious to read it. Even that most intimidating branch of seventeenth-century science, mathematical mechanics, found a place of at least mild charm in the *Histoire* as well as the *Mémoires.* The most frequently published mechanician during the first decade of the academic journals was Fontenelle's friend Pierre Varignon, professor (simultaneously) of mathematics at the Collège de Mazarin and of classics at the Collège de France.[34]

Varignon read widely. His papers reflect a careful reading of Newton's *Principia* as well as his contacts with the Parisian community of the 1680s and 1690s—a community that by the early eighteenth century had been dispersed throughout Europe. Varignon readily acknowledged his debts; nearly every paper began with an account of an earlier solution, published perhaps without proof or in a style of mathematics no longer deemed valid, now set right by the prolific professor. Fontenelle not only gave tremendous play to this material in the *Mémoires;* he offered extensive introductions to many of Varignon's articles. The *Histoire*'s account of these researches communicated two messages above all. First, mechanics was making great strides every year. Second, Fontenelle's generation of mathematicians was working out the final foundational details of the new mechanics, setting the record straight, and had just about finished with the whole project. New analytic methods allowed even a mathematician of modest ability to detect the tiniest of inconsistencies in existing physical theory.[35]

In 1707, for example, Varignon took on the two cherished gifts Galileo had given to the science of mechanics. Fontenelle's summary, "On the Hypothesis of the Turning of the Earth, Complicated with That of Galileo Touching the Weight of Bodies,"[36] set out the problem. Galileo had suggested that a body falling from rest toward the center of the earth would suffer a constant acceleration, and would therefore pass through distances proportional to the square of the time of the fall. Yet the proof of this proposition assumed that bodies fall in straight lines. In fact, as Galileo had convinced the thinking world, the earth really rotates, so a falling body must trace a spiral toward its center. Varignon took this spiral as a mathematical challenge. He constructed a diagram that elucidated it in excruciating detail, labeled a dozen points on the diagram, and produced a series of infinitesimal equations replete with terms both squared and cubed. Varignon's report concluded that it was not possible that Galileo's law of falling bodies and his hypothesis of the rotation of the earth could both be strictly true at the same time.

Fontenelle noted that the difference between Galileo's propositions and Varignon's demonstration is insensibly small unless the distance through which the body falls is immeasurably large. It is precisely the inconsequential nature of the difference between Galileo's simple, elegant solution and Varignon's labored and cluttered correction that Fontenelle most admired: "See what uses Geometry serves. It gives us the truth in all its purity, which physics and experiment always alter, and it causes us to see at what point we who cannot avoid confusion fool ourselves with impunity."[37] The point of the article was not to allow anyone to solve real problems more effectively—both Fontenelle and Varignon understood full well that for any actual falling body the difference between Galileo's solution and Varignon's was undetectable. Nor did either of them extend the problem to a thought experiment concerning bodies falling from unattainable heights, even to the realm of the moon, from whence the difference might be measurable. (This was, of course, the extension of the problem that Newton would claim led him to the law of universal gravitation.) Instead, for Varignon the whole question represented a bit of pedantry, a point that, although it might confuse the novice and bore the practitioner, could nonetheless be made, showing the superiority of modern techniques to the mere genius Galileo had brought to the problem.

It was in elucidating this peculiar, theoretically possible, mechanics that Varignon reveled. His attitude is perhaps best reflected in a passing remark that Fontenelle made in an article by a chemist during this same period. The chemist in question, "following the example of the geometers, who often augment the difficulty of their problems from the gaiety of their hearts, has proposed a second, more difficult synthesis."[38] No one found more gaiety of heart in taking on difficult extensions to problems already solved than Varignon. Yet as Fontenelle never made the step that Huygens made in matters of Martians—that if God wanted them to see, he would fit them with appropriate eyes, not phosphorescent mountains—Varignon never made the step that Huygens made with respect to falling bodies and mathematics. Math for Huygens was a tool to solve problems suggested by mechanics; for Varignon it was also a toy for solving problems contrary to fact, problems that a mathematician might imagine.

The vision of mathematics and mathematical mechanics shared by Fontenelle and Varignon has never enjoyed great popularity among historians of either subject. It did not, to be sure, produce any significant technical advances to be chronicled in the conventional developmental accounts. Rather like Fontenelle's *Conversations*, however, Varignon's style of mathematics did have a certain impact in polite culture. The seventeenth century saw a small but steady stream of works in a genre known as "recreational mathematics." Generally based on the works of Claude-Gaspard Bachet, they consisted mostly of problems in number theory, along with a bit of algebra.[39] Varignon's academic colleague Jacques Ozanam produced a new *Recréations mathematiques et physiques* in 1694. Problems of the sort that so delighted Varignon—unrealistic but mathematically solvable questions in mechanics, variations on classic but long-solved applications of differential calculus to falling and sliding and rolling bodies— were among the most common in this new work. The work of *académie*, seen by a gentle audience through the perpetual secretary's accounts of it, was of a piece. If the mathematical recreations did not do quite so well for Ozanam as the *Conversations* had for Fontenelle, Ozanam did manage three Parisian editions within a decade in addition to one reprinted in Amsterdam.[40]

Despite the frequent appearance of *Mémoires* by Varignon, mathematics and technical mechanics did not play the largest role in the *Histoire*. Pride of place in the academic journal, as in the *Conversations*, went to astronomy. A reader familiar with Fontenelle's fictional account of the world would have had no trouble if she encountered explanations of the sort offered in the summary of a 1707 report that described the appearance of Jupiter and Saturn:

All the principle planets turn around the sun, and the satellites around the principle planets, and the sun around itself, from west to east. That is the universal motion of our whirlpool. But we are the center of the motion of the moon, and the sun is our center, so these appear to move from east to west. Jupiter's satellites seem to move east to west on the near side of the planet, and west to east on the far side. Sunspots seem to go east to west, since we see only the near side of their orbit. This same reason extends to the retrograde motion and the stations of the planets.[41]

This is not to say that the vortex theory was a closed or completed topic. Fontenelle portrayed physical astronomy, like mathematical mechanics, as a vital, developing field.

In 1707, the *Histoire* noted the publication of *A New System, or, New Explanation of the Motion of the Planets,* by a Cartesian theorist called Philippe Villemot.[42] Villemot's efforts justified one more go at the topic, Fontenelle argued, since they for the first time provided a physical cause for the forces that hold the planets in their orbits. In fact Villemot's reasoning and Fontenelle's account of it—not always the same thing[43]—present great difficulties of interpretation. Villemot's derivation revolved around the fact that the surface area of a sphere is proportional to the square of its radius. Each layer of the great celestial whirlpool about the sun must therefore spread its tendency to circular motion over a region proportional to the square of its distance from the sun; thus the speed of circulation of the subtle matter ought to be inversely proportional to the square root of its distance from the sun.

This rule is equivalent to Kepler's third law, that the square of the periods of planetary orbits must be proportional to the cube of the orbit's radius. "This is not only a response to a difficulty in Kepler," Fontenelle concluded, "but also an a priori demonstration of his rule."[44] For the first time, Descartes's physical account of the construction of the heavens agreed with Kepler's mathematical description of planetary motion. But the story in the *Histoire* did not end with Kepler. Fontenelle's account turned to Cassini. After his arrival in France, the Italian astronomer had pursued calculations further than the German mystic had done. Armed with superior mathematics, Cassini had been able to determine that the planetary orbit is not exactly Kepler's standard ellipse but a very similar shape, which Fontenelle appropriately called Cassini's ellipse. The classical ellipse is the collection of points traced by drawing lines from two points—the foci—to a third point, such that the sum of the length of those two lines is the same for each point on the ellipse. Cassini's ellipse, by contrast, was constructed so the *product* of the two distances is the same for each point on the ellipse. This a shape purely analytical in nature—one cannot draw it with a few tacks, a bit of string, and a pencil the way a standard ellipse is (in theory) constructed. Cassini followed Kepler in placing one of the foci of the planetary ellipse in the sun. For ellipses with foci close together compared to the distance between the foci and the ellipse (and all the planetary revolutions have such closely spaced foci), the difference between Kepler's ellipses and Cassini's are so small as to almost escape notice. Nevertheless, Fontenelle could inform his readers, the assiduous efforts expended at the Royal Observatory had managed to discern this difference and allowed the further progress of astronomy.[45]

Cassini was not, incidentally, the only working astronomer who understood and also attempted to improve upon the work of Kepler. Here the modern, standard story might benefit from following Fontenelle. One of the clichés of the history of celestial mechanics has it that Newton's greatest accomplishment was discovering Kepler's three laws in the rambling works of the German astronomer. In fact the laws were well known and available in a number of places. Cassini was the most obvious source in France—Villemot apparently found Kepler's third law from Cassini's papers, without consulting the original source. In Germany, the work of one of several important women astronomers, Maria Cunitz, also both clearly enunciated and offered modifications to Kepler's laws. Like Cassini in the next generation, Cunitz's *Urania propitia sive tabulae astronomicae mire faciles* (*Urania,* or astronomical tables made easy) offered correction and simplification of Kepler's work.[46] Indeed, since all tables of planetary position through the middle of the eighteenth century took the German mystic's *Rudolphine Tables* as their basis, any astronomer worth her salt would have put forth the effort to understand the mathematical theory behind them. Newton, although he took the normal precautions, was hardly exceptional in this regard.

Nor did advances in astronomical calculation end with modifications of the orbital ellipse. Fontenelle could also report that Cassini's careful theoretical work had allowed him to develop a straightforward scheme for calculating tables of planetary position. He needed to know only the time and speed at which a planet reached a few crucial points—the point closest to the sun and two or three other specified positions on the ellipses—to determine the time and speed at which the planet would traverse every portion of the orbit. This work, tedious development of mathematical methods to save the practitioner even more tedious calculations, lacks the glamour of orbital theory and has rarely merited much attention in histories by anyone but working astronomers.

As Fontenelle's imaginary marquise looked to her tutor for a certain expertise that would guide her own understanding of and conclusions about the physical world, so her real models could find guidance through the technical difficulties in the *Histoire*. This is what it meant to be a professional natural philosopher in the latter years of the reign of Louis XIV—to master the technical minutiae, to communicate general theories to the social elite, and to grind through the calculations. It was Fontenelle's mission to leave the impression that technical mastery was but a matter of self-discipline. In the preindustrial world that he inhabited, astronomical calculations were performed by people of greater or lesser value and talent in the same way that a thousand other tasks were performed for the ladies and gentleman of Paris. These calculations were hardly the sort of thing that ladies and gentlemen needed to do themselves, except perhaps as an eccentricity. The real pleasure of philosophizing came in discussing the implications of the theory without any particular concern for the details—as it so often does to those twentieth-century philosophers who concern themselves with the "meaning" of quantum mechanics without any but the most passing acquaintance with how one might go about solving the differential equations.

Nonetheless, these technical developments were hardly the ethereal musings of astronomers with their thoughts lost in the heavens. The analysis of eclipses of Jupiter's moons, for example, turned out to have signal importance for earthly observers, since accurate tables of these events provided the key to a world-wide determination of Paris time—and therefore of longitude.[47] All observers on earth must see the frequent eclipses of Jupiter's moons simultaneously. Anyone equipped with a telescope and Cassini's tables could set a clock to Paris time—under good observing conditions as often as several nights a week. Reasonably educated European travelers—a description more or less synonymous with Jesuit missionaries—determined Paris time from the eclipses of Jupiter's moons; local noon was easily established from the time at which the sun reached its highest point in the sky. The difference between Paris and local time—an easy period to determine with even a rather crude clock, since it only needed to keep good time for something like half a day—allowed a simple calculation of the local longitude. Fontenelle drew the moral for earthly observers of Jupiter's moons as clearly in the *Histoire* as he ever had done in the *Conversations.* He reported, for example, that missionaries to Siam determined their longitude using Cassini's techniques. "We know that knowledge of this world of Jupiter, 165 million leagues distant, produces for us knowledge of the earth, and indeed practically changes her face. Siam, for example, is 500 leagues closer to us than we had previously believed."[48]

Despite the startling niceties that celestial observations allowed in measurements on earth, the dimensions of the solar system remained one of the most elusive problems in astronomy. There was no easy way to determine the distance between the sun, the moon, and the planets in terms of terrestrial measure. To be sure, the timing of planetary motion appeared all but solved, and Kepler's laws tied the relative sizes of planetary orbits to questions of time. These accomplishments did allow the astronomer to calculate exactly what fraction of the earth's orbit Mercury's orbit might be, and exactly what fraction of Mars's orbit the earth's orbit might be. Yet no strictly astronomical measurement could say how many leagues or miles the earth is from the sun or the moon or Mars. To complicate matters further, the determination of the shape of our planet and others had theoretical interest as well as implications for astronomical observation. The earth is not a perfect sphere. According to the Cartesians, the subtle matters swirling around the earth's axis must press more firmly at the equator than at the poles, producing an elliptical profile, with the axis of rotation a bit larger than the equatorial diameter.

The two problems of determining the shape of the earth and the parallax of the planets inspired a century-long series of philosophical expeditions.[49] These voyages became something of a rite of passage for young astronomers. The *Mémoires* for 1700, for example, contained letters from "M. Couplet Jr."—one of many academic offspring who assumed their fathers' places.[50] Couplet explained that he first intended to go to the "East Indies," but Jesuits dispatched by the king had already determined the longitudes there and made observations of the natural history of that part of the world. The "West Indies," by contrast, remained largely unknown. (The tone of the letter suggests that for the young Couplet the term *Indies* was more or less synonymous with "places far away.") Upon his arrival—in Brazil—he performed his appointed tasks. In what would become classic eighteenth-century style, he also made a series of observations in natural history. He wondered at a poisonous snake whose flesh could be consumed—at least by "Brazilians and Blacks"—without any ill effects. He marveled even more that manioc, whose root (which he characterized as "grain") constituted the staple of the Brazilian diet, had a poisonous "sugar." Couplet tested this claim directly, feeding the sugar to a basset hound who consumed the sweet meal at eight of an evening and was dead the next morning. "I made an infinity of other observations of physic," Couplet concluded his last letter, excusing their absence with another all too common eighteenth-century refrain— "which were lost with my memoirs when I was shipwrecked."[51]

The distance between technical astronomy and natural history was hardly greater at the Académie royale des sciences than in the *Conversations on the Plurality of Worlds.* The new world of the Americas, especially, produced the same sort of fascination for Europeans who visited them as did the new worlds of the heavens made accessible by the telescope. The peoples and natural history encountered seemed so overwhelmingly different from the old world, the social structure so completely alien—there wasn't even a proper emperor or king to take the central place in the political vortex of the Native Americans—that voyages like Couplet's resembled cosmic adventures to bold new worlds "where no one has gone before." There was, in the eyes of Couplet, no culture at all to study, only a natural history to observe.

The message in the *Histoire* and *Mémoires* never became so explicit as the morals supplied in the *Conversations.* For the reader immersed in the message and the milieu of the novel, however, passages like those from the young Couplet were of a piece with the musings of Fontenelle's philosophical lady and gentleman. The world outside of Paris was nasty, brutish, mean, and cruel. Its denizens were barely human, somewhere closer on the cosmological and gastronomical great chain of being to dogs and poison snakes than to His Majesty's astronomers. For those who had read the *Conversations,* it required no great leap to conclude that His Majesty's representatives should rule over the savages they encountered, as Jupiter does his moons. Natural right, once learned, is an easy lesson to apply.

Ironically, the Jesuits in the Orient faced exactly the opposite sort of problems in their proselytizing for the new science. One missionary, Father Perennin, wrote that his host, a Chinese prince, expressed "surprise that all of these observations and researches extend even to things most vile in appearance, more worthy to be neglected, to cobwebs for example." Yet the Chinese monarch ordered that the Jesuit "should translate into Tartar everything that M. Réamur had said" about the contemptible matter so that his three sons could study this nook of Western science and tell him about it. The three agreed that "to have such a great ardor for discovery, *it is necessary to be European.*"[52] (Jonathan Swift's satire in *Gulliver's Travels* reflected the reality of his times; one "projector" at the Academy of Lagado inhabited a disgusting, cobwebbed room for researches into spider webs, intended to compete with Chinese silk.) Perennin, to be sure, despaired above all that Western science would be stifled in China because the Chinese would no longer be willing to receive capable Westerners who carried "the double enlightenment" of science and religion. The general tone of his report suggested that they might otherwise continue to be occasionally interested and openly amused by further reports of the compulsive, delving activities of European philosophy.

Fontenelle's *Histoires* and the *Mémoires* they introduced would scarcely have silenced the sniggers of Perennin's Chinese hosts. The perpetual secretary and his academic colleagues busied themselves with a wide range of questions, nearly always cast in a broadly Cartesian framework. Like the astronomical discourses these questions accompanied, accounts of "general physics" and natural history often wandered a bit from the apparent point at hand and sprinkled morals and aphorisms liberally among technical questions. In the *Histoires,* these discussions also present a fundamentally literary view of the philosopher's relationship with the physical world.

The birth of a new Cartesian Physics

The continuing conversation with the real marquises of Louis XIV's France through the vehicle of the *Histoire* is perhaps best illustrated by periodic reports of developing theories of thunder and lightning. The series began in 1700 with a discussion of "earthquakes, volcanoes, lightning, and thunder."[53] Fontenelle, as was his habit, provided a summary of a report prepared by the chemist Nicolas Lemery—one-time lecturer to that curious admixture of apothecaries and ladies of polite society. A casual reader could peruse developments in the more popular style of the *Histoire;* serious students could read the technical account in the *Mémoires* that followed. In the case of the discussion at hand, either article leaves the reader with the same clear impression.

The discussion is striking in that it offered a fundamentally chemical account of all the noisy natural disasters it covered. Since philosophers had wrested such phenomena from theologians, the usual approach had been mechanical. In the Cartesian system, ponderous subterranean matters in motion, expansively flowing heated gasses, colliding rigid clouds of ice, and raging whirlpools of subtle matters had provided the tremendous powers necessary to explain geological and meteorological devastation. At the dawn of the eighteenth century, however, chemists believed themselves to be on the verge of understanding and even harnessing the powers necessary to wreak havoc both military and natural. Lemery's report explained that the motive force for the rare, tremendously damaging natural phenomena must be "a particular preparation of sulfur, called the 'Sugar of Mars,' which I gave to the public several years ago."[54] Nothing else, he explained, was sufficiently flammable to explain nature's occasional fury. Lemery pointed out that a new edition of his textbook in chemistry, taken from his lectures and just published, included an expanded explanation of the preparation of this deadly stuff.

For the reader not ready to venture into the technical *Mémoires* at the back of the volume, Fontenelle's *Histoire* explained that sulfurous matters in the bowels of the earth could contain the motive force behind the rare phenomena. Direct action of these materials in situ naturally accounted for earthquakes. When the activity of the sulfurs occurred close enough to the surface, their great convulsions produced volcanoes. According to this theory, airs spewed forth during eruptions provided materials in the atmosphere capable of creating thunder and lightning. The great destructive promise of chemistry—an art removed from the sole province of the apothecaries and miners and set to the problem of gunpowder—here provided the first theoretical spin-off of military research. How except through the most destructive mechanism invented by the mind of man might nature unloose its destructive powers?

Nor did Lemery's speculations prove the last word of the chemists on the powers of sulfurs in earthquakes. Theoretical chemistry continued apace. In 1703 Fontenelle could report that Lemery's colleague Guillaume Homberg had decomposed the explosive sulfur and analyzed its constituents;[55] the next year, a third royal student of chemistry, Étienne François Geoffroy, confirmed the analysis by synthesizing sulfurs from the constituents that Homberg had described. Their accomplishment proved quite a feather in the royal cap that was the *académie,* since "Boyle and Glauber, two great chemists" (notably British and German) had both believed that they could make common sulfur, but both had fooled themselves—without impunity. "The error of these great men," the *Histoire* concluded, "raises up the merit of M. Homberg's discovery."[56]

The work at the *académie* represented something more than empty theories. Between October 1702 and July 1703 a series of tremors stuck in Italy; the worst, which occurred on 2 February, killed 5,000 people. The *académie* collected accounts of the destruction, which seemed to confirm Lemery's ideas and Homberg's additions completely. Huge fissures rent the earth; when they opened, flames leapt out, and heavy smoke followed for several days. Waterspouts burst forth from the bowels of the earth. Often, the academicians discovered, tremors were accompanied by great noises in the air, and often people heard the noises without experiencing tremors—"even when the sky was most serene." These terrible accounts lent great credence to Lemery's extensive theory of earthquakes, volcanoes, and thunder.

A few years later the record of the *académie* returned to meteorology.[57] Despite the success of aerial explosions, Fontenelle acknowledged that the mere discovery of a suitable chemical admixture that might be accomplished "in the air as well as in our laboratory" did not suffice to account for anything so complex as a meteorological phenomenon. In the laboratory, the mixture of the explosive combination occurred only once—new supplies were required for each new bang. Yet thunder occurs repeatedly. Fontenelle, in a passage that he might have lifted practically without alteration for a new edition of the *Conversations,* explained Homberg's extended theory. In the laboratory, he suggested, the materials required for the explosion are blown away by the very explosion they produce. Dispersed in this manner, they rise through the heavy, chaotic air near the surface of the earth and come to rest on top of that layer, separated sufficiently to prevent further contact. The material that causes thunder, in contrast, must rise gently as exhalations from the earth and settle in a concentrated region at the bottom of the homogenous air above the heavy surface layer. In the more tranquil reaches of the upper atmosphere, the sulfurous matter and acidic spirits would simply settle back to their resting place after each explosion and mix again to produce a new thunderclap. The same exhalations thus come into contact again and again—apparently without combining—until they are washed out of the air by the rains that invariably accompany thunderstorms.

Consideration of this extensive interchange offers at least some answers to the question of what natural philosophy was at the Académie royale des sciences during the first decade of the eighteenth century. On the one hand, it was new and changing; discovery followed explosive discovery and system followed explanatory system. On the other, in a significant sense these rapid developments represented orderly progress rather than a revolution in science. Even the aggressive intellectual growth of chemistry is of a piece with the accounts offered by the likes of Rohault or Mlle de Chetaignieres. Fontenelle's ultimate story in the long series on chemical meteorology provided a discussion completely in character with Descartes's *Meteorology* even as it modified the Cartesian meteorological system. Homberg explained the great explosive powers of his sulfur in terms of the second matter dispersed in the interstices of the third matter of the air.[58] The province of a philosophical system for explaining thunder remained the same as the province of the system that Descartes had required to produce an explanation of the appearance of multiple suns—the problem that had prompted him to prepare his manuscript *World.*

The incursion of chemistry into matters meteorological by no means represented a general retreat of the Cartesian system. It rather served to illustrate one-half of an interchange that occurred in both directions between physical experiments and chemical investigations. That Descartes's own work had relatively little to say about chemical matters did not concern his disciples half a century after the works of the master had appeared. The Cartesian system was not in 1685 or 1700 or 1715 a static description of the natural world. Instead, it represented an ongoing research program. Cartesianism did not even represent much of an orthodoxy. The many self-proclaimed disciples of Descartes and the larger school of rationalist philosophers who believed that they had broken with Descartes but who still held beliefs distinctly Cartesian in character quite freely changed even essential details of philosophy both natural and metaphysical. Solutions to fundamentally Cartesian problems like the connections between the mind and the body that were offered by characters like Benedict Spinoza and Nicolas Malebranche and Gottfried Leibniz have always been seen as part of a lively and diverse tradition; Fontenelle held the same view of the productive natural philosophers whose work he summarized in his *Histoires*.

A contemporaneous discussion that represented change in the other direction, the absorption of a fundamentally chemical problem into the Cartesian system of subtle matters, may be found in the *Histoire*'s discussion of luminescence. Fontenelle presented various sorts of glowing light, independent of the sun or fire, as a source of inquiry as persistent as thunder. The most famous of these eerie glows, associated with phosphorescent materials of various sorts, belonged primarily to the world of the chemists. This branch of learning—it is not clear whether even in the last years of the seventeenth century the study of phosphors could be dignified with the title of philosophy—still had discernible foundations in the tradition of natural magic that had so distressed Somaize as he contemplated its role in the *Dictionnaire des précieuses* half a century earlier.

The most famous of the phosphors, the Bologna stone, had been prepared in secret by a German practitioner from a mineral found near the Italian city. It had the property that once it was exposed to light, it would glow for some time in the dark. The secret of production appeared to die with its inventor, however, and encouraged a lingering fear about the magical overtones of chemistry. During the last quarter of the seventeenth century the secret of the Bologna stone was rediscovered and eventually made public—although the literal and figurative prices extracted for the disclosure of the recipe caused great moral (if not financial) anguish in the philosophical community. The stuff remained a rarity even then, in part owing to the difficulty of obtaining the mineral source of the Bologna stone.

The dual fashions of astronomy and barometry provided the first generally accessible and reproducible source of luminescence that did not require previous exposure to light. Concern about the effects of atmospheric refraction on astronomical observations, coupled with the philosophical astronomer's compulsion to record things, dictated that any self-respecting observatory place a barometer in a position accessible to those making observations. This combination presented the elements of many broken barometers and a repeated chance discovery. As stargazers literally bumped into their mercury tubes, a few noticed a dim light emanating from the empty, so-called Torricellian space in the top of the tube. The first clear report of such an accident had come in 1675 from the astronomer Picard, himself a member of the *académie*. "Right away," Fontenelle would later report, "all Observers of nature tested their barometers, but very few had the privilege"[59] of seeing them glow. Some barometers, it seemed, produced this effect, and others didn't; no one could really say why. The phenomenon appeared nearly as unpredictable as Saint Elmo's fire.

The phenomenon in fact had not been as widely reported or tested outside the *académie* as Fontenelle's account might lead one to believe. Indeed it was the *Histoire* that first brought it to the attention of the philosophical community and that rendered the tricky phenomenon somewhat tractable. In 1700, the very year Fontenelle first reported Lemery's system of earthquakes and thunder, he could also announce the first thorough account of barometric luminescence. The report came in a letter to Fontenelle's friend Varignon from Jacob Bernoulli, a brilliant mathematician who had studied in Paris until the political situation became untenable for Protestants. Bernoulli had run across two accounts of Picard's chance observation and accepted a public invitation in one of these accounts to "perfect this discovery."[60]

Bernoulli offered both a set of careful instructions for producing the effect and a theoretical system for explaining it. In addition, he suggested the name "mercurial phosphor" to describe the glow. The name would stick for several decades, indicating the fundamental acceptance of Bernoulli's approach if not of all the details of his theory. His instructions seemed simple enough. To produce the new luminescence, the barometer tube needed to be thoroughly clean and dry and the mercury likewise clean, pure, and purged of air. An important indicator of success in these precautions appeared on the surface of the mercury at the top of the tube, where it came into contact with the Torricellian space. Any impurities in the system caused this surface to show imperfections. With reasonable care, Bernoulli suggested, the glow could be seen quite strongly.

The letter explained the effect with a Cartesian mechanism worthy of Rohault. The space above the mercury contains no air or other gross matter; instead, it is completely full of the finest bits of Descartes's most subtle matter, the first matter, ground off the edges of the microscopic elements of the universe. This is the same situation Descartes had ascribed to the sun, or to the little pores of explosive materials. When the tube is shaken, Bernoulli explained, the particles of the mercury strike the bits of first matter smartly. These tiny, hard particles in turn send off a shock though the second matter, which our eyes detect as light. As Descartes had explained, such illumination does not occur in our normal experience because the little bits of first matter are dispersed among the more flexible materials of the gross world, made up of the third matter. If the mercury has bits of impurities on its upper surface or mixed among its particles, these impurities absorb the bulk of the shock, so the first matter remains relatively undisturbed and sends forth no waves of light. "Everyone," Fontenelle reported, "must be touched by the genius of discovery which shines through this system."[61]

The ideas were put to the test at the observatory by Cassini and Philippe de La Hire.[62] Unfortunately, these trials seemed not to confirm either Bernoulli's recipe or his theory. A number of barometers made in "the ordinary way" produced a quite noticeable light. When new instruments were made according to Bernoulli's admonitions, however, they failed utterly to produce the faintest glow. In the end Fontenelle had to acknowledge that such a novel idea requires a great deal of discussion and that without this discussion the idea will not succeed.

This precipitous, public response to the Swiss letter did eventually produce the requisite discussion. The French failure to reproduce

Bernoulli's results revolved around their interpretation of "clean" mercury. Bernoulli meant that the liquid metal should be filtered; the French, attempting to follow the directions, washed theirs with water and alcohol. The question of which mercury was really clean was not resolved in this round of discussion, but Fontenelle was eventually able to report that if Bernoulli's initial instructions were interpreted according to his meaning, the experiment would succeed as its inventor had suggested. The brilliance of the Cartesian system used to explain the effect was at last illuminated by the glow of the mercurial phosphor.[63]

Such an explanation clearly extended the province of Cartesian optics to a completely new branch of "particular physics." In the same way that Huygens's theory of color had extended Descartes's theory, Bernoulli's expanded its province to account for the mercurial phosphor. The two extensions in fact followed the same general pattern. Huygens's depended on the sharpness of disruptive shocks in the second matter to account for the perception of different colors. Bernoulli's depended upon the sharpness of the shocks transmitted to the first matter to produce light waves in the second. The Cartesian system, in Kuhn's parlance, had achieved something like the level of "normal science," providing a paradigmatic framework within which its adherents could solve the puzzles that nature presented.

What is most striking about Bernoulli's work, in light of our own understanding that the world just doesn't operate through subtle matters, is the way in which the Cartesian theory interacted with the empirical investigation of an elusive effect. No one before Bernoulli had been able to control the mercurial phosphor with any consistent results, and no one had offered any extensive theory of its cause. Yet Bernoulli integrated the shape and rigidity of the particles of the various theoretical matters with his manipulations of real bowls of quicksilver and long glass tubes to produce a simultaneous advancement of the natural history of light and the system that explained it. It hardly seems fair, if the science wasn't true, that this socially constructed theory allowed Bernoulli to construct a dependable technology out of an irreproducible result. Such is the archaeology of knowledge.

In 1701 Bernoulli sent another letter on "phosphors," noting that certain stones when rubbed in the dark also glowed. This phenomenon had been observed, in one special case, by the Englishman Robert

Boyle, who had a very particular diamond that he rubbed in the dark to produce a phosphorescent effect. Bernoulli, however, generalized the experiment and showed that several other materials exhibited the effect as well. In a pattern the *académie* would repeat again and again, Fontenelle's colleagues proved eminently successful in replicating, expanding, and improving the state of the art. With an empirical fanaticism usually associated with British natural philosophy in the seventeenth century, they pursued the phenomenon relentlessly. Their results appeared in the *Histoire* for 1707. The academicians showed that a large number of combinations of materials when rubbed produce little sparks of light. Cat's fur if stroked with a number of ordinary laboratory materials like sulfur or exotic ones like sugar (still in the early eighteenth century a luxury) shone brightly, especially in the winter. Glass buffed with gold gave the best metallic sparks. Diamonds above all could be made to exhibit light when they were massaged with a large range of materials. Fontenelle's conclusion to this article cited Bernoulli's letter of 1701: "From all this, M. Bernoulli concluded that M. Boyle, as accomplished as he was in experimental physic, regarded as a sort of prodigy something that was not. This was a Diamond which, being rubbed in the dark, threw out a spark, to which he gave the superb name of *Adams Lucidus*. It has no particular privilege."[64] The *académie*, in short, by dint of its collective persistence, could do even such an experimental genius as Boyle one better.

As with mathematics or astronomy, this foray into natural history was of a piece with the attitude toward the physical world that Fontenelle expressed through his character in the *Conversations on the Plurality of Worlds*. The results provided an appropriate topic of polite conversation; the materials belonged to *le monde*, the world of *politesse* and wealth and glamour in which the marquise and her philosophical gentleman moved. They could, with a minimum of effort and a great deal of self-satisfaction, repeat the experiments if they wished, using furs and diamonds at hand. The expertise of the academicians came not from any technical mastery they had over some abstruse science of materials; rather, it depended upon their assiduous pursuit of the mundane. One can, to be sure, gain a certain proficiency at rubbing glass and cat's fur to produce sparks, but it is a proficiency rather quickly mastered and easily communicated. Like other servants of the royal household, the academicians performed the endless tasks required to maintain all aspects of regal *gloire;* the king and his court could easily witness or indeed master the few aspects of burnishing and buffing that produced charming results.

Examples could be extended and multiplied, but the point is perhaps already made. The picture of the Académie royale des sciences that the ladies and gentlemen of Fontenelle's Paris would have gleaned from its *Histoires* had evolved from the little philosophical salon closeted in the king's library to a true scientific institution producing an understanding of the physical world. Lest we feel too familiar with this institution, however, we must not picture a university department or an institute of science and technology from our own experience. The knowledge that the *académie* produced was the knowledge dispensed by Fontenelle's charming philosophical voice to his imaginary marquise. The chemists produced glowing phosphors; their success served as a point of national pride. Astronomers dashed off to exotic lands, braved the dangers of a savage diet, and debated the constitution of celestial vortices and their subtle matters. Students of *la physique générale* and mathematical mechanics alike pursued their subjects in an accessible and conversational tone, more likely to inspire recreational mathematics than theoretical breakthroughs. The topics that held sway at Renaudot's Bureau d'adresse—What is the ultimate constitution of matter? What is the cause of thunder? How are the heavens arranged?—continued to provide a source of fascination for both philosophical practitioners and curious amateurs. The elaborate arrangement of subtle matters managed with such care by Christiaan Huygens, and with such panache by Jacques Rohault, received careful attention at the *académie* and abroad. This work came alive— no longer in the apartments of a man with the most philosophical hat in Paris or the salon of a *précieuse* gentlewoman, but in the elegant pages of the academic periodical, in the words of a most charming and knowledgeable philosophical gentleman. Fontenelle presented a style of science more to be read than to be practiced, but an accessible philosophy in this literary context.

The worlds that Fontenelle inhabited—the social *monde* of Paris, the astronomical worlds of the *Conversations* and the Royal Observatory, the worlds of Académie française and the Académie royale des sciences—together formed a literary continuum that flowed from the same pen. All were bathed in the same light from the Sun King, all provided him with *gloire,* and all offered some vague metaphorical support to his state and (what was the same thing) to his self. Planets and falling bodies, philosophical ladies and their charming beaux, all swam in a literal and in a figurative vortex: One revolved about the earth and the other about the court. This image so filled the world of Western thought that even Christiaan Huygens or John Locke, refugees from absolutism, played out the same metaphors and beliefs as Fontenelle and his colleagues and characters. The melding of philosophies natural and political is usually attributed to the mind of the Enlightenment by both its adherents and its detractors—for those who concern themselves with this discourse nearly always join it. The philosophy of the Enlightenment took this peculiarly modern confla- tion of unrelated realms (or republics) of thought as its cornerstone. Yet the theme of modernity setting right the study of both nature and statecraft entered the discourse in France a generation earlier than Enlightenment in questions of politics. Like the little flock of philosophes of the next generation, the ladies and gentlemen of Fontenelle's Paris and indeed of his Europe took natural philosophy as at least a part and occasionally the central character of this elaborate ballet danced in the physical and cultural spheres.

For the philosophes, of course, absolutism would become anath- ema; Fontenelle's connection between Louis XIV's *"l'état, c'est moi"* and Descartes's *"cogito, ergo sum"* would become an albatross around the neck of the philosopher's school. It is easy to forget when one looks through the liberal eyes of Anglo-American political theory that absolutism had rescued France from the political fragmentation and cultural crudity of the early seventeenth century. These problems still vexed both British and German culture as late as the time of the publication of the *Conversations.* Likewise, the Cartesian system had rescued philosophy from the fragmentation of the Bureau d'adresse and rendered it suitable for polite conversation. Even Voltaire from his Enlightened perspective could look back and see in the age of the Sun King a flowering of culture and learning. It has been the aim of the previous and present chapter to characterize the philosophical bud of that most literary flower.

From the time of the death of Colbert in 1683 through the end of the reign of Louis XIV, we may take Fontenelle as our exemplar of the French natural philosopher. Like the age of Colbert, the latter part of the reign of the Sun King was a distinctive moment in French history, a time of decadence after brilliance, a time of intolerance and frittering away the intellectual and artistic patrimony that *colbertisme* had bestowed upon Western culture. Fontenelle was not Molière or Voltaire, he was not Huygens or Maupertuis, and he was not Locke or Hume. His age was not one of blazing scientific accomplishment in France. Yet this is not to castigate the age or the character who best represents it. Although it could not compete with the work of Newton, the French scientific community managed to hold its own in the international community. We must not see the long generation of Louis XIV and Fontenelle as the last gasp of the early years of the revolution in mathematics and mechanics accomplished by Galileo, Descartes, and Kepler, nor as a weak precursor to the Enlightenment. Instead, it represents the first generation that saw itself as a group of working scientists who believed their theoretical framework was largely correct and essentially complete. They could reasonably imagine that they were on the way to solving the outstanding technical problems that confronted them, and they offered their own community to the rest of the thinking world as an exemplar of how an intellectual enterprise ought to operate. It is that self-confidence that Fontenelle left as his legacy to both the scientific and the larger cultural communities—a legacy that has been accepted by generations whose scientific distinction has been greater than Fontenelle's, and also by generations whose scientific distinction has been more illusory than that of the nearly perpetual secretary of Louis XIV's *académie*.

PART THREE

Science in the Reign
of Louis XV

6

The Demonstration of Enlightenment

ONE OF THE WONDERFUL and undoubtedly apocryphal stories in the history of the reception of scientific theory has John Locke calling on Christiaan Huygens. Both of them were exiled in Holland, Huygens as a Protestant no longer welcome in France and Locke as a member of the party about to bring William and Mary to England. Locke was in the midst of writing the *Essay Concerning Human Understanding,* the philosophical basis of that Glorious Revolution and of the Enlightenment. It was shortly after the publication of Isaac Newton's *Principia.* According to the story, Locke said that he had read Newton's work and had only one question. He wanted Huygens to tell him if the math was right. "Yes," Huygens answered, "but," he began as Locke stood to leave, "if you don't understand the math," he continued as Locke walked out the door, now shouting to try to catch the departed philosopher's attention, "you don't understand the *Principia!*" Thus, "the great Mr. Locke was the first who became a Newtonian without the help of geometry."[1]

Western thought since the earliest years of the Enlightenment has followed Locke's example in adopting natural philosophy as a paradigm for human understanding without adopting a requirement that Western thinkers have any particular familiarity with its details. Locke was not swayed by the internal logic or elegance of the *Principia*'s argument, for he could not follow it. Nor can it be argued that any astronomical or mechanical prediction might have so struck Newton's lay contemporaries that it brought them into his camp, for Newton made no such predictions. This raises the question of why the thinkers of the early Enlightenment so vigorously embraced natural philosophy as a model for political philosophy, and for the contemplative life in general. The scientific theory of universal gravitation leads no more logically to liberalism than Cartesianism does to absolutism.

The most likely source for the great stock that the mind of the Enlightenment placed in its science is, improbably, the demonstration-lecture. Intellectually mundane, diminished in modern times to the accompaniment for the droning of often bored professors turned elementary physics teachers in spite of themselves, this locus for the demonstration of Enlightenment must prove a bit of a disappointment for those who love great ideas. Surely, Fontenelle's younger contemporaries—one could be considerably younger than Fontenelle and still be his contemporary—came to know science as a grand philosophical system largely from writers. Although it is the literary legacy of the Enlightenment that has naturally enough attracted the attention of historians, this was hardly the source of the philosophes' understanding of nature. What they knew about scientific practice, about how experimental philosophers confronted their world, they came to know in the demonstration-lecture.

A clear line of successors to Rohault metaphorically donned the most philosophical hat in Paris and taught their generations how to see the world. Experiment in the Ages of Reason and Enlightenment served as a demonstration of what was known rather than an investigation into what was not. The lecture hall remained above all a place to show well-rehearsed and thoroughly predictable effects to those who sought Enlightenment.

The lecture-demonstration was by no means an exclusively French phenomenon. Much more than the developments discussed in the other chapters, these scientific entertainments represented a broad European movement. The discovery or refinement of a particularly striking illustration of one scientific principle or another was easily transported from lecture hall to lecture hall, and the patter that accompanied it could change in its ideology as easily as in its patois. What is more, the lecturers universally disclaimed allegiance to any philosophical school, arguing that they interfered not at all with nature as they worked their wonders. The high philosophical disputes among Cartesians and Newtonians and Leibnizians—disputes that play a significant role in the history of ideas and the geography of the mind of the Enlightenment[2]—could not impinge on the path of ivory balls in the lecture hall. The great Parisian practitioners presented Enlightenment with a French accent, to be sure, but the instruments they used and the experiments they performed were the same as those in Leyden or London or Berlin, or even Philadelphia.

It was owing to the great fashion of demonstration-lectures and experimental cabinets that the Enlightened philosophes in France and the French-speaking cultural sphere in Germany, as well as the British Empiricists and their Dutch contemporaries, came to believe the peculiar claim of natural philosophy to tell the truth about the world. Demonstrators could make balls jump through hoops—literally. They could project pictures on the wall with elaborate precursors to slide projectors and crank little painted planets about toy suns on tabletop clockwork mechanisms. It was this manipulative facility that made Locke's successors believe that natural philosophers spoke the truth, as the commonplaces of television or the airplane make us all believe that scientists speak with some authority.

The project of the demonstrators is not so simple as might at first appear. It turns out to be extremely difficult to devise an experiment that isolates and illustrates a particular physical principle. The hundreds upon hundreds of mechanical demonstrations worked out by lecturers in the early decades of the eighteenth century remained at the core of science pedagogy well into the twentieth century, and many bits of apparatus devised during that period persist in regular use—and in scientific supply catalogues—to this day.[3] The philosophical lecturers who were at such pains to assure their auditors that nature itself operated their demonstrations in fact arranged nature's actions with great care and had to have considerable skill as well as ingenuity to make things work. Elaborately staged spontaneous behavior of laboratory apparatus was rather like the extemporaneous verses Molière's characters had so carefully composed. The execution had to seem simple and natural.

This group of lecturers, purveyors of Enlightenment in a century whose collective mind embraced natural philosophy with an enthusiasm and innocence imaginable only in a preindustrial age, have never received much attention in the historical literature.[4] Their role was to make self-evident the truths that their generation took to be so, and their methods were sufficiently effective that their contribution has been largely overlooked. The eighteenth-century successors to Rohault nonetheless form a coherent tradition as easy to identify as the rationalist or Empiricist philosophers or the school of mathematical adepts who developed rational mechanics, if rather more obscure than any of them.

Those who uphold the validity of the literary and philosophical canon of the Enlightenment will undoubtedly be ready to do battle with this rival foundation for the certainty of science embraced by the philosophes. It might seem that this elevation of the demonstration-lecture attempts to raise something like vocational education to the status of high culture. The lecturers played the part of purveyors of public entertainments whose philosophical thoughts were so mundane as to have found no place in the history of ideas. Their mathematical expertise was sufficiently limited that none of them merited mention in the technical development of what is sometimes called rational mechanics,[5] the brilliant eighteenth-century mathematical extension of the work of Huygens and Newton and their colleagues. The arguments always presented by those who embrace the traditional canon can be offered again: that those who attack the canon simply fail to understand Western culture, that they hope to put in the place of the great books a series of pretty dumb books by second-rate authors, that the only notable connection among those authors is that they fit the conception of culture held by those who proclaim the importance of the alternative tradition. To open up the present discussion for a broadside from the defenders of the canon, the conception of culture being pushed in this chapter is one in which the little flock of Enlightened thinkers might actually have needed to be convinced of the claims of natural philosophers to speak the truth about the world—that those truths might not have been self-evident, at least until they were demonstrated.

The most philosophical hat in Paris passes to Pierre Polinière

The first of the demonstration-lecturers of the eighteenth century to provide fodder for the canon was Pierre Polinière. Polinière was born in the provinces in 1671.[6] He studied for a time in Caen and apparently acquired a medical degree, although its source is unclear; he did not use it except to decorate the title pages of his books. He ended up in Paris in the 1690s, studying philosophy at the university, mathematics with Varignon, and experimental philosophy on his own. Like his contemporaries Varignon and Ozanam (both destined for membership in the Académie royale des sciences), Polinière offered private math lessons in the capital. In 1704 he further emulated them by publishing an elementary text in the field. Word of his experimental prowess spread to the university; several professors of philosophy invited him to perform demonstrations by way of introduction to their lectures on natural philosophy. Within a few years these evolved into a two-month-long course, including about a hundred demonstrations. The university's medical school picked up Polinière's series as well. As his reputation grew, private individuals attended the lectures, straining the capacity of the college halls. Beginning in the decade before 1720, Polinière offered his course independently; Fontenelle sent a nephew to the lectures and was mightily impressed. It was perhaps owing to this connection to the Académie royale des sciences that in 1722 Polinière was invited to present the course to the young Louis XV. No greater success could be imagined.

In 1709 Polinière published his lectures as the *Expériences de physique.* He claimed that he hoped only to make the material available to those outside of Paris; the lectures, he assured his readers, were much better than the text. An experimental philosopher at heart, Polinière's admonition should probably be taken seriously—although tempered by the observation that demonstration was a remunerative occupation in an age before authors collected royalties on books. The *Expériences* presents a coherent exposition of nearly five hundred pages, richly illustrated with hundreds of engraved figures on dozens of plates. If one must exercise the imagination a bit to capture the flavor of the Polinière's performance, the content of the demonstrations can be straightforwardly reconstructed. The preface recited the first variation of what would become a familiar claim in the genre:

I did many simple experiments, and many that were less well known. I persisted and often repeated my operations over a long period of time. I applied myself to the mastery of experimental researches and to the discovery of their uses, to the acquisition of appropriate instruments, and to the creation of more numerous and different proofs. I tried experiments which are known to few people, or only in foreign lands; reproducing them frequently, I carefully examined the conditions, operations, and variations which allow an understanding of their causes.[7]

The seventeenth-century British term *virtuoso,* used to describe the experimental philosopher, captures the part Polinière would play in Paris. He not only possessed the cabinet of philosophical instruments required to demonstrate truths in a manner that made them self-evident; he could bring forth from them just the right result every time, and he could make it seem easy.

Polinière's text sets the tone in another way as well for demonstration-lectures published during the first half of the eighteenth century. It was limited to a description of the phenomena and avoided philosophical theory. To be sure, it was deference to the faculty at the university and the medical school rather than philosophical enlightenment that dictated that Polinière avoid framing his own hypotheses[8]—his was hardly a Humean disavowal of the connection between the constant conjunction of events in the laboratory and the philosophical opinions he held about them. Indeed, Polinière saw fit in his introduction to quote Fontenelle at length concerning the new, systematic style of science swept in with the new century.[9] The lectures themselves began with a series of experiments in mechanics that supported a Cartesian exposition of the system of the world. The thrust of the lectures nonetheless set a clear early Enlightenment tone of deference to phenomena over theory, an example quite different from the literary style presented by Fontenelle, in which all phenomena were made to fit into a world of vortices and subtle matters undetectable through any direct experiment.

In the first experiment, Polinière simply tied a bucket of water to a rope and swung it around to demonstrate that the water would be held in the bucket by centrifugal force. (Like Rohault, Polinière depended upon the laws of nature to save himself the undignified work of mopping up.) The second showed the collision of ivory balls rolling on a table—billiards for science; the discussion provided a qualitative description of the quantity of motion of the colliding objects.[10] These together Polinière deemed sufficient to assert an essentially Cartesian theory of gravity, but he did not dwell on it. He went on in this series of half a dozen experiments to discuss fluid equilibrium, Archimedes' principle of buoyancy, and fluid pressure—effects all vaguely related to the way in which a whirlpool of gravitational ether might force bodies toward the center of the earth, but clearly demonstrable in the motions of gross bodies handled in the lab and in everyday life.

This bit of basic mechanics served by way of preface to the longest series of experiments in the collection, fifty demonstrations occupying nearly two hundred pages of text, dealing with barometry, the spring of the air, and the pneumatic pump. Polinière in fact rivaled Rohault in his manipulations of the barometer. Still more impressive were his operations with the pneumatic pump. In Rohault's generation, this device had represented a cantankerous custom-built luxury more suited to the inquiries of a serious philosopher with substantial material support like Christiaan Huygens or Robert Boyle than to those of a struggling philosophy master. Only a few years after the death of the man with the most philosophical hat in Paris, however, the pneumatic pump had become a commodity available even to those of relatively modest means.[11] It became in Polinière's hands a fantastic source of special effects.

Polinière began his exposition with a description and demonstration of several types of pneumatic machines.[12] This introduction included a number of demonstrations that Polinière treated as familiarization with the equipment rather than full-blown experiments. He placed a barometer in the "receiver" (that is, the jar that served as the vacuum chamber) of the pump to show that evacuating the air causes the column of liquid to fall; he showed that if the handle of the pump is released at midstroke, it is pulled back sharply into its cylinder; he made his auditors familiar with the sound of air rushing into an evacuated receiver. The copious illustrations that accompany the text— only about half of a single page is reproduced here (see Figure 6.1)— communicate a sense of crowded apparatus brought forth to examine the void.

The experiments proper began with a favorite of seventeenth-century inventors and purveyors of air pumps. Polinière took two polished cylinders of crystal, wet their surfaces, and pressed them together. He held the upper piece by an attached hook and showed his audience that the two stuck together. Next, he hung the pair in the receiver of the pump and evacuated the air. As the pressure decreased, the lower crystal dropped to the floor of the receiver. Polinière

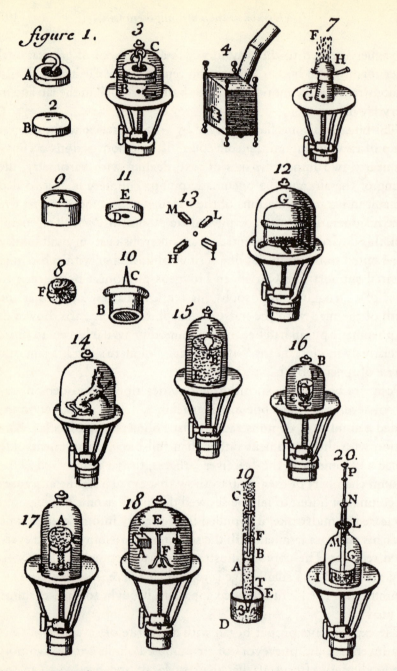

Figure 6.1 Some devices used in Polinière's demonstrations. Polinière's figures 1–3 show that in a vacuum two marble plates stick together firmly enough to lift the pair by a hook attached only to the top plate. Figures rearranged and reproduced from Pierre Polinière, Expériences de physique *(Paris, 1734), plate 5 (all editions used the same foldout plates). Courtesy of the Bakken Library, Minneapolis, Minn.*

explained to his audience (plausibly, but not entirely correctly) that the pressure of the atmosphere held the two cylinders together initially; when the air was removed from the receiver of the pump, this pressure ceased to operate and the bottom plate fell away.[13]

The opening experiment added a patina of philosophical theory to the pneumatic experiments. This tone was quickly replaced by a more common repertoire of household objects that were subjected to the vacuum. Polinière began with an apple.[14] As the air is pumped out of the receiver, the tempting fruit's skin ruptures. This served as the first of myriad examples of the fact that most foodstuffs and living things contain some air, which erupts from them in one way or another when they are placed in vacuo. Surely these "experiments," immensely popular from the invention of the air pump in the 1660s on, bear closer filiation to the collecting and cataloguing instincts of the natural historian or the collector of antiquities than to the theoretical bent of the natural philosopher.[15] Polinière's experimental collection included wine (which effervesces), liquor (which forms little bubbles), beer (which produces a wonderful head of extremely fine bubbles of a volume greater than that of the beer that produced it but that disappointingly collapses when the air is readmitted), and eggs (which burst). Sponges, he observed, float higher in buckets of water when they are placed in a vacuum than when the buckets sit in open air.[16]

Such was the outcome of the great seventeenth-century science of the void. There were, to be sure, two bits of theory that informed the long series of demonstrations: The atmosphere exerts pressure, and air is naturally expansive—in seventeenth-century terms, it has "weight" and "spring." Direct proofs of both principles found a place in Polinière's exposition. To illustrate the latter, for example, Polinière made an elaborate bit of glass tubing, straight at one end and branching at the other.[17] The straight end fitted snugly into a bottle, extending almost to the bottom. Polinière inverted this bottle, with the tube and its branches, in a larger, open jar filled with water (see Figure 6.2). He placed the whole apparatus in the receiver of his pump and removed the air. When the valve was opened, the pressure of the atmosphere pushed a considerable quantity of water up through the branching tubes and through the single tube, so that it made a little fountain in the inverted bottle. Polinière opened his receiver, removed the bottom jar, and placed the bottle, replete with its fancy tubes, in the vacuum chamber. As he pumped the air out, the pressure inside the

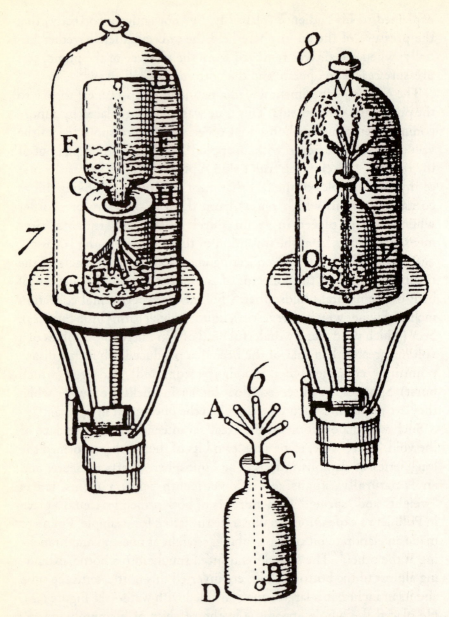

Figure 6.2 Illustration of Polinière's apparatus to create a fountain in a vacuum. His figure 6 shows a branching glass tube inserted in a bottle. His figure 7 shows the same tube inverted in a vessel of water inside a large, evacuated bell jar, drawing up water as air is allowed to reenter the jar. His figure 8 shows the operation of the fountain as the jar is pumped down again. Figures rearranged and reproduced from Pierre Polinière, Expériences de physique (Paris, 1734), plate 6. Courtesy of the Bakken Library, Minneapolis, Minn.

bottle sent little streams of water squirting out of each of the branches of the tube—an effect that his auditors found most diverting.

Despite the consistent reference to the two fundamental physical principles that Polinière and his contemporaries believed govern all the experiments in the air pump—a facile belief, as it turns out—it is difficult to imagine that the same thing was going on in his lecture hall that goes on in the modern university research laboratory. His experiments, repeated ad infinitum by the ladies and gentlemen who bought air pumps and carted them home, served to delight the observer and to illustrate the basic principles, easily mastered, that were required to explain all the action taking place in the receiver. These experiments were repeated, not in the interest of discovering subtle variations, or even of confirming facts already established to fulfill some requirement of the scientific method, but out of the sheer joy of demonstrating once again the way that natural philosophy accurately depicted nature. The few demonstrations designed to illustrate the weight and spring of the air were presented willy-nilly among those that simply displayed the behavior of the stuff of the household in vacuo; one has to read and consider the experiments rather carefully to arrive at the twin principles.

Contrary to modern notions of the immensity of scientific research and its continuous nature, Polinière's demonstrations and the ease with which he explained them seemed to show that experimental philosophy could be grasped and mastered quite simply and that its description of the phenomena was thorough and complete. In the lecture hall, as in Fontenelle's writing, the world was a pretty novel of physics. Demonstrations above all served to produce a faith in the certainty of natural philosophy, in the universality of its conclusions, and in the solidity of its method. There was a predictable connection between cause and effect, always perfectly understood and explained by the natural philosopher. The purpose of demonstration was confirmation of this intellectual success, not the innocent exploration of phenomena in search of new knowledge. Polinière certainly projected the sense that he could toss almost anything into the air pump and describe its expansion or its bubbling—or its diminution and its drooping—in terms of his minimal principles. His own role was that of the virtuoso, capable of doing it right every time, infallible in his operation of the machinery, and as spectacular in his own setting as Rohault had been in Molière's Paris.

Apart from experiments involving the air pump, the most extensive section of Polinière's lectures concerned chemistry. This is hardly surprising in light of Fontenelle's reports in the *Histoire* of the Académie royale des sciences during the first twenty years of the eighteenth century. To be sure, the dignity accorded natural philosophy had still not completely embraced the chemical community. Polinière felt compelled to distinguish his work from that of alchemists seeking to change base metals into gold or silver, or seeking the philosophers' stone.[18] The specter of the chemist as magician, benign, as Somaize had portrayed her, or sinister, as in the eyes of the witch hunters, was not yet completely removed from the collective consciousness of the early Enlightenment. Polinière indeed conceded that chemists for their own part had often written obscurely out of fear of persecution. Yet he declared that in the free-thinking atmosphere in which he lived, such concerns were no longer significant.[19] Beginning with the second edition of the *Expériences de physique,* Polinière in fact adopted the term *pyrotechnic* in place of *chemistry* in order to differentiate his demonstrations from those of the alchemists. He defined this new science as "the art of separating the different materials which make up bodies, in order to choose those which are useful."[20] By 1720, at least, Polinière believed that the revolution in that science had already come.

Like the experiments with the air pump, those in the section on pyrotechnic offer an eclectic series, one coming after another without any clear theoretical or developmental progression. Polinière demonstrated the dissolution of metals in acids, the chemically induced coagulation of the blood, and the glowing of phosphors. When he occasionally ventured to offer theoretical explanations, despite the presence of the learned professors, Polinière presented a miscellany more reminiscent of the discussions at the Bureau d'adresse or in the *Journal des sçavans* than the pretty novel of physics offered by the Cartesians. In the early portion of the lectures, those concerned with mechanical questions, Polinière offered the sort of micromechanical explanation one might expect from a contemporary of Descartes or Boyle. One experiment, for example, simply illustrated the way in which an inverted bottle of air submerged in a goblet of water remained full of air—the air in the bottle and the water with which it was in contact did not mix. Polinière told his auditors, "The smaller the parts of different mixed bodies are, the more friction there is between them." Since the little bits of air are much smaller than those of water, the particles of water are unable to wedge their way in.[21] This mechanism was of a piece with the analysis that Polinière offered as he described the Cartesian system of the world, but equally of a piece with Robert Boyle's mechanical philosophy. Polinière's eclecticism offers evidence that his mind was not so small as to be haunted by the hobgoblin of consistency.

The section on pyrotechnic proper went considerably further. It opened with a radically different, Paracelsian, account of chemical combination. Polinière told his auditors of the four chemical principles of salt, sulfur (or oil), earth, and water. It was within this system that he described the new chemistry developed by the likes of the younger Lemery at the Académie royale des sciences. The revolution accomplished there was significant—to hear Polinière tell it, almost as much so as the Cartesian system. Everything, Polinière told his auditors, belongs to pyrotechnic: Rain, hail, tempests, lightning; congealing, distilling, fermenting, and dissolving are all pyrotechnic operations.[22] Gunpowder owes its explosive effects to pyrotechnic, and antimony, its vomitive virtue. Pyrotechnic teaches about nutrition, the absorption of nutrients, the formation of chyle, its conversion in the blood, its distribution to the parts of the body, and its role in nourishment, growth, and the formation of animal spirits and nervous sugars.[23] It allows one to turn the corrosive sweet.[24] Among the most striking of the demonstrations that Polinière performed under the rubric of pyrotechnic was imitation thunder. His introduction followed Lemery's theory, which had been described in the *académie*'s *Histoire* by Fontenelle: Thunder represents the quick, violent rarefaction of acidic, alkaline, and sulfurous matters in the middle region of the air. Polinière included an extensive recipe for the explosive concoction and treated his auditors to a demonstration of its efficacy.[25] Indeed, his exposition included a number of other simulated "meteors"—the northern lights, falling stars, and the like.

Polinière, in short, played the role of Rohault in his own time and place. He presented a pastiche of experimental diversions, accompanied by a philosophical patter driven by the demonstrations. Those who observed the lecture series must certainly have believed that they learned a number of true things about the physical world. Like

Rohault's audiences half a century earlier, they took away a sense that Polinière could manipulate the stuff of the laboratory to startling and charming effect. Above all—this was Polinière's innovation—the demonstrations showed that experimental philosophers could simulate large-scale natural phenomena. Owing mostly to advances in chemistry, these lectures at the dawn of the Enlightenment reenforced the rhetorical claim of natural philosophy to explain not only artificial demonstrations like those in the air pump but also less abstruse questions like the causes of the weather.

The understanding of natural philosophy an auditor would have taken away from Polinière's lecture must nevertheless have been rather different from that acquired through literary forays into the field. It is hard to imagine that Polinière's audiences would have gained a sense that natural philosophers had discovered a coherent system of the world of the sort Fontenelle's readers found in the *Conversations on the Plurality of Worlds* or in the *Histoire* of the *académie.* Those literary efforts presented a fully integrated Cartesian theory of heavens and earth. This was not the story that emerged from the lecture hall. These two presentations of the physical world, one literary and the other experimental, converged in many ways— witness their conclusion that chemistry had undergone revolutionary change. Yet in the generation of Polinière and Fontenelle there were still two distinct styles of natural philosophy even within the relatively unified Parisian scene. It is not plausible to suggest that the philosophe's faith in the ability of the natural philosopher to discover the truth about the world came exclusively from the lecture hall. Rather, Polinière's demonstrations lent credence to the system to be learned from the philosophy faculty or the literary expositor. Through the first quarter of the eighteenth century, the experimental virtuoso remained a sort of entertaining sidekick to the natural philosopher.

All this seems rather far from the today's understanding of empirical research. Modern philosophers of science would cringe at the notion that what Polinière did was science—indeed, they have available a tool to deny it. Aimed, it would seem, at Freudian explanations that seemed to explain too facilely every psychological outcome in terms of the same experiences of childhood sexuality, modern philosophers of science have proposed the criterion of "falsifiability" as a way to trip up the explainer. Simply put, this is the idea that in "real" science one might perform an experiment that contradicted existing theory— a contradiction that would lead in turn to substantial changes in or even total rejection of that theory.[26] This attempt at discovering at least one characteristic of a scientific method would have seemed as foreign to Polinière as his own activities must appear to us. The suggestion that his experiments ought to have provided falsifiability for his theory would to him have seemed simply perverse. What Polinière hoped to do was to set out a series of truths about nature, not to discover how the world behaves when nature or the philosopher is confused. This is not to say either that falsifiability is an inappropriate tool for assessing scientific research or that Polinière deceived himself or his audience. It is rather to point out that he was doing something different from modern scientific research. His different project, his scheme to demonstrate the truth of natural philosophy, had its consequences in the culture rather than in the content of science. About the culture of science modern philosophy has little to say.

Indeed, the only area in which Polinière might have been counted anything like a scientific researcher in the modern sense of the term, looking for something he didn't already know, occurred in researches that are retrospectively identified as electrical. Like his contemporary Francis Hauksbee,[27] the demonstrator for the Royal Society of London, Polinière undoubtedly saw in Bernoulli's mercurial phosphor— the strange glowing observed in the top of barometer tubes—a new entertainment for his audience of gentle amateurs of science. The two professional philosophical exhibitors made what might be characterized as a series of "simultaneous discoveries" in a field that has since acquired the wonderfully eighteenth-century-sounding name *phospholuminescence*. As sociologists of science have recognized for some time now, simultaneous discoveries almost always indicate that two (or more) researchers hit upon a more or less obvious next step in a "hot topic" in their own specialized community.[28] Polinière and Hauksbee represented such a little flock; a few decades later they would have been fated to correspond and even call upon each other, and a few centuries later they would have been fated to attend the same industry- or government-funded meetings. The lecture-demonstration business in 1705 did not carry such perks, although the sociology of simultaneous discovery is in other ways unscathed by their activities.

Despite their lack of a professional organization, both demonstrators developed essentially the same extension to the work that Bernoulli reported; both used the independent developments to their professional advantage.[29] The "phosphor," or glowing, in a barometer shaken by a philosophical observer (or stumbled over by one in a dark observatory) seemed to both Polinière and Hauksbee to be associated with mercury, vacuum, and motion. Both were struck with the notion of placing a bit of mercury in the evacuated globe of an air pump, spinning the globe, and rubbing its surface with their fingers in order to agitate the mercury (see Figure 6.3). Both succeeded in producing a more striking light this way than with the barometer. Both experimental philosophers also noticed that globes spun and rubbed in this manner, even when they were not evacuated, attracted little bits of dust and threads, although Hauksbee pursued this effect with more tenacity than did Polinière.

The two demonstrators found the discovery sufficiently striking that each reported it to the appropriate scientific body—the Royal Society in England, and the Académie royale des sciences in France. Hauksbee's presentation in the more amateur British setting came in the normal course of his duties as the Royal Society's demonstrator. Notwithstanding the presence of the society's president, Sir Isaac Newton, the display of the apparatus and its effect had no noticeable impact on the experimental community in Britain. Polinière's presentation of his effect to the Académie royale des sciences in Paris was an event rather more out of the ordinary. Since the lecturer was not a member of the august royal institution, his presentation required a special invitation; the academicians must have taken at least cursory notice because the demonstration required a darkened room. Nonetheless, Polinière's contribution merited no special mention from Fontenelle in the *académie*'s *Histoire,* even though it occurred during the period in which the perpetual secretary took an interest in the mercurial phosphor.

The simple experiments made their way not only into academic circles but into a more general experimental literature as well. Polinière included a brief description of his experiments in the *Expériences de physique.* In the same year, Hauksbee published his results more extensively in a work whose descriptive title page exudes an enthusiasm evident throughout the work: *Physico-Mechanical Experiments on*

Plate VII.

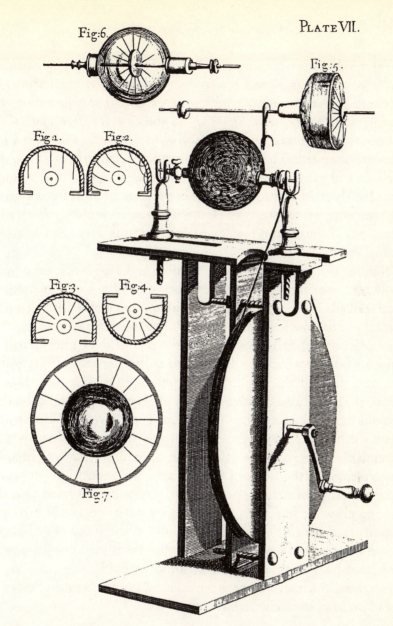

Figure 6.3 Hauksbee's electric machine, an elaborately mounted glass globe, capable of being emptied of air and spun rapidly; when Hauksbee touched the spinning globe with his fingers, he produced effects of electrical attractions. His figures 1–5 and 7 show various large hoops with light threads attracted to the electrified glass; his figure 6 shows threads inside the globe similarly attracted. Reproduced from Francis Hauksbee, Physico-mechanical Experiments on Various Subjects (London: R. Burgis, 1709), plate 7. Courtesy of the Bakken Library, Minneapolis, Minn.

Various Subjects, containing an account of several surprising phenomena touching on light and electricity, producible on the attrition of bodies, with many other remarkable appearances not before observed, together with the explanations of all the machines (the figures of which are curiously engraved on copper) and other apparatus used in making the experiments.[30] The two demonstration-lecturers, in short, did produce and publish significant new discoveries in experimental philosophy. To be sure, the importance of these researches into phospholuminescence for the study of electricity became clear only some time after both Polinière and Hauksbee died, but this does not negate the claim.

Neither the discoveries that Polinière and Hauksbee simultaneously made nor the announcements they offered of their experiments produced any activity on the part of either French or British circles of natural philosophers. Indeed, on careful consideration, these simultaneous discoveries offer evidence for the role of the demonstrator as purveyor of that which was known rather than pursuer of that which was not. Both of the public natural philosophers saw their experiments as illustrations of the mercurial phosphor, a phenomenon that was old hat by the time they took it up. They developed the experiments for the purpose of enlivening their lectures with a dramatic and dependable display of the effect. The community that is generally characterized as the locus of serious scientific enterprise—the community that published in professional journals—assumed that the strange glowing had been carried to its most elegant end by the demonstrators.[31] If it ever occurred to that community of gentlemen amateurs and royal academicians that the effects might be improved, they must have assumed the demonstrators would be the ones to improve them. Such efforts were the domain, not of scientific research, but of philosophical entertainment.

Demonstration-Lectures: Enlightenment without Hypothesis

In the first decade of the eighteenth century, the Anglo-European scene offered no demonstrations more coherent than those in Paris. Yet by the 1720s there was a lively community of demonstrators in both England and Holland that had developed a more complete description of the physical world than what could be gleaned from Polinière's lectures. On Hauksbee's death in 1713 the position of demonstrator at the Royal Society went to John Theophilus Desaguliers.[32] It was Desaguliers who first told the story about Locke and Newton with which this chapter opened. Desaguliers's lectures were not in fact particularly mathematical; they provided an alternative path to the *Principia* for the student who wanted to learn about natural philosophy. But they were extensive. Rather than consulting Huygens, the amateur of nature could hear and see Desaguliers's discussion, taking the truth of philosophical description on something more solid than faith.

Indeed, Desaguliers offered in addition to Newtonian astronomy some discussion of the three Cartesian matters.[33] He achieved a sufficient reputation that by the middle of the decade he could present a private series of lectures in addition to his duties at the Royal Society. Sometime before 1719 he printed up a series of copperplate engravings featuring some of his apparatus and optical diagrams—by their look, the plates were not all prepared at once—to save his auditors the trouble of sketching while he spoke.[34] These early diagrams depict the same sort of materials as that which Polinière had presented—air pumps and mechanical devices—and a fairly extensive discussion of optics was included.

One real innovation clearly attributable to Desaguliers's lectures came in his use of the "orrery," a clockwork mechanism used to illustrate the motion of the planets in the solar system (see Figure 6.4). By the time he had his illustrations printed up, Desaguliers could show his students a fairly sophisticated instrument.[35] Indeed he continued to improve the orrery—as well as his understanding of its history—so that in the 1730s he claimed to offer his students instruction on the best available instrument, which he had taken to calling a "planetarium."[36] Desaguliers's version had dozens of interchangeable pieces. In the planetarium's simplest form a brass sun stood on a post in the center and smaller metal balls represented the earth and the five known planets. Turning a crank on the front, Desaguliers could cause the planets to revolve about the sun, each describing its orbit at a different rate. All the planets were removable and could be replaced one at a time by other globes fitted with little hooks on top. Desaguliers fitted in each planet in turn a rod attached to the top of an appropriate

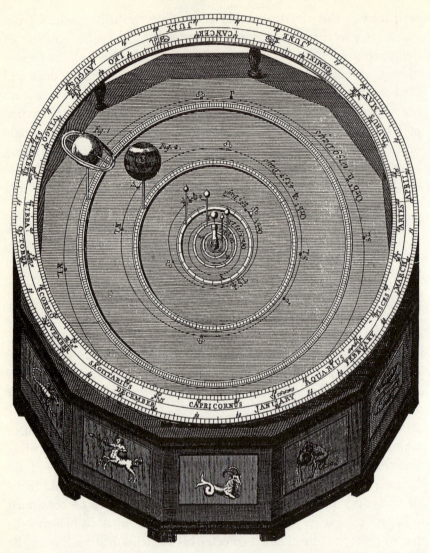

Figure 6.4 Desaguliers's orrery, or planetarium. Reproduced from J. T. Desaguliers, Lectures of Experimental Philosophy, *"second ed." (London, 1719), last plate. Courtesy of the Bakken Library, Minneapolis, Minn.*

model earth. Imagining this rod as a line of sight, Desaguliers could show how the planets appear to move first forward and then backward through the fixed stars of the heavens, refuting the strongest argument in favor of the Ptolemaic system and reenforcing the Copernican view of the solar system.

Prized by collectors and fascinating even to modern observers jaded by all sorts of mechanical contrivances, these philosophical machines seem to me to capture the spirit of Desaguliers's lectures. Planetaria offered a solid demonstration of the Enlightened view of the solar system, a triumph of the moderns over the ancients. They fix forever in the mind of the beholder that seventeenth-century British metaphor of the clock-work universe—a belief in a regularity, predictability, and comprehensibility, the naïveté of which is charming, at least within the context of the Enlightenment. Nevertheless, with their circular paths and their mechanical epicycles, orreries froze astronomical theory in the mid–sixteenth century. The selection of appropriate rod lengths and gear ratios represented a completely empirical notion of how the motion of the heavenly bodies might be determined, a problem with physical meaning only in a purely Copernican view of the world. Desaguliers's magnificent example captures the tension between philosophical theory and the trade of the demonstration lecturer.

It is the planetarium, perhaps, that best illustrates the place of the demonstration-lecture in England on the brink of industrialization. The scale of and demand for the instrument were appropriate to the burgeoning trade in clocks and watches. This was an industry that the British came to dominate during the eighteenth century. Increasingly elaborate astronomical toys clearly represent an effect rather than a cause of the excellence of British chronometers. Moreover, Desaguliers's attitude toward improvement of his instruments reflects the behavior of eighteenth-century British clock- and watchmakers. Blessed with an incredible technical skill and a market prepared to pay for luxury, the builder of planetaria as well as of chronometers "solved his problems by adding parts, not subtracting them."[37]

Much has recently been made of the importance of Desaguliers's lectures for the development of a sort of mechanical consciousness, first in Great Britain and then Holland. This familiarity with machines allegedly fed the fires of the industrial revolution.[38] One suspects that, as with the steam engine, cause and effect were more important in the other direction: Technology supplied the material for analysis by natural philosophers.[39] It is certainly true that Desaguliers devoted several lectures to machines, although his analysis did not proceed beyond the application of the law of the lever—the observation that the speed with which a weight is raised is inversely proportional to the power that raises it. Yet what he analyzed were existing machines; he tried to explain how it was that men or horses might pull heavy loads in carts that rode on steel wheels turning on iron rails. Although he expressed fascination from the time of his early lectures with inefficient, fire-powered Newcomen engines, he provided more significant arguments concerning the limitations on work that men or horses could complete in a day. These arguments came only in response to reckless claims that machinery could accomplish an unreasonable multiplication of effort, and this only in the last year or so of his career.[40] It is ironic that his definition of these limits might seem to set the stage for the industrial revolution: The great motor of industrialization was the steam engine, capable of delivering more power than men or horses ever could. Apart from standard analyses of simple machines, available from the earliest years of the seventeenth century, Desaguliers's lectures generally explored the transmission of human or animal power rather than the application of great powers mechanically produced.

More important, any attempt to explain differential rates of industrialization in terms of Desaguliers's lectures fails to take into account the similarity of demonstration apparatus throughout Europe. The air pump, especially, is cited as a significant instrument. The maintenance of the seals, operation of the piston, and manipulation of valves certainly did provide worthwhile experience for mechanics who might work on the steam engine. In some general way, the demonstration-lectures, and in particular the individuals who bought air pumps and had to maintain them, helped to spread what is oxymoronically called "mechanical literacy." Yet Polinière's lectures and those by his successors in Paris offered demonstrations on the air pump as extensive as the ones in Britain and the Low Countries. Disseminated through the university as well as in popular private settings, those lectures (were the hypothesis that mechanical literacy hastens industrial revolutions falsifiable) should have fomented the industrial revolution in France before it occurred in other lands.[41]

Whatever his role in the history of industrialization might have been, by the latter part of the 1710s Desaguliers was offering a new style of lecture series, more coherent and connected to philosophical theory than Polinière's had been. In 1717 Desaguliers published a

short summary as his *Physico-mechanical Lectures*,[42] intended merely
to relieve his students of the burden of taking notes; it is the topics
covered rather than the content of the lectures that can be gleaned
from the summary. Two years later, one of the students published his
own, fuller notes as an unauthorized "second edition" of *Lectures of
Experimental Philosophy*,[43] which Desaguliers officially disavowed.
Confronted with a fait accompli, however, he added a hasty preface,
in an attempt to correct the more egregious errors.

The filiation of ideas becomes rather clouded here, since another
early spectator was a young Dutchman named Willem 'sGravesande,
who (like Huygens two generations earlier) had arrived as a member
of a diplomatic family dispatched to a foreign capital and had been left
with considerable time on his hands. 'sGravesande fell in with the
community of natural philosophers in London; in about 1714 he re-
portedly observed one of Desaguliers's early performances.[44] The
next year a young instrument maker named Petrus van Musschenbroek also traveled from the Netherlands and observed Desaguliers's
lectures.[45] In 1717 'sGravesande was chosen as professor of natural
philosophy at Leyden. In about 1719 Musschenbroek took up a faculty position in Duisburg; in 1723 he moved to the university at
Utrecht. It is not clear, and will probably remain one of those questions debated despite a lack of evidence, how much 'sGravesande's or
Musschenbroek's lectures owed to Desaguliers's. The experimental
debt was considerable, doubly unsurprising since Petrus van Musschenbroek's older brother Jan served as instrument maker for
'sGravesande shortly after Petrus returned from England.

The first of the Anglo-Dutch lecturers to publish a full transcription of his lectures on his own initiative was 'sGravesande, in 1720.[46]
The work was sufficiently successful that Desaguliers himself prepared an English translation from 'sGravesande's Latin. (French editions followed shortly.) Musschenbroek, too, began publishing versions of his lectures. By the time Desaguliers published a full,
authorized volume of his own lectures in 1734 they bore much the
same character as 'sGravesande's; the direction of the influence was
undoubtedly a two-way street. The three series of lectures, pitched at
slightly different levels, would all appear in numerous versions and
editions through three decades. Desaguliers's presentation was the

easiest and most popular; 'sGravesande's the most rigorous; Musschenbroek's fell between the others. Whatever intellectual debts they may have owed to one another, they had a great deal in common.

One conspicuous feature of the Anglo-Dutch lecturers is that they all professed to be Newtonian.[47] That word became in the Enlightenment so commonly bandied about that it is difficult to tell what it meant. Among the demonstrators considered here, it seems to have signified three things. First, they (along with a number of French Cartesian lecturers, including Polinière and his successor, Jean Antoine Nollet) professed not to "feign hypotheses" but rather to confront nature empirically and without prejudice. Second, they took mathematical mechanics as the basis of natural philosophy, claiming that their position ran counter to a prevailing philosophical culture that placed a Fontenelle-style "novel of physics" ahead of specific physical principles. Finally, they took Newton's side on two debates in which he became engaged: They adopted his position on the conservation of what is now called "momentum" in collisions and accepted his theory of universal gravitation. Historians have too frequently accepted these professions of the Newtonian faith at face value. As shall appear upon more careful consideration, all three claims are more or less universal Enlightenment rhetorical flourishes. French Cartesians as well as British Newtonians adopted the whole of the program except for Newton's law of universal gravitation.

The novelty of their collective approach was nonetheless profound. On the one hand, the new experimental philosophers integrated their demonstrations fully into their university-style lectures, which they organized along theoretical lines. On the other, they provided an experimental illustration of nearly every proposition. This was true not only for obviously empirical fields like "the void" and chemistry but also for problems traditionally considered mathematical and abstract. The exact contribution of Desaguliers, 'sGravesande, or Jan or Petrus Musschenbroek is, of course, an interesting puzzle—though not one whose pieces are easy to put together. However this system of teaching may have evolved, by the early 1720s a clear school of demonstration had evolved.

The first claim to Newtonianism—the renunciation of "hypotheses"—might as well be seen as a claim to crush philosophical infamy. Each of the new demonstrators, including those of clearly Cartesian or Leibnizian leanings, took the part of advocate for a new philosophical party, composed of those who "have wisely restrained that once prevailing and licentious custom of feigning hypotheses, of which former ages had been so fond."[48] It is now clear to all who study Newton's work that he in fact held opinions on the cause of gravity and other sources of hypothetical physics; the occasion for his philosophical modesty was that he preferred not to air them. Although many Enlightenment Empiricists and philosophes took Newton's claim at something like face value, the lecturers were more sophisticated about the Great Thinker they adopted as mentor. Newton and his disciples were seen as feigners of hypotheses as elaborate and unjustified as those of the most ardent Cartesians. The words were aimed as sharply at the disciples of the British genius as the disciples of the French. They are professions of adherence to a radically experimental philosophy. Petrus van Musschenbroek, for example, declared:

> I am attached to no party, but to that of truth only. Such things as have been well demonstrated by the most acute *des Cartes* I have retained. The very many and great discoveries of the illustrious *Newton* (the glory of *England,* to whom no age has produced an equal) by which he has so much advanced Philosophy, I have readily embraced. I have adopted the opinion of the noble and excellent *Leibniz.*[49]

The new experimental philosophers believed that they could settle the arguments among the mathematical and the philosophical.

The mechanical basis of the demonstration-lectures presents an appropriate antidote to the elaborate theorizing of Pierre Varignon. Whereas the French mathematician may have been carried away with mathematical solutions to physically impossible problems, the British and Dutch experimentalists offered physical demonstrations of problems generally considered abstract and mathematical. One of the most striking demonstrations of principles generally viewed as mathematical came when 'sGravesande spoke about the trajectories traced by objects hurled with some initial velocity. There are, of course, an infinite number of such trajectories, depending on the infinite variety of speeds and directions and initial positions with which objects can be hurled. The mathematical mechanicians had shown that all such paths ought to trace parabolas. For Varignon, such a statement was all the discussion one needed. Yet 'sGravesande actually traced out a particular parabola on a board and attached a series of hoops spaced equally in the horizontal direction and lying on the parabola (see Figure 6.5) so that their distance below a horizontal line grew as the square numbers 1, 4, 9, 16. 'sGravesande demonstrated to his audiences that for this one trajectory, a ball rolling down a ramp and allowed to fly off the end passed through hoops that encircled the theoretical path and landed in a container of sand placed at the theoretical end of the path. The parabolic trajectory, for Varignon a product of pure intellect, was thus made concrete.

The experimental apparatus is really very clever. It illustrates the parabolic path clearly and fixes that path in the observer's mind. Yet one has to be serious about the goal in order to build such a piece of furniture. Mechanical contrivances generally demonstrate first of all the recalcitrance of matter, and nothing looks sillier than a demonstration of universal principles that fails. The launching ramp and ball need to be completely smooth, the starting point must be clearly fixed, and the whole massive board must be completely level for the demonstration to work. The placement of the sand must be just right. Moreover, the theory that describes rolling objects is more complicated than the launch theory presented, which (following the example Galileo and the tradition of Varignon) assumes dimensionless objects sliding down frictionless ramps. "The distance," as Desaguliers observed in his discussion of the apparatus, "must be found by trials."[50]

Such a single example of parabolic motion cannot, of course, prove anything so general as the theory of projectile motion. To the great analytical mathematicians of the previous generation—Huygens and Newton and the Bernoullis, who had worked out the solutions to such problems in rigorous detail—'sGravesande's demonstration would have been little more than a plaything. Whether such a toy might have amused them would have been a question of personal temperament. As a demonstration of a mathematical proof, however, the apparatus would never have satisfied those with acutely mathematical temperaments. Yet for ladies and gentlemen of uncertain arithmetical or geometrical expertise seeking enlightenment about the great accomplishments of their philosophical contemporaries, the picture 'sGravesande offered would have counted more than a thousand technical words.

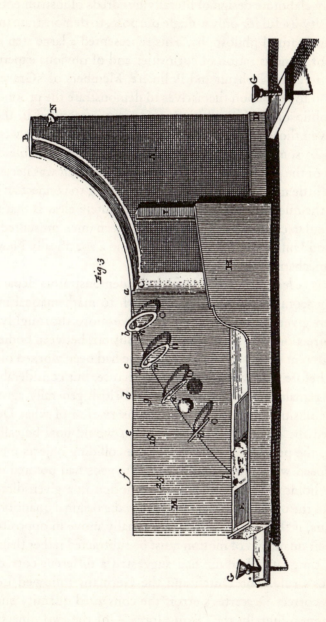

Figure 6.5 Apparatus designed to demonstrate the parabolic nature of trajectories of objects thrown horizontally. Reproduced from Willem 'sGravesande, Élémens de physique (Leyden, 1744), vol. 1, plate 19, figure 3, facing p. 142. Courtesy of the Bakken Library, Minneapolis, Minn.

'sGravesande and his contemporaries were doing something novel when they introduced experiments of this sort. They undertook the incredibly elaborate design of literally hundreds of instruments, often by necessity useful for only a single purpose, to demonstrate the truth of the new natural philosophy. This represented a large step beyond the sort of demonstration of curiosities and of obvious experimental effects offered by Rohault and Polinière. Members of 'sGravesande's generation took it upon themselves to demonstrate the proof of all of natural philosophy through the experiments presented in their lectures—even those aspects of mathematical mechanics that were most abstract. In some cases, to be sure, they offered reasonable demonstrations of the principles they discussed; in others, it was necessary to resort to little more than elaborate hand waving to connect an experiment to the question at hand. What is absolutely clear is that there is no particular connection between the mechanics presented in the British and Dutch texts on the one hand and a specifically Newtonian style of mechanics on the other.

There is at least one case in which the demonstrators departed significantly from the Newtonian approach to mathematical mechanics—even given an opportunity to move more thoroughly in the British direction. The rules governing collisions between bodies moving at different speeds along a straight line had been worked out half a century before 'sGravesande began to lecture, but considerable controversy remained. The French and the British generally agreed that in such collisions there should be a conservation of what Descartes had called the quantity of motion—what would now be called *momentum,* the product of the mass of the colliding objects multiplied by the speed with which they move. Huygens had pointed out that this rule holds only if it is applied to motion in a given direction—motion in the opposite direction opposes the original quantity of motion. Thus, if the colliding bodies originally move in opposite directions, their quantities of motion must be subtracted rather than added. A short time later, Leibniz had suggested a different correction to Descartes's rule. The Dutch and the Germans followed Leibniz's claim to correct Descartes's error; the conserved quantity should be the *vis viva*—literally the "living force"—of the two objects, computed by multiplying the mass of each body by the *square* of its speed.

Unlike Huygens's quantity of motion, the "living force" is always counted as positive, no matter what direction the bodies move.

This vexatious debate had been raging for half a century when the lecturers began to comment on it, and it represented one of the most divisive issues in natural philosophy. The reason that the difficulty could not be simply decided by experiment is bound up in the apparatus used to demonstrate collisions from the time Huygens worked on the problem on. In France, the device was usually attributed to Huygens's colleague at the Académie royale des sciences, Edme Mariotte. Two ivory balls were suspended by pairs of strings, so they could move only in one plane. One or both of the balls could be pulled away from its resting place. When released simultaneously, the two balls collided and rebounded. The speeds with which the balls moved before the collision were determined by the height from which they were released; the speeds after the collision could be calculated from the height to which they rebounded: Galileo had determined that the speed of a pendulum bob at the bottom of its swing was proportional to the square root of the height from which it fell or to which it rose. (In the terms of Leibnizian theory, as the body descended, it converted the "dead force" of gravity into the "living force" of motion—vestiges of this theory remain in the common language phrase "dead weight.") Since the ivory balls bounce quite well against each other, and since the direction of their motion is always in one dimension, both quantities—quantity of motion and living force—are conserved in the experiment.

In the early 1720s 'sGravesande set about empirically determining a distinction between quantity of motion and living force in collisions. He managed to design a new apparatus for a "crucial experiment" (see Figure 6.6). A slight variation on the Mariotte instrument, it depended on an elaborate modification of the bob of the pendulum. 'sGravesande constructed bobs made with removable clay inserts so that they would stick together after the collision. In a second variant, he used a small, rough board suspended as a pendulum. After setting the board swinging, he dropped a rough weight on top, again providing an example in which the colliding objects stuck together. These new devices settled the question unequivocally. The pair of bobs and the weighted board both moved off with speeds consistent with the

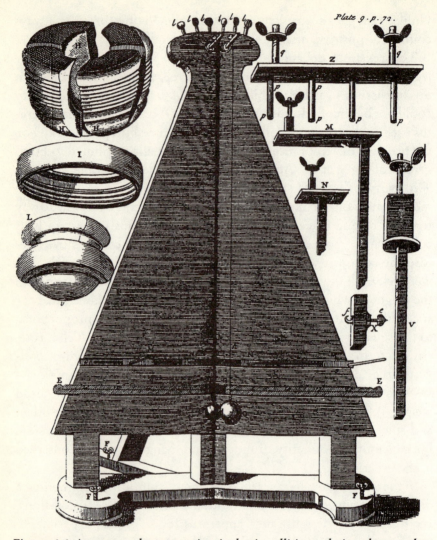

Figure 6.6 Apparatus demonstrating inelastic collisions, designed to resolve the dispute between partisans of vis viva *and those of quantity of motion. Reproduced from Willem 'sGravesande,* Mathematical Elements of Natural Philosophy *(London, 1747), plate 31. Courtesy of the Bakken Library, Minneapolis, Minn.*

conservation of quantity of motion; they lost "living force." Newton and his British and French collaborators were vindicated.

Yet the situation was not so simple as to make Huygens and Newton winners and Leibniz a loser. Another series of experiments in which 'sGravesande dropped ivory balls into little pots of clay showed that the size of the indentation grew with the square of the velocity—that the living force governed some aspects of collisions, and the quantity of motion others. Thus even in this victorious Newtonian moment, the demonstrator adhered to the principle of teaching only the phenomena and not the dogma of one or another philosophical camp.

The exact meaning of the philosophical, mathematical, and experimental debate represents a sufficient historiographical quagmire that I shall not pronounce upon the validity of 'sGravesande's solution.[51] I shall simply suggest that in this example the demonstrators in fact did succeed in devising a workable explanation of a problem that had perplexed the best mathematical minds of the day. They presented this explanation in classic Empiricist style, showing how disputes about words could lead to misunderstandings. Locke himself could not have hoped for a more sound and commonsensical approach to this little corner of human understanding.

The contribution of 'sGravesande and his colleagues has never been well understood by historians of science. He has seemed to the mathematically inclined always to have been on the edge of new developments in analytical mechanics, but never to have made any significant contributions of his own. It is clear that his demonstrations added nothing to the mathematical theory worked out during the previous generation. To devotees of experimental philosophy as it was practiced by the likes of Robert Boyle, it seems that early-eighteenth-century practitioners just didn't find very much new. In fact, the lecturers were doing something very different from either their contemporaries working in theory or their predecessors in experiment. They were demonstrating the truth of the new philosophy; they had determined a new method to spread Enlightenment.

All too often, innovation of this sort is dismissed, especially by technical histories, as meaningless dabbling—a charge that is rarely leveled, for example, at Varignon. That which is true is identified as that which is discovered and demonstrated mathematically, and great stock is put in such truth. The tenor of most historical accounts of eighteenth-century demonstrators ranges from apology for their lack of originality to ridicule for missing the point of mathematical physics. Yet 'sGravesande, the even less mathematically adept Desaguliers, and their imitators clearly played a crucial role in the development of natural philosophy in the eighteenth century. They provided access to the study of nature beyond the literary style that Fontenelle offered in the *Conversations on the Plurality of Worlds* or even in the *Histoire* of the Académie royale des sciences. They gave their audiences a sense of actually witnessing the truth of natural philosophy. Their students did not have to take the impenetrable technical details on faith, as the demonstrators believed that Locke had done.

In addition to the signal technical solution to the problem of collision, the school of philosophical demonstrators in fact made important contributions of three sorts to the culture and content of natural philosophy during the Enlightenment. Most significant for the present purpose is that their spectacular visual confirmation of the abstruse technical accomplishments of the seventeenth century made those accomplishments real to the educated public. The ladies and gentlemen of Louis XV's Paris and of other major European cities, introduced to natural philosophy through the literary style of Fontenelle, could make it their own when they saw its truth demonstrated on the stage of 'sGravesande and his imitators. Second, the lecturers had to work out a consistent account of natural philosophy, free of the bickering between partisans of Descartes, Leibniz, and Newton that increasingly dominated the discussion of the philosophes and the literati. It was through the agency of these so-called popularizers that the fragmented mathematical physics that emerged from the late seventeenth century evolved into a consistent story about nature. Although the mathematically adept could pick and choose among the available and competing notions about the laws governing interactions between bodies—especially collisions in the terrestrial realm and the operation of the planets and their moons in the celestial one—unseemly arguments among the experts could hardly have inspired the sort of confidence in natural philosophy evidenced by the mind of the Enlightenment. The cultural place of natural philosophy as an example of how to discover the "truth" owed no more to obnoxious pedants in the eighteenth century than it did in the seventeenth. Finally, the demonstrators of the midcentury developed most of the significant apparatus in the evolving science of electricity in order to present more excitement in their lectures.

Jean Antoine Nollet and the Enlightenment in Paris

We are, however, getting ahead of our own Parisian story. Polinière's lectures early in the century did offer a few experiments to introduce the uninitiated into the truth of the mathematical description of nature. His restraint from philosophical comment did set the tone for the demonstrator as the transparent window into nature, which became so important for Enlightenment beliefs about natural philosophy. Yet his lectures never offered either a complete or a coherent view of nature. Upon Polinière's unexpected death in 1734, an obvious opening existed for a successor. This place was taken by a young provincial abbé, Jean Antoine Nollet.

Like both Polinière and Varignon before him, Nollet came to the capital without any great fortune and determined to make his way as a natural philosopher. Following their example he served for a time as a tutor. In the late 1720s he joined a little band called the Société des arts, set up to offer instruction to artisans. (Again, the French seem to have beaten the British to this bit of Enlightenment rhetoric, although to no apparent industrializing effect.) It would serve as a stepping-stone for a whole generation of future members of the Académie royale des sciences.[52] In the context of this group Nollet met both Polinière and a number of academicians. With Cassini's blessing, he worked in Réaumur's laboratory and assisted Du Faye.[53] Through some informal mechanism Nollet became the heir apparent to Polinière. The academicians sponsored a tour in which the abbé visited the great lecturers of Holland and Britain—'sGravesande, Musschenbroek, and Desaguliers.[54] By about 1735 he was offering a full-blown series of lectures patterned after those he had visited.[55]

Nollet matched the British and Dutch lectures both in terms of presentation and intellectual sophistication. Yet at least in its early years the Parisian version maintained an intimacy similar to that which philosophical salons had achieved in the glorious years of the reign of Louis XIV. The philosophical guests sat around a table in a spacious apartment fitted out with appropriate experimental apparatus (see Figure 6.7). The afternoons chez Nollet retained the tone of easy sociability that Christiaan Huygens had encountered as a young gentleman visiting Paris with his diplomat-father and in the company of

Figure 6.7 A demonstration-lecture in Jean Antoine Nollet's cabinet de physique *in Paris. Reproduced from Jean Antoine Nollet,* Leçons de physique expérimentale *(Paris, 1745), vol. 1, frontispiece. Courtesy of the Bakken Library, Minneapolis, Minn.*

philosophical gentlemen, or that is present in the aristocratic *Conversations on the Plurality of Worlds,* which Fontenelle had offered. The ladies and gentlemen who joined the colloquies in the rooms of the king's most visible philosopher during the mid–eighteenth century enjoyed the sort of participatory enterprise that their predecessors had chez Guédreville. Like Rohault, Nollet welcomed women to his lectures, and from the beginning they came in numbers large enough to be remarked upon. Nollet indeed admonished potential auditors that "the path had been cleared by people of condition and merit so respectable" that no woman needed fear for her reputation by enrolling in the course.[56] (In this he imitated Desaguliers as well, who noted that persons of all ranks and professions and "even Ladies" could and did understand natural philosophy with the help of experiments.[57])

He got his message across. As early as April 1736, Émilie du Châtelet wrote to a friend that Nollet's lectures attracted "the carriages of duchesses, peers, and lovely women. Voilà then how pretty philosophy can make a fortune in Paris. I hope to God that this will endure."[58] Indeed the joke around Paris had it that "all the women had their *bel esprit*, next their geometer, and finally their abbé Nollet."[59] Stories circulated portraying Nollet as a sort of courtly absentminded professor. Voltaire would write to a friend, "Let us do like Nollet, who had imagined that he regularly slept with a Mme Truchot; when he saw her he made excuses to her for not sleeping with her any more."[60] This gentle ribaldry should serve to illustrate that Voltaire saw Nollet as part of the little flock of philosophes that inhabited his Enlightened world.

If Nollet did not adopt the sort of spectacular haberdashery Rohault had affected, he nonetheless cut an oddly striking figure, draped in an oversized lab coat and hat (see Figure 6.8). More than once he had himself portrayed in the lavish engravings included with published lectures, almost always among women or girls. Often he appeared at the bottom of a diagram, a sort of personal touch to cut through any clinical coldness that might be associated with science. Nollet's audiences were treated to many of the spectacular pieces of apparatus Desaguliers, 'sGravesande, and the Musschenbroeks had pioneered, as well as those that Huygens's contemporaries had observed in the apartments of Rohault and that the generation between had witnessed in Polinière's hall. Captured in the quintessentially eighteenth-century art form of the illustrative engraving, the abbé and the beautiful equipment available to his patrons can be seen: crystal bowls, blown and drawn glass, elaborate mechanical contrivances of wood and brass and leather in the style of Louis Quinze furniture (which in fact they were), all available for examination by those who sat at the table with the philosophical gentleman, as the future king

Figure 6.8 Nollet, wearing his lab coat and hat, and a student, both working at microscopes. Reproduced from Jean Antoine Nollet, Leçons de physique expérimentale *(Paris, 1745), vol. 5, lesson 17, plate 5, figure 20. Courtesy of the Bakken Library, Minneapolis, Minn.*

Louis XVI had himself sat. Nollet managed, as the political pollsters say, to define himself.

The first substantial evidence for the content of Nollet's lectures came when he circulated a *Programme* of the course along with a complete and detailed listing of the instruments he used. In this, too, Nollet followed the example set by the Anglo-Dutch lecturers. 'sGravesande had noted in the published version of his work, which was replete with engraved illustrations of each of his implements, that readers could obtain reproductions for their own use by indicating to Musschenbroek what they required.[61] The book became a catalog as well as a text; readers could order by plate and figure number. Later, Petrus van Musschenbroek even included the prices that Jan commanded for each of the illustrated instruments in his plates.[62] The demonstration of Enlightenment was not only witnessed in the lecture hall; it could be repeated in the parlor.

Like Jan Musschenbroek, Nollet offered for sale copies of his philosophical instruments. The more than fifty pages of instrument descriptions in the *Programme* of 1738 began with a clear sales pitch for the equipment.[63] He claimed that at first he sold copies out of necessity, financing his own collection on the profits—profits that he characterized as a "voluntary tribute" offered by the Enlightened patrons who purchased them.[64] By 1737 he had an excellent assistant, one Cousin, who "writes with a good hand, draws, is a machinist, studies mathematics, applies himself to experiments; he is going to learn to operate the observatory."[65] It seems Nollet also had a repair business for instruments made by amateurs or other makers, which weakens the impression that his only commercial interest was to improve his own collection.[66]

Nollet set out his priorities in designing the apparatus. Above all, he insisted that the instruments be very exactly made: Expense was not wasted, he said, if it saved errors. Yet he assured potential customers that beyond the necessaries he kept things as simple as possible: The price of his instruments would not be inflated by superfluous ornamentation. To the contrary, he continued, construction was the simplest, the easiest, and the sturdiest possible so that the instruments could be reproduced and repaired with the least expense, the least study, and the least inquiry. Finally, Nollet assured his customers that whenever possible he added multiple functions to his equipment, as long as these did not compromise utility, in order to keep the total cost of equipping a lab as low as possible.

This no-nonsense approach does not mean that Nollet provided shabby or rough-hewn equipment. The exquisite workmanship and finish one expects in artifacts of eighteenth-century furnishings were justified in terms of utility. Nollet assured his customers that all wooden and metal surfaces were carefully smoothed and polished to ensure proper operation. Most of the equipment involved sliding or rolling surfaces, and these had to be carefully finished for scientific rather than aesthetic purposes. With an assurance that must brighten the day of the curators of science museums, Nollet also informed his customers that varnishes were required to keep wood from swelling and shrinking; unsealed construction would lead to distortions in the apparatus and consequent inaccuracies in experiments. The French polish on antique instruments can be maintained for reasons of scientific utility as well as aesthetics.

Even with these bare necessities, Nollet's equipment did not come cheap. In May 1737 Voltaire and Mme du Châtelet purchased a telescope from him for 2,000 livres.[67] A year later they set out to furnish a philosophical cabinet from the anticipated *Programme* and reckoned,

"It will take perhaps nine or ten thousand francs for the abbé Nollet and our *cabinet de physique*. We live in a century where one cannot be learned without money."[68] This investment would have supported a modest bourgeois household for a year. The estimate was not far off the mark; a few months later Voltaire was asking for a copy of 'sGravesande's newest edition on credit, since "the abbé Nollet has ruined me."[69]

Nollet's commercial success and popularity in society did not brand him as a mere purveyor of cut-rate Enlightenment. To the contrary, in 1739 he won admission to the Académie royale des sciences. He had no significant discoveries to his name; he certainly had no familial clout to help him along in his peculiar career. It was on the basis of his abilities as an expositor and demonstrator that he achieved membership in the *académie;* his colleagues and the royal household deemed the diffusion of science a goal sufficiently worthy in its own right to merit inclusion in the little band of the king's philosophers.

The Enlightenment Nollet offered is not difficult to determine. After the fashion set by 'sGravesande and Desaguliers, Nollet determined in 1745 to publish the text of his lectures. When they appeared in print Nollet's version filled six octavo volumes of several hundred pages and several dozen illustrative plates each. In these texts we find the clear traces of lectures accompanied by three or four major pieces of apparatus in each of three sections. The great Dutch demonstrations of the latter part of the eighteenth century and the British lectures at the Royal Institution in the early part of the nineteenth would indeed become big business, an outlet for the commercialization of leisure in the industrializing societies that pioneered such enterprises. The elaborate preparations must elicit in the modern reader a sense of mass spectacle. Yet Nollet's illustrations and his tone retained the more intimate feel of the salon. The guests were entertained in the philosopher's apartments, seated at the experimental table next to the learned abbé, and served by assistants operating the heavier apparatus.

Like Rohault and Polinière before him, Nollet offered his course to a wide variety of audiences. The usual draw, it seems, included women and men from the polite society of Paris. Children were accommodated as well: The published version of the lectures, the *Leçons de physique expérimentale,* offered a graceful apology to those who have spent "a certain time in the world" for the apparent triviality of some observations and examples; the lectures were intended also for "young people of one or the other sex" to whom even the ordinary experience of daily adult life was mysterious.[70] Not the least of these was the crown prince of Nollet's early career, later Louis XVI: The title pages of Nollet's books were adorned with not only the title of academician but also "Tutor to the Dauphin." As heir to Polinière, Nollet achieved sufficient prestige to enlighten royalty.

The philosophical approach of the *Leçons* would likewise offer standard demonstration-lecture fare with a French accent. In the preface to the published version of the work, Nollet repeated the experimental philosopher's perpetual claim: "I present myself under no auspices but that of a philosophe; it isn't Cartesian Physics or Newtonian or Leibnizian that I have prescribed to follow particularly."[71] Yet the protestation can be taken no more literally than Newton's claim to frame no hypotheses. Nollet's own Cartesian leanings are as easy to glean from the preface as from the lessons that follow. Fontenelle, for example, he cited as "a *savant* well respected and well worthy of being so"; those interested in metaphysics, he suggested, might consult the *Recherche de la vérité*, which Malebranche had written. The formulaic philosophical disclaimer indicated simply that metaphysical considerations had no place in Nollet's own studies.[72] The physical aspects of the Cartesian world, however, Nollet assumed implicitly. His was a world filled with subtle matters as definitely as it contained air pumps and orreries. Consistent with the philosophy of the Enlightenment, however, Nollet did have an open mind toward Newtonian and Leibnizian formulations, as long as they did not challenge the basic tenets of his Cartesianism.

Like Polinière before him, Nollet began his discussion of mechanics with the principle of inertia, first formulated by Descartes: A body tends to remain at rest, or to remain in motion in a straight line, until something pushes it to move it or change the course of its motion. Yet the explanation and the experiment were rather more sophisticated than Polinière's version. Nollet followed Newton in arguing that the inertial property is proportional to the quantity of matter and used an apparatus suggested by Newton, whose priority he acknowledged: a massive ball hanging from a frame and a billiard ball hanging next to it. Nollet showed that the small object could strike the large one with considerable speed without producing any noticeable movement on the part of the larger one. The passage continued in a Newtonian vein. Nollet acknowledged that we do not ordinarily observe things continuing in motion but explained that they are generally retarded by the medium through which they move. Dropping balls into long tubes filled with water, Nollet showed that they soon slow down to some constant velocity. Again he turned to the works of Newton for theoretical justification, citing the proof in the second book of the *Principia* that objects moving through resisting media will lose half their velocity in a distance equal to two diameters of the object—a controversial claim, as it turns out, in the eyes of most of the mathematical mechanicians of the Cartesian persuasion.[73]

The collision of two moving bodies required an extensive theoretical preamble. The controversy between advocates of "quantity of motion" and those of the *vis viva,* or "living force," had not yet been resolved when Nollet began his lectures. In good French fashion, he expressed his own preference for the conservation of quantity of motion; an Enlightened demonstrator, he also acknowledged that there were strong arguments to be offered on the other side for the conservation of the living force. Unlike his Dutch and British colleagues, however, he did not present any empirical evidence for this position. Nollet adopted neither the new experiments devised by 'sGravesande to demonstrate the inadequacy of the Leibnizian view for collisions in which the impacting bodies stuck together nor those that illustrated the success of *vis viva* in explaining the impressions left by balls dropped into clay. In the first complete published edition of the *Leçons* in 1745, he suggested that readers seeking information on the Leibnizian point of view consult the *Institutions de physique,* which had been composed by "a woman as respectable by her enlightenment as by her birth."[74] Maintaining a polite decorum, he did not name his customer in the instrument trade, Émilie du Châtelet, as the author of that volume. She, like 'sGravesande in Holland, had come to believe that both the living force and the quantity of motion are conserved in different ways. Yet the Parisian lectures (or the text that survives) give the strong impression that living force is more a metaphysical than a physical concept.

The next lecture considered the motion of objects subject to "compound forces"—simultaneous forces in different directions—and "central forces." This theoretical material went well beyond the old Cartesian notion of the quantity of motion, perfected by Huygens and Mariotte at the *académie* two generations earlier and involved original equipment. Nollet's first apparatus might be titled "the marriage of billiards and croquet" (see Figure 6.9). It offered a clearer and more dependable illustration of compound motion than variations on Mariotte's collision apparatus used by most of the other lecturers. Two ivory-headed mallets were suspended from pivots on wooden arms that could be rotated so that the mallets could strike an ivory ball from any angle. The height to which the mallets were raised determined their speed as they struck the ball, converting the dead force of weight to the living force of motion. Thus Nollet could manage the quantity of motion applied to the ball from each direction. He noted that if the two mallets struck from equal angles on opposite sides of

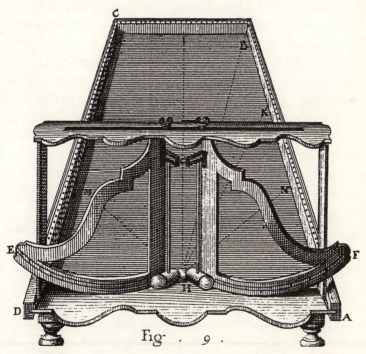

Fig . 9 .

Figure 6.9 Apparatus for demonstrating "compound forces." Reproduced from Jean Antoine Nollet, Leçons de physique expérimentale *(Paris, 1745), vol. 2, lesson 5, plate 2, figure 9, facing p. 24. Courtesy of the Bakken Library, Minneapolis, Minn.*

'the center line, and with the same speed, the ball would move down the center of the table. By launching the ball with the mallets directed at different angles, or moving with different speeds, or both, he could send the ball off in any direction he chose. Newton's theory, already translated into the French language and Leibnizian mathematical notation by Varignon, explained the demonstrations completely.

Given this understanding of bodies subject to two short-lived forces applied in different directions, Nollet turned to bodies subject to the continuous forces of their inertia and their weight. Just as two mallets directed the ball in the previous experiment, Nollet explained that an object thrown into the air feels a push in one direction from its inertia and in another from its weight. Rather than suffering an abrupt change in motion like that caused by collision, however, the object moved in a gradual curve, the change caused by continuous forces. Nollet repeated 'sGravesande's demonstration of a ball launched from a ramp, which jumped through hoops, for the delight of the spectators. An alternate demonstration used a small "cannon" mounted on a board that slid along two taut wires (see Figure 6.10). Nollet used a third wire to pull this apparatus along at a constant speed of about eight or ten feet per second—which required an extremely steady hand—and tripped a wire that fired the cannon while the motion continued. Throughout the trajectory, the ball's horizontal inertia carried it along above the board, which Nollet continued to pull with a constant speed. The spring sent the ball in a vertical direction, as if a mallet had struck it from below. The weight of the ball pressed it downward; it slowed, stopped, and finally fell back into the moving cannon. Nollet explained that the ball traced a parabola as it moved through the air. (A lecturer who produced this patter would look extremely silly if things did not transpire according to plan; Nollet required a considerable virtuosity to be able to get it right year after year.)

It is hard to imagine a series of experiments—leading from collinear collision through compound impacts to projectile motion—more thoroughly tied to the development in the first book of the Newton's *Principia*. Thus, although Nollet remained consistently Cartesian in his picture of the world, his view of mechanics in the lecture hall, if not in the heavens, followed the developments of British school. The exposition continued through a standard discussion of the rules gov-

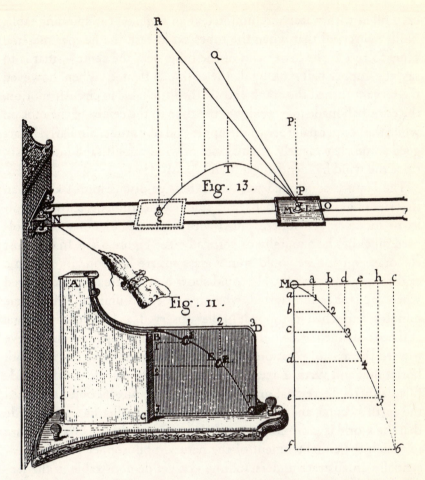

Figure 6.10 Apparatus for demonstrating the parabolic path of objects in free fall and graphical representations. Reproduced from Jean Antoine Nollet, Leçons de physique expérimentale (Paris, 1745), vol. 2, lesson 5, plate 5, facing p. 42. Courtesy of the Bakken Library, Minneapolis, Minn.

erning circular motion, presented in much the same manner as Rohault had done for the ladies and gentlemen of his generation.

Like Rohault and Huygens three-quarters of a century earlier, Nollet used the rules of circular motion as his point of departure in his explanation of the cause of gravity, explicitly citing the theory of great celestial whirlpools that Descartes had "ingeniously imagined."[75] Nollet also mounted new attachments to his rotational apparatus. Two tubes, one containing a cork and the other a copper ball, were each filled with water and mounted at an angle on the spinning table. Nollet observed that when the tubes sat at rest, the heavier material came to rest at the lower end of the tube, near the center—that is to say, the copper ball sank while the cork ball floated. When, however, the servant turned the crank and set the little table in circular motion, the cork ball made its way down the tube to the center of the motion while the copper ball rose to the upper end of its tube. Similarly, he argued somewhat vaguely, a whirlpool of wind can lift sand into the air, since the wind has centrifugal force.[76]

The lecture concluded with an extensive discussion of Cartesian theories of gravity. Another series of lovely instruments allowed Nollet to rotate crystal spheres filled with water and bits of wax or colored oil either horizontally or vertically (see Figure 6.11). In the most elaborate version he could spin a glass sphere horizontally within a cage that spun vertically. He could show how the floating bits moved when the circulation started, when it proceeded uniformly for some minutes, and when it stopped. Nollet observed, as Huygens had done at the Académie royale des sciences, that the floating bits could move toward the axis of rotation—Nollet could demonstrate this for both horizontal and vertical axes—but not toward the center of the fluid-filled sphere. Terrestrial gravitation of course directs objects toward the earth's center and not toward its axis, so Nollet had to concede that the world is more complicated than his models. This was one case in which the enlightenment of the natural philosopher remained essentially an abstract understanding, not yet demonstrable in the lecture hall:

> While these hypotheses and these experiments that we have just repeated don't have the advantage of explaining in a satisfactory manner how sublunary bodies tend toward the center of the earth, nonetheless we know, beyond doubt, that a fluid material which circulates can precipitate not only light bodies, but also heavy ones. If this principle, which is incontestable, has not yet been applied with happy results, that is not a reason to despair that it cannot be one day. It seems more reasonable to believe this than other things.[77]

The "other things" looming on the French horizon were, of course, the Newtonian theory of universal gravitation. Nollet acknowledged

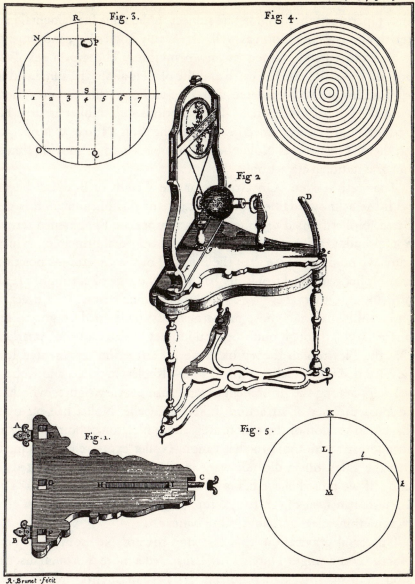

A. Brunet fecit

Figure 6.11 Nollet's apparatus for demonstrating the gravitational vortex with water and bits of wax in a spinning glass globe. This plate is similar to a more crowded one in the Leçons de physique expérimentale. *Compare this apparatus to Hauksbee's electrical machine (see Figure 6.3). Reproduced from* Histoire de l'Académie royale des sciences, avec les Mémoires de Mathématique et de Physique *(1741), plate 4, facing p. 198. Courtesy of the Bakken Library, Minneapolis, Minn.*

that superlunary bodies must be subject to the same fundamental materials and laws of motion as well: "Heavenly bodies have movements which must be explained on my principles. The moon revolves around the earth, and the earth and the planets about the sun, making revolutions so well regulated that an astronomer understands them with the utmost precision."[78] Their motions, too, Nollet assured his auditors, must be explained in terms of the central forces that operate on them. These forces Nollet believed to be caused by moving fluids, not gravitational attraction.

The sixth lesson, "On Gravity or the Weight of Bodies," began with the acknowledgment that the cause of this phenomenon is debated. Nollet framed the question in appropriate Enlightened terms. Some think gravity is an "inherent and primordial principle," which can have no other cause than the free will of the Creator—a position that Nollet remarked ironically had the advantage of cutting short all difficulties. Others (here we count Nollet) think that it is the effect of an invisible material whose properties must be learned (in good Empiricist style) through philosophical inquiry. As an aside he remarked that the Newtonian theory of universal attraction represented less novelty that was usually ascribed to it—Kepler, Frenicle, and Roberval were among the prominent seventeenth-century figures who had adopted theories of attraction. Like Fontenelle, Nollet had his own Cartesian version of the canon. Regarding Newton, whom he saw as an interesting footnote to that canon, Nollet expressed puzzlement that the Englishman did not want his attractionist view imputed to him, "if we must believe his own claims" to abjure hypotheses. The Cartesian analysis of centrifugal forces, he went on, must at least give us something clear and physical to believe.

Universal gravitation, that last step toward Newtonianism embraced by the Anglo-Dutch school, inspired a more thorough discussion than *vis viva* had required. As perhaps befits the practical demonstrator, the argument was at first essentially based on simple observation—although it rather quickly assumed an ad hominem character. Nollet observed that dropping objects in open spaces doesn't tell us much about free fall, since their fall will be diminished by air resistance. Only in the confines of the air pump are simple observations accurate; there, all things always fall according to the same laws. Now, the lecturer went on, Newton had argued that objects fall toward the earth because of some hidden power and that objects falling from points farther from the surface of the earth must fall at a slower rate than those dropped near the earth. He had dared to predict this diminution in weight mathematically, claiming that a stone dropped from the height of the moon would fall 3,600 times more slowly than one dropped from the surface of the earth. Nollet, in what seems to have been a sincere effort to understand how such an intellect as Newton could have misled himself so egregiously, referred to experiments of which Newton knew. British observers had dropped objects from the top of St. Paul's Cathedral and timed the period of free fall. Nollet assured his auditors that such descents must necessarily have taken longer than Galileo's rules had predicted, because even the massive objects dropped at St. Paul's must have been slowed by air resistance. This result might lead the incautious observer to believe that the rate fall from this great height was a bit smaller than expected, and to extrapolate this misunderstanding all the way to the sphere of the moon. Were it not that Newton had never made such an argument, Nollet's analysis might have provided a serendipitous explanation for the formulation of the law of universal gravitation—a formulation that in Cartesian eyes needed more to be explained away than to be explained.

Having determined, at least implicitly, why Newton might have imagined a need to see the gravity of bodies decrease as they were placed farther from the surface of the earth, Nollet spent a few moments to refute the notion. The fundamental problem, Nollet suggested, was that for an object to move in a circular path there had to be two balanced central forces, one pointing out and the other pointing in. The *centrifugal* force, the one that presses the object outward, is supplied by the matter of the body itself, its tendency to move in a straight line, pulling away from the center of the circle. The *centripetal* force, the force that pulls the body toward the center of motion, must balance this outward tendency inherent in the matter of the body. Yet Newton claimed that it is the matter of the body itself, the very thing that supplies the centrifugal force, that also supplies the centripetal force. One could say in anachronistic terms that Nollet grasped the fact that Newton claimed that the inertial mass and the gravitational mass of a body are the same thing. Since these two sorts of mass have opposite effects, Nollet felt justified in dismissing the claim as absurd. (Were it not that Newton's claim is true, this logic would undoubtedly serve as an excellent argument against it.)

The great debate concerning universal gravitation that so fascinates those who would analyze the mind of the Enlightenment was a real one. It was not a question for which the experimental philosophers could provide a demonstration, and on this one question even these radical Empiricists offered arguments essentially philosophical. It seems that the only hypothesis that either side framed concerned the cause of gravity; it was Nollet who offered the most extensive series of experiments to try to demonstrate the mechanism in which he believed—fluid whirlpools—to his audience. Yet the tenor of Nollet's argument was hardly that of a Cartesian ideologue railing against a self-evident truth. Most important, it was a single item of disagreement. Otherwise, the Parisian lecturer shared the main tenets of what might be identified as Newtonian experimental philosophy in the Anglo-Dutch tradition. He adopted the radical Empiricism visible in Desaguliers, 'sGravesande, and Musschenbroek. In the same way as the Newtonians, he presented a picture of the world that took as its paradigm the mechanics of ordinary bodies like billiard balls and croquet mallets. In the other great debate, the quantity of motion versus *vis viva,* he took the same side as the Newtonians, against the Leibnizians—all the while recognizing the possibility that the latter might have something worthwhile to offer.

Once again, however, we are getting ahead of our story. The relationship between Newtonianism and Cartesianism is a different problem from the demonstration of Enlightenment offered in the eighteenth-century lecture hall. Both schools offered Locke's successors a better reason to believe in the truth of natural philosophy than the testimony of experts. The philosophically curious ladies and gentlemen in Louis XV's Paris could witness, without recourse to sophisticated mathematics, the way in which natural philosophy correctly predicted the motion of bodies and the behavior of light. Lectures opened windows into the far-off worlds of the planets or the tiny realms visible through the microscope. They made manifest the power of chemistry to produce thunder and of the air pump to discover the world of the void, which is in many ways more natural than our own.

The debate over the cause of weight, insofar as it was not simply a philosophical dispute, was a problem in theoretical astronomy. Yet

Nollet took up the question of Newtonian gravitation at the end of his extensive series of lectures on mechanics. Astronomy, by contrast, he put forth as a primarily observational rather than a theoretical exercise. The field was rendered simpler, Nollet suggested, through the device of the "planetarium," or "orrery," the clockwork mechanism that carried little painted balls representing the planets about a large, central ball representing the sun. After acknowledging that such instruments had been perfected by "the late Dr. Desaguliers," Nollet went on in characteristic form: "I can't avoid saying that the planetarium I use has a very considerable advantage over the moving spheres made in France and elsewhere for fifty or sixty years."[79] In his lectures Nollet used a magnificent model five feet in diameter; he was willing to sell copies or a more modest two-foot-diameter version for more private settings.[80] That is to say, the only dispute concerning astronomical theory that surfaced in the interchange between Nollet and his Anglo-Dutch rivals concerned the commercial value of their instruments.

The conflict between the Newtonians and the Cartesians, often touted as the first salvo of the Enlightenment, appears to have influenced the astronomy implanted in the mind of the Enlightenment not at all. Those who called on Nollet's salon came away with the same Copernican picture of the solar system as did the auditors at Desaguliers's lectures. Otherwise, the essential elements of Nollet's demonstrations were practically identical to those of the Anglo-Dutch experimental philosophers. The picture of the universe emerging from the lecture hall did significantly elaborate that drawn in Fontenelle's *Conversations on the Plurality of Worlds* and his *Histoires* of the *académie*. A reader could construct in her mind a physical world rooted in the great Cartesian system; if the popular expositions did not provide all the details of that system, they provided enough examples that she could believe herself competent to understand them. Both Desaguliers and Nollet supplemented this vague but firm fundament with an essentially empirical view of the world.

This transition from the science Fontenelle presented for the benefit of polite society in Louis XIV's Paris to the Enlightenment demonstrated by Polinière and Nollet resulted from internal developments in eighteenth-century experimental philosophy. The experimental philosophers, to be sure, include a number of thinkers who described themselves as Newtonians, but the primary meaning of that label was the Enlightenment ideal of Empiricism, adopted by the Cartesian lecturers as well. Members of both philosophical camps on the one hand denied their membership in any ideological school and on the other explicitly embraced accomplishments of the Cartesians, the Leibnizians, and the Newtonians. All represented the ideal that Enlightened thinkers advocated, to reject ideology in favor of the senses and to reject authority in favor of reasoned judgment.

Even as the middle of the century drew near, the Enlightenment already well and irrevocably launched, it was possible to be a natural philosopher, an experimentalist, a popular public figure revered by Voltaire, and a Cartesian. Universal gravitation is not the only path to Enlightenment. The acceptance of natural philosophy as an exemplar for human understanding did not emerge uniquely from Locke's reading of Newton—perhaps, if we believe Desaguliers, it did not emerge by that route at all. Instead it became an idea in the air, discovered continuously and repeatedly, evolving in France as well as in England—in Fontenelle's literary assurances, in Polinière's demonstrations, and again in Nollet's, in the fashions followed by the ladies and gentlemen of their Paris, and in the philosophical instruments and cabinets displayed throughout the kingdom. That is to say simply that the Enlightenment was French as well as English.

7

The Discovery of the Newtonian World; or, Flattening the Poles if not the Cartesians

NOLLET'S SKEPTICAL VIEW of Newton's theory of gravity does not fit the classical historiography of the Enlightenment. The standard story of the scientific revolution as told in general histories and by the traditional history of ideas skips rather hastily from the mathematical triumphs of the seventeenth century to the complete description of the solar system achieved by what is generally known as classical physics. According to this historiography, the greatest task of the eighteenth century was the Newtonians' convincing Cartesian ideologues in France of the truth of universal gravitation despite an ignorance and prejudice bordering on infamy. This process of forcible paradigm shift is broadly associated with the French Enlightenment, a movement more properly literary and cultural than scientific. The liberalism of the Enlightenment, like universal gravitation in science, was essentially a British import: This political philosophy was rooted in the writings of John Locke, just as the new science was rooted in the *Principia* of Sir Isaac Newton. The purpose of the present chapter is to understand how it was that Paris became Newtonian—to what extent the philosophes, the writers who formed the core of the French Enlightenment, followed Locke and "became Newtonian without the help of geometry."

Part of the difficulty in understanding the way in which Newtonianism insinuated itself into the Parisian scene derives from the fact that the role of natural philosophy was tremendously complex by the time the new British science arrived. We have observed Cartesianism as a technical framework for solving problems in mathematical physics, as a cosmological system that allowed people to make sense of their physical world, as a literary device and a subject of polite conversation, and as a requisite of a cultivated individual in a highly mannered society and an avenue of social progress into that society. It has been the object of this book to show how the interplay of these various aspects of Cartesianism made a scientific worldview part of Western culture in the Age of Reason. During the first generation of the Enlightenment, roughly contemporary with Desaguliers, 'sGravesande, and Nollet, the central role played by Cartesian natural philosophy in all aspects of Parisian elite culture was challenged by Newtonian analogues. Newtonianism remained a technical approach to mathematical science, to be sure. Yet it also became a metaphor for the liberal political philosophy of the Enlightenment, a source of literary allusion and polite conversation, and a route into both the Académie royale des sciences and the salon culture of Louis XV's Paris. This chapter will offer a brief sketch of the story, not so much to add to the historical record as to interpret it in light of the understanding suggested in the preceding chapters of what science was.

The French Enlightenment was a sufficiently diffuse movement that it is often characterized through the examination of a single individual rather than through the statement of generalities. In literary circles the place of the paradigmatic philosophe is almost always assigned to Voltaire. Ernst Cassirer, seeking a symbol for the "mind of the Enlightenment," chose Jean Le Rond d'Alembert as his representative, largely owing to d'Alembert's multiple roles as a mathematical prodigy delving into questions of the celestial mechanics, as a literary lion at the Académie française and in the salons, and as an editor and champion of the great *Encyclopédie*. The present account will likewise adopt a single, representative character as a sort of tour guide through the first generation of the Enlightenment in France, a member of the little flock of philosophes who all knew one another so well. Our window into the mind of the Enlightenment will be Gabrielle Émilie Le Tonnier de Breteuil, Marquise du Châtelet.

Émilie du Châtelet
and the Mind of the Enlightenment

Émilie de Breteuil[1] grew up in the world of the salons. Her parents' house was an important literary salon; the middle-aged Fontenelle called there on Thursdays during her childhood, and the young Voltaire was an occasional visitor. Émilie de Breteuil was given a proper literary education, largely by her parents. Her father tutored her in Latin and Italian; her mother's salon provided an incomparable education in French poetry and prose. The girl also studied English—a language more studious than recreational, as Fontenelle's remarks in the *Conversations on the Plurality of Worlds* might indicate. The young Émilie further took up mathematics and natural philosophy. The family friendship with Fontenelle makes his novel a rather obvious guess as a source for this study, although the details of this aspect of her education are no clearer than the vague statements about her introduction to French and foreign literature.

In 1725, the nineteen-year-old Émilie married the Marquis du Châtelet. It was an arranged alliance, which Mme du Châtelet maintained—despite what is always described as a genuine lifelong mutual spousal affection—simultaneously with a series of lovers. This sort of arrangement was fairly common in France in the eighteenth century, and indeed Mme du Châtelet's sustained affair (and even longer cohabitation) with Voltaire was quite public and quasi-official, and in the mores of the time reasonably respectable. The two played cards as a couple at the royal table and shared an apartment in the complex at Versailles. In an age in which the male aristocracy was excused, in light of the political nature of marriage, for its official and its casual womanizing, Mme du Châtelet played by the same rules. She was a manizer. She was also a passionate student of mathematics, physics, and metaphysics, a stunningly successful character on the social scene in Paris and at court, an inveterate gambler (often of Voltaire's money), a fluent speaker of Italian and English, and an accomplished Latinist. There is a great debate in the literature concerning the quality of her appearance—one can hardly imagine such discussion of a man, and it is hard to understand why it matters. Clearly she did not rely on her looks to make her way in the world, and her looks did not impede her progress. It was her intellect, character, and social éclat (as it was the intellect, character, and social éclat of her male contemporaries) that established her at the heart of the little flock of the philosophes.

With her husband posted to administrative or military duty most of the time, Mme du Châtelet took up permanent residence in his house in Paris during the early 1730s. She became one of the most popular women in the social scene of the *salonières*. A dazzling conversationalist, discreetly erudite, vivacious and energetic, she played the appropriately updated role of Molière's learned ladies. She also could be, when she chose, ridiculously *précieuse*. Following the standard formula, she acquired first her *bel esprit*, then her geometer, and finally an acquaintance with the abbé Nollet. Her first public affair was with a notorious older gentleman and has no particular bearing on our story. She soon met the mathematician Pierre Louis Moreau de Maupertuis. Shortly after her permanent settlement in Paris, Mme du Châtelet sought Maupertuis's services as a tutor in mathematics and physics. She also took him as a lover and made something of a scene when she tried to get seating with him in a fashionable café that served only men. Indeed, she had to come back dressed in men's clothing (which fooled no one) to accomplish this feat. The couple then carried on an animated discussion about geometry. The escapade made a wonderful story around Paris.[2]

Maupertuis[3] had joined the Académie royale des sciences in 1723 at the age of twenty-five. He had taken up natural philosophy and mathematics when he was about twenty, having first rejected philosophy and tried his hand at music. By the time he joined the *académie*, he had to his credit not only a formidable mathematical reputation but also a minor research paper on the anatomy of salamanders. Like Nollet, Maupertuis had traveled to England to learn what he could of the British scientific scene. He returned from this voyage in 1728 as the first serious mathematician in France to embrace Newton's celestial mechanics. He also parlayed his position in the *académie* into an entrée to the world of the salons.

The technical details of Mme du Châtelet's early studies are not well known; they must be inferred from the work of her teachers. In 1732 Maupertuis published the first significant extension to Newton's work, a *Discourse on the Different Shapes of Stars*. The book aimed primarily at determining the shape of the earth in a manner reminiscent of Varignon's Newtonizing—it translated the peculiar British mathematics into the more familiar notation of Leibniz and expanded the development in ways that were, perhaps, a bit easier in the continental than the English style. Fontenelle's introductory description in the *académie's Histoire* for 1732 captured the essence of the technique, which would be developed more and more extensively through the course of the eighteenth century. Fontenelle described how Maupertuis, in his calculations of the shape of a rotating star, considered the behavior of an infinitesimal bit of matter—an "atom"—located on the surface of the star. This technique allowed the calculation of the attraction of the large body for the atom on its surface while ignoring the effect of the infinitesimal piece on the large body.[4] Calculating the effect of increasing layers on the formation of the body, the French disciple determined with much greater precision than Newton had done the geometrical form that a uniform blob of rotating liquid would assume when subjected to the centrifugal force of its spinning and to the gravitational attraction described by Newton's law.

Mme du Châtelet began her studies with Maupertuis at precisely the time he prepared this first book of French Newtonianism. She proved a capable student. Although biographers feel compelled to point out that she made no significant original contributions herself to the mathematical mechanics of the eighteenth century, it is clear that she could speak intelligently with those who did. This is not to damn her with faint praise; those with whom she conversed on technical questions of mathematics and mechanics were among the most brilliant of her generation and indeed among the most rigidly mathematical physicists of the eighteenth century. Her competence exceeded not only that of more literary philosophes like Voltaire but also Nollet's and that of the other experimental philosophers discussed in Chapter 6. As will appear in the present discussion, she assimilated what she learned, she engaged in published commentary and debate, and she provoked considerable response in the learned community.

After a few years with her first tutor, as their romantic relationship for a time soured, Maupertuis suggested that Mme du Châtelet might look to another mathematician, Alexis-Claude Clairaut,[5] for assistance. Clairaut had studied with Maupertuis's teacher, one Father Le Castel; it seems likely that the elder student promoted the younger one's interests at the *académie*. The two were certainly close friends.

Clairaut read his first *mémoire* to the *académie* about the time Maupertuis joined the body, in 1725. Clairaut was at the time twelve. Only a year later, he took up with the Société des arts, the short-lived institution where Nollet had won his introduction to the scientific community. This association was the first of many in which Clairaut was accepted, apparently as an equal, in a group of men virtually all twice his age. By the time he was sixteen he had proven himself among the greatest mathematical minds in France; the *académie* put him forward for membership, although the minimum age for admission was officially twenty. The crown refused to confirm the appointment before the young man reached his eighteenth birthday in 1731.

In 1734, Mme du Châtelet turned to Clairaut as her new instructor in mathematics. Suffice it to say for the present that the lessons that he prepared for his first advanced student would be published as the *Elements of Geometry*—a title borrowed from Euclid, whose *Elements* has been the most famous mathematics textbook (perhaps the most famous textbook in any field) in the history of Western thought. In this polished form, Clairaut's became the standard advanced introduction to the subject, the first step along the road to Newtonian celestial mechanics for two generations of physicists. Mme du Châtelet clearly mastered its contents. She also formed a genuine friendship with the shy young man who wrote it—Clairaut in fact brought about a reconciliation between his new student and her first teacher. The three of them shared both social and intellectual conversation; Clairaut and Maupertuis were frequent visitors at both her town and country houses.

Mme du Châtelet thus got off to a early start as a French Newtonian. What that meant at the time was to take an interest in the mathematical consequences of universal gravitation, investigated through the methods of Leibniz's calculus. At this stage, even Fontenelle took the exercise as no more serious a threat to Cartesianism than Varignon had posed. Maupertuis, Clairaut, and Mme du Châtelet, to be sure, had a very different view. They believed they were doing physics. They did not adopt Varignon's concern about how a world might operate in which there was a central force proportional to the third or forth or fifth power of the distance from the center. They believed that Newton's inverse square law described the universe as it is—that disciplined, directed development of the analysis of the forces and motions it predicted would lead to a complete solution to the solar system.

Just as important as this technical paradigm was the social status of the membership of the little community of Newtonian thinkers. Theirs was not a fanatical revolutionary cell, either inside the *académie* or in the larger world of the Parisian elite. Maupertuis had encountered his stunning student in the social world of the salons and he continued to move in those circles; his biographers often remarked that he remained popular with the ladies of polite society. Mme du Châtelet, too, continued as a lioness of the salons; her relations with Fontenelle, the Cartesian secretary of the *académie,* remained cordial. Newtonianism in this academic and social setting (for the spheres intersected in the circles of the salons) was no more outré than Cartesianism had been when it first entered the *académie* under the leadership of Chapelain, Huygens, and Claude Perrault.

This innocent Newtonianism in the context of Louis XV's France was not to continue. The young writer François Arouet, who took the pen name Voltaire[6] in 1718 at the age of twenty, would shatter Fontenelle's world in a number of ways more serious than the challenge offered by Mme du Châtelet and her tutors. During the early 1720s Voltaire made quite a reputation and a surprisingly substantial income as a poet and playwright in Paris; he managed to win a pension from the crown like those that Chapelain had handed out in Fontenelle's youth. He moved in the same salon circles as Fontenelle—the two apparently met chez Breteuil at a fairly early stage in the younger man's career. In a style reminiscent of the *précieux* during the minority of Louis XIV, Voltaire pushed the bounds of polite behavior during the minority of Louis XV. His first significant indiscretion was a poem that celebrated a widely circulated scandal of the regent's incestuous affair with his daughter. Yet Voltaire played by the rules—the poem was clever rather than vicious; the poet denied his authorship in a formally plausible manner; following the peculiar logic of the old regime he nonetheless agreed to a short and reasonably civilized imprisonment in the Bastille and a seemly exile from Paris, only to return and resume his literary success. By the time he reached his middle twenties, he seemed destined for the life of a courtier sufficiently brilliant to get away with a certain naughtiness.

All this *précieuse politesse* came to an end in 1726 when Voltaire aimed eloquent insults at a young chevalier called Rohan, who was clearly his social superior. Voltaire undoubtedly expected a clumsy response in kind; he might even have feared a duel. In the event, however, he suffered injury, insult, and ignomy. The poet was hauled away from the dinner table of a duke, who sat by apparently undisturbed by the proceedings; in the street in front of the house he was beaten up by Rohan's servants. The insulted gentleman supervised the thrashing from his carriage and then drove away—soon to file charges of public nuisance against the injured commoner, who ended up back in the Bastille because of the ordeal and then in exile in England. In the parlance of the newest Left, such an incident is bound to radicalize a person.

Voltaire's radicalization did not bring about a rejection of literary or courtly ambition. Nor did it drive him into the timidity of seeking the security of the eighteenth-century equivalent of academic tenure. Instead, it instilled in him a tremendous intellectual courage, a resolve to hate what is evil and to speak out from the privileged position his talent and the tremendous wealth it generated would earn for him. This debonair and cultivated Frenchman had little trouble establishing himself in intellectual circles in England. Within eight months of his arrival there in 1726 he won an introduction to King George I; a few months later he attended Newton's funeral at Westminster Abbey—one of the most sought after tickets of the season. He spoke in English, he wrote in English, he studied English literature and manners and political philosophy, and he became the leading French Anglophile of the eighteenth century. He again parlayed his literary capabilities into considerable income and invested successfully.

Having arrived bruised in body and ego, Voltaire breathed in England an air at once rusticated and free. He delighted in the liberties extended by the government to his hosts and in the toleration they extended to their fellows. In his fascination with the British there was a certain disdain for the coarseness of their manners and especially for their literature—it is not clear whether the French will ever accept the graveyard scene from *Hamlet*—and something of the bewilderment Fontenelle had shown when he wrote in the *Conversations on the Plurality of Worlds* of the serious Englishmen overly concerned with politics. In Voltaire's case, however, the bitter experience of the chastening rod inspired a respectful study of the political philosophy of the British rather than the bemused dismissal that Fontenelle had offered.

Voltaire returned to France in 1728. Despite his intellectual transformation, his style of life changed not at all. Once again, he established himself in the center of Parisian society. He set about making a great monetary fortune—in part through a lottery scheme worked out with the assistance of the Maupertuis's colleague Charles-Marie de La Condamine, an early student of probability.[7] In 1733, he met Mme du Châtelet; the two immediately fell in love. (Indeed, this relationship contributed to the tension between her and Maupertuis, initiating Clairaut's lessons.) Among the many things they shared was a fascination with things English in general, and with Newton's science in particular. Voltaire continued to press at the boundaries of intellectual propriety. Mme du Châtelet met him just as the publication of his *Letters Concerning the English Nation* had thrust him again to the center of controversy. Within a year of their encounter, she felt compelled to provide him with a safe refuge at Cirey, an abandoned estate owned by her husband's family. A year later she decided to leave Paris (and a renewed affair with Maupertuis) to join the poet at her husband's ancestral home. The couple settled down, indulged in the great eighteenth-century vogue of remodeling, and (as we have already seen) set up a large laboratory eventually furnished at great expense with instruments by Nollet. They filled their home with visitors both literary and scientific. And to a large extent they presided over the construction of French Enlightenment Newtonianism.

Voltaire had composed his series of *Letters Concerning the English Nation* upon his return to Paris, although he withheld publication until 1732. This tremendously influential book introduced the virtues of British liberalism to France, turning its precepts into the basis for the European Enlightenment. Voltaire opened his exposition of English ways with four letters about the Quakers, not so much because he admired them (although, in a strange way, he did), as because he admired the English for tolerating them. From this example of toleration in action—so different from France after the revocation of the Edict of Nantes—he moved on to the Parliament, the government, and thence to the free commerce of the British Isles. Through all these letters, he wrote as if still abroad, offering his compatriots something between a travelogue and an anthropological study of an inscrutable people. Yet his admiration for the liberal alternative to the decadent absolutist state he had left was obvious.

It was in the history of ideas that Voltaire saw the reasons for British liberalism. Voltaire conflated Bacon's accomplishments with those of the whole seventeenth century, praising the Lord Chancellor as "the father of experimental philosophy."[8] In this intellectual progression, which Voltaire imagined to be full of empirical information, he placed the nongeometrical Newtonian, John Locke. From Locke and his empirical philosophy, Voltaire moved on (backward through time) to Newton, the provider of the great analysis of observations that would lead to an understanding of the physical world:

> A Frenchman who arrives in London finds things as much changed in philosophy as in all the rest. He left the world full; he finds it empty. In Paris, he saw the world composed of whirlpools of subtle matter; in London, he doesn't see them at all. Among us, it was the pressure of the moon which caused the tides; among the English, it is the sea which weighs toward the moon, in a way that when you [in France] believe that the moon makes the tide high, these gentlemen believe the tide must be low; which unhappily cannot be verified, since it would be necessary, in order to clarify the matter, to examine the earth and the moon at the first instant of creation. . . . In Paris, you shape the earth like a melon; in England, it is flattened at both ends.[9]

Voltaire went on in a series of three letters to compare Newton's physics to Descartes's in the same favorable light in which he compared Locke's commonsense philosophy to Cartesian metaphysics. The main point of contention in questions of astronomy to which Voltaire addressed his second letter came in the theory of universal gravitation.[10] He began with the famous account of Newton's epiphany in the garden: Apples fall toward the earth according to Galileo's law; why shouldn't the moon obey the same law? This led Newton to calculate the rate at which the moon "falls" toward the earth as it describes its orbit. Reflection on this question inspired the law of universal gravitation.

Voltaire suggested that despite his brilliant deduction, Newton ran into problems.

> They had in England only very poor measurements of our globe; people used the uncertain estimate of sailors, counting sixty English miles to the degree, while there are really nearly seventy. This false calculation

didn't agree with the results Newton expected to find, and he abandoned the work. A poor philosopher who cared only for his own vanity would have made the measure of the earth fit his system one way or another. Newton preferred to abandon his project. But as soon as Picard measured the earth exactly, tracing the meridian which gave such honor to France, Newton returned to his earlier ideas, and found his calculations in accord with Picard's.[11]

Again, at least by implication, Newton reversed the Cartesian procedure. He put empirical data ahead of theory—even when his theory was correct and the empirical data turned out to be wrong. The Cartesian system builders, by contrast, constructed a world filled with the materials that they imagined their theories required.

It is also worth noting in passing that Voltaire counted Picard's as the first of a long series of eighteenth-century geographical measurements that supported the Newtonian system. According to the first generation of philosophes and Newtonian astronomers, the truth of universal gravitation was not so much calculated as it was discovered. The theory was there before Picard set out to make his measurements of the meridian; his surveying party found the evidence for the British theory in the same way that they might have found a lake or a mineral deposit. Again, this geographical procedure reversed the Cartesian system in the *Meteorology* or Descartes's old *Principia*, where the theory of the formation of the earth "discovered" that mineral deposits ought to lie at the feet of mountains—the usual locations for mines.

Voltaire, in short, found in the Newtonian world technical accomplishments that were linked broadly to a Lockean philosophical stance. Like Fontenelle's connection between Cartesian science and absolutist politics in the previous generation, this new conjunction of philosophies natural and political justified the politics of the author. A world at once unfettered by unreasonable deference toward the nobility and uncluttered by whirlpools of subtle matters allowed the dignified simplicity of the Quakers and the mathematically elegant simplicity of the law of universal gravitation. The new connection was as subtle in the *Letters Concerning the English Nation* as the old one had been in the *Conversations on the Plurality of Worlds;* once again, the analysis of the position must seem clumsy in comparison to its initial assertion.

The style of Newtonianism adopted at Cirey, with this additional philosophical burden, was significantly different from what Mme du Châtelet had studied with Maupertuis and Clairaut. Her work after she began her long relationship with Voltaire took on an increasingly philosophical tone. Nor was her intellectual interchange with Voltaire's Lockeanism the only way in which she broadened her understanding of natural philosophy. During the middle 1730s, she attended Nollet's lectures. These she apparently fitted into her picture of a Newtonian world, for both Mme du Châtelet and Voltaire continued their rhetoric in support of the British natural philosopher even as they expressed their admiration and affection for Nollet. As we have seen, experimentalists of every stripe joined Newton in the rhetorical rejection of hypotheses. Alongside the sort of mathematical translation and elaboration of Newton's celestial mechanics practiced by Mme du Châtelet and her math tutors, then, we see a style of experimental philosophy that we must characterize as more generally that of the eighteenth century than of Newton. Although there is no particular inconsistency between the theory of universal gravitation and the mathematical analysis of motion on the one hand, and experimental philosophy as practiced in the first half of the eighteenth century on the other, there is no particularly significant connection between them either.

The laboratory at Cirey indeed consisted mostly of the sort of demonstration apparatus examined in the previous chapter. From an early date they kept a magic lantern—a slide projector—with which to amuse their guests. Clearly, Mme du Châtelet and the poet she protected adopted Nollet as the exemplar for the experimental philosopher. Their substantial orders discussed in the previous chapter arrived during the very period in which Nollet prepared his *Programme* of lectures along with the apparatus catalog. The philosophical enlightenment that his apparatus demonstrated included subtle matters along with simple observation. The battle between the Cartesians and the Newtonians—between the corrupt absolutists and the tolerant liberals—was fought out in Voltaire's books, not Nollet's. It was Voltaire, insisting that he was following the English master as he manipulated Nollet's machines, who acted the part of the ideologue.

The militant Newtonianism adopted by Voltaire had no particular effect on the experimental program Mme du Châtelet shared with him at Cirey. It appears that they, like the Parisian lecturer they knew and teased, concentrated more upon demonstrating what was known than investigating what was not. Even when the installation did produce one fling of attempted original research, it had no discernible Newtonian flavor. The Académie royale des sciences set a prize problem in 1736 concerning the nature of fire. Voltaire determined to win it and spent considerable effort weighing things, burning them, and weighing the residues—fairly standard sorts of experiments—with the confusing results that materials sometimes gain weight and sometimes lose it when subjected to the indignities of fire. He wrote up his results anyway and went through the elaborate ritual of submitting them anonymously to the *académie*. This style of research owed a certain amount to the work of the Dutch chemist Hermann Boerhaave,[12] but bore no more particularly Newtonian stamp than did the work of the Dutch demonstrators considered in Chapter 6.

Mme du Châtelet, meanwhile, determined to compose her own essay for the competition. Not wishing to upset Voltaire, she kept her work a secret from him. She eschewed the laboratory, wrote late at night (without more than a few hours' sleep), and conspired with her husband to manage her own anonymous submission. The *Dissertation on the Nature of Fire,* which resulted from her nocturnal recreations, nonetheless has the tone of experimental philosophy in the style of Nollet and the other demonstrators of Enlightenment.[13]

The essay began with a series of "experiments"—mostly observations from common experience—concerning the relations between light and heat. These preliminaries allowed Mme du Châtelet to dismiss the Cartesian notion that light is a manifestation in the second matter of what we call fire, and heat a similar manifestation in the first matter.[14] She assured her readers that she introduced this idea only because it was current. The real investigation, observations of the phenomena, followed. It is worth noting that Mme du Châtelet offered a perfectly Enlightened discussion, based on Locke's sensationalist philosophy and on empirical claims, without any new experiments performed especially for her own investigation. The cry of Empiricism embraced the recitation of facts from everyday experience as well as the results of new research from the laboratory.

The collection of relevant facts mimics the method Bacon suggested in his *New Organon.* Bacon's single example of philosophical research presented in that book had considered the nature of heat and presented a lengthy list of examples as a sort of model for the *Dissertation on the Nature of Fire*. Like Bacon, Mme du Châtelet gathered not only straightforward instances of fire but also those that might mislead the naïve researcher. She began this table of instances with the rays of the moon and phosphorescent materials, which present us with examples of light in the absence of heat. Conversely, she observed, metals often display heat without any light. Other tricky differences must be considered as well. Light is transmitted in straight lines, whereas heat diffuses through bodies; light can be extinguished instantaneously, whereas heat always persists for some time.[15] These Baconian tables presented an empirical style no more successful than Voltaire's combustion experiments, but just as philosophically correct.

Observations of this sort would have been at home as preliminary material in Nollet's lectures as well as in Mme du Châtelet's investigation. The mind of the Enlightenment was by no means entirely British. Yet the *Dissertation on the Nature of Fire* did move on through the series of authors Voltaire had named in his *Letters Concerning the English Nation*. The discussion that Mme du Châtelet presented next turned to the senses, passing from Bacon to Locke.[16] She urged empirical research but stressed the need for caution. Borrowing the standard example, she noted that when we first place our hands in separate vessels of hot and cold water and then quickly move them to a lukewarm vessel, the cold hand senses hot water, the other cold. Mme du Châtelet warned that the senses might deceive, that heat can be measured only with a thermometer. Moreover, she noted that the two attributes of fire, heat and light, are perceived by different senses. The investigation of the nature and propagation of fire included several points on which Mme du Châtelet offered more specific experimental evidence. She refuted the notion that fire naturally rises, with the same experiment Nollet employed in his lectures: In the receiver of an air pump, smoke falls like any other material.[17] Again, scientific instruments refuted the naïve evidence of the senses.

The *Dissertation* concluded that fire has extension and divisibility in common with matter, but neither impenetrability nor weight. On this last point she felt compelled to consider Voltaire's primary point of interest, the problem of calcination of metals. She acknowledged that in these experiments the application of heat apparently causes a gain in weight, but she suggested that another material must be responsible for this change, not fire.[18] Although Mme du Châtelet's weightless material has a great deal in common with a number of other eighteenth-century subtle matters, the argument leading to it fits the generic category of experimental philosophy much more neatly than it does any specific Newtonian theory. Indeed, she explicitly rejected the notion that the rarefaction of heated materials results from a repulsion of their parts, pointing instead to the simple "action" of fire.[19] Her description of that action depended upon three main claims: Fire, ordinarily distributed uniformly through all matter, is insensible in this state of equilibrium. When bodies are condensed or compressed, fire is driven out, causing the bodies to feel cold. Finally—adding Newtonian rhetoric, but no particularly Newtonian meaning—she suggested that when the "action" of fire overcomes the "reaction" of bodies, we perceive heat or light, depending on the circumstances, as well as the rarefaction already discussed.[20]

This qualitative discussion reads quaintly to an audience familiar with nineteenth-century experimental physics, but so do practically all essays in experimental physics from the early eighteenth century. The *Dissertation* was firmly in the mainstream of experimental philosophy. By the standards of gentle amateurs, Mme du Châtelet's work was first-rate. In the event, however, neither essay from Cirey won the contest. The prize went instead to Leonhard Euler, the leading mathematical physicist of the great Swiss school. Euler's contribution, like the pair of essays from Cirey, was essentially qualitative; his philosophical position belonged to the style of elaborate Cartesianism favored by Fontenelle. The *académie*, with its leadership still anchored in the spirit of systems, found the vortex-based explanation appealing.

Almost immediately correspondence flowed out of Cirey bemoaning the poor taste of the judges and the bad luck of the competitors there. Mme du Châtelet told Voltaire of her clandestine essay; she wrote to Maupertuis informing him of her little plot. Voltaire was sufficiently comfortable with Nollet's liberality of spirit that he remarked in a fit of pique in a letter otherwise devoted to the business of Enlightenment—Nollet was dunning him for overdue bills—"we both competed for the prizes and it was the servants of whirlpools who won. *O tempora! O mores!*"[21] (This was hardly the sort of thing

one might send to a bill collector of undue Cartesian persuasion.)
Nollet's scientific patron Réaumur, whom we have met as the student
of spiders inscrutable to the Chinese nobility, a good friend of
Voltaire, ensured that the two essays from Cirey received honorable
mention in the contest. Voltaire was sufficiently impressed with their
work that he eventually published the pair together.

The prize essays composed by Voltaire and Mme du Châtelet have
little significance for the development of either science or the Enlightenment. Yet they do open a window into the scientific and the more
broadly philosophical communities in France in the middle 1730s.
Most significant for the former, they help to delineate positions
within the Académie royale des sciences. On one side, the leadership
of that body was still decidedly Cartesian: Euler's work bore the un-
mistakable stamp of the vorticist. The other side included the familiar
Newtonians Maupertuis and Clairaut, as we might expect. Yet this
empirical camp, set on crushing hypotheses as well as infamy, also included Réaumur and Nollet. The latter was a Cartesian in the sense
that he believed that forces are transmitted by subtle matters, that the
heavens follow celestial vortices, and that the weight of terrestrial
bodies is owing to the motion of another vortex. Réaumur, although
not a Cartesian ideologue, never embraced a strong Newtonian position either. To be sure, the forgetful philosophical abbé and his patron
at the *académie* also embraced up-to-date views, especially in questions of chemistry and collision. In light of these views, apparently,
they were not painted with the brush of the vorticist. It appears that
for Mme du Châtelet and her poetic companion, it was possible for a
reasonable, Enlightened thinker to manipulate subtle matters in the
manner of the Cartesians. The "new" science need not always have
been in any strict sense Newtonian; mechanical systems as well as attractions found a place in the discussion at Cirey.

These putterings in the laboratory, these dabblings in philosophical
theory, also make it clear that members of the French as well as of the
British elite kept their cabinets and fancied themselves capable of contributing to the natural as well as the political philosophical enterprise. The presence of an ostensibly professional *académie* staffed by
mathematically adept experts did not intimidate Mme du Châtelet in
her generation any more than it had Mme de La Salbière in the glorious years of Louis XIV. Voltaire counted himself a full participant in,

as well as an elegant popularizer of, the new science. What we might anachronistically call research scientists of the stature of Maupertuis and Réaumur took at least a polite interest in their work. In short, the kind of professionalization that is usually attributed to the Académie royale des sciences throughout the eighteenth century had simply not occurred before the middle third of that century—and the sort of disdain that the *académie* would routinely show to amateurs of natural philosophy during the last years of the old regime had not yet found its way into the body.[22]

This is not to suggest either that science at Cirey was really in a class with that of the Paris professionals or that it was practiced with a professional seriousness. The amateurs at Cirey also indulged in a lighter-hearted Newtonizing of a more literary sort. On more than one occasion their elegant gardens served as a setting for an updated conversation on the plurality of worlds. A young Italian, one Francesco Algarotti, called on Mme du Châtelet in 1735 and again in 1736. On something of a grand tour, polishing his French and his English, he spoke with his hostess and with Voltaire of his own project for popularizing the new British theories. He prepared a dialogue, clearly in the tradition of Fontenelle's *Conversations on the Plurality of Worlds,* which he called *Newtonianism for the Ladies.* Mme du Châtelet shared with Maupertuis a proposed passage in which Algarotti described love as decreasing in inverse proportion to absence and to the cube of the distance.[23] Algarotti's text, soon translated into French, simply updated the charming dialogue of Fontenelle's philosophical gentleman. The original Italian edition of 1737, dedicated to Fontenelle, showed as its frontispiece a scene in which Algarotti and Mme du Châtelet conversed as they strolled in the gardens around a large country house. As in the case of the essays on fire that emanated from that country house, the Newtonizing of Algarotti's Cirey was firmly rooted in Fontenelle's vision of science as a gentle pastime rather than a professional discipline.

All these styles of "Newtonian" science found their place before any clear evidence emerged for the correctness of Newton's science over that of Fontenelle and his school. As Voltaire had observed in the passage contrasting the Paris he had left and the London in which he had arrived, the French Cartesians and the British Newtonians each maintained that their own system presented a tremendous advantage over the other. Quite independent of any evidence for the new system, Mme du Châtelet and her poetic companion had adopted a fully "Newtonian" natural philosophy that filled most of the niches that Cartesianism had occupied in Fontenelle's world.

The Discovery of the Newtonian World

Newtonianism at Cirey, like Fontenelle's Cartesianism before it, meant a number of things. There was, of course, the mathematical mechanics, which hypothesized universal gravitation, as well as laws of motion largely shared with the French Cartesians since Huygens had come to the Académie royale des sciences three-quarters of a century earlier. There was an experimental style of science, indistinguishable, perhaps, from either Dutch or British Newtonianism, but hardly connected with questions of tides or celestial whirlpools or the shape of the earth, questions that separated Voltaire's London from Fontenelle's Paris. There was in the *Letters Concerning the English Nation* a hypothetical connection between Newtonian natural philosophy and Lockean political philosophy and epistemology, comparable to Fontenelle's link between Cartesian natural philosophy and Louis XIV's absolutism. Both Mme du Châtelet and Voltaire, by their very interest in Newtonianism, introduced it into the culture of the salons as firmly as Cartesianism had been insinuated into that context in the early years of the reign of the Sun King. Finally, with Algarotti's work, Newtonianism made its way into the more clearly literary realm, which Cartesianism had entered with the *Conversations Concerning the Plurality of Worlds.* Enlightened Newtonianism, in short, stood ready to replace rationalist Cartesianism on every front.

It was not until 1737, however, that there was the first significant evidence that Newton's mathematical mechanics, with its theory of universal gravitation, offered advantages over the Cartesian system championed by Fontenelle and Cassini. The point is, on the one hand, that the adoption of the Newtonian system was well begun before any such clear evidence existed, and, on the other, that simple technical evidence of the superiority of a single detail of the Newtonian system over the Cartesian would not have shaken the great scientific and social system. Indeed the first "crucial experiment" offered between the two chief world systems turned on the question of the shape of the earth. This was one of a number of questions in which Cassini had offered a new, French solution in opposition to the existing opinion in the Cartesian system. Huygens had suggested, as Newton did, that the earth's rotation should cause it to bulge at the equator; Cassini suggested, to the contrary and in light of new measurements, that the ether spinning around the equator must compress the equatorial diameter.

Maupertuis's book on the shape of the earth set in train a pair of expeditions to extend Picard's geodesic measurements and to determine once and for all the real shape of the planet. The first set out for Peru in 1735 in order to determine the length of a degree of latitude at the equator. The next year, Maupertuis and Clairaut departed for Lapland, where they were joined by Celsius (of thermometric fame) to determine the length of a degree near the North Pole. Their data, they all believed, would provide the crucial experiment required to determine whether Newton's theory was correct.

In 1737 Maupertuis and Clairaut returned to France; before long, the older mathematician came to call at Cirey. Maupertuis was very full of himself, confident that his measurements demonstrated the truth of Newton's ideas about the shape of the earth. He impressed his hosts sufficiently that Voltaire recommended Maupertuis to Frederick the Great as president of the Berlin Academy of Sciences—over the head of Euler, already in Frederick's court. The adventure in Lapland enjoyed by Voltaire's and Mme du Châtelet's philosophical friends certainly produced a good story; even Fontenelle's account in the *académie's Mémoires* presents a heroic search through ice and snow, threatened by the desolation of the Northland and the intractability of reindeer.[24] In classic eighteenth-century style it even involved a shipwreck on the return voyage. The tale told at Cirey also included a good deal of scatological as well as technical swashbuckling, which the secretary of the *académie* ignored. I too, shall leave it aside for the present; it is a story best told by Voltaire.

Despite some controversy over the measurements,[25] the ascendant Newtonians at last had something to point to in order to demonstrate their superiority over the Cartesians. The success of the voyage to Lapland, finally acknowledged when it was confirmed irrefutably by the results of the equally arduous and substantially longer expedition to

Peru reported in 1739, thoroughly established a Newtonian foothold in questions technical. To be sure, it still competed with the Cartesianism of Fontenelle and Nollet. Indeed, as Huygens had argued, one could construct a Cartesian argument that produced an explanation in qualitative agreement with the results of the expeditions. Moreover, Maupertuis's calculations left enough to be desired that Clairaut took up the theoretical problem. Dispensing with Maupertuis's assumption that the earth is relatively uniform in density, he published his own, improved solution in 1742.

As Newtonian theorists began to establish more and more successful applications of the law of universal gravitation, the mathematical community increasingly accepted its utility. In 1740, Daniel Bernoulli was able to reconcile Newton's theory of the tides with the observations. Even as thoroughly Cartesian a thinker as Leonhard Euler, the nemesis of Cirey in the essays on fire, directed his unparalleled mathematical skill to the new celestial mechanics. Cassini, with his ellipses, was the last important astronomical calculator to work without the law of universal gravitation.

Nevertheless, it is important to recognize that in 1740 the theories set forth in the *Principia* still could not produce predictions about the motion of the planets or their moons in a manner demonstrably superior to Cassini's—or even to Kepler's. None of the principals on either side of the debate questioned this fact. Although no one seriously doubted that the law of universal gravitation offered something more than a hypothetical justification for Kepler's rules of planetary motion, there were still legitimate questions about how successfully mathematical thinkers might extend the material presented in the *Principia*. In short, the technical achievement of the calculation of the shape of the earth—celebrated as crucial to the acceptance of the theory of universal gravitation—could only have won over those already firmly leaning in Newton's direction. It was a combination of the various aspects of Newtonianism—the social prominence of its advocates, its connections with an increasingly popular political philosophy and sensationalist epistemology, and the technical stature of its practitioners as well as the single success—that invested in the voyage to Peru the near mythical significance it acquired in the rhetoric of the Enlightenment.

The new philosophy did successfully make its way into the mainstream. The last major element of Newtonian philosophizing to appear in France, ironically, was a replacement for one of the first elements of the Cartesian system to make its way into polite society—the textbook. Originally provided by Rohault, the *System of Natural Philosophy* had been prepared in the 1660s and first published in the early 1670s. The demonstration-lectures that we have considered provided an alternative to Rohault's experiments, but without a firm enough Newtonian framework for the tastes of the new Anglophiles. Voltaire himself produced the first Newtonian replacement; he published his *Elements of the Philosophy of Newton* in 1738. The work was more didactic than the *Letters Concerning the English Nation* had been, closer to Rohault in tone than to Fontenelle. The style of science presented in the *Elements* was largely experimental philosophy of the sort offered in the essays on fire, salted with philosophical comments tying this ostensibly Newtonian science to Lockean epistemology. It was sufficiently contentious that Mme du Châtelet became concerned once again about Voltaire's safety as he sent the work to press; the great poet was as anxious as ever to use his British lessons as a hammer with which to crush infamy. Natural philosophy was for him, as it was for Fontenelle, a part of the larger intellectual milieu.

The best of all possible worlds; or, the marriage of Newton and Leibniz

Voltaire's safety was not all that concerned Mme du Châtelet when he published his *Elements of the Philosophy of Newton.* The mistress of Cirey found her lover's ideology extreme. She set out to provide a slightly different point of view—as she had done when Voltaire prepared his essay on fire. She had her *Institutions de physique* ready for the press by the end of the year that Voltaire had published his *Elements,* but she held it back for a few more corrections. Like Voltaire, Mme du Châtelet explicitly intended the *Institutions* as a replacement for the dated *System* of Rohault.[26] Yet her plans were temporarily interrupted. In 1739 Maupertuis returned to Cirey, this time bringing with him a mathematician, Samuel Koenig, who had studied with Johann Bernoulli. Koenig had worked through Newton's mechanics in the early 1730s, when Clairaut and Maupertuis and Mme du Châtelet had taken up their joint inquiry into Newtonian science. In the intervening years Koenig had worked under the guidance of the great Leibnizian Christian Wolff and developed a clear statement of what would now be called the conservation of kinetic energy of a system of particles interacting without friction.[27] The German mathematician hit it off with his host and hostess—Voltaire took him on a trip to meet the naturalist Réaumur, and Mme du Châtelet shortly hired him as a tutor. Koenig undoubtedly fulfilled his obligations to instruct her in mathematics, but he also introduced her to Wolff's version of Leibniz.

To Voltaire's great consternation, Mme du Châtelet found Koenig's arguments convincing. In her *Institutions* she gave a polite nod in the direction of Voltaire's *Elements,* which she said provided an excellent introduction to Newton, but she suggested that a complete survey of natural philosophy needed to include still-potent Cartesian developments as well.[28] She prepared an additional section, which she inserted in front of her existing, largely Newtonian text, to bring this new Enlightenment to the world. The *Institutions* offered a complete examination of natural philosophy.

The new chapters set out the basis not only of Leibnizian physics but Leibnizian metaphysics as well. Mme du Châtelet's text took on a cast decidedly antagonistic to the Lockean foundation on which Voltaire had erected his Newtonian edifice. Whereas the British philosopher had grounded all understanding in the senses, Mme du Châtelet restored the Cartesian primacy of the mind. All necessary truths, she asserted, evolve from the principle of contradiction—the logical principle that it is impossible to affirm and deny a thing at the same time. Mathematics, she claimed, derives from this metaphysical starting point. And mathematics served for Mme du Châtelet, as for the theorists who served as her tutors, as the basis of science.

Contingent truths, matters not grounded in the certainty of mathematics (the stuff of natural philosophy, and in Voltaire's view the realm of the Empiricists), for Mme du Châtelet required in addition to noncontradiction only the equally metaphysical principle of sufficient reason. It was the principle of sufficient reason, introduced by Leibniz into mechanical thought, that allows us to understand the physical world. Analysis based on Leibniz's philosophy distinguishes the sorts of unrealistic but possible truths that got the Cartesian system builders into such trouble from actual truths like those discovered by sound physics. Thus the solution to the very real problems confronted by Descartes came not, as Locke had claimed, from experience but from metaphysics. Mme du Châtelet was quite prepared to accept the German philosophy on the same broad basis—epistemological, mathematical, and physical—as Voltaire had embraced his British theories.

The *Institutions* have a significance for the present story primarily because Mme du Châtelet introduced Leibnizian physics alongside her account of Newton. She considered both *vis viva*, the living force, and Newton's quantity of motion in her discussion. As 'sGravesande would do a few years later, she came to recognize that the Newtonian definition (the momentum-like quantity of the early eighteenth century) was not incompatible with the Leibnizian one (related to what is now called kinetic energy). Undoubtedly she came to this realization with help from Koenig and perhaps from Maupertuis or Clairaut as well—this I will grant to those who find it impossible to attribute originality in science to women—but it was Mme du Châtelet who first published the conclusion. It would be the *Institutions,* for example, that Nollet would cite in his *Leçons de physique* as the best source for the Leibnizian position on collision—although since it was a woman he did not, for reasons of delicacy, mention the author's name.[29]

The *Institutions* went on, in good Newtonian form, to embrace the theory of universal gravitation; its author had not abandoned all her British teachings in favor of the German. Rather, like the demonstrators, she attempted to integrate the two theories. Gender could certainly have played a role in her decision; it has been suggested that Leibniz's metaphysics, which stresses the interconnected nature of the world, is attractive to women's sensibilities.[30] More generally, women are perhaps less pigheaded than men and more willing to see the complexities of an issue and acknowledge the strengths and weaknesses of more than one point of view. Along these same lines, women perhaps see less necessity to find a loser for every winner; Mme du Châtelet could accept the correctness of universal gravitation without needing to see the defeat of the theory of living force. We might also point to Mme du Châtelet's intuition—her mathematical intuition. In the event, the solution to the remaining substantial shortcomings of Newtonian theory would depend significantly on a Leibnizian style of mathematical physics. It is just possible—and here we must part company with those who would deny Mme du Châtelet's originality—that she understood that the mathematical physics of the next generation would evolve from a synthesis of the two competing theories.

Voltaire, who hated Leibniz with the same passion that he hated infamy, was disturbed by this turn of events. He warned Maupertuis sarcastically that Mme du Châtelet "will arrive together with sufficient reason and surrounded by monads."[31] One might offer a number of speculations concerning the different views of the residents of Cirey. Voltaire could simply have been huffy that Mme du Châtelet had prepared a work in competition with his own *Elements of the Philosophy of Newton*. His was, after all, the more mercurial and fickle personality. Yet we also need to observe that Voltaire remained the Newtonian ideologue, even after Mme du Châtelet adopted a more pluralistic view of things. His defense of the position he had adopted in his youth and integrated into a sociopolitical view of the world seems rather like Fontenelle's continuing defense of the Cartesian system against a Newtonianism that challenged the political implications he had developed for his own view of the natural world. Perhaps gender played a role here as well. These scientifically informed but decidedly amateur men, having constructed their own interconnected worlds, saw the technical success of rival theories they really didn't understand as the source of the contradictions that would lead to the deconstruction of those intellectually secure worlds.

Maupertuis, the recipient of Voltaire's warning, was at a stage in his own intellectual development where he constructed a Newtonian system verging on baroque Cartesianism. It is perhaps worth pausing briefly to examine this development, if only to show that Mme du Châtelet and Voltaire were not atypical in their lax, evolving philosophies natural and otherwise. In 1745, Maupertuis published a work called the *Venus physique*—the physics of love, loosely translated—in which he put forward a theory of procreation. The book opened in character, with the erotic aspect of insemination a bit more prominent than most serious authors on reproductive biology have chosen to make it.[32] After these preliminaries, Maupertuis presented an extensive history of theories of procreation and embryology. Finally, he turned to his own "Hypotheses on the Formation of the Fetus."[33] It is difficult to present the argument without appearing to pun, for it was based on the attraction of the male and female parts for each other. Maupertuis suggested that the male and female seminal materials contained little bits of all the organs of the contributing organisms. In the womb, the bits of liver from the mother and the bits of liver from the father found their way together through this attractive force; all the other organs were similarly assembled. From these parts a whole embryo could be formed, again through some appropriate attractive law.

Apart from the naïve Newtonizing represented by this hypothesis, it is interesting for several reasons. One is the way in which a number of authors in the twentieth century have found in the *Venus physique* a precursor to molecular genetics, praising one of Maupertuis's silliest intellectual diversions as though it were serious science.[34] Another is the fact that Maupertuis gave an unusually equal and symmetrical role to the contributions of women and men to their offspring. Maupertuis in fact found himself rather puzzled by the presence of the "spermatic animalcules" in the "male semen"; he saw no particular reason for these little beasts so often put forth as the great triumphal discovery of the microscopists of the seventeenth century. "I have looked in vain with an excellent microscope for similar animalcules in the fluid emitted by the female."[35] He hypothesized that they might serve to stir the male and female fluids together and remained open to the possibility that female reproductive fluids contained similar spermatic particles.

This Newtonian reproductive system—for surely, it must be characterized as a system, with all the overtones that term bore in the middle eighteenth century—came not from some literary tyro, but from a natural philosopher with serious mathematical credentials and considerable experience in natural history. Indeed Maupertuis was joined in his enthusiasm by his colleague at the *académie,* Georges Louis Leclerc, comte de Buffon, the author of a tremendously popular *Natural History* and the most distinguished zoologist in France. Newtonianism turned up in places and guises as improbable as any natural philosophy produced by the Cartesian systematists in earlier generations.

Nor was this Newtonian system building justified by any decisive refutation of the Cartesian natural philosophy it was meant to replace.

Even as late as the mid-1740s, more than a decade after Voltaire had declared his espousal of the British viewpoint and five years after the return of the expedition to Lapland, Maupertuis and his mathematical colleagues had not managed to solve a single substantial problem in celestial mechanics. The Paris *académie* underlined this point when it set as its prize problem for 1748 a complete theory of the motion of the moon.

The mathematics behind the Newtonian elaboration of the theory of the moon were much more difficult than those encountered by Maupertuis and Clairaut in computing the shape of the earth. The moon presents the classic "three body" problem. Fifty years earlier, Varignon had already elaborated Newton's solution to the problem of a single body orbiting about a fixed center according to the inverse square law of attraction. The "two body" problem—the motion of two bodies free to move in space and pulled only by their mutual gravitational attraction—can be reduced to two problems in which each body is treated as if it were independently attracted to a fixed point at the center of mass of the two bodies. To describe the motion of the moon, however, it is necessary to take into account the gravitational forces with which both the sun and the earth pull the moon. The problem can be solved at any given instant for one of the three bodies: The two forces exerted by the other bodies can be calculated independently and added together. But since all three bodies are in constant motion, the forces change from instant to instant; it is impossible to calculate the cumulative effect of their interaction. This problem has never been reduced to simple, soluble parts in the way the two-body problem was. Instead, its solution depends on new mathematical approximation techniques developed during the middle third of the eighteenth century.

Three important solutions to the motion of the moon arrived at the *académie;* the three solutions presented the same conclusion. One was Clairaut's. The second came from Leonhard Euler, whom we have already met as the vorticist who beat out Mme du Châtelet and Voltaire for the prize on the nature of fire. Euler was the most prolific mathematician of his generation—perhaps the most prolific important mathematician in the age of printed works. Swiss by birth, he had studied with Johann Bernoulli and spent his professional career in Berlin and St. Petersburg; he was the strongest mathematical physicist of the German-speaking world and vied with the French on the important problems of the mid–eighteenth century. The third solution came from Jean Le Rond d'Alembert, the youngest of the brilliant generation of French mathematical physicists represented by Maupertuis and Clairaut. Only about four years younger than the latter, he did not make his reputation until nearly fifteen years after the precocious Clairaut first read his paper to the *académie*.

To the consternation of the Newtonians, all three solutions predicted that the axes of the ellipse described by the moon should move around the earth at about half of the observed rate. It was Euler's essay that once again won the prize. He remained, as Voltaire had called him after losing the earlier competition, a "vorticist." Euler suggested that the difficulty, which persisted despite the successful Newtonian solutions, lay in the physical mechanism of the heavens:

> I am able to give several proofs that the forces which act on the moon do not exactly follow the rule of Newton . . . since the errors cannot be attributed to the observations, I do not doubt that a certain derangement of the forces supposed in the theory is the cause. This circumstance makes me think that the vortices or some other material cause of these forces is very probable, since it is then easy to understand that these forces ought to be altered when they are transmitted by some other vortex.[36]

That is to say that Newton's law offered an approximate, empirical description of the motion of the planets in the vortex in a slightly more accurate version than Kepler's laws had done. Yet the vortex behaves in subtly different ways; the only path to improving Newton's approximation would involve a thorough understanding of the vortex. A second competitor, d'Alembert—apparently on the suggestion of the naturalist Buffon—toyed with the idea of "another force besides gravity," possibly magnetic, which "deranged" the action of the inverse square law. Indeed, he went as far as suggesting that it might be worthwhile to search for correlations between magnetic variations on earth and the position of the moon.[37]

Clairaut, following the same sentiments in a different direction, calculated that he could bring his analysis—and those of Euler and d'Alembert—into agreement with observations by introducing a slight modification to Newton's law. In addition to the inverse square term, he suggested, there is also a term that depends on the inverse of the fourth power of the distance between the attracting bodies. Clairaut was not playing diverting mathematical games as Varignon had done when he altered the form of Newton's investigation of central forces; he was attempting to correct an inaccuracy in physical theory. The new term he introduced would be relatively large when operating on bodies close by astronomical standards—the earth and the moon or other planets and their satellites—but negligible over the longer distances that separate the planets from one another and from the sun.

Thus, despite the firm establishment of a Newtonian contingent among the strongest mathematicians of the *académie,* it appeared during the late 1740s that universal gravitation did not provide a sufficient solution to the problem of the solar system. No one had been able to use Newton's theory to improve upon Kepler's laws before the solution to the problem of the moon, and the improvement put forward by d'Alembert, Euler, and Clairaut seemed imperfect. Their efforts, like Cassini's ellipses, did a better job than Kepler's laws at explaining the phenomena, but not sufficiently so for one to take Newton's law of gravitation as unquestionable fact. In response to this failure in the details of technical minutia, all the major actors turned away from the sort of strong Newtonianism suggested by Maupertuis's *Venus physique,* Voltaire's *Elements of the Philosophy of Newton,* or Buffon's rhetoric. One might choose, like Euler, to reject universal gravitation as a physical cause; like d'Alembert, to accept that it was only one physical cause among several; or, like Clairaut, to modify the mathematical rules governing universal attraction. The decision was more a matter of philosophical taste than of technical investigation. Yet all the most technically adept students of mathematical physics believed that Newton's work, like Kepler's, represented a brilliant empirical rule but failed to reflect a great truth about the universe.

Only Clairaut continued to work at the problem left over after the prize was awarded in 1748. In 1749 he recognized that the three solutions had all made the same approximation at a crucial juncture and that by carrying the calculation one term further he could arrive at a solution that agreed with observations. He announced his results—

without disclosing his methods—and d'Alembert was able to confirm the calculations independently once he realized the problem was soluble. It was d'Alembert who got his solution into print first; the question of priority as it would appear in the historical record became a source of friction between him and Clairaut. The latter also prepared a *Théorie de la lune*, published in 1752, and a set of *Tables* predicting the position of the moon on the basis of that theory in 1754. It is significant to note that these were the first tables calculated anywhere that depended on theoretical developments beyond Kepler's laws; they appeared more than half a century after Newton had published the *Principia*. At last, however, everyone with any technical competence at all came to accept the correctness of Newton's law.

While Clairaut had been struggling with the solution to the three-body problem, Mme du Châtelet had returned to her study of the *Principia* with his assistance. She determined in the mid-1740s to prepare a French translation of the work. She also planned a commentary that would at once present Newton's abstruse mathematical style in more comprehensible terms and provide up-to-date explanations of the problems, which had developed beyond the point to which Newton had brought them. In this project she made public the individual, private accomplishment of mathematicians like Clairaut, Maupertuis, and d'Alembert who had translated Newton's cumbersome mathematics into Leibniz's notation. This was the same problem that Varignon had set himself in the decades around the turn of the century. Varignon had missed the point of Newton's accomplishment, expanding the mathematical solution of physical problems into the realm of mathematical recreations without applications. Mme du Châtelet by contrast got the solution right, illuminating the way in which Newton's accomplishment allowed the mathematical mechanician to describe the motions of bodies in our real, instantiated world.

Critics feel compelled to point out that she only assimilated this work, that the progress that she reported was made by others. This is certainly true, and Mme du Châtelet acknowledged it. It is the importance and the range of the work that she assimilated that is impressive about her edition. By the time she prepared the commentary, she had a solid command of the solutions worked out to most of the problems, which, for example, Voltaire had recognized in his *Letters Concerning the English Nation* as unresolved points of disagreement between the Newtonian and Cartesian systems. The French *Principes mathématiques de la philosophie naturelle*[38] included a summary of the theory of tides worked out by Daniel Bernoulli in 1740, demonstrating (without access to the state of the oceans at the time of the formation of the earth) that attraction rather than the pressure of the moon on the terrestrial vortex caused the phenomenon. Mme du Châtelet further discussed the three-body problem in a passage written with Clairaut's guidance; of course she gave full credit for his cooperation. The quality of the translation and commentary was sufficiently high that no French historian of science has ever prepared a new version. The work should be recognized for what it was—a magisterial exposition of the seminal work in mathematical physics, with a review of the progress made in the half-century after its publication.

The translation of the *Principia,* like the composition of the *Institutions,* continued for two years after Mme du Châtelet sent the manuscript to the publisher. She began reading proofs in spring 1747; two years later she was still making corrections and additions. During this period she took a new lover, the poet Saint-Lambert. She realized she was pregnant by him in January 1749 and feared greatly for her health. During the pregnancy she redoubled her efforts on the publishing project. The first volume of the work on Newton was published on 1 September; a daughter was born on 4 September and "laid on a quarto tome of geometry";[39] five days later Mme du Châtelet took ill. The next day she dated the manuscript of the remaining commentary on Newton, and died. The text was not put in order and published for another ten years. By the time it appeared, Paris was largely in the same philosophical world as London.

Émilie du Châtelet's death, owing to complications of childbirth following an unplanned and unwanted pregnancy, supplies the somber occasion for reflection on the ways in which her role as a woman influenced the natural philosophy she practiced. To be sure, hers was not a distinctly feminine style of philosophizing in the tradition of the *salonières* of the early reign of Louis XIV. She did not find a place in a community of women like that of Mme de Guédreville or Mlle de Scudéry two generations earlier. Moreover, her titillating personal biography, her delight in her prolific sexuality, and her tremendously public persona present a problematic character study for the feminist historian. In some sense it was by adopting an outwardly masculine lifestyle that Mme du Châtelet made her way in Voltaire's and Maupertuis's world.

There are a number of ways in which Mme du Châtelet's scientific career was disadvantaged by her gender. First we should observe that premature death, among its other consequences, puts an end to a career; neither Voltaire nor Maupertuis, both of whom enjoyed their sexuality in a manner parallel to that of their (sequentially) common lover, needed to fear the problems of pregnancy. Moreover, the accomplishments that Mme du Châtelet managed in her shortened life were always harder won than similar accomplishments by men. It was not Voltaire who stayed up night after night, following a late evening's entertainment, to compose an essay on fire. These accomplishments were often treated dismissively. Voltaire's teasing about his lover's fascination with monads has a different tone than his invective directed against men. Nollet did not deign to name his customer and friend as the author of the *Institutions de physique*. Traditional histories have always concentrated on Mme du Châtelet as Voltaire's lover first and as an intellectual figure in her own right second. Her importance in the canon of the history of science should certainly outrank that of men like Varignon; although her name might be better known than his, her reputation as an interpreter of Newton is generally not acknowledged.

Finally, we should return to the point made during the discussion of the *Institutions*. Mme du Châtelet did seek a compromise that embraced both Newtonian and Leibnizian elements. She did so from within a community polarized and vindictive in questions of natural philosophy. Her experience as a woman living in a world of men with very big egos, men whose angry disputes frequently embroiled her, men with whom she maintained intimate friendships after she ended affairs, left her with a very different perspective on arguments than that held by those men in her world. Her philosophical position in the *Institutions,* ironically, was one that placed the theoretical, the philosophical, and the mathematical before the empirical, the sensual, and the intuitive, embraced by Locke and Voltaire. It was of course this entirely theoretical, mathematical approach that Lagrange and Laplace would employ in the next generation to finish the solution of the solar system, a task that was not accomplished, despite the swaggering rhetoric of the participants, in the voyages of exploration launched to discover the Newtonian world. Mme du Châtelet turned out in this instance to be more prescient not only than Voltaire but also than Maupertuis.

.

A new conversation on the plurality of worlds, in which Fontenelle is both panned and glossed

The story of the establishment of Newtonianism in France seen though the career of Émilie du Châtelet seems rather more evolutionary and less contentious than accounts by the philosophes often made it appear. The Cartesian vortex system cohabited with Newton's mathematical description of attraction into the late 1740s. Experimental philosophy of the sort practiced by Nollet, too, allowed the peaceful coexistence of subtle matters and attractive powers—as long as the Cartesian aspects did not require any particular ideological explanation. The technical developments in celestial mechanics Mme du Châtelet witnessed and documented required a thorough integration of Leibniz's mathematical style, and indeed of his theoretical mechanics, into Newton's physical system of universal gravitation. It was Voltaire, the scientifically naïve poet, who sang the praises of the connection between liberalism and universal gravitation against the conspiracy of absolutism and Fontenelle's Cartesianism. It was Voltaire who could not accept the fact that Mme du Châtelet—for reasons largely technical—had changed her mind about technical problems.

In the context of this new, part Leibnizian, part Newtonian, and part original, style of science, the mathematical mechanicians of the eighteenth century continued their work after Mme du Châtelet's death. From the time of the calculation of the lunar tables in the early 1750s, celestial mechanics based on universal gravitation saw one triumph after another. Clairaut determined to apply the solution to the three-body problem to a new question, and in 1758 he set to work calculating the exact time of the return of Halley's comet. As happened so frequently in the middle eighteenth century, he found himself in a race. This time the race was with the comet; it became necessary to enlist help with his calculations. A young astronomer, Jérôme Lalande, and one Mme Lepaute, the wife of a clockmaker for the scientific community, set to work under Clairaut's supervision; in November they were able to announce that the heavenly body would make its once-in-seventy-odd-year appearance in April 1759. The calculation proved accurate to within less than the month's uncertainty Clairaut had allowed himself; it was this feat that Nollet would eventually use in his *Leçons de physique* to convince his auditors of the efficacy of the law of universal gravitation.

The decade after the completion of Mme du Châtelet's translation of Newton in 1749 saw the consolidation of the solution to the motion of the planets and moons in the solar system initiated by Maupertuis, Clairaut, and their contemporaries. Pierre Simon Laplace worked out a mathematical formulation of gravitational attraction, which has been known since the early nineteenth century as "potential theory." It is a system based on what modern science calls energy—related to Leibniz's *vis viva*—rather than on momentum—the current name for the Newtonian quantity of motion. Yet the style of science of the last third of the eighteenth century and the first third of the nineteenth is more properly called "Laplacian" than Newtonian or Leibnizian or Cartesian. This style of science was a departure from the natural philosophy known by Mme du Châtelet or Voltaire or Fontenelle. It was no longer a science for polite society; it offered a demonstration of Enlightenment only indirectly, through the testimony of the technically adept who practiced it and not through information accessible to the senses in the lecture hall.

Cartesian science and the styles of philosophical discourse it engendered disappeared from the French scene around the middle of the eighteenth century for more than technical reasons. The philosophy of the Enlightenment and the literature of the philosophes drew a great deal from the sort of connection between philosophies political and natural with which Fontenelle had consolidated the place of Cartesianism in the social and political worlds of Paris. Yet the style of the philosophes would undermine the naïve way in which Fontenelle had placed Cartesian natural philosophy at the center of his literary and social worlds. Science would become for the Enlightenment a symbol of rationality and a method for solving problems in political and social philosophy, not a source of explicit and simplistic metaphors for those solutions. In this larger intellectual movement, it was not Mme du Châtelet but her longtime lover and intellectual collaborator, Voltaire, who fired the fatal volleys at Fontenelle's Cartesian fortress.

The connection between natural philosophy and the sort of literary world Fontenelle inhabited is best illustrated by a minor piece by Voltaire. He composed the philosophical romance of *Micromégas* around 1739—at a time when Maupertuis was a close friend of the couple at Cirey and a regular visitor there. A sort of burlesque of the celestial voyage genre so popular in the seventeenth century, it lampooned both the *Conversations on the Plurality of Worlds* and the voyage to Lapland. The story did not appear in print until 1752, after the law of universal gravitation had gained acceptance on its technical merits. Nonetheless, the text may serve as an appropriate summary of the way in which Newtonian science made its way into the Académie royale des sciences and into high culture in Paris during the decade before Clairaut's solution of the problem of the moon. Voltaire's romance gives rather short shrift to the technical development of Newtonian theory, but this is perhaps appropriate for the way in which British celestial mechanics actually penetrated the consciousness of the Parisian technical and cultural elite.

Micromégas, the protagonist of Voltaire's story, hailed from a giant planet that revolved around the star Sirius. Unlike Fontenelle's unfortunate planetarians, Micromégas assumed the gigantic proportions appropriate to his home—"his stature amounted to eight leagues [twenty-four miles] in height."[40] He was a gentleman, handsome, university educated, and a person of parts. A child prodigy, the Sirian (as Voltaire called him) proved a more successful mathematician by the age of eighteen than had Blaise Pascal on earth. As a young man Micromégas dissected insects tiny by the standards of his planet— though hundreds of feet long by our measure. Here he got himself into trouble, Voltaire reported, for inquiring into the question of whether the substantial form of a snail differs from that of a flee. His defense of his philosophy "made all of the female sex his proselytes"[41] but also won him expulsion from the planet. "Not much affected at his banishment from a court that teemed with nothing but turmoils and trifles, he made a very humorous song upon the prince, who gave himself no trouble about the matter, and set out on his travels from planet to planet in order (as the saying is) to improve his mind and finish his education."[42]

Micromégas as introduced in this opening sketch formed a peculiar composite of the mathematical prodigy Clairaut, the anatomizing physicist Maupertuis, and Voltaire himself. Whereas all three had been at the center of numerous intellectual controversies, it was Voltaire, of course, who had been banished from court for slander. Indeed it was Voltaire who had suffered criticism for his statement in the *Philosophical Letters* that the human soul develops with the body in the same way as animal souls develop with their bodies—although he hadn't gotten into any particularly serious trouble for that. Like Micromégas, Voltaire considered himself a man of parts; he devoted great energy to philosophies natural and political, as well as to his more notable literary endeavors. Throughout the story, the fictional protagonist would voice opinions of the author, as Fontenelle's philosophical gentleman had done in the *Conversations on the Plurality of Worlds.*

It was a talent for calculating the effects of gravity that Voltaire next attributed to Micromégas. "Our traveller was a wonderful adept in the laws of gravitation, together with the whole force of attraction and repulsion, and made such seasonable use of his knowledge that sometimes by the help of a sunbeam, and sometimes by the convenience of a comet, he and his retinue glided from sphere to sphere, as the bird hops from one bough to another."[43] Voltaire in this passage did Fontenelle one better: On the one hand, the conveyance of Micromégas from place to place depended upon the science-fictional manipulation of physical law rather than the simple fantasy presented in the *Conversations on the Plurality of Worlds;* on the other, the physical law embraced was Newtonian attraction rather than the Cartesian mechanism with which the earlier dialogue had set the stage.

Voltaire eventually directed his exiled giant to Saturn. As he had done for Micromégas, he endowed the Saturnians with stature appropriate to their planet—a somewhat less gigantic height of a thousand fathoms, for Saturn, he reckoned, was nine hundred times larger than the earth. Like Huygens, Voltaire equipped his planetarians for their surroundings. Indeed, the *Celestial Worlds Discovered* apparently merited Voltaire's notice—and suffered his implicit ridicule. A poke at Fontenelle hit the Dutch author as well: "In short, Micromégas at first derided those poor pygmies, just as an Indian fiddler laughs at the music of Lully, at his first arrival in Paris; but as this Sirian was a person of good sense, he soon perceived that a thinking being may not be altogether ridiculous, even though he is not quite six thousand feet high."[44] As Huygens had moved beyond Fontenelle's colonial out-look, Voltaire extended the Dutch philosopher's recognition of the natural rights of foreigners celestial (and by implication terrestrial) to a general relativism.

Micromégas presents the new ideology with a literary deftness and subtlety every bit as successful as Fontenelle's. Voltaire pointed up his more pluralistic view by at first attributing to Micromégas the sort of narrower position Fontenelle had adopted. He then praised the gigantic planetarian for his liberality of spirit when he repented of this self-centered view of culture. Likewise, it was the Indian of the simile who first displayed an ignorant disregard for Parisian music and then showed good sense to acquire a taste for Lully; Voltaire did not bash his audience for ignorance of things Indian. Yet he did in this passing reference to music point out, against Huygens's assertion that plane-tarians elsewhere in the solar system must develop the same sort of harmonies as we do on earth, that art and taste may differ in different cultures—that these matters stand outside the jurisdiction of natural law.

In a more personal reference to Fontenelle, Voltaire favored his fic-tional giant with an intimate friendship with the secretary of the Academy of Saturn: "a man of good understanding, who, though in truth he had invented nothing of his own, gave a very good account of the inventions of others, and enjoyed in peace the reputation of a little poet and great calculator."[45] Voltaire's own overly didactic interest in the popularization of science, along with his unequaled reputation as a poet, makes this extremely fair judgment all the more admirable. (The peaceable enjoyment of a reputation, which Voltaire likewise ac-curately attributed to Fontenelle, was something the later, greater lit-erary figure would never achieve for long.) When *Micromégas* was composed, the aging secretary of the Académie royale des sciences in Paris was still a figure to be reckoned with in the literary scene.

Voltaire was not squeamish about criticizing his predecessor in the popularization of science. The great satirist also captured the clash of the philosophies between Fontenelle's generation and his own in a conversation between Micromégas and the Saturnian secretary:

"It must be confessed," said Micromégas, "that nature is full of variety."
"Yes," replied the Saturnian, "nature is like a garden, whose flow-ers—"

"Pshaw!" cried the other, "a truce with your gardens."

"It is," resumed the secretary, "like an assembly of fair and brown women, whose dresses—"

"What a plague have I to do with your brunettes?" said our traveller.

"Then it is like a gallery of pictures, the strokes of which—"

"Not at all," answered Micromégas, "I tell you, once and for all, nature is like nature, and comparisons are odious."

"Well, to please you," said the secretary—

"I won't be pleased," cried the Sirian, "I want to be instructed; begin, therefore, without further preamble, and tell me how many senses the people of this world enjoy."

"We have seventy and two," said the academician, "but we are daily complaining of the small number, as our imagination transcends our wants, for, with the seventy-two senses, our five moons and ring, we find ourselves very much restricted; and notwithstanding our curiosity, and the no small number of those passions that result from these few senses, we have still time enough to be tired of idleness."[46]

Voltaire continued on this grander scale to endow Micromégas with more than the Saturnians—a thousand senses, three hundred fundamental properties of matter, thirty-nine primary colors, a million-year life span, and so on—though even the relatively puny Saturnians had immensely more than we on earth. Moreover, the Sirian visitor had constantly to inform the Saturnian secretary that other planets that he had encountered orbiting other stars showed greater variety still. The message of cultural relativism—like Fontenelle's message of cultural hegemony, more subtle in the story than in the analysis—informed every passage of the story.

Voltaire chose to separate in other ways as well natural philosophy from the sort of cultural norms to which Fontenelle had tied it. Most obviously, Voltaire ridiculed the way in which Fontenelle had integrated philosophical discourse into literary culture. The flowers and ornaments of Louis XIV's France had no place in Voltaire's picture of an Académie royale des sciences. He disdained the polite style and poetic pretensions of Fontenelle's *précieuse* philosophy, philosophers, and "philosophesses." In a discussion of science, one gets down to business; the first order of business for Voltaire, as for the demonstration-lecturers, was observation rather than system. Voltaire saw scientific popularization as a didactic rather than a literary endeavor.

After this extended visit to Saturn, in which Micromégas shared with his hosts his views of what science should be, he set off, accompanied by none other than the secretary of the Academy of Sciences from that planet, who left his weeping mistress "to console herself with a minor official of the country."[47] (Voltaire was sufficiently public about his affair with Émilie du Châtelet—who had taken Maupertuis as a lover before the mathematician's departure for Lapland—that this passage might well have been read in the context of these amorous adventures.) The philosophical pair first traveled by comet to Jupiter, although Voltaire claimed he could not report their fascinating activities there, owing to the censors.

Again, the method of conveyance served to the cognoscenti as a subtle attack on the Cartesian system. Descartes's cosmology had placed the comets on the edges of celestial whirlpools, moving from the province of one star to another but necessarily always removed by some distance from the stable orbits of the planets. Newton had suggested that the comets observed in our solar system instead orbit the sun, obeying Kepler's laws, simply tracing extremely elongated elliptical orbits. On this theory, the wandering bodies must pass through the spheres of the planets, wandering quite close to the sun before streaking away as invisible specks beyond Jupiter. Such a path, of course, is incompatible with the Cartesian view of the planets floating along in a celestial ether—a comet in Saturn's or Jupiter's region of the heavens should trace the same path as Saturn or Jupiter does. Here again, however, the Newtonians had been unable to compute the path of any particular comet, so the question of who was right about their paths remained unresolved. Voltaire's literary device served as an ideological assertion rather than a legitimate public declaration of a philosophical discovery.

The next stop Micromégas made with his Saturnian friend continued the implicit commentary on the earlier, imaginary voyage described by the secretary of the Parisian *académie*:

> Coasting along to the planet Mars, which is well known to be five times smaller than our little earth, they described two moons subservient to that orb which have escaped the observation of all our astronomers. I know Father Castel will write, and that pleasantly enough, against the existence of these two moons; but I entirely refer myself to those who reason by analogy. Those worthy philosophers are very sensible that Mars, which is at such a distance from the sun, must be in a very uncomfortable situation, without the benefit of a couple of moons.[48]

Voltaire, of course, offered this ironic argument for the presence of these moons, even though he supposed that they did not exist. He was making fun of Fontenelle's description of Jupiter's moons, and the ring and moons of Saturn, as objects placed to reflect light on those great planets for the benefit of their inhabitants. It is a wonderful irony that in this mockery of Fontenelle's argument for phosphorescent mountains on the planet, Voltaire produced from his imagination moons that a century later appeared in telescopes.

Apart from its twin moons, Mars held few attractions for the planetary visitors. Voltaire reported that they set off promptly, like travelers subjected to the accommodations of a tiny village heading to the next market town, for our own little planet. The pair arrived riding the tail of a comet "on the northern coast of the Baltic on the fifth day of July, new style, in the year 1737."[49] The choice of alternative accommodations turned out not to be a terribly good one for travelers of their proportions:

> "This globe," said the dwarf [as Micromégas called his companion from Saturn], "is ill contrived, and so irregular in form as to be quite ridiculous. The whole together looks like chaos. Do but observed these little rivulets; none of them runs in a straight line; and these ponds which are neither round, square, nor oval, nor indeed of any regular figure; together with these little sharp pebbles (meaning the mountains) that roughen the whole surface of the globe, and have torn the skin from my feet. Besides, pray take notice of the shape of the whole, how it flattens at the poles, and turns round the sun in a awkward oblique manner, so that the polar circles cannot possibly be cultivated. Truly, what makes me believe there is no inhabitant on this sphere is a full persuasion that no sensible being would live in such a disagreeable place."[50]

Again Voltaire provided both literary and technical contention against his predecessors in the genre. Fontenelle had taken the earth as the model planet, suited in every way to the needs of its inhabitants, and had offered every variation from its features on other planets as detrimental. Huygens had offered a corrective to the problem of what literary critics have taken to calling "the Other," presenting a world in which the munificence of God provided all creatures with their wants. Voltaire looked instead to his usual cynical relativity, casting aspersions on the physical attributes of our own planet in contrast to the wonders and conveniences of the others.

The mention of the flattening of the poles referred to the work that Maupertuis and Clairaut had done to calculate the shape of the earth on Newtonian principles and to confirm the calculations by measurement. This, too, Voltaire included in his story. The return of the academic adventure to Lapland occurred at the very time the Sirian and Saturnian voyagers arrived in the Baltic. Voltaire—here more reminiscent of Molière than of Fontenelle—arranged a meeting with appropriate representatives by having Micromégas spot and collect a tiny speck on the sea.

It is well known that at this period a flock of philosophers were upon their return from the polar circle, where they had been making observations, for which nobody has hitherto been the wiser. The gazettes record that their vessel ran ashore on the coast of Bothnia and that they with great difficulty saved their lives; but in this world one can never dive to the bottom of things. For my own part, I will ingeniously account the transaction just as it happened, without any addition of my own; and this is no small effort in a modern historian.

. . . The passengers and crew, who believed themselves thrown by a hurricane on some rock, began to put themselves in motion. The sailors, having hoisted out some casks of wine, jumped after them into the hand of Micromégas; the mathematicians, having secured their quadrants, sectors, and two young women from Lapland, were overboard at a different place.[51]

Here, perhaps, Voltaire proved a more accurate historian than Fontenelle. A more decorous account of the sexual adventures of the members of the philosophical expedition to Lapland remarked that it was carried out "in an atmosphere of youthful gaiety for which some reproached them."[52] This purely fictional recounting of the shipwreck captured the flavor of Maupertuis's expedition, and his rehearsal of it at Cirey, appropriately.

The passage continued to deflate the heroics of the adventurers. Voltaire's satire, which supported the scientific merit of the expedition, offered a rather more pedestrian critique of the swashbuckling philosophers than the *académie* had recorded in its *Histoire*. He dwelt extensively on the difficulty that the visiting planetarians had in even discerning creatures so small as men. (In this, too, Voltaire wrote at the expense of Maupertuis, who was short—the *Micromégas* always set the height of men at a mere five feet, quite small even by eighteenth-century standards.) Only through the ingenious use of diamonds in his jewelry as magnifiers did Micromégas manage to observe the members of the expedition—an accomplishment Voltaire compared to the observation by Hartsoeker and Leuwenhoek of sperm in human semen, "the seed of which we are formed."[53] Again, Voltaire offered an implicit but specific jab at Maupertuis, whose theory of reproduction discounted the importance of the sperm—as well as the more general ribaldry directed at microscopists' fascination with seminal fluids.

Micromégas, blessed with acute hearing and intelligence, soon managed to understand and communicate with the tiny creatures he had discovered. Asked to describe their occupation, the philosophers responded, "We anatomize flies, we measure lines, we make calculations, we agree upon two or three points which we understand, and dispute upon two or three thousand that are beyond our comprehension."[54] The discourse reported by Voltaire touched on a number of questions, including a long passage on the exquisite precision with which the members of the philosophical expedition were able to use their instruments to measure the giant and his rather less gigantic companion from Saturn. Impressed by the philosophers' competence, Micromégas inquired of them the sizes of and distances between a number of celestial objects. Taking the side of Maupertuis and Clairaut against Cassini, Voltaire had his planetary visitor marvel at the accuracy and precision of each result.

The larger question of the implications of the measurements and their role in natural philosophy in general likewise found a place in the story. Voltaire closed *Micromégas,* as Fontenelle had opened the *Conversations on the Plurality of Worlds* two generations earlier, with the disputes between various schools of philosophers. The passage came in response to the Sirian's inquiry about human theories of the soul. The responses, in which Voltaire displayed his ability to at once pan and gloss his opponents at its sharpest, makes delightful reading. The first respondent, an Aristotelian, quoted the Philosopher in Greek. When Micromégas complained that he didn't understand the language, the Aristotelian replied that he did not either, "but it is reasonable that we should quote what we do not comprehend in a language we do not understand."[55] After next tripping up the Cartesian on the immateriality of the soul, Micromégas quite reasonably inquired into the nature of matter, choosing as an example a stone. The Cartesian described the properties of the stone—its size, its color and shape, and so on. Micromégas probed further, inquiring after nature of the stone independent of its properties, to which the Cartesian had to admit ignorance. In *Micromégas*, as in the *Philosophical Letters*, Locke refuted Descartes. A student of Malebranche next offered his explanation for the soul—claiming that in order for his body to operate in consonance with the immaterial world, he acted merely as God willed. To this doctrine of occasional causes Micromégas responded, "That is being a nonentity indeed!"[56] Voltaire, as was his habit, heaped the greatest scorn on the follower of Leibniz, for whom he penned the response: "'In my opinion,' answered this metaphysician, 'the soul is the hand that points at the hour, while my body does the office of a clock; or, if you please, the soul is the clock, and the body is the pointer; or again, my soul is the mirror of the universe, and my body the frame. All this is clear.'"[57] The matter could not have been stated more elegantly by Candide or his famous teacher, Pangloss.

Having thus dispensed with his opponents, Voltaire was ready to state his own position. Like Fontenelle's Cartesian observing that Phaethon in the opera was lifted by ropes attached by pulleys to heavy weights, Voltaire introduced a partisan of Locke to clear up the matter:

> I do not know by what power I think; but well I know that I should never have thought without the assistance of my senses. That there are immaterial and intelligent substances I do not at all doubt; but that it is impossible for God to communicate the faculty of thinking to matter, I doubt very much. I revere the Eternal Power, to which it would ill become me to prescribe bounds. I affirm nothing, and am contented to believe that many more things are possible than are usually thought so.[58]

With this Micromégas agreed.

The story closed as the giant prepared an account of what he knew of philosophy for the tiny creatures he had met on Earth:

> Before his departure he made a present of the book, which was brought to the Académie des sciences at Paris, but when the old secretary came

to open it he saw nothing but blank paper, upon which—"Ay, ay," said he, "this is just what I suspected."[59]

This passage, this personal attack on Fontenelle's competence, brought to a close *Micromégas*. In a broader sense, it also brought to a close the genre of the celestial voyager, and indeed the literary style of science that had emerged in the court of Louis XIV nearly a century earlier.

The satire of *Micromégas* was scattered toward a large range of targets. To be sure, it took clear and specific aim at Cassini's astronomical system through the mathematical sights of universal gravitation. Voltaire, without ever appearing heavy-handed or polemical, demonstrated his mastery of the satirical form, as Micromégas at every turn opted for the Newtonian rather than the Cartesian solution to each detail. Voltaire was every bit Fontenelle's equal in the ability to pass over difficult technical material in a pleasant alternative to pedantry.

Yet Voltaire's account of the celestial voyage also made light of the project of literary exposition of serious natural philosophy. Voltaire believed himself to stand astride both literature and the scientific enterprise, as he clearly understood Fontenelle had done, and Molière as well. An educated Parisian in Voltaire's generation, as in Fontenelle's or Molière's, needed to be conversant with natural philosophy in order to understand civilized discourse—and to know who was making fun of whom. But Voltaire assumed that this understanding came, not from polite conversation or light literature, but through disciplined study of a text like Nollet's—or like his own *Elements of the Philosophy of Newton* or (despite its Leibnizian leanings) Mme du Châtelet's *Institutions de physique*. Philosophical disputation was a matter for discussion informed by expertise, not for polite conversation informed by speculation. Fontenelle, with his flowery language and his appeal to the untutored marquise, Voltaire implied, had abandoned all pretensions to competence. The great irony of *Micromégas* is that it works, despite the fact that Voltaire was the dilettante, whereas Fontenelle could claim a reasonable mathematical competence and an unparalleled command of the doings of the scientific community through three-quarters of a century.

As we look to the mind of the French Enlightenment, especially in the second half of the eighteenth century, we see that the philosophes increasingly assumed that science was the province of experts rather than an aspect of polite culture. The Académie royale des sciences—not to mention a half-dozen other institutions—closed ranks and stood on its expertise. The government began to enlist science, and more frequently scientists, to solve problems both technical and general. There is no question that the style of science Voltaire lionized, the mathematical physics of his and the next generation, produced a more successful description of the heavens than Fontenelle's generation had done. Yet it is also true, as the Marxists would point out, that in claiming science for their own, the scientists expropriated discussion of nature from the general population. The new, "Newtonian," science imagined by the mind of the Enlightenment—applauded by some of Voltaire's contemporaries and rejected by others but accepted as defining science by nearly all—was a science for scientists. Those scientists might deign to offer examples of their discipline as a demonstration of their own Enlightenment, but they could not make it into a science for polite society.

This view of science as a matter for experts has largely dominated Western thought since the Enlightenment. Except for a few peculiar moments in the history of science—Britain in the early nineteenth century springs to mind—the lay elite has not indulged itself in scientific entertainment. Science has stood as a symbol of rationality, a model of methods by which men might come to know, a discipline rather than a pleasure. It has demanded a manly rationality over feminine intuitive intellectual styles. Above all, in terms of a rhetoric much more British than French, science has made its claim to importance because it is useful, because of its "special success" in answering the questions that society's needs have posed for it. The present study should make clear that science announced its achievement before it achieved any notable successes. Newtonians both British and French celebrated the intellectual vanquishing of the heavens long before it occurred.

This rhetoric of the certainty and rationality of science, of its objectivity and its independence from the whims of cultural change, emerged largely in the Enlightenment of the eighteenth century. It was a rhetoric designed to replace the rhetoric of the Cartesian world, a world in which science played a role as an intellectual diversion, a topic accessible to women and suitable for polite conversation in mixed company. In the seventeenth century, science had become a part of French culture, a source and subject for the literary imagination, something that sophisticated women and men held in common, a metaphor for political philosophy, and a source of moral lessons. Fontenelle's vision of science, or Claude Perrault's, was one that provided an all-encompassing framework, a way to make general sense of the world, into which the myriad details uncovered by natural philosophers and natural historians might be placed. Only in the context of such a vision thoroughly ensconced in polite society, an intuitive belief that science constituted an integral part of culture and a dependable route to demonstrable Enlightenment, can we imagine that the tenuous claims to expertise in abstruse technical areas by contentious men might have been taken seriously by an intellectual elite still essentially literary and philosophical.

8

Electricity in the Eighteenth Century; or, The Philosophy of Shocks and Sparks

THE DISCOVERY OF THE NEWTONIAN world was a story that, from the point of view of the Enlightened thinkers who pursued it, had a happy ending. Truth triumphed, albeit rather belatedly, over false hypotheses. Liberality won its just victory over absolutism. The promise of the scientific revolution of the seventeenth century was finally fulfilled, enabling the creation of a canonical account of the progress of the human mind from Kepler and Galileo through Newton and beyond. The Newtonians, led by Voltaire, convinced the public of the truth of their system over the ideology of the Cartesians. Yet the classic historiography of the eighteenth century does not give any large place to the technical details of the consolidation of the Newtonian picture of the solar system—the assumption is that everyone with any sense should have done as Locke and Voltaire did and adopted the theory of universal gravitation as soon as it was articulated. Fifty years of hard work by the mathematical community are written off as tidying up the details. Instead, the canon attributes to the scientific world of the eighteenth century a consolidation of the still shakier seventeenth-century science of experimental philosophy. This does not refer to the sort of demonstration of Enlightenment we considered in the chapter by that title (Chapter 6). According to the standard story, first electricity and then chemistry came under the purview of the scientific method, a method perfected by Newton and adopted by the investigators of the Enlightenment.

The whole question of experimental philosophy as an investigative field has received, by the standards of existing historiography, rather short shrift in this book. Indeed, the interpretation that has been offered so far, treating experiment as the plaything of Molière's model modernists or as the province of the demonstrators of Enlightenment, would seem to dim the bright light of experimental progress that the philosophes claimed illuminated their century. Yet that is not my intention. Instead, I hope to suggest that experimental philosophy was something different in the eighteenth century than modern experimental scientific research—to be sure, something important enough to justify the elaborate claims made on its behalf by the philosophes and their disciples, but something peculiar to the eighteenth century. The present study of science in polite society must therefore turn to the first of the new eighteenth-century experimental sciences—what we now call static electricity—to understand how it was that Enlightened scientists discovered new, true things about the world.

My own reading of the eighteenth-century tradition is that the experimental philosophy had a purpose largely unrecognizable to the modern practitioner. From the era of Jacques Rohault through the full-blown development of static electricity in the third quarter of the eighteenth century, experimental philosophers sought to illustrate and to elucidate natural philosophy. To this end they designed ever more charming and dramatic effects; they presented cabinets of natural history and collections of philosophical instruments. Yet they did not closet themselves individually or in small teams within the laboratory in order to probe nature and take its measure, to push back its veils, to obtain the sort of personal intimacy with the phenomena sought by modern denizens of the lab.

The present, idiosyncratic account of the demonstration of the Enlightenment through the efforts of the lecturers of the eighteenth century might at first seem irrelevant to the standard story about the history of eighteenth-century electricity. As we have seen, experiment in the Ages of Reason and Enlightenment was a decorous public exercise, a performance, a demonstration of what was known rather than an investigation into what was not. Although vestiges of the eighteenth-century tradition may persist in the lecture halls and laboratory exercises of high school and elementary college courses, this pedagogical remnant is hardly what students of laboratory life refer to when they write about the modern experimental sciences. Thus in terms of the standard historiography, the present chapter must offer a surprising observation that it was this demonstrative style of experimental philosophy rather than any "hard" experimental research that produced the great advances in the study of electricity in the eighteenth century.

This is not to say that the demonstration-lecturers spurned the new findings that their work turned up or to denigrate their efforts in isolating, amplifying, and illuminating the electrical phenomena that found a place, willy-nilly, in their demonstrations. It is simply to insist that none of the important students of electricity in the eighteenth century set out to discover new things about the world, to disrupt an existing paradigm, or to explore brave new theoretical worlds. Whether the important and brilliant phenomena produced by this collection of characters—improbable discoverers according to any philosophy or sociology of scientific progress—should be counted more or less significant in light of their source I leave as a question for those who concern themselves with philosophies and sociologies of science. The history of electrical studies in the eighteenth century is sufficiently fascinating without considering its implications for broader questions.

Indeed, we might model our investigation of electrical researches on the presentation of the void offered by the demonstrators. The genuine advances that occurred in inquiries into physics, chemistry, and biology through the instrument of the air pump usually appeared in spurts inspired by new devices or even by accidental discoveries no more systematic than the observation that when one trips over a barometer in a darkened observatory the barometer sometimes glows. It was discovered that animals and fires expire in the absence of air, that sounds are not transmitted through the void, that most animal and vegetable matter contains air (or airs), and so on. A few nicer points made their way into the literature as well—the anomalous suspension of mercury in a properly prepared barometer in an air pump, which Huygens pointed out against Boyle's initial denial comes to mind—but by the turn of the eighteenth century the repertoire was pretty well standardized. Pierre Polinière or Francis Hauksbee or Willem 'sGravesande could put on the show with equal facility and conviction. So it was too with the history of electricity.

The characters in the history of electricity through the 1750s are those we have already encountered in the lecture hall: Pierre Polinière, Francis Hauksbee, J. T. Desaguliers, Willem 'sGravesande, Petrus van Musschenbroek, and Jean Nollet. We need add only Desaguliers's protégé Stephen Gray and Nollet's patron Charles Dufay to complete the cast of electricians in France, Holland, and England. Apart from the important developments of a decidedly amateur school in Germany, the demonstration-lecture circle accounted for all the major discoveries in classical electrostatics. These developments at first commanded the attention primarily of the demonstrators—and of their audiences—and remained remarkably independent of the mathematical scientists, who devoted themselves to questions of mechanics celestial or terrestrial. Indeed, the dramatic new electrical effects probably did more to expand popular interest in science during the High Enlightenment than even the contemporaneous swashbuckling voyages in search of the shape of the earth and the size of the solar system. If the mechanical and optical lectures served to demonstrate the Enlightenment, electrical displays provided the hook required to pull audiences into the halls. The delay between experimental design, execution of a new investigation, and presentation of the resulting phenomenon as a commonplace was typically measured in weeks or months; new effects, although they frequently spawned elaborate theories, never inspired a noticeable paradigm shift on the part of either the major senior scientists involved in electrical studies or the major junior scientists who would succeed them.

It is not that electrical researches somehow constituted illegitimate experimental philosophy. The field properly serves as the paradigm laboratory science of the Enlightenment; the standard historiography has got that right. Yet the tradition to which it belongs is one of public demonstration and amateur amusement rather than of laboratory research, as anyone who reads its delightful sources could scarcely fail to recognize. That these lighter characteristics have been dismissed by many of the histories that examine them must remind us of the story told by many an academic lecturer disturbed by an inability to elicit any response in a popular audience, despite the most obvious attempts to win them over with humor. The story inevitably ends up with the lecturer overhearing one listener tell another, "That was so funny I could hardly keep from laughing." The philosophy of shocks and sparks worked out during the middle third of the eighteenth century was probably more fun—and funnier in the recounting—than any other sustained episode in the history of science.

Unfortunately, the story has been told with such a dry turgidity that the reader is made to feel guilty for seeing the humor in grown women and men sharing electrified kisses before recognizing their activities as part of the great Enlightenment debate between the *esprit de système* and the *esprit systématique*. This great Enlightenment distinction, between the Cartesian—read clever French—enthusiasm for building a theoretical edifice (according to critics for its own sake) and the Lockean—read practical British—insistence on a measured, logical approach to questions of natural philosophy undeniably played an important role in the rhetoric of electrical debates. It provided a ready-made moral for the outcome of a dispute engineered to place competing electrical theories on opposing sides in the philosophes' crusade against Cartesianism, absolutism, and infamy. Historians have ever since sought to find an example and a moral for the larger intellectual debate in the natural philosophy on which the distinction was ostensibly based. The present account will offer a rather different sort of *esprit* for electrical studies.

From the beginning of the eighteenth century the development of electrical experiments came in the lecture hall. Accidental discoveries and public reconsideration of striking effects found their ways into the demonstrations we have already considered (Chapter 6). Pierre Polinière's electrical studies came in the course of genuine attempts to master Bernoulli's "mercurial phosphor," the glowing at the top of agitated barometer tubes reported so faithfully by Fontenelle in the annual *Histoires* of the Académie royale des sciences. Like his contemporary Francis Hauksbee, the demonstrator for the Royal Society of London, Polinière undoubtedly saw in Bernoulli's effect a new entertainment for his audience of gentle amateurs of science.

Improvements to the electrical demonstrations of the first decade of the eighteenth century were extremely slow in coming. Polinière continued to show his audiences the effects without developing them any further for nearly thirty years, until his death in 1734. The glowing and attraction of dust produced by rubbed glass also took a part in most of the philosophical demonstrations developed during the period spanned by Polinière's career. Desaguliers kept the tradition going in England, and his imitators carried the effects to Holland—it has been observed that British and Dutch demonstrators who counted themselves Newtonian usually referred to Hauksbee's publication of the results, whereas French and Germans cited Polinière.[1] When 'sGravesande, Musschenbroek, and Desaguliers brought out the texts describing their lectures, standard accounts of the experiments pioneered by Polinière and Hauksbee found a modest place.

The world is full of a number of things, most of them electric

The most significant character in electrical researches for some decades was the Englishman Stephen Gray, dyer and amateur scientist—an unusual combination, for tradesmen rarely dabbled in the relatively aristocratic domain of natural philosophy. Gray was befriended by Desaguliers; some accounts have him occasionally assisting the demonstrator during lectures, and others have him boarding in Desaguliers's quarters.[2] Gray moved in Royal Society circles as a sort of second-class citizen, acting more frequently as an assistant to gentleman amateurs than as an equal. Moreover, he seems to have been the only one in his circle interested in the little electrical attractions that Hauksbee had discovered; he pursued them on his own. Investigations in 1708 led Gray to observe that a down feather that is attracted to an electrified wand after coming into contact with the glass will a moment later suddenly fly away from the tube and thenceforth be repelled by it. Gray composed a letter to the Royal Society in which he reported spending hours chasing bits of down about his room with an electrified glass rod: Science represented a simple pleasure. Yet the society's secretary did not see fit to publish the correspondence, so the discovery did not make its way into the literature;[3] no feather chasing took place in the British or Dutch or French demonstration-lectures.

Connections with scientifically inclined gentlemen allowed Gray to retire from his unhealthy and unseemly occupation of dyer in 1719 and to take up a pension at the Charterhouse of London, an institution that otherwise served primarily as an orphanage. In this unanticipated leisure he joined and assisted his patrons in astronomical observations and the pursuit of experimental philosophy. He determined in 1729 to return to his electrical researches, apparently on his own initiative. Gray obtained a long, hollow glass cylinder to rub in order to excite electricity. To keep dust from being drawn by electrical attraction into the tube, he closed the ends with cork stoppers. Unexpectedly—here, as all the standard histories follow Gray in pointing out, Fortuna smiled upon a prepared mind—he observed that the cork seemed to acquire an electric virtue exactly the same as that in the glass. It attracted bits of dust and metal leaf, as did the rest of the tube. Yet cork itself, Gray confirmed, is not "electric"; that is to say, no amount of direct rubbing will cause it to attract bits of dust. Somehow, he had managed to transmit, or conduct, the electrical property from electrified glass to the cork. Gray showed the effect to Desaguliers, who communicated it to the Royal Society of London on 1 May 1729, although the demonstration seems to have aroused no great interest.

Gray, along with a few gentlemen friends, indulged himself for two years in a leisurely examination of the transmission of electrical effects to and from different materials.[4] The story is a delightful one, all the more so since Gray had no particular interest in publishing his discovery. In addition to cork, Gray tried a number of other materials close at hand. First he wedged a stick about four inches long into the end of the hollow tube and found that an ivory ball attached to its distant end still attracted lightweight materials. He quickly tried another stick twice as long as the first, and then a two-foot piece. Transmission of the electric virtue continued. He hung a two-foot section of iron wire from the corked end of his wand and determined that when he attached the little ball to the wire, it still demonstrated the properties of electrified objects. Brass wire worked as efficaciously as iron, and a yard-long piece of packthread transmitted the effects too. Gray tied to this string in turn a guinea, a shilling, a half-penny, a piece of tin, and a piece of lead. Still during the first flurry of experiments he proceeded to try out the hardware from his fireplace: A fire shovel, tongs, and an iron poker all acquired the electric virtue. Heading next to the kitchen, he found that a copper teakettle would attract metal leaf when suspended from the increasingly elaborate train of materials. This was true whether or not the pot was filled with water, whether or not the water had already been warmed. A silver pint pot worked too, as did "vegetable substances both green and dry." Next he sacrificed his walking stick, trimming the end so that it fitted snugly into the glass tube. This he followed with a two-piece fishing rod fourteen feet long, one section made of Spanish cane, the other of wood and whale-bone. A cork ball impaled on the end of the contraption still attracted metal leaf.[5]

Shortly thereafter, Gray called on his gentlemen friends to show them the results of his researches. On 2 May he visited one John God-frey; the pair rigged a twenty-four-foot pole and transmitted the elec-tric virtue down its entire length. They could construct nothing longer that would fit into the end of Gray's glass tube. On the six-teenth of the month, Gray collaborated with a new host, Granvil Wheler. Wheler first witnessed the electrification of household ob-jects: A poker from his fireplace, both cold and hot, and a chicken dressed for roasting acquired the electric virtue.[6] The grander house-hold allowed wider-ranging transmission; from materials at hand Gray made a rod thirty-two feet in length, still capable of transmitting the ability to attract bits of metal leaf. Three days later they returned to the method of packthread, hanging a twenty-six-foot length out of an upper window. Our intrepid investigators suspended an ivory ball from the bottom of the thread and observed that it attracted brass leaf in the courtyard below. On the last day of May they rigged an eigh-teen-foot pole, one end of which they inserted into the glass tube. To the other end they tied thirty-four feet of thread; Gray stood in the balcony, rubbing the rod while Wheler observed an ivory ball at-tached to the thread attracting lightweight objects in the courtyard below. The pair resolved to try the same experiment, with a longer thread, from the cupola of St. Paul's cathedral.[7]

The planned marriage of science and religion never occurred. In June, the electricians hit upon an alternative approach. They deter-mined to suspend a wire horizontally. The upper floor of Wheler's house was a large, open room, the sort of thing now used as a picture gallery for the amusement of tourists. It is wonderful to imagine peo-ple sufficiently comfortable in such surroundings to go pounding nails into the exposed oaken beams in order to string a wire from one end to the other for an amateur philosophical experiment. They at-tached an ivory ball to one end of the wire so that they might see if, standing at one end of the room and rubbing a glass rod, they could make the ball attract bits of dust and metallic foil at the other end of the room. (The ball was undoubtedly close at hand; such spaces were, after all, used as gaming rooms in the eighteenth century and usually came equipped with the instruments of billiards.) A first attempt, suspending a long piece of iron wire from the nails, using short lengths of brass wire, failed. A second attempt using silk thread to hold up the iron wire—silk chosen because it was finer than brass, not because of its composition—succeeded marvelously. When Gray rubbed the glass rod at the far end of the room, dust and metal leaf jumped to the ivory ball and clung to it, as if it were by remote control. Wheler's top-floor room allowed a straight transmission of 80 feet; with the iron wire doubled back to where the rod was excited, the virtue passed through a distance of nearly 150 feet. The avid experimenters proceeded to the barn, and thence to the great outdoors, stringing wires through the garden; they discovered that their ability to transmit electrical effects over distances was limited more by the difficulty in draping their iron wires over the countryside than by any electrical limitations (see Figure 8.1). Pounding wooden poles into the ground and attaching metal wires to them by means of silk ribbons (here we must see a precursor to the telephone pole), they eventually extended electrical transmission to a distance of 765 feet. These were the delights that rewarded the charming eccentricity of the British gentry and those they patronized.[8]

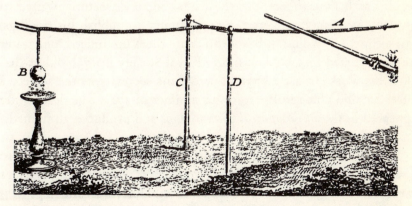

Figure 8.1 A wire strung across a field to demonstrate transmission of the electric virtue. Reproduced from Jean Antoine Nollet, Leçons de physique expérimentale *(Paris, 1745), vol. 6, plate 3, figure 13. Courtesy of the Bakken Library, Minneapolis, Minn.*

The different behaviors of brass, silk, and iron suggested a new series of experiments aimed at determining what objects could acquire the attractive properties associated with "electric" materials. Wheler assisted in experiments with another group of objects suitable to the grander household—a tablecloth, a globe with a map of the world, and so on—which they hung from strings attached to the ceiling. Each in turn demonstrated the attractive virtue as the electrified wand brushed against it.

Gray continued to test new objects in his apartments. The human body suggested itself for electrification, so the experimental philosopher made loops in the ends of two "clothes ropes" and hung them from four stout hooks—again fixed to a beam in the ceiling. He persuaded one of the boys from the Charterhouse to lie on the ropes, face down, supported under his chest and his thighs (see Figure 8.2). It is not clear just how Gray struck the arrangement; the only record of the orphan is that he was "between eight and nine" years of age, and that he weighed forty-seven pounds at the time. Gray rubbed his glass tube with his hands to electrify it and then touched the boy's feet with the tube; the boy was able to attract dust and down to his fingers. The human body, like cork, ivory, and iron, acquires the electrical virtue by communication.[9]

This great electrical adventure remained a private pleasure for Gray and his friends. The retired dyer did apparently share his continuing results with Desaguliers, but the Royal Society's lecturer waited to give the amateur discoverer an opportunity to publish his findings. For a time, Gray did not bother to write them up. Indeed, only after he was granted membership in the Royal Society in 1730 did he disclose his work. In early 1731 he wrote the secretary of the society a letter detailing his results from the summer of 1729. The description appeared in the *Philosophical Transactions* and produced an immediate response.

The standard histories of electricity here point most prominently to a series of experiments performed by Charles Cistern Dufay, Nollet's mentor at the Académie royale des sciences. Dufay's thorough professionalism offers a stark contrast to Gray's delightful amateur investigations. Indeed in this aspect the French research is reminiscent of the way in which Lemery had managed a generation earlier to move from the secret of Glauber's phosphor—a single, practically alchemical

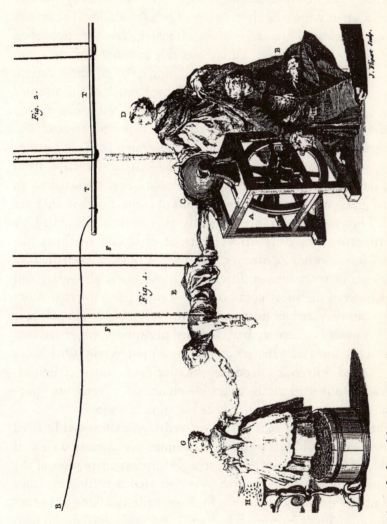

297

Figure 8.2 Illustration of a boy, like Gray's orphan, used to collect the electric virtue. This example of the genre is from Recueil de traités sur l'électricité traduits de l'allemand et de l'anglois (Paris, 1748), plate 11. Courtesy of the Bakken Library, Minneapolis, Minn.

recipe for a substance that would glow in the dark—to a routine extraction of a plethora of phosphors from dead fish, urine, and excrement. (Dufay himself took an interest in phosphors as his first major scientific research; it is said that he caused a depression in the trade in the material when he published his results.[10]) The French royal academician spent many months electrifying all sorts of things. The results of this work appeared in a series of six extensive *Mémoires* published in the *académie's* collection.[11] Dufay was able to show that most materials could be made electric either by rubbing or by communication. According to the standard story, this work took much of the mystery and magic out of electrical attraction, as Lemery's work had moved phosphors from the alchemical realm to the province of science.[12]

Even greater play goes to Dufay's announcement of Gray's earlier discovery, which had remained unpublished—the observation from the first decade of the century that feathers are first attracted to an electrified glass rod, but after a few seconds of contact with it, they are repelled. Dufay showed more generally that objects electrified by communication not only attract bits of dust and feathers but also repel one another. Moreover, lightweight objects electrified by communication with certain different electric materials—glass and resin cakes were the most common pair—attract one another more strongly than they attract dust and down. Dufay, classifying electric materials as avidly as Lemery had classified phosphors, suggested that there are two sorts of substances that become electric. One kind, which he called "vitreous," produces the species of electricity first associated with rubbed glass; the other, which he called "resinous," produces the same species of electricity as his cakes of resin.

The theoretical views that Dufay offered are less frequently cited and never dwelt upon. His was a rather primitively Cartesian view of the world, and his theory offered a straightforward adaptation of the vortex theory of gravity to electricity—celebrated as further evidence for the embattled theory of vortices by Fontenelle's gushing introduction in the *académie's Histoire*.[13] Indeed Dufay was joined in this project by Joseph Privat de Molières, the last and most elaborate theoretician in the Cartesian vortex tradition.[14] Dufay suggested yet another subtle matter be added for electricity to those for gravity, magnetism, anomalous suspension of fluids in barometers, capillary action, and so on. His example might perhaps serve as a corrective to the Enlightenment view, too often perpetuated in the historical literature, that those who worked diligently in the laboratory refrained from formulating elaborate hypotheses and that those who backed the wrong theoretical horse were deficient in every other way as scientists.

With this intensive work in Dufay's laboratory, the main phenomena of classic electrostatics were established, despite the Cartesian leanings of their author. There are two sorts of electrification that can be excited by rubbing various "electric" materials (now known as insulators); both sorts can be transmitted by contact to "nonelectric" (conducting) materials. Objects electrified either by rubbing or contact repel other bodies with the same sort of electrification and attract things electrified the other way. Indeed, Dufay recognized that electrical attractions could be communicated to objects by induction—that is, by bringing an electrified object near a material that could acquire the electric virtue by communication. For the strong positivist tradition in the history of science, there remained little but the mathematization of this information to complete the science of electrostatics. According to the standard story, Dufay rates with Gray as one of the great heroes of eighteenth-century electrical science: Each sought to uncover the phenomena for the glory of science, without the prejudices that so frequently afflicted the ideologues in natural philosophy.

Yet Gray's and Dufay's contemporaries saw things in another way. On the one hand, Dufay's driven pursuit of the phenomena and his extensive empirical generalizations had almost no direct effect on the practice of electricity. This is not to deny the importance of Dufay's discoveries; they were crucial to the development of electrical theory in the eighteenth century. It is simply to indicate that the sort of painstaking work that observers then and now recognize is necessary (though not sufficient) for scientific progress did not strike the audience for electricity as terribly significant—it was dreadfully boring. On the other hand, Dufay's development of Gray's discovery that people suspended from ropes could acquire the electric virtue swept polite European society by storm.

In the course of his investigations, Dufay constructed a somewhat more comfortable version of the clothesline loops Gray had rigged for his orphan boy, providing a wooden board for support. The French academician then had an assistant operate the electric wand and took the place of the human conductor himself. During one experimental session, his helper reached out to touch him, and both Dufay and the assistant on the floor felt a noticeable (indeed an unpleasantly noticeable) sensation. They also observed a dim spark; when they repeated the experiment in a darkened room, this spark became quite striking. Neither of these observations, of course, adds to the positivists' requirements for new phenomena to construct a new science of electricity, any more than Dufay's theoretical work does. Yet Dufay's experiments as a human conductor made electricity into a popular science.

The *système Nollet*

For our story, the most important aspect of Dufay's work is that it introduced his new assistant, Jean Antoine Nollet, to the science of electricity. Nollet would eventually make electrical demonstrations the centerpiece of his lectures and of his professional career. In Dufay's lab he gained practical experience manipulating electrified objects, testing the electrical properties of hundreds of materials, and generally acquiring the sort of intimate laboratory acquaintance with electrical phenomena that he came to show in his mechanical and optical demonstrations as well. He became, after Dufay and Gray, the most skilled electrician in Europe. Nollet's lectures, designed in the first few years after Gray had announced his discovery, offered the most up-to-date presentation of static effects from the early 1730s through the middle of the century. The *Programme* of 1738, which served as a catalog of equipment for sale, included a complete electrical kit[15] that contained not only a glass wand for rubbing and bits of lightweight conducting materials suitable for electrical attraction but also stout silk cords capable of suspending a full-grown human conductor of electricity. The demonstrations offered in Nollet's apartments from the beginning offered a delightful reprise of Gray's work and of Dufay's observations as a personal conductor of electricity.

The experimental developments in electricity, the natural philosophy of shocks and sparks, might have been tailor-made for the sort of lectures Nollet and his colleagues in the demonstration-lecture business offered throughout Europe. Like the air pump or the pyrotechnic kit, the electric wand and associated materials provided a spectacular visual effect; the added sensations of sparks and the "spider web" feeling induced by the electrified wand[16] added a further diversion, at least in the small, intimate setting of the Parisian style. Thus Nollet transferred the serendipitous results from the most serious experimental physics laboratory of the eighteenth century to the more common, and distinctly less research-oriented, locus of scientific entertainment.

By contrast, there is no evidence that Nollet ever shared Dufay's theories. Indeed, he did not even dwell upon the distinction between vitreous and resinous electricity in his lectures.[17] From the mid-1730s—perhaps even from the very first years of the lectures—Nollet put forth his own theory of electrical action. The *système Nollet*, as it eventually came to be called, condensed a complete explanation of electrical phenomena into a single phrase, striking in its simplicity and completeness: Electricity is the "simultaneous efflux and influx of a subtle matter."[18] A bit less cryptically, the lecturer explained that the world is filled with a material that finds its appropriate place in the pores of gross matter (see Figure 8.3). This extremely fine stuff, similar to the matter of fire—perhaps even the same thing as ordinary fire—can be forced out of the pores when they are squeezed. Under normal circumstances this local motion of the subtle matter produces no noticeable effect. Yet the electrical discoveries of the eighteenth century made it clear that there are certain materials that, when rubbed, deform in such a manner as to send the subtle electrical matter out of their pores in quite a strong stream. The elasticity of the gross matter quickly restores the shape of the pores, and the electrical matter seeps back into the interior of the object from which it had been expelled. Nollet, working with Dufay, had found the materials that most readily display electrical effects. In terms of the system that the discoverer announced in his lectures, these materials have the peculiar property that the pressure of the inflow of the electrical matter as the pores are restored to their original volume keeps a certain amount of the subtle matter flowing out in little jets. Therefore, near an electrified object, there is a general flow of the electric material into the excited electric, with a few tiny pores from which the matter is vigorously ejected.

The Enlightenment attack on indulgent Cartesian systems was in the air, and Nollet felt compelled to respond to it. He acknowledged that his theory did represent a system, requiring imagination as well as observation in its construction. Yet Nollet asserted that his imagination

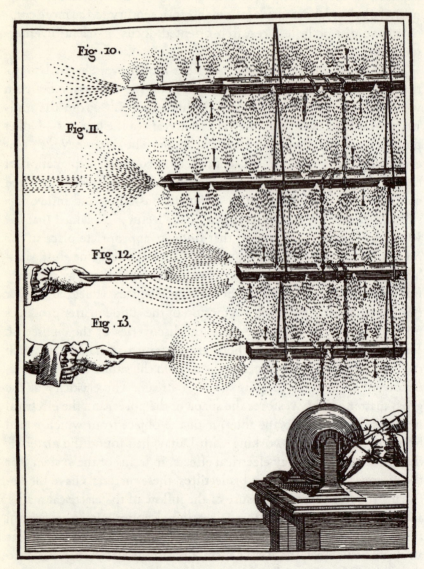

Figure 8.3 Illustration of Nollet's subtle matter. The arrows pointing toward the metal bars indicate the influx of the matter into pores between the particles that compose solids; the diverging dotted lines indicate its rapid efflux from the bars. Reproduced from Jean Antoine Nollet, Lettres sur l'électricité (Paris: Guerin, 1753), vol. 1, plate 3, facing p. 152. Courtesy of the Bakken Library, Minneapolis, Minn.

built on phenomena and that his system was solid. The word *system* did not, in his case at least, indicate that the theory represented an "assemblage of mere possibilities, or speculations barren of proof."[19]

Nollet's explanation clearly took as its paradigm experiment Gray's old observation, rediscovered as Nollet worked with Dufay in the early 1730s, that a bit of down or dust will first be attracted to a rubbed glass rod; it will come to rest for a time against the electric material, but soon it will wobble a bit and then suddenly flee from the rod. A skillful experimenter like Gray or Nollet himself could chase the downy feather around the room for some minutes; the exhibit became a standard in demonstration-lectures. In terms of the theory of simultaneous efflux and influx, objects like down and dust first enter into the general motion of subtle matter toward an excited electric, as though they were caught in a wind or a stream. As a dusty bit comes to rest on the glass, the general motion of the influx of electrical matter moves it gently around on the surface until it is nudged by chance over one of the little jets of subtle matter in efflux. Caught up in the vigorous stream receding from the excited electric, light objects can be thrown some distance. Indeed, careful manipulation of an electric wand and its associated jets could hold a feather suspended in the efflux for some time.

Nollet's theory offered more than an account of a single experiment. It brought electricity into the mainstream of the sort of explanations offered for other phenomena in the demonstration-lecture school that, as we have seen, became associated with Newtonianism. Nollet turned away from the obvious Cartesian vortex theory his mentor Dufay had offered to a self-consciously modern sort of theory that swept the vortices away. We can understand, in light of this theory, why it is that Voltaire felt comfortable writing to Nollet upon the rejection of the essays from Cirey on fire about his disgust that the prizes had gone to vorticists. The explanation in terms of a material responsible for the effects of both electricity and fire—an explanation that, as we have seen, Émilie du Châtelet adopted at about the same time—had the advantage of simplifying the physical world in which Nollet worked. If Dufay's theory was the last gasp of orthodox Cartesian ideology, Nollet's was the first attempt in French experimental physics to adopt the new style of the international community of demonstrators of Enlightenment.

True to the tradition of these demonstration-lectures, the presentation of the system offered a tone more akin to Gray's delighted amateur pursuit of feathers than to Dufay's serious academic *mémoires.* The spirit as well as the content of Nollet's early electrical lectures are captured in the frontispiece (see Figure 8.4) to his *Essai sur l'électricité.*[20] A young man lies on a board suspended from the ceiling by silk ropes. Someone—we assume it is Nollet himself—wields the electric wand, rubbing it with his hand and then wiping it against the boy to electrify him. A young woman decorously draws a spark from his nose with her finger (electrified kisses were also a commonplace at the time[21]), while the boy attracts bits of paper from a small table placed below him. The background shows the same setting illustrated in the early volumes of the *Leçons de physique expérimentale,* which Nollet published at exactly the same time. Even more than those illustrations, this frontispiece communicates a sense of the delight taken by audiences in electrical demonstrations.

Similar scenes were repeated in all the important lecture halls of Europe. Electricity took its place in the demonstration of Enlightenment and offered a better advertisement for the new science than articles in mathematical physics ever could have done. The equipment required for these recreations was quite simple, especially once Dufay (with Nollet) had performed exhaustive tests of the electrical properties of materials. The results were so striking that as news of the discoveries spread, electrical shows popped up throughout Europe and even in America. Characters with little or no experience in philosophical matters presented demonstrations in the salons of their patrons, playing the part of Nollet or Desaguliers or perhaps Rohault. They believed that in a few weeks they could repeat and master all the electrical research performed anywhere up to that point, and demonstrate it in any circle no matter how prestigious. (Such immodest claims are occasionally repeated at face value in histories of electricity, ironically including some that describe with great admiration the months of struggle devoted to the subject by Dufay.) It was in fact the very ignorance of standard techniques and experiments that allowed this wonderful amateur community to produce a string of discoveries that transformed electrical science from a delicate plaything to a boisterous spectacle.

Figure 8.4 A young man lying on a board suspended from the ceiling by silk ropes. Someone (Nollet?) wields the electric wand, rubbing it with his hand and then wiping it against the boy to electrify him. A young woman decorously draws a spark from his nose with her finger while the boy attracts bits of paper from a small table placed below him. Reproduced from Jean Antoine Nollet, Essai sur l'électricité des corps *(Paris: Guerin, 1746), frontispiece. Courtesy of the Bakken Library, Minneapolis, Minn.*

The first new electrical discoveries emerged in Germany in the early 1740s. It is extremely difficult to sort out just which of the enthusiasts in the exploding electrical community hit upon which particular electrical demonstration or apparatus. Members of that community followed Gray's example of sharing new discoveries with friends in informal settings, and news passed from one city to the next as observers traveled through the German-speaking world. Many experiments and innovations must have spread by word of mouth—that worst nightmare of historians—since they appeared in several different accounts published during the years 1742 to 1744 as commonplaces. Nor was there any particular discussion of priority in most of these publications. Indeed when we consider the style of the accounts of the new experiments that emerged, it is hardly surprising that such information is not included. Georg Matthias Bose, for example, presented his account as a German poem; even the footnotes rhymed.[22]

Nollet, extremely careful about such matters of precedence, was probably the scholar in the best position to have discovered the answers to questions of priority. Close to the sources and well connected in the international philosophical community, during the 1740s he had no particular ax to grind concerning the accomplishments of amateur electricians. Yet even Nollet despaired when it came to the work of the Germans; his tentative attributions were always hedged with comments about how difficult it was to provide proper recognition when researchers did not include the date of their work in their reports of that work. (In this he emulated Dufay, who had the same complaints about the amateurish researches that had preceded his entry into electrical studies.) Much of the historical background presented by the Germans is patently absurd—one book reports that Otto von Guericke inspired the work of William Gilbert,[23] although the German had not yet been born when the Englishman published his study. It is modern scholars who have taken partisan positions on these developments; the field has become something of a quagmire. More important, arguments about experimental priority miss the point of the German researchers. Like Stephen Gray they reveled in the phenomena; members of the experimental community usually offered their discoveries quite voluntarily to the public domain.

Suffice it to say that Nollet was aware of the work of all the major German electricians. Christian Hausen, a professor of mathematics at

Leipzig,[24] and Georg Matthias Bose, who had published an analysis of Claude Perrault's essay on sound,[25] are usually cited in the secondary literature as the most important researchers. Clearly, Leibnizian lecturer and author Christian Wolff, who was Koenig's teacher and whose work thus indirectly inspired Mme du Châtelet to look into the theory of living force, was the most influential intellectual who took up the new studies. Although his own contribution in the technical development of the field may not have been significant, his interest certainly helped to make the field respectable, and word of his repetition of the demonstrations others had developed spread quickly. Likewise, publications by the influential classical scholar Johann Heinrich Winkler were translated into both French and English, and therefore represented a more important influence for the transmission of the new science than is generally recognized.[26] The fact that scholars of such note from such disparate fields took up electrical experimentation must serve to indicate that the Renaissance Man was alive and well into the German Enlightenment.

The German experimenters, taken as a community, made three significant if accidental technical contributions to the development of static electric generators. They introduced the "rubber"—usually a leather pad, but sometimes just a sheet of paper—to excite electricity in glass. They reintroduced large spinning globes like those Hauksbee had constructed; in combination with the rubber, these produced larger quantities of electricity than tubes of the sort Gray and Dufay had used in their researches. Finally, they collected the electric virtue on metal "prime conductors" to store the electricity created by the new machines—a virtue sufficiently potent to produce more discomfiture than delight in the human conductors popular during the late 1730s.

The rubber is perhaps the most obvious of the developments and therefore the most difficult to document. A number of people distressed by the idea or the reality of working their fingers to the bone to produce electricity rubbed glass with paper or leather pads. Winkler (see Figure 8.5) presented a rather complicated version to excite electricity in a wand. The glass tube was mounted in brackets lined with a leather cushion that was stuffed with wool. The pulley and string arrangements allowed Winkler to pull the tube to and fro, producing prodigious quantities of electricity.[27] Nollet is of little help

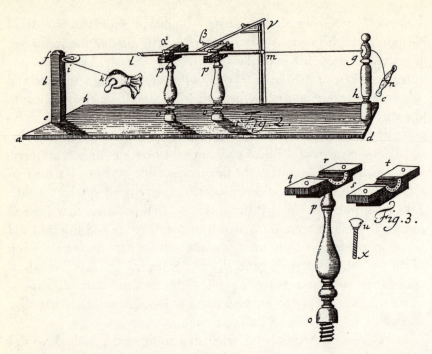

Figure 8.5 Probably the first apparatus with a leather and horsehair "rubber."
Winkler's figure 3 illustrates the brackets Winkler constructed to support the
glass wand LM in Figure 2. Reproduced from Johann Heinrich Winkler, Die
Starke der electrischen Kraft des Wassers in glasernen Gefassen *(Leipzig:*
Breitkopf, 1746). Courtesy of the Bakken Library, Minneapolis, Minn.

concerning precedence in the innovation of the rubber, for he refused
to adopt the innovation. His occasional mention of the device served
only to dismiss it as a sort of accessory for sissies.[28] The French
demonstrator observed that Gray had done his brilliant, pathfinding
work with nothing between his hand and the electric material it excited, and indeed the Frenchman felt compelled to defend the Englishman's honor in the face of slights by aristocratic Germans, who
suggested that only hands toughened and dried by years in trade
might produce electrical effects without insulating leather. The royal
academician suggested that Gray had shared with him such a delicacy
of touch that they had no need of bits of leather or paper to produce
large electrical effects from glass.

The second German advance in design came ironically with the return to the sort of globe generators that Hauksbee had devised twenty

years earlier. In this case, the development came out of ignorance rather than sloth. The large, complicated engines that Hauksbee had illustrated early in the century had no particular advantage over the electric wand when either was rubbed by hand, as Gray had done in his researches and as all the major British and Dutch demonstrators had described in their books. Yet when the announcements of exciting new electrical experiments confusedly made their way to Germany, they did not come with instructions to use a glass tube. The history got so confused that Winkler's account, the first to be published in France, explained that Hausen had come up with the idea of using a spinning globe.[29] (On the next page it was granted that this novelty was inspired by Hauksbee's accounts of the apparatus used to induce the mercurial phosphor, although Winkler appeared not to realize the role Hauksbee's researches had for the history of electricity.[30]) Christian Wolff had a copy of Hausen's machine made, and Wolff's influence caused his version to serve as the basis for the "new" German design.[31] In short, only the absence of any expertise in matters electrical caused the Germans to try a globe—Bose in fact prepared his by breaking the neck off a large chemical retort. (In another irony, the spout of the retort later served as an electric wand.[32]) Yet rubbers similar to those Winkler had devised, when applied to such rotating globes made in imitation of Hauksbee's original machine, produced even more electricity than Winkler's mechanically operated wand.

The third innovation came in the way the Germans collected electricity. Human conductors remained popular, but with the increasing power of electrical generators the job became uncomfortable. A whole series of metal household objects—gun barrels and swords were among the most common—could be suspended near rubbed glass globes to serve as what later came to be called "prime conductors" in the system (see Figure 8.6). At first these objects were suspended, like Gray's orphan boy and his successors in the role, from silk strings; later they came to be mounted on glass rods. Unabashed curiosity and delight drove electricians all over Europe to try to produce larger sparks, stronger attractions, and more attractive demonstrations.

Many of the German demonstrations simply repeated or expanded upon the sort of transmission experiments Gray had done—already extensively explored by Dufay, whose work was apparently not

310

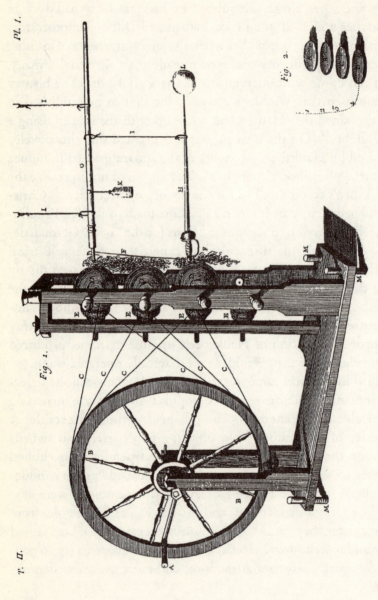

Figure 8.6 Illustration of a gun barrel and a sword used to collect electricity. The apple on the end of the sword prevents accidental leakage of electricity from the sharp point. Reproduced from Recueil de traités sur l'électricité traduits de l'allemand et de l'anglois (Paris, 1748), plate 1. Courtesy of the Bakken Library, Minneapolis, Minn.

known in the German-speaking world. Winkler, for example, transmitted electricity through a glass tube successively containing water, milk, beer, aqua vitae, and mercury. He also presented extensive examples of the way in which the virtue is transmitted through the human body.[33] This rather haphazard sort of display produced no new results—except to literally and figuratively electrify new audiences for science.

Yet with the introduction of the rubber, especially when it excited a large sphere, electricity was transformed from an amusement with dust and down to a philosophy of shocks and sparks. Like Dufay, the Germans discovered that a suspended human conductor could produce sparks large enough to cause a "lively pain."[34] Larger sparks produced other effects as well. The first new manifestation of the vastly increased power of the new generators came during a demonstration in Berlin in 1744. According to Winkler, a Prussian army doctor named Ludolf originated the experiment.[35] In the most romantic version of the story, natural philosophy turned the world upside down, since the discovery came as the electrician handed a snifter of brandy to the servant who was employed as the human conductor. When the electrician brought the drink to the waiting lips, a spark jumped from the servant's tongue to the liquor—which immediately burst into flame. The spectacular flaming of spirits begged for an audience. A Mr. Reinhard told Winkler of the effect; Winkler went to the famous Wolff at Halle and the pair repeated the experiment. Winkler himself climbed into Wolff's conducting apparatus hung from silk ribbons, touched a spinning glass globe, and used his fingers to set spirits on fire.

The effect was immediately described in the gazettes of the German-speaking world. The German phenomena were transmitted with hasty theories, generally variations on Cartesian vortex theories of the sort Dufay had formulated. Winkler's account, the first to appear in French, again provides a typical example.[36] He suggested that electricity might be caused either by a material of the sort Newton had hypothesized in the *Optics* as responsible for the refraction of light in transparent materials or else by an ether like that responsible for central forces. Winkler proceeded to dismiss the Newtonian material and concluded that since the electrical virtue results from a central force, it must come from the action of a whirlpool.[37] This is the rather mysterious message of the mind of the Enlightenment as it manifested itself in Germany.

With the news of the new German discoveries, Nollet stepped forward in Paris as the European dean of electrical studies. The move was by no means presumptuous. His mentor, Charles Dufay, was dead, as was Stephen Gray. The work of the Germans was so thoroughly, delightfully, and innocently amateur that even the community of demonstration-lecturers could hardly take the German discoveries as evidence of any serious philosophical concern with the phenomena. Neither 'sGravesande nor Musschenbroek had demonstrated a serious interest in the development of electrical experiments in the wake of Gray's discoveries; Desaguliers, who had displayed such an interest, died in 1744. Nollet, a royal academician with ten years' experience in electrical studies, was the natural candidate for the role of Europe's leading electrician. And he was prepared.

The German discoveries presented a brilliant affirmation of the theory that Nollet had developed and offered in his lectures for a decade. Nollet's (and Émilie du Châtelet's) suggestion that electricity was the manifestation of a second effect of the material responsible for the action of heat allowed the straightforward explanation of this new phenomenon in terms of existing theory. The dramatic demonstration that electricity causes spirits to burst into flame demonstrated that powerful electrical effects were sufficient to produce enough heat to ignite extremely flammable substances. This was not something that other current theories—especially the Cartesian theories involving whirlpools of a new matter—would have been able to explain.

Nollet's opportunity to tout his success came soon enough. Each Easter, the Académie royale des sciences held a grand public meeting. These occasions are more frequently remembered in histories of the science from a period near the end of the eighteenth century (Antoine Laurant Lavoisier announced his discovery of oxygen at one of those public meetings), but the *académie* seems to have held high hopes for Nollet's discussion of electricity. At the public presentation in 1746, Nollet brought to a close a yearlong presentation of new discoveries from Germany and added considerable information on his own researches. The papers he read would eventually be published in the *Mémoires* for 1745 and 1747, although publication was so slow that the first would not appear until 1748. Nollet therefore published the substance of the two lectures, together with more elementary materials, in an *Essai sur l'électricité des corps*,[38] which appeared shortly after the speech at the plenary session of the Académie royale des sciences.

In these publications, Nollet did more than merely report the empirical findings of the Germans. The *Essai*, especially, became something of an electrician's bible, offering extensive advice based on the experience that the lecturer had gained in Dufay's laboratory and in his own preparations for demonstrations. Nollet provided extremely detailed instructions for the production of electrical instruments and effects. He noted which materials proved most efficacious for the production of electricity. He described in detail how conducting materials should be constructed and electrically isolated from the ground in order to transmit the electrical virtue most successfully from one place or object to another. He even set forth what weather and rooms are most conducive to the repetition of various experiments. Even after Nollet's publication of several further works in the field, the *Essai* remained available for twenty years.

Nollet's grand public lectures, and the *mémoires* and *Essai* that followed, also put forth his own theory of electrical action—a theory that until that point he had offered only in the privacy of his demonstration-lectures. The prefatory remarks that he presented make it clear that he was preoccupied with the philosophy of the Enlightenment—or at least with its rhetoric. Nollet acknowledged that his explanation represented a system. Yet, he argued, it was not a rash system like those many electricians were offering, since he had formulated it many years before, as the auditors of his lectures could attest.[39] Moreover, he pointed out, it was not a system constructed to explain a single phenomenon. Instead, his system simplified the discussion of electricity. In a single phrase, he could account for the broad spectrum of effects—his own account provided thirty-three classes of attractions, repulsions, transmissions, sights, sounds, and tactile sensations.[40]

It has been the fashion since the generation after Nollet to dismiss his work as the insubstantial musings of an ideologue. Yet in his own generation, he was the undisputed master of electrical theory and practice. The *Essai* and the volumes of *Recherches* and *Lettres sur l'électricité* that followed it proved the most popular works on the subject in the 1740s, and all were republished for decades. Nollet's theories were the center of attention from both adherents and detractors and survived a number of new discoveries. It is perhaps the vituperativeness of his enemies—a commonplace in eighteenth-century discourse—that has caused so many histories, especially in the Anglo-American tradition, to disparage the theory of simultaneous influx and efflux; in fact, it proved a remarkably successful and adaptable explanation for static effects.

There would be a great deal for the system to adapt to. Events moved more quickly even than Nollet. Following on the heels of the German improvements to electrical machines and the phenomena these more powerful devices allowed came yet another discovery that changed the face of electricity. Even before Nollet could publish his *Essai,* news arrived more or less simultaneously from Germany and from Holland of a new device, an instrument that could store the electrical virtue more efficaciously and over a much longer period of time than a simple prime conductor. The first word came in a letter from Petrus van Musschenbroek in Leyden to Nollet's senior colleague Réaumur, describing the Dutch version of the accidental discovery. Musschenbroek was experimenting with methods of storing electricity in water. He attached a wire to his prime conductor and placed the wire in a jar of water, which he held in his hand. An assistant spun the handle of the generator; Musschenbroek reached for the prime conductor (see Figure 8.7). As his hand neared the metal bar, he sustained the worst electrical shock of his career: never, he vowed, would he repeat the experiment. He was thrown to the floor, and his arms ached. The charming sparks and little shocks that had served as the basis for amusements like the electrified kiss were suddenly supplanted by a virtual weapon of terror.

Nollet rushed a description and illustration of the experiment into print in the *Essai.*[41] In honor of Musschenbroek, he named the device the "Leyden jar." (Nollet's authority in matters electrical may be gauged by the fact that the moniker stuck; through the end of the eighteenth century all major electricians referred to the device by that name.) What is more remarkable, the French academician apparently repeated the experiment himself and suffered a shock every bit as severe as the one Musschenbroek described. His colleague at the Académie royale des sciences, Louis-Guillaume Le Monnier, soon began to offer shocks from the Leyden jar—not so strongly charged as Musschenbroek's had been—as a public amusement.[42] A visiting

*Figure 8.7 The apparatus that gave Musschenbroek an unforgettable shock
(bottom picture) and Nollet's explanation of the flow of electrical matter (diagram at the top). Reproduced from Jean Antoine Nollet,* Essai sur l'électricité
des corps *(Paris: Guerin, 1746), plate 4. Courtesy of the Bakken Library,
Minneapolis, Minn.*

Englishman, one Turberville Needham, went for a try. He first asked
a lad of sixteen who experienced the shock ahead of him what to expect; the boy said that it didn't really hurt, but that the strong sensation that the jar produced left him without any feeling in his arms.

Encouraged, apparently, by this report, Needham too, decided to subject himself to the shock. "I observed particularly upon the trial of this," he wrote, "that the operator, who appeared to be very expert, and quite familiarized with every former effect, showed however some apprehension, and was unwilling to lead the way, as he had done in all the other experiments."[43] After the fact, Needham reported that the strong and unpleasant sensation was indeed quite painful in both arms.

The Leyden experiment, like the use of the human conductor to collect the electric virtue, quickly swept Europe. It was determined that a metal foil could be used on the outside of the jar, replacing the hand of the experimenter. Likewise, a metallic conductor like lead shot or foil could be used inside the jar in place of water. (In this form, the Leyden jar is fairly easily recognizable as a modern capacitor or electric condenser, used for short-term storage of electric charge.) Nor was Le Monnier the only natural philosopher who, for a price, allowed visitors to experience the Leyden experiment. Nollet himself subjected others to the experience as well. He discovered that the effects of the jar could be passed through more than one person. Rather like Gray and Wheler transmitting the electric influence through increasingly long pieces of packthread, the Parisian electrician set about shocking increasingly extensive chains of human conductors. In one public spectacle arranged for the king, Nollet had 180 soldiers line up in horseshoe formation, holding hands, so that those at either end of the line could grasp a pair of wires coming from the jar. As they did so, the jar discharged and the whole line jumped as one man. Not to be outdone, the grand Convent of the Carthusians lined up its entire community and formed a chain nine hundred paces long; again, "the whole company, at the same instant of time, gave a sudden spring, and all equally felt the shock that was the consequence of the experiment."[44]

Nollet also pursued a less spectacular series of investigations into the Leyden jar in the years between its invention and 1748, when he prepared the results for the *académie*'s *Mémoires* and then hurried them into print in a new volume, the *Recherches sur les causes particuliers des phénoménes électriques*[45] of 1749. He devised a glass globe fitted with brass connectors at the ends so that he could seal one end over the prime conductor of an electric machine and then empty the glass vessel by means of an air pump fitted to the other end. When Nollet reached for the evacuated globe he felt a shock "similar to that which one feels in the Leyden experiment,"[46] suffering a severe headache and complaining that he felt sick for days. The shock was accompanied by sparks inside the tube, which Nollet believed looked like "the lights which precede or accompany thunder."[47] This new demonstration spawned a device known as the electric egg, since oval-shaped globes were favored for its implementation (see Figure 8.8). The egg was constructed with a stopcock on a pipe at one end so that the glass globe could be evacuated by an air pump, and both ends were fitted with electrical connectors to allow electrification of the residual air. These devices joined the electrician's cabinet, allowing for the production of an eerie glow associated with what is now known as a gas discharge—an effect closely related to the "mercurial phosphor" that inspired the machines that had initiated the study of electricity.

With his new demonstration, Nollet could explain the action of the Leyden jar in terms of his system. It was clear that in the new experiment there was no air to impede the motion of any subtle matter inside the jar. Owing to this freedom of movement, he said, the jets of electrical matter expelled from the glass flew out more vigorously than when rubbed glass was surrounded on both sides by air. These extra-strength jets explained the greater power of the evacuated jar to produce sparks, shocks, and light. In the same way, Nollet suggested, the Leyden jar allowed extremely strong jets to escape from the outside of the jar. Although he provided no precise mechanism for the operation of the jar, he suggested that the conductors on the inner and outer surfaces of the glass served a function analogous to the pieces of iron used to "arm" a magnet, increasing its strength.[48] (The small magnets used today in order to hold metal doors closed, for example, are usually "armed" with two pieces of iron that protrude slightly beyond the faces of the magnet.) Somehow the arming conductors provided a clear path for the subtle matter responsible for electrical effects by displacing the air that ordinarily impedes its motion. The plausibility of this explanation depends upon the fact that electric effects are ordinarily transmitted through conductors—the shape of the microscopic pores in the bodies is conducive to the motion of the jets. The Nollet system had survived its first major public, empirical challenge: It absorbed an important new apparatus and phenomenon

318

Figure 8.8 Nollet's "electric egg," in which sparks in low-pressure air produce large flashes like lightning. Reproduced from Jean Antoine Nollet, Recherches sur les causes particuliers des phénoménes électriques (Paris: Guerin, 1749), third discourse, plate 2. Courtesy of the Bakken Library, Minneapolis, Minn.

without modification to any important aspect of its explanatory mechanism.

Moreover, the investigation of the electric egg, which came in response to the discovery of the Leyden jar, uncovered an important new chain of phenomena. Nollet observed that the sparks inside his egg appeared like miniature versions of the major meteorological displays of lightning. Like Lemery a generation earlier, Nollet hoped to explain that violent activity in terms of the extremely energetic new effects that experimental philosophers had created in the laboratory. Lemery, of course, had looked to chemistry; Nollet, in his turn, saw the explanation for thunderstorms in electricity. The desire to explain the noisy and dangerous meteor in terms of the new science had begun with Descartes; the alternative explanations offered by members of the first two generations of natural philosophers in the eighteenth century captured the slightly different spirits of their contemporaries. Lemery offered a system even more elaborate than the original Cartesian explanation: Volcanoes belched forth inflammable airs, which found their way between atmospheric layers and, in concert with rain clouds, burst into flame. The system had depended upon the newest researches into chemistry, but the spirit of Fontenelle's *Conversations on the Plurality of Worlds* informed the broader mechanism. Nollet, living in Enlightened Paris, eschewed the baroque elaboration of extensive hypotheses so popular in the previous generation. For him, it was the simplicity of the mechanism and the minimalism of the conditions his system required that lent credence to his explanation of the weather.

Of kites and coonskin caps: a noble savage for electricity

The publication of the *Researches on Electricity* in 1749 represents the zenith of Nollet's career. Shortly after its appearance he set out on a triumphal tour of Europe, meeting with all the important electricians and debunking the claims of a number of overly ambitious enthusiasts. He was, without doubt, the most famous experimental philosopher of his generation, a darling of the philosophes, and tutor to royalty in both France and Italy. In the same way that Fontenelle had stood as the personification of natural philosophy in polite society around the turn of the eighteenth century, Nollet occupied that role at its midpoint. His style of science was completely modern, in tune with Parisian social tastes, with the experimental style that, as we have seen, emerged throughout Europe during the middle third of the eighteenth century, and with the antivortex sensibilities of the High Enlightenment.

As was the case with Clairaut in celestial mechanics, however, there were those outside the community of experimental philosophers who believed in a higher standard for politically correct science. Georges Louis Leclerc, comte de Buffon, donned the mantle in electrical studies, as he had done in astronomy. The naturalist's case for a more thoroughly Newtonian electricity came from a strange and unexpected quarter. A Philadelphia printer and amateur of science named Benjamin Franklin had taken up electrical experiments in the wake of the demonstrations developed during the early 1740s. Buffon would adopt Franklin's electrical theories as the most thoroughly Newtonian ideas on the subject, and would promote them as more Enlightened alternatives to Nollet's.

News moved rather slowly to the provinces. Not until late 1746 did Franklin learn of the electrical phenomena discovered since Gray's work in the early 1730s, which had thrust the science into the limelight. Like the Germans five years earlier, Franklin and his circle received rather confused information; they developed a small repertoire of experiments and shared their discoveries by word of mouth. Like Gray, Franklin hit upon a series of phenomena, most of them standard fare in Europe, that he demonstrated for the amusement of his friends.[49] He described these in letters to Peter Collinson, a member of the Royal Society in London, who gathered the correspondence into a book, *Experiments and Observations on Electricity*, published in 1751. It was this book that Buffon discovered and had translated into French the following year as the newest Newtonian word in experimental philosophy.[50]

Nollet was certainly used to seeing the sort of enthusiastic amateur study that Franklin presented. His own work, indeed, showed up in a vestigial way in the *Experiments and Observations*. The earliest letter was concerned primarily with the "power of points"—the property that electrical sparks jump most readily to and from pointed objects, a fact noted by Nollet in his *Recherches*. Franklin recounted a pair of little demonstrations of the special properties of points: "We had even discovered [the electrical fire's] afflux to the electrical sphere, as well as its efflux, by means of little lightweight windmill wheels made of stiff paper vanes, fixed obliquely, and turning freely on fine wire axes."[51] The American later noted that the success of these experiments, which had been suggested to him by one Philip Syng, "was not owing to any afflux or efflux of the electric fluid, but to various circumstances of attraction and repulsion."[52] It is clear that the American electrical community had some access to Nollet's work and owed the French academician some intellectual debt. Moreover, Franklin called the material to which he attributed electrical effects an "electric fire," echoing Nollet's opinion. "Common matter," he claimed, "is a kind of sponge to the electric fluid."[53] Again, Franklin's original picture of his electrical fire appears rather like the fluid Nollet had already taught about for fifteen years when he saw the work of the American. The colonial letters must have seemed to belong to the genre of work by enthusiastic and untutored amateurs who needed above all to master the literature—advice that Nollet would explicitly extend to the Philadelphian.

Within a few months of taking up electrical studies, however, Franklin advanced his own hypothesis. The starting point was quite close to Nollet and half a dozen other more senior electricians. Rubbing glass rods forces the electrical fire out of the spongelike holes that contain it. Here, however, Franklin departed from standard European fare. He suggested that the fire is transferred to the rubber (Franklin favored buckskin for this purpose), leaving the glass with a deficiency of electric matter and the buckskin with an excess. Once the two materials were separated, the glass rod's pores were left unfilled and an "atmosphere" of excess electrical fire formed around the buckskin. Franklin, in good Newtonian form, suggested that there is a mutual attraction between common matter and the electrical fire, and a mutual repulsion between the bits of electrical fire.

It is difficult for the sympathetic modern reader not to assume that Franklin meant by the bits of electrical fire something quite similar to electrons, and by common matter something akin to the positively charged nuclei of atoms. Viewed this way, the Franklinian theory of course explains all the phenomena and vanquishes all reasonable criticism. Nollet did not have the advantage of this insight into the American's work. His immediate reaction was that Franklin, like a host of other amateurs infected with the electric bug, would benefit from a bit of instruction. From Nollet's point of view, Franklin compounded the ordinary sins of the most enthusiastic Newtonians. Whereas the *Principia* had attributed to ordinary matter two contradictory properties—an inertial force that prevented a body from changing its state of motion and a gravitational force that caused a body to move toward other bodies—Franklin added at least two new forces. Electrical matter, which is contained in all ordinary bodies, carried both a mutually repulsive force and an attraction for the common matter. The theory offered a Newtonianism as baroque as Dufay's Cartesian explanation concocted a decade earlier.

More troubling still was a consequence that Franklin had not apparently worked out. Franklin attributed electrical effects to two states of matter—bodies with either deficient or excessive amounts of electrical fire. Nollet had seen a similar claim in Dufay's two sorts of electricity. Yet Dufay had attributed to each sort essentially the same sort of properties—in the Cartesian theory he worked out, two sources of vortices. Thus pairs of either resinously or vitreously charged bodies display a mutual repulsion. Franklin's two states must likewise explain the similar behaviors of positively and negatively charged bodies. It is easy enough to understand the repulsion between two positively charged bodies—the excess electrical fire on one body repels the excess fire on the other. Similarly, the attraction between oppositely charged bodies is easy to understand; excess fire on the positive body is attracted to the common matter in the other body.

The repulsion between negatively charged bodies, however, is quite a different problem. Franklin would have to posit an extremely strong force of repulsion between pieces of common matter. Yet the very Newtonianism that his theory ostensibly embraced posited a weak attraction between all the bits of ordinary matter in the solar system. Nollet had found it difficult enough to accept ordinary Newtonian attraction, since the Newtonians agreed with all other students of mechanics that the mass of matter also carries with it an inertial force that resists any change in motion. Franklin—whether he knew it or not—was introducing yet another, contradictory, property attributable to common matter. Indeed, this third, repulsive, force outrightly contradicted the very basis of the mathematical mechanics that had finally convinced Nollet to accept the Newtonian hypothesis of universal gravitation.

There is no evidence that Franklin had considered the question of how negatively charged bodies repel when he published his theory. Indeed, the further into the *Experiments and Observations* Nollet might have read, the clearer it would have become that Franklin was a thinker in the old style of the spirit of systems, a maker of hypotheses who was prepared to write a pretty novel of physics. The *Experiments and Observations* offered a suggestion that electricity might be responsible for the phenomenon of lightning—an observation that Nollet had previously published in his own *Recherches sur l'électricité*. The American letters did include a casual suggestion that one might confirm this hypothesis by erecting a tall metal pole with a point at the top underneath a thundercloud and testing the lower end of the pole for signs of electricity—but the tone of the comment does not indicate that he took his idea terribly seriously. What did follow upon the lightning hypothesis were some thirty-four paragraphs of "Opinions and Conjectures" on the weather, a system comparable in its scope and speculative character to Descartes's *Meteorology*.

Franklin's meteorology invoked yet more interparticulate forces. Air, he asserted, is composed of small, hard, round particles that are mutually repulsive, whereas the particles of water are ordinarily mutually attractive. Ordinary evaporation occurs when particles of water are surrounded by common fire—a material, like electrical fire, composed of tiny bits of mutually repulsive material. Once evaporated, particles of water become attached (through a mechanism Franklin did not specify) to particles of air—Franklin suggested that up to twelve particles of air might surround each bit of water. Upon the compression of these elaborate structures, caused by the loss of common fire or by winds forcing the water-laden air against mountains, the particles of water would fall from the air as dew or rain. Franklin further observed that seawater is composed of water (which conducts electricity) and salt (which produces electricity when rubbed). Thus he asserted that evaporation of water from the sea depended not only upon the action not only of common fire but also of the electrical fire. Clouds formed from seawater thus come equipped with electrical properties. When these clouds are compressed by cooling or the pressure of the wind, the electrical fire that surrounds the bits of evaporated water can jump from the sea cloud to a cloud composed of electrically neutral water evaporated from freshwater sources, as we often observe in thunderstorms. When clouds formed over tropical oceans make their way north and encounter thin bits of vapor, the electrical fire—visible only when it is in motion—leaps from water droplet to water droplet, forming the northern lights. Like Descartes, Franklin found evidence for his theory in the facts it was meant to explain. The Andes Mountains, serving as a barrier to the warm clouds blown in from the Pacific Ocean, suffer tremendous rains and violent thunderstorms, whereas ships at sea rarely encounter lightning.

If there are no nearby freshwater clouds or vapors to attract the excess electrical fire in ocean clouds, the energetic material might jump instead to the earth as that most destructive meteor, lightning. Franklin here reflected that the matter of electrical fire must be extremely like the matter of common fire, for the devastation produced by lightning strikes is similar to that created by intense fire. In many cases, he suggested, the lightning bolts might ignite sulfurous vapors or the vapors from moist hay or rotting vegetation—just as electrical sparks will inflame spirits—accounting for the fires that accompany lightning strikes. Another possibility, he suggested, is that lightning striking buildings might find its way through bits of metal, like nails, and cause such a repulsion among the metallic parts that these would burst apart and ignite the wood into which they were hammered. Bits of melted metal, dripping onto the floor, might also set a building ablaze.

This peculiar combination of "Newtonian" forces and the most outrageous Cartesian system building must have seemed incredible to Nollet. Franklin himself mentioned that the French electrician at first thought that the American was an invention of his enemies,[54] and the *Experiments and Observations* a parody of philosophical research. In light of the eighteenth-century setting for the work such a reaction would hardly have been surprising. In his eventual response to the American, at any rate, Nollet suggested that Franklin had probably never heard of him.[55] The great irony in the historical accounts of the French expert's response to the American amateur is that Franklin is generally cast as the Enlightened experimental philosopher pitted against Nollet's obtuse Cartesianism—a sort of repetition of the seventeenth-century scientific revolution in which Galileo had challenged the outmoded Aristotelian system with new truth gleaned from experiment.

Yet Franklin's work, like the German researches that preceded it, merited more than passing interest for two reasons. First, he devised a clever demonstration that lent tremendous plausibility to his theory of balanced excesses and deficiencies of electricity. He constructed a Leyden jar with the usual rod coming out of the top terminated with a sphere, or "button." To the foil he used as a conductor on the outside of the jar he attached a wire, which he bent so that it came to the same level as the wire from the inside of the jar, and he terminated this wire with a second button (see Figure 8.9). Franklin charged his apparatus and placed it on a resin cake to isolate it. Then he suspended a cork bob on a thread and suspended the thread so that the cork was free to move back and forth between the buttons. The cork, he said, "will play incessantly from one to the other, 'till the bottle is no longer electrised; that is, it fetches and carries the fire from the top to the bottom of the bottle, 'till the equilibrium is restored."[56]

This new experiment with the Leyden jar was a variation on an already popular demonstration in which a metal clapper was suspended on a chain attached to the prime conductor of an electric machine and allowed to discharge by banging into a bell connected to the ground. Indeed, the buttons of the Leyden jar were soon replaced by small bells, and the cork by a brass ball. The transportation of the electrical fire from the top to the bottom of the jar was accompanied by the tinkling of little bells. This variation ensured that the experiment made its way into the standard demonstration-lectures. What Franklin's experiment showed was that equal amounts of electricity were contained on the inner and outer conductors of the Leyden jar—that the quantity of electricity removed by the cork from one conductor, when deposited on the other conductor, was just the right amount to neutralize the second surface.

The second brilliant speculation in the *Experiments and Observations* concerned the electrical nature of lightning. Nollet, of course, had made the same suggestion himself in the *Recherches sur l'électricité*. Franklin, however, offered in passing an empirical confirmation. In the midst of his elaborate meteorological system he wrote:

To determine the question, whether the clouds that contain lightning are electrified or not, I would propose an experiment to be tried where

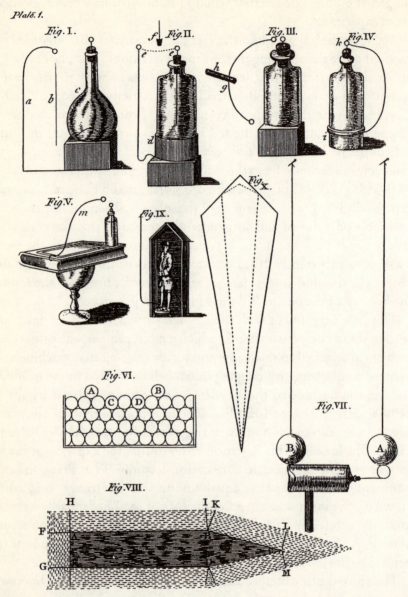

Figure 8.9 Franklin's Leyden jar experiment: to demonstrate that the jar holds equal but opposite charges on its inner and outer surfaces (his figure II); and the famous sentry box experiment: the first demonstration that lightning represents an electrical phenomenon (his figure IX). Reproduced from Benjamin Franklin, Experiments and Observations on Electricity *(London, 1751). Courtesy of the Bakken Library, Minneapolis, Minn.*

it may be done conveniently. On the top of some high tower or steeple, place a kind of sentry-box big enough to contain a man and an electrical stand. From the middle of the stand let an iron rod rise and pass bending out of the door, and then upright 20 or 30 feet, pointed very sharp at the end. If the electrical stand be kept very clean and dry, a man standing on it when such clouds are passing low, might be electrified and afford sparks, the rod drawing fire to him from the cloud. If any danger to the man should be apprehended (though I think there would be none) let him stand on the floor of his box, and now and then bring near to the rod the loop of a wire that has one end fastened to the leads, he holding it by a wax handle; so the sparks, if the rod is electrified, will strike from the rod to the wire, and not affect him.[57]

Franklin did not construct an appropriate sentry box; indeed the description comes across as something of a throwaway, a thought experiment whose theoretical consequences Franklin was sufficiently certain about that there was no need to try it. Within a few months he devised a more famous experiment, the one in which he employed a kite to bring electricity down from the clouds.

It was nonetheless the sentry box experiment that made Franklin's reputation in France. In the Paris suburb of Marly, Buffon enlisted the assistance of Jean Dalibard to construct the apparatus. Fortunately they took the precaution Franklin suggested and chose to detect the presence of the electrical fire using a metallic rather than a human conductor. An obscure demonstration-lecturer named Delor, a serious competitor to Nollet only after Delor became involved in the debate initiated by Buffon, provided electrical apparatus. On 10 May 1752, Dalibard had the good fortune to be at Marly as a thundercloud passed, and he detected electricity. Buffon promptly had his protégé report the success to the Académie royale des sciences. A week later Delor, using an even higher pole, confirmed the result.

The experiment was quite naturally a sensation. Nollet determined to repeat it himself; with Cassini he rigged a pole outside their apartments at the Royal Observatory. Not wishing to have to go outside in the rain, they suspended a heavy iron wire on silk ropes and brought one end inside so as to be able to conduct their experiments in civilized comfort.[58] As he had done with the Leyden jar, Nollet quickly prepared a description of the new demonstration. In imitation of Franklin's book, Nollet published his reflections on lightning and on

Franklin's theory as a series of letters. Most were addressed to Franklin, although the first letter was a response to inquiries from a young Italian woman, Maria-Angela Ardinghelli.

Not yet twenty years old, Ardinghelli had translated Stephen Hales's *Haemastaticks* to Italian—several years before Buffon performed the same service for the French. Another of the forgotten female practitioners of science, Ardinghelli was surely of a Newtonian stature comparable to Franklin's before the success of the sentry box experiment. Better informed than the American about philosophical expertise, she quite naturally looked to Nollet for information on this new electrical spectacle. The royal academician took advantage of the inquiry from this up-to-date apostle of the English Enlightenment to offer his own account of the Marly experiment.

Nollet wrote as one certain he was establishing the canonical account of the proof of his own suggestion in the *Recherches sur l'électricité* that lightning was an electrical effect. He expressed an understandable bewilderment that Franklin was given credit for the identification, in light of the fact that the American had not tried the experiment himself—it wasn't terribly difficult or elaborate even for a colonial amateur (see Figure 8.10). (In what must be seen as a generous interpretation of Franklin's failure to act on his idea, Nollet agreed that it was possible, "as some have said," that there aren't as many thunderstorms in Philadelphia as in Paris.[59]) However, he expressed a serious concern over the dangers such an experiment presented. Noting that one proficient amateur had, during the course of a sentry box experiment, received a painful shock of a magnitude that the Leyden jar had never displayed, he wrote to his philosophical correspondent: "Mademoiselle, we have arrived where we touch the fire of the sky, but if ignorant or profane hands touch it we might well repent. . . . We have come to understand Prometheus of the fable."[60] Nollet's concerns were legitimate. Georg Wilhelm Richmann, an experienced experimentalist in Russia, would later attempt the experiment following Franklin's first set of instructions. Richmann was killed when lightning struck.[61]

In the same passage in which Franklin had tossed off the sentry box experiment, he also proposed erecting pointed rods atop buildings, connected to the ground by means of wires, to save them from lightning strikes. Franklin believed that the high points would cause the

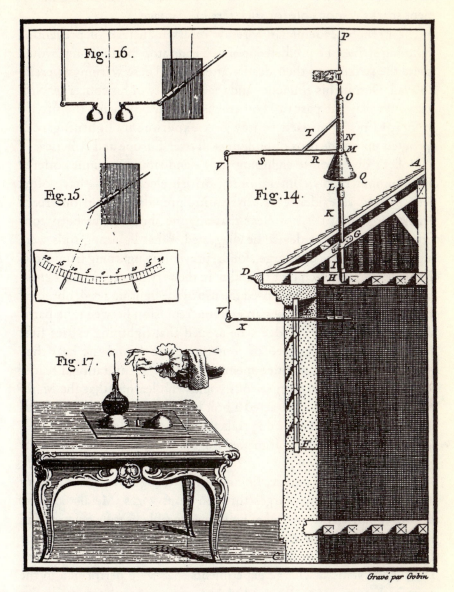

Figure 8.10 Nollet's devices for his repetitions of Franklin's experiments. Nollet's Figures 16 and 17 relate to Franklin's theory about the Leyden jar; Figure 14 offers Nollet's version of the sentry box experiment demonstrating that lightning is electrical. Reproduced from Jean Antoine Nollet, Lettres sur l'électricité *(Paris: Guerin, 1753), vol. 2, plate 4. Courtesy of the Bakken Library, Minneapolis, Minn.*

electric fire to leak slowly from the clouds without producing the violent sparks responsible for such terrible damage.

The French academician foresaw disaster. Instead of preventing lightning strikes, he predicted, pointed rods atop tall buildings would invite the strikes and their deadly aftermath. These warnings were to no avail. Despite his eminence and the extremity of his concerns, Nollet would play the part of Prometheus bound. Following the success of Franklin's proposed sentry box experiment, lightning rods sprouted up on the tops of buildings all over Europe and America.

Nollet's objection to lightning rods—and similar critiques offered by a number of his contemporary British electricians—have often been offered as evidence of unscientific prejudice. Yet if one reads Franklin's book, it is not clear that anyone should have been convinced to try out the device he suggested. What lightning rods were supposed to do was discharge clouds, preventing lightning from striking at all. We have seen that Franklin, in the very passage in the *Letters and Observations* that proposed the use of the lightning rod, observed that the electrical fire causes an extreme repulsion between the particles that form metals. Indeed, he argued that lightning causes fires when metallic objects used in construction melt and the heat they generate sets nearby wooden members ablaze.[62] Any rational reader who took this explanation seriously and who learned that the Marly experiment had in fact attracted a bolt of lightning must have arrived at the conclusion that lightning rods themselves would be likely to become so hot as to throw off melted fragments and ignite nearby parts of a building.

As it turns out, of course, Franklin was wrong about the effects of the huge electrical discharges through stout wires. Metals conduct electricity sufficiently well that no unmanageable heating occurs. Had Franklin chosen a less effective conductor with which to connect the lightning rod to the ground, the outcome might have been different. The sort of static discharge experiments that were performed in the eighteenth century are not good at determining the relative resistivity of various materials. Iron and copper wires were undoubtedly selected for their mechanical properties rather than their electrical advantages over other materials that conduct electricity in static experiments—materials that, we should remember, include wood and water and packthread and vegetable matter as well as human beings. That the American's two miscalculations, one concerning the power of points to discharge the clouds without lightning and the other concerning the effects of lightning on metals, had the effect of canceling each other out is hardly another example of Fortuna smiling upon the prepared mind; Nollet's hesitancy cannot be written off as the sign of reactionary Cartesianism. There was a legitimate question to be answered, whether lightning rods would increase or decrease the likelihood of damage, and the stakes were very high in terms of risk to human life and destruction of property. Franklin, and those who took his advice on the matter of lightning rods, were lucky—much luckier than Richmann had been.

Be that as it may, lightning rods did of course protect buildings from the most disastrous effects of thunderstorms. Owing to this fact more than any other, Franklin's theory of a single electric material, made manifest when present in excessive or insufficient quantities in ordinary matter, won fairly wide acceptance in France. Nollet's books continued to appear in new editions, but after the demonstration of the electrical nature of lightning there were no substantial discoveries of electrical phenomena before Volta's invention of the direct current battery forty years later. By that time all the principals in the competing Franklinian system and the *système Nollet* were dead and a new generation had set out to grind its own ideological axes. It was a story bound up in the politics of the French Revolution and animal electricity and magnetism, a postscript to the Enlightenment or a prelude to the nineteenth century. Our own story had come to an end.

The lesson in the story of Franklin's theory of electricity, and its reception in both France and England, is usually cast as one of truth vanquishing an ignorance backed up only by ideology. It is clear that Nollet's opinions were informed by experience. To be sure, Franklin's innocence turned out to produce an important innovation—perhaps the most successful application of Enlightenment science to the amelioration of human suffering. Yet the bitter polemics and the portrayal of good guys and bad guys in the community of Enlightened experimental philosophers also had the effect of removing the technical aspects of science from the public realm in which demonstrators from Rohault to Polinière had placed it.

It was the visible demonstration of the truth of natural philosophy that had allowed practitioners to set the field up as an exemplar of rationality even in the face of high philosophical debates among Cartesian, Newtonian, and Leibnizian theorists. If none of them could agree on the precise quantity conserved in collisions or the nature of light, all could point to the actual collisions between suspended ivory balls and predict the outcome, or project the images of paintings on glass onto the wall to illustrate that they knew whereof they spoke. Indeed, in the context of the Enlightenment, the success of the Empiricism of the lecture hall showed itself even more clearly in light of the philosophical bickering that all who followed Voltaire or Locke knew was going on behind the scenes. Demonstrators of every stripe—British, Dutch, and French—had professed to take what was good and true from Newton and Leibniz and Descartes without regard to ideology. The claim that science made, that it told the truth about the world, was a claim that all who practiced natural philosophy believed they could demonstrate in the lecture hall. Anyone willing to look must be compelled to grant the claim.

The dispute between Franklin and his partisans on the one hand and Nollet on the other turned on a different source for the establishment of truth. Both agreed on the phenomena—the Leyden jar and lightning behave the same way in France as they do in Philadelphia. Both Franklin (with Buffon's full support and encouragement) and Nollet made the dispute into an argument about the expert interpretation of the phenomena. The lay observer could no longer, as Locke and Voltaire had done, depend upon a straightforward observation of the behavior of the natural world to grasp the validity of the philosophy that described that world. The great clash of electrical systems did what the bickering of Newtonians, Cartesians, and Leibnizians could not do. It brought to an end the cozy Enlightenment view that any educated person could, on the basis of sensory data and common sense, judge the truth for herself.

The truth of the matter, in retrospect, is fairly easy to apprehend. The debate between the advocates of electrical motions involving Nollet's matter of fire on the one hand and Franklin's on the other has been cast in many terms: Cartesianism against Newtonianism, the *esprit de système* over the *esprit systématique*, mechanism versus action-at-a-distance, and so on. All of these things may in some manner be valid. Yet it is equally clear that the transition from the Nollet system to Franklin's electric fluid was a transition from one experimental paradigm to another. Both experiments in fact survived; Joseph Priestley's *History and Present State of Electricity,* itself the canonical text in the generation after Nollet's works had failed to attain that status, presented them in 1767 in this way (see Figure 8.11):

> Suspend one plate of metal from the conductor, and place a metal stand of the same size at the distance of a few inches exactly under it, and upon the stand put the figures of men, animals, or whatever else shall be imagined, cut in paper or gold leaf, and pretty sharply pointed at both extremities, and then, upon electrifying the upper plate, they will perform a dance, with amazing rapidity of motion, and to the great diversion of the audience. . . . To the dancing figures above-mentioned, it is very amusing to add a set of electrical bells. These consist of three small bells, the two outermost of which are suspended from the conductor by chains, and that in the middle by a silken string, which a chain connects to the floor; and two small knobs of brass, to serve instead of clappers, hung by silken threads, one between each two bells. In consequence of this disposition, when the two outermost bells, communicating with the conductor, are electrified, they will attract the clappers, and be struck by them. The clappers, being thus loaded with electricity, will be repelled, and fly to discharge themselves upon the middle bell. After this, they will be again attracted by the outermost bells; and thus by striking the bells alternately, a continual ringing may be kept up as long as the operator pleases. In the dark, a continual flashing of light will be seen between the clappers, and the bells; and when the electrification is very strong, these flashes of light will be so large, that they will be transmitted by the clapper from one bell to the other, without its ever coming into actual contact with either of them, and the ringing will, consequently, cease. When these two experiments of the bells and the figures are exhibited at the same time, they have the appearance of men or animals dancing to the music of the bells, which, if well conducted, may be very diverting.[63]

In the electric dance we quite literally see the jets in Nollet's matter of fire causing "an amazing rapidity of motion"; the bells, by contrast, Priestley described as being "loaded with electricity." Neither experiment is easy to picture in terms of the competing theory. Nollet's system was a theory for the phenomena of electric wands; Franklin's fluid presented an explanation for the violent motions occasioned by the completed electric machine and the Leyden jar. Nollet's breeze

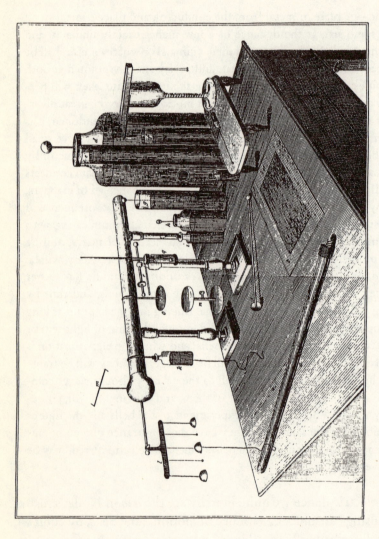

Figure 8.11 Illustration of common electrical demonstrations, including the electric bells (l) and the plates between which figures danced (n–o). Reproduced from Joseph Priestley, History and Present State of Electricity (London, 1767), plate 2, facing p. 479. Courtesy of the Bakken Library, Minneapolis, Minn.

fitted best with the delicate and hesitant wanderings of paper bits and downy feathers, and Franklin's fluid spilled onto brass clappers and propelled them smartly from bell to bell. The increasing magnitude of the available electric virtue made Franklin's picture more plausible, although it never provided anything like the delicacy of Nollet's gentle breezes.

It might seem at first glance that the story of eighteenth-century developments in electricity told in this chapter echoes the confirmation and elaboration of universal gravitation. When Voltaire embraced Newton's theory of celestial mechanics, there was no particular technical justification for his choice. To be sure, Maupertuis and his cohort rapidly provided that justification, and Laplace eventually far exceeded the expectations that Voltaire entertained for Newton's work. The canonical reading of electricity during the same period tells how Franklin put forth a bold, new theory around the midpoint of the century; this theory replaced Nollet's elaborate system. If it took a few months for French Franklinians to confirm and elaborate the theory of positive and negative charges and the electrical nature of lightning, that matters little. The truth did out in electrical studies, as it would in mechanics.

The difficulty with this minor repair to the usual account comes in locating the kernel of Franklin's theory that ostensibly provided the basis for classical electrostatics. Electrical potential theory was worked out by Dennis Poisson in the early nineteenth century on the model of Laplace's celestial mechanics—indeed, Laplace had first set the problem for Jean-Baptiste Biot in the last years of the eighteenth century.[64] Yet what survived from Franklin to Poisson is rather different from what survived from Newton to Laplace. In the mechanical case, it was the basic mathematical formulation of the law of universal gravitation. What Laplace demonstrated was that there was a tremendous mathematical subtlety behind the law that Newton formulated—that the mathematics took on a life of its own and provided answers to questions that early students had not yet dreamt of. Franklin's electrical theory by contrast was at its core verbal—it offered, against Nollet's claim that electricity is the effect of a simultaneous influx and efflux of a subtle fluid from ordinary matter, the claim that electricity is the effect of an imbalance of a subtle fluid present in excessive or deficient amounts in common matter. The spirit of

Franklin's explanations—his system of meteorology comes most readily to mind—belongs more to the style of Descartes than to that of Newton. This is not to criticize Franklin's results or to deny their genius and creativity. It is simply to observe that, lodged in the mind of the Enlightenment, there is a willingness to accept both the *esprit de système* and the *esprit systématique.* There is, in Franklin's theory and in the widespread adoption of the lightning rod, as much of Descartes and Fontenelle as there is of Newton and Locke.

9

The Conclusion, in which the Author Draws a Moral

THIS RATHER IDIOSYNCRATIC INVESTIGATION of the scientific revolution in France tells a story sufficiently far from either traditional or revisionist accounts that its point may not be entirely clear. First and foremost, the issue with which the book began, is the fascination that the science of the scientific revolution continues to hold. The idea is not to return to the sort of hagiography that animated most histories through the post-Sputnik era or to enter into the continuing tradition of history for scientists, usually by scientists, which assumes that science is inherently worthwhile and fascinating. Instead, this book has attempted to provide an explanation for the very real interest that a rather broad segment of the tiny educated public had for science during the seventeenth and eighteenth centuries. That interest came not from some moral sense that understanding science was a good thing, a patriotic duty or a self-imposed discipline, but from the sheer enjoyment that the practice of science brought to its amateurs. If the story told has made that science come alive, has captured the sense of public spectacle and private pleasure it offered to its practitioners, this account has succeeded in its main end.

Yet there are other points as well that bear comment. One is the woman question, the nexus of issues surrounding the gender of science and of scientists, and the feminine or feminist side of the scientific revolution. A second is the way in which connections were constructed between scientific discourse and political or philosophical discourse in the late seventeenth and early eighteenth centuries. Finally, there is a historiographical question about what the history of

337

science is—an implicit plea that the fields of intellectual history and even the history of ideas might still be interesting.

Each of these issues of course presents a two-edged sword. The treatment of science as a charming and amusing field in the intellectual landscape of the seventeenth and eighteenth centuries risks trivializing the work done and the scientific practitioners who so enjoyed their labors. The possibilities for caricature seem endless: From dilettantes at play to decadents at work, the pleasant side of these serious matters is for too many of us in our modern, professionalized world the sophomoric side of science. It seems that advocates and critics of modern science agree in taking the disciplined analysis of nature terribly seriously and in assuming that science is above all hard work for a technical elite. The discoverery that it was something different causes a clash of values for many practitioners of science studies. It seems they suppose that the clever amusement of the eighteenth century was not real science, and that the real science of the scientific revolution could not have been a clever amusement. That is to say, it produces cognitive dissonance in the modern mind to imagine that Cartesian science could have been, in the eighteenth-century common-language meaning of the term, Cartesian—clever, like Puss in Boots.

Some scientists still offer their sheer delight in their work as the reason they pursue their chosen field, although such protestations are more often the stuff of shy excuses than sincere explanations. In the context of modern science, of the "brain" and the pocket protector and above all of the professional scientist, fun as the motivation for science is at best a conceit, an excuse for the unnatural act of liking one's job or a declaration of alienation from "the real world." Yet in an age more technically innocent than our own atomic world, an age in which the educated classes generally had sufficient independent means that an eccentric hobby was a reasonable alternative to anything that might pass in the modern world as gainful employment, the fascination that nature holds for something like the human spirit might have served as a more plausible explanation for scientific pursuits than it does today.

Certain styles of science can hardly be seen as anything other than sources of delight and wonder. We might marvel that historians of electricity have managed to find in their field the stuff of potential theory, in the same way that historians of astronomy wondered that

Newton found in Kepler's work his three laws of planetary motion. Yet each generation produces its own big, square book on the history of electricity, tracing the canonical development of the static generator from von Guericke's sulfur globe through a studious line of experimenters, none of whom is ever credited with the development of the electrified kiss. Only a firm conviction that science is serious, and a fear that making it seem like fun might demean it, seem to explain the dry accounts of eighteenth-century experimental science usually offered. Histories of the field have continued to follow the broad outlines of the stories first written for polemical purposes, casting Franklin as a Newtonian foe of the Cartesian Nollet.

The notion that electrostatics might have grown out of a fascination with the obscure phenomenon of phospholuminescence, tangentially related to sparks, rather than out of a meticulous inquiry into a tiny attractive force, tangentially related to Newton's gravitation, did not further the nineteenth-century historians' purpose of providing a history that recapitulated contemporary theory. Thus von Guericke replaced Bernoulli as the instigator of electrical studies. The philosophies of science that took as their models the stories told in these theoretically constructed histories produced a hypothetico-deductive method that required that the story must have occurred as it was usually told. A tradition grew up surrounding the history of electricity in which the mark of a real scholar became the ability to find the traces of the serious business of scientific research in books that perversely offered bits of this research in the midst of long, repetitive, and theoretically uninteresting demonstrations that served no purpose but to amuse the decadent ladies of Europe and their foppish admirers.

The rather different relationships between the historian and the history in the cases of Kepler's laws and static electricity grow out of the different relationships between the texts and the practices in those fields. The work of astronomy primarily involved reducing astronomical observations mathematically. Kepler's philosophical speculation, his astronomical and astrological angst, will always be fascinating to a certain sort of historian more concerned with the philosophical implications of science than with the seventeenth-century practice of natural philosophy. Yet working astronomers knew Kepler's rules and they knew how to apply those rules, whether or not they waded through the verbiage in which the three laws were concealed. This knowledge was passed along in the astronomical spaces of the seventeenth century, the observatories and households in which astronomers taught and learned, apprentice style, and in which they spent most of their time in the dreadfully dull practice of calculation. It is in the choice of the canonical texts—Kepler and Newton—and in paying attention to the admittedly more colorful philosophical aspects of those texts that many historians of the subject have lost track of what astronomers did. The textbooks of the demonstration-lecturers, however, described in great detail the daily practice of electrical studies. The lack of interest shown by historians in the repetitious, slowly evolving natural history of shock and sparks, a natural history that grew up in fits and starts driven by accidental advances in technology rather than by theoretical considerations, likewise reflects modern interests rather than early modern practice.

The astronomy of the early eighteenth century has suffered much the same fate as that of the seventeenth. The abstruse mathematics of the French successors to Newton has always seemed the most dignified and significant work of their generation. The canon wends its deliberate way from Newton to Lagrange and Laplace, mathematical theoreticians of the most rigorous sort. Yet it was the generation of Maupertuis and Clairaut and a host of less spectacular mathematicians that set out at once to derive and discover the construction of solar system. Their swashbuckling exploration of the Newtonian world, and the other astronomical voyages that preceded and succeeded it, practically demand a romantic interpretation. It was on the decks of French and British ships that all the early skirmishes between the Cartesians and the Newtonians were fought; on land, the astronomical observers comported themselves more visibly as sailors than as scientists. The bold attempts to literally measure the world with surveyors' chains in Lapland and Peru proved much more impressive to those who followed astronomical debates in the eighteenth century than did the quiet calculations of mathematicians that eventually settled the technical issues. These expeditions captured the public imagination; the scientist appeared in roles from the gallant to the cad, but never played the social misfit.

The dry, unproductive mathematics of Varignon also produced a delight in the practitioner and commanded a wider audience than Maupertuis's technical work would. The attraction in this case was not quite so obvious as in the case of experimental philosophy or the voyages of discovery, and clearly not so ribald. Indeed, Varignon's analytical musings represented an amusement with no more progressive an end in sight than Nollet's electrical explorations had. In both cases, the pleasure was an end in itself. Recreational mathematics has never been so widely pursued as popular science, but it bears a clearer relationship to Laplacian theory than do most experimental demonstrations. Fontenelle's mathematical friend played at mathematical physics in much the same way as Nollet played at experimental philosophy. Without making too much of this—surely we don't want to shift to the Latinized *ludi*—we might make "play" a synonym for "enjoyably work." Thus Mme du Châtelet enjoyably worked through Newton's *Principia* as well as through Nollet's *Programme*. Huygens discovered the rings of Saturn, adopted Descartes's system, discovered the laws of centrifugal force, mused on the reactions of extraterrestrial beings, and parlayed it all through the milieu of the salon into an appointment at Louis XIV's court. It was, for him, enjoyable work.

Scientific developments in the seventeenth and eighteenth centuries often grew out of an attachment not only to the pure intellectual pleasure of science but to the vaudevillian aspects of natural history and experimental philosophy as well. It was a very physical sort of humor. Thanks in large part to the serious and ponderous histories that have preceded this one, it is clear that the philosophy of shocks and sparks, the displays of the man with the most philosophical hat in Paris, and the exploits of the voyagers so struck with the brave new worlds they encountered all did constitute important scientific developments. Had these points not been established, the present history would have had to present an extensive argument along these lines. Yet the ways in which the science of the scientific revolution—especially the astronomical disputes between the Cartesians and the Newtonians, and the experimental development of electricity—have affected the world in which we live are well enough established that not even the fact that they were fun can displace their importance.

The kinder, gentler face of science in the Ages of Reason and Enlightenment presented in this book is a face more feminine than is usually painted. This is an empirical rather than a stereotypical claim. My own route to the interpretation of science presented here began with an exploration of the role of women in science, and of science in feminine culture, in the court of Louis XIV. As is so frequently the case when the traditional historian turns his eye to the mirror of women, he sees the reflection of all humanity. The more literary, more metaphorical, more polite and charming circles of science in the salons provided the background necessary to understand the ways in which the Académie royale des sciences served as a source of *gloire* for Louis XIV. The women in Rohault's or Nollet's audience provided each with an occasion to explain how his lectures would amuse and fascinate as well as enlighten. Once the reader assimilates this message as it applied to the women in the audience, it is not a long distance to the conclusion that Chapelain or Locke or Voltaire had the same motivation. Indeed, we find in Huygens or Perrault or Maupertuis the same naïve fascination with the implications of the science they, with Madelaine de Scudéry and Émilie du Châtelet, had wrought.

As we move from the feminine to the feminist, this analysis may seem to fall short of the politically correct. If we see science as more feminine only insofar as we see it as a more accessible, more entertaining, more charming, and less technical science, then we see the feminine side of science as the least like what science is supposed to be—and the most like what stereotypical characterizations claim women are supposed to be. This is a slippery slope down which I hope this account of science in the seventeenth and eighteenth centuries will not in its last pages slither. Yet there are several sorts of responses to this putative objection to the present characterization of science as in some way feminine. One concerns the delicate subject of what we might characterize as masculine and feminine; others concern what effects these ostensibly gendered sides of science might have had on the development of the field and on its place in the larger culture.

The simplest response to the admittedly problematic conjunction of feminine sensibilities and the style of science characterized in this story is to observe that women played a significant role in its development. Especially at the crucial junctures of the early personal reign of Louis XIV and the beginnings of the great school of French mathematical mechanics in the early reign of Louis XV, the distinctly feminine milieu of the salons had important influence on who practiced science and how they practiced. Many women engaged in philosophical exploration of nature. Their involvement ranged from the serious study of Mlle de Chetaignaires or Mme du Châtelet, the academy of Mme de Guédreville and her friend Mme de Bonneveau through the *précieuses* elegies for Madelaine de Scudéry's chameleons to simple attendance at the abbé Nollet's lectures or the reading of Fontenelle's *Conversations on the Plurality of Worlds*. At some gross empirical level, then, women are implicated in this science; to characterize it as feminine in this sense serves merely to identify the unexpected gender mix of its practitioners.

The fact that women participated in the creation of modern science, at least in France, somehow cries out for a more interesting analysis than to state that it happened. This is especially true, since part of the traditional understanding of gender characteristics undoubtedly evolved from a tacit assumption that science is masculine. This gender identification is often coupled with the construction of a scientific method by philosophers and other students of the practice of science that embraces the virtues of logical thinking, consistency, deductive argument, and so on. As we have seen, this philosophy, itself largely a product of the Enlightenment, does not bear close scrutiny. The histories of electricity and astronomy, not to mention of that of natural history, were reinvented before they were mature. Yet it is this older style of the history and philosophy of science that for the most part has turned issues of gender and science into a major front in the culture wars.

Two feminist critiques, not entirely consistent, have been launched on this front. On the one hand, the scientific community is criticized for excluding women for arbitrary, sexist reasons, even when those women are perfectly capable of the sort of rational thought required by science. On the other hand, science is criticized for being too masculine and therefore both alienating to women and deficient in the answers it is able to give or to accept owing to its narrow-mindedness.

The present story should make clear the ways in which women participated in the practice of science in France in the seventeenth and eighteenth centuries, as well as the ways in which they were excluded. That is to say, the first of the feminist critiques, concerning the exclusion of women from the practice of science, needs to be modified to account for the very real participation of women at every level except for membership in the Académie royale des sciences. That exception is certainly enough to count the glass as half empty, but active participation of women in essentially every other philosophical or experimental venue, even to the joint inquiry into the chameleon carried out by the *académie* and the salon of Mlle de Scudéry, must count as a glass half full.

More important, the participation of women and their role in the formation of the science of the scientific revolution must temper our notions of the manly character of science. Science is often cast as a playing field on which there are winners and losers. This characterization is projected backward to the scientific revolution. One of the key debates between the Newtonians and the Cartesians, for example, concerned the conserved quantity associated with moving bodies. The beginnings of that debate—extremely philosophical and theoretical and logical, concerning the very essence of scientific method—receive a great deal of coverage in most accounts of seventeenth-century science. The resolution of that debate, however, does not usually enter into the story of eighteenth-century rational mechanics. The debate seems to have just petered out. In fact, the disputants came to realize that both Huygens's quantity of motion and Leibniz's living force are useful concepts. There were no losers; everyone profited from the flexibility offered by alternative methods for approaching the class of problems governed by the laws of motion. It was some time after both came into common use that the technical relations between these concepts—the notion that quantity of motion is a force applied over a time, whereas living force is a force applied over a distance—were clearly articulated. Indeed, the community showed a remarkable tolerance for dissent. There were well-known, ongoing disputes among the Cartesians, the Newtonians, and the Leibnizians.

If we examine the venues in which the competing theories came to be accepted, we see that both show a more feminine face than usually appears in the portraits painted of science in the eighteenth century. One was the demonstration-lecture, the locus for science farthest from philosophical or foundational discussion; it was, in terms of traditional gender stereotypes, the least masculine, the least rigorous, the least prestigious place in which science was practiced. The other place in which the reconciliation between the Cartesians and the Newtonians became explicit was Mme du Châtelet's *Institutions de physique,* a work usually mentioned, if at all, as a sort of female curiosity. Neither of these sources of conciliation fitted the nineteenth-century notion of a rigorous and thoroughly consistent science, derivable in a nearly Euclidian fashion from a series of easily articulable hypotheses. Even in the wake of *The Structure of Scientific Revolutions,* when rigor was removed as a requirement and a party line replaced articulable hypotheses as the cornerstone of a scientific school, the idea that competing paradigms might long coexist seemed beyond the pale. Yet this is exactly what happened in the early-eighteenth-century study of collision. That is to say, insofar as women or institutions welcoming to women contributed to science in a way that traditional gender roles would characterize as feminine, those contributions have been ignored or undervalued.

Nor have more recent feminist critiques done much to portray the seventeenth- and eighteenth-century beginnings of modern science in a light more sympathetic to women. The construction of the gender of science, of course, represents a development as self-conscious as the construction of the logical development of electrical studies. The construction of the gender of science, too, largely derives from the late nineteenth century, in which professionalization changed the practice of science inexorably. Yet feminists have, for the most part, bought into the characterization of seventeenth-century science as a manly discipline. The feminist project in studies of the scientific revolution has been one primarily of pointing out the ways in which the undesirable masculinity of science—sexist recruitment practices, undue competition, and a single-mindedly businesslike approach to nature—trace their roots to the scientific revolution. As in the case of electrical studies, it has become the mark of the student of gender studies to find in the science of the scientific revolution the same gendered cast as scholars have determined for the modern scene.

Indeed, the argument that science is unduly and unhealthily masculine, that it counts rigor for more than connectedness with the world, logic for more than emotion, consistency for more than compassion—that it artificially separates the mind from the body, that it has a brain but no heart, an intellect but no soul—is often laid at the door of Descartes. This argument seems to me simply ahistorical. Whatever interest the relations between the mind and the body may hold for modern philosophy, Descartes himself placed the connection between the mind and the body in the pineal gland. His mind-body dichotomy was a straw argument. Although the solution in the essay *On Man* may not satisfy the modern reader, it kept its author from being pre-occupied with the divide between the worlds of the body and the soul. It is one of the delicious ironies of the history of philosophy that Descartes's solution was so banal and so wrong.

In terms of the larger enterprise, as well, natural philosophy in the seventeenth century was hardly masculine in the conventional sense. Curious civility counted for more than pedantic talent as an entrée into philosophical circles. The stereotype of the natural philosopher as driven and socially inept, insofar as it existed at all, was more connected to notions of magic than of science; it applied in Somaize's *Dictionnaire des précieuses* to women as well as to men, and by the golden age of the court of the Sun King, it had evaporated entirely. Nor did the community adopt a patriarchal hierarchy. Senior scientists showed at least a polite interest in the work of rank amateurs; the royal academician Jean Antoine Nollet at first sent a kind and only mildly condescending letter to the unknown Philadelphian, Benjamin Franklin.

Not only the organization of the scientific community, but also the content of the science it generated and embraced, displayed characteristics now usually cast as feminine. Especially among the Cartesians, the coherence of the system played a more significant role than any particular point of detail, and competent scientists were willing to tolerate conflicting details. There was, in short, a diversity of views recognized by all significant practitioners and an uneasy tolerance of that diversity. Newton and Leibniz, Newtonians and Leibnizians and Cartesians, lecturers of all stripes, and any informed person who read the journals recognized that there were a number of competing philosophical underpinnings for legitimate natural philosophy.

Within this diverse community, in some cases because of the different points of view pursued by its members, science flourished in a peculiarly early modern way. It was precisely the conflicts between the Newtonians and the Cartesians and the Leibnizians, the ideological and nationalistic rivalries among experimentalists, that stimulated the explosive growth of science in the eighteenth century. As is so often the case, the addition of a new point of view, another voice in the discussion, made the community more successful in solving its problems. Women certainly played this role from the middle of the seventeenth at least through the middle of the eighteenth centuries in

France. If the visions and voices of Mlle de Scudéry or Mme du Châtelet were different from those of Claude Perrault or Voltaire, those visions and voices were not ignored. If, ultimately, the views adopted and published by the men were not those of the women, neither were they views that the men had adopted in isolation from and with arrogant disregard for the thoughts and opinions of the women with whom they enjoyably worked.

This is not to offer the period of the scientific revolution as a womanly paradise. The feminine audience for science, to be sure, by and large did not play as active a role in research as the circle of natural philosophical men traditionally considered in accounts of the scientific revolution in France. Most of the most technical work, most of the most famous work, and most of the most important demonstrations were the enjoyable work of men. Such a statement is simply a matter of fact; I hope that the reader will not grant it moral value of any quality.

Here, too, it may at first appear that we are conceding to traditionalists their stereotypical interpretation of gender roles: What was crucial about science in the scientific revolution was more masculine than feminine. Once again, however, the situation is not quite so simple as that. Enlightenment philosophes claimed as their great intellectual accomplishment the adoption of science as the exemplar for human understanding and the adaptation of the methods of science to all problems, especially to problems of polity. Yet it seems to me that this adoption and adaptation arose from the more feminine style of assimilation of science than from the traditional, masculine style of scientific accomplishment. The notion that Franklin invented electricity and American political democracy in more or less the same way has a sort of poetic romanticism to it. Yet the real architects and expositors of Enlightenment political philosophy, Locke in England and Voltaire in France, had a much more distant appreciation of the accomplishment of their technically adept contemporaries. Locke, the first to become Newtonian without the aid of geometry, did so on the advice of the Cartesian Christiaan Huygens. No greater irony could be imagined by those who saw the Cartesian and the Newtonian schools as irreconcilable rivals rather than as members of a diverse community. Voltaire had the aid of Nollet and his ilk for the demonstration of the scientific basis for Enlightenment. Yet the great writer's grasp of the

Newtonianism he embraced pales by comparison to that of Mme du Châtelet. That is to say, the appreciation that Enlightened writers had for science was the very appreciation that its purveyors generally peddled explicitly to women.

Nor is the style of science embraced by Locke the only evidence for the vaguely feminine connection between Enlightenment natural and political philosophy. The kind of argument that British liberalism put forth to offer a scientific basis for the claim that all men are created equal belonged to a tradition that grew out of the salons of Louis XIV's France. From the morals so delicately drawn by Perrault's investigation of the chameleon in Mlle de Scudéry's salon through Fontenelle's *Conversations on the Plurality of Worlds* to Huygens's *Celestial Worlds Discovered,* the models for foundations for political theory in natural philosophy all derive from authors at once better informed about science, further from Newtonianism, and more comfortable in the company of women than the British successors to that tradition. That is to say, this peculiarly modern interpretation of the idea that the truth will set us free, an interpretation that sees science as the source of liberating truth and that sees the Enlightened republic as the manifestation of freedom, derives from the feminine rather than from the masculine side of the science of the Enlightenment. It is this observation that the author offers as a moral to the story.

Notes

CHAPTER 1

1. The standard story originated in the eighteenth century; Jean Le Rond d'Alembert's "Discours preliminaire" to the *Encyclopédie, ou, Dictionnaire raisonné des sciences, des arts, et des metiers,* is as convenient a starting point as any. When standard stories begin with Enlightenment thought, I shall not cite extensive secondary literature. A few frequently cited more recent sources from which the story might be gleaned include Ernst Cassirer, *The Philosophy of the Enlightenment,* trans. Fritz C. A. Koelin and James Pettegrove (New York: Beacon Press, 1951); Alexandre Koyré, *From the Closed World to the Infinite Universe* (New York: Harper, 1958); Thomas S. Kuhn, *The Copernican Revolution: Planetary Astronomy in the Development of Western Thought* (Cambridge: Harvard University Press, 1957); I. Bernard Cohen, *The Birth of a New Physics* (New York: Anchor, 1960); Richard S. Westfall, *The Construction of Modern Science: Mechanisms and Mechanics* (New York: Wiley, 1971); J. L. Heilbron, *Elements of Early Modern Physics* (Berkeley: University of California Press, 1982); Thomas L. Hankins, *Science and the Enlightenment* (New York: Cambridge University Press, 1985); and Margaret C. Jacob, *The Cultural Meaning of the Scientific Revolution* (New York: Knopf, 1988).

2. Thomas Kuhn, *The Structure of Scientific Revolutions* (Chicago: University of Chicago Press, 1964).

CHAPTER 2

1. Quoted in J.-J. Denonain, "Les Problems de l'honnête homme vers 1635: *Religio Medici* et les *Conferences* du Bureau d'adresse," *Etudes Anglaises* 18 (1965), pp. 235–257, on p. 236. The authoritative source is Howard M. Solomon, *Public Welfare, Science, and Propaganda in Seventeenth-Century France: The Innovation of Theophraste Renaudot* (Princeton: Princeton University Press, 1972).

2. Extracted from Solomon, *Public Welfare,* appendix A. On the dromedary see p. 54.

3. On the *Conferences,* see ibid.; Denonain, "Les Problèmes de l'honnête homme"; and Harcourt Brown, *Scientific Organizations in Seventeenth Century France (1620–1680)* (Baltimore: Wilkins and Wilkins, 1934), pp. 17–50.

4. On the audience at the *bureau,* Solomon, in *Public Welfare,* pp. 67–69, reviewed the literature but offered very few specifics. On the question of women, he cited G. Reeynier, *La Femme au dix-septième siècle* (Paris, 1929), pp. 142–149.

5. Solomon listed fifteen in *Public Welfare,* pp. 144–146. He did not include the edition I cite, *Recueil general des questions traitees és conferences de Bureau d'adresse, sur toutes sortes de matieres, par les plus belles esprits de ce temps* (Paris: I. B. Loyson,

1658–1660), 5 vols., or a single-volume collection under the same title by the same publisher (1655). The translation *Another collection of philosophical conferences of the French virtuosi, upon questions of all sortes, for the improving of natural knowledg. Made in the Assembly of the beaux esprits by the most ingenious persons of that nation, Rendered into English, by G. Havers* (London: T. Dring and J. Starkey, 1665), which contains *Conferences* 101–140, is apparently a continuation of the 1664 translation cited by Solomon, which I have not seen. Brown, *Scientific Organizations*, p. 26, offered another edition under a completely different title; quite possibly others of this sort exist. I have not searched extensively for other editions.

6. This term comes from Daniel Roche, *La Siécle des lumières en province: Académies et académiciens provinciaux, 1680–1789*, 2 vols. (Paris: Mouton, 1978).

7. *Conferences*, vol. 1, *Conf.* 1, "De la méthode," pp. 6–10, quote appears on p. 6.

8. Ibid., 1, 9, "De la terre," first speaker.

9. Ibid., 1, 6, pp. 90–101, first topic, "Du feu," pp. 90–93.

10. Ibid., pp. 93–97.

11. Ibid., pp. 98–99.

12. Ibid., pp. 99–100.

13. Ibid., pp. 100–101.

14. Quoted in R. R. Bolgar, *The Classical Heritage* (New York: Harper Torchbooks, 1964), p. 273. My discussion of pedagogy follows closely from Bolgar's in chapter 7, section 1, and from conversations with JoAnn Morse and Anthony Grafton.

15. *Conferences*, 1, 1, "De la méthode," pp. 8–9.

16. *Conferences*, 4, 204, "De l'art de Raymond Lull."

17. *Conferences*, 2, 53–58.

18. For the distribution of the topics discussed, see Geoffrey Sutton, "A Science for a Polite Society: Cartesian Natural Philosophy in Paris During the Reigns of Louis XIII and XIV" (Ph.D. dissertation, Princeton University, 1982), appendix A.

19. *Conferences*, 1, 44, pp. 728–735, "Comment croissant les mineraux?" The other two conferences directly addressing this problem were 3, 136, pp. 447–455, "De l'origine des pierres précieux"; and 3, 137, pp. 457–466, "De la generation des metaux." Also of interest are 1, 93, pp. 712–721, "De la pierre philosophale"; and 3, 110, "Des eaux minéraux."

20. Ibid., 1, 29, pp. 498–504, "D'ou vient la saleur de la mer?"

21. Ibid. 1, 10, pp. 162–170, "Du mouvement ou du repose de la terre." First speaker on pp. 163–167.

22. Ibid., p. 167.

23. Ibid., pp. 167–170.

24. The condemnation came on 22 June 1633, some four months before the *Conference* on the motion of the earth. Renaudot did not find out about the action of the Church until November, after the discussion and the publication.

25. Solomon, *Public Welfare*, pp. 73–74. The arm of the Church did not, however, reach far into France. Nowhere in the published reports of the *Conferences* did the question of Galileo's problems appear, or even Renaudot's hasty apology. Indeed, the frequent reprintings of the discussions included the offending tenth *Conference* in full.

26. *Conferences*, 1, 41, first topic, "Des comets," pp. 682–689.

27. Ibid., first speaker, pp. 682–683.

28. Ibid., 2, 93, "Des taches de la lune et du Soleil," pp. 697–712.

29. On Chapelain and the scientific community, see A. J. George, "A Seventeenth-Century Amateur of Science: Jean Chapelain," *Annals of Science* 3 (1938), pp. 217–236. Much more useful are Huygens's journal and correspondence, cited extensively in Chapter 3. The larger literature on Chapelain as *homme de lettres,* lion of the *précieuses,* and cultural adviser to the crown under Louis XIII and XIV, although rather tedious, gives a wonderful insight into the organization of polite society in the seventeenth century. See Antoine Fabré, *Chapelain et nos deux premières académies* (Paris: Perrin, 1890), and Fabré, *Les Ennemis de Chapelain,* 2 vols. (Paris: Thorin et fils, 1897).

30. On the salon movement in France in the ministry of Richelieu, see Antoine Adam, *Grandeur and Illusion: French Literature and Society, 1600–1715,* trans. Herbert Tint (New York: Basic Books, 1972), or David Maland, *Culture and Society in Seventeenth-Century France* (New York: Charles Scribner's Sons, 1970). On the Hôtel de Rambouillet especially, see Leon H. Vincent, *Hôtel de Rambouillet and the précieuses* (New York: Houghton, Mifflin, 1900).

31. On the foundation of the Académie française, see Adam, *Grandeur and Illusion;* Maland, *Culture and Society;* and D. Maclaren Robertson, *A History of the French Academy* (New York: G. W. Dillingham, 1910).

32. The regulations are published in Robertson, *The French Academy,* pp. 10–16.

33. Quoted in ibid., pp. 20–21.

34. See the statistics on performances from 1680 to 1966 compiled in the introduction to Pierre Corneille, *Seven Plays,* trans. Samuel Solomon (New York: Random House, 1969), pp. xxxiii–xxxiv.

35. Maland, *Culture and Society,* pp. 109–112.

36. In this discussion I am indebted to Adam, *Histoire,* vol. 1, pp. 513–518; Geroges Collas, *Jean Chapelain, 1595–1674* (Paris: Perrin, 1912), pp. 131–145; and the introductions to the editions of the *Sentimens de l'Académie françoise sur le tragicomedie du Cid,* one by Georges Collas (Paris: Picard, 1912), and another by Colbert Searles (Minneapolis: University of Minnesota, 1916).

37. The decree appeared in 1624. Cf. Lee Davis Lodge, *A Study in Corneille* (New York: Burt Franklin, 1970, from the 1891 ed.), p. 109.

38. Ibid., pp. 75–76.

39. Robertson, *The French Academy,* p. 38.

40. Quoted in Searles's introduction to *Sentiments de l'Académie,* p. 1. Georges Mongrédien, *Madelaine de Scudéry et son salon* (Paris: Tallandier, 1946), p. 18, claimed that Scudéry's charges came "at the instigation of Richelieu himself." Lodge, *Corneille,* p. 113, suggested that Richelieu intervened only after Scudéry had written the *Observations,* when the cardinal suggested Scudéry should submit it to the *académie.*

41. See Collas's edition of the *Sentimens,* pp. 71–72.

42. Chapelain's draft is published in Collas's edition of the *Sentiments.* It also appears with later manuscript versions in Searles's less readable, but tremendously valuable, edition. References will be to Collas's edition unless otherwise noted. *Sentiments,* p. 12.

43. On erudition in French culture in the seventeenth century, see René Pitard, *Le Libertinage erudit,* 2 vols. (Paris: Boivin, 1943); John S. Spink, *French Free-Thought from Gassendi to Voltaire* (London: Althone Press, 1960), pt. 1; and Ira O. Wade, *The*

Intellectual Origins of the French Enlightenment (Princeton: Princeton University Press, 1971), pt. 3.

44. *Sentiments*, pp. 24–25. Chapelain cited Francis Bacon as a debunker of mistaken readings of Aristotle; see p. 26. Cf. also pp. 17–18.

45. Ibid., pp. 34–35, 75–77.

46. Chapelain spoke of the "solid doctrine founded on the authority of Aristotle, or, to say it better, on that of reason" (ibid., p. 31); or, "in these matters where the poet is at liberty to do anything, we believe that to imitate or to invent is the same thing" (p. 78).

47. Ibid., p. 79.

48. Searles presented a detailed account of the history of the manuscript in the introduction to his edition of the *Sentiments*.

CHAPTER 3

1. The major biographical sources are Adrien Baillet, *La Vie de monsieur Des-Carte*, 2 vols. (Paris: Horthemels, 1691; reprint, Hildsheim: Olms, 1972); and Charles Adam, *Vie et oeuvres de Descartes*, vol. 12 of the authoritative edition of Descartes's works, *Oeuvres de Descartes*, ed. Adam and Paul Tannery, 13 vols. (Paris: Cerf, 1897–1913). Citations of Adam's biography will appear as Adam, *Vie;* those referring to other volumes of the works are abbreviated as AT followed by volume and page numbers: E.g., AT.X.213 corresponds to vol. 10, p. 213. I have also consulted Pierre Frédérix, *Monsieur René Descartes et son temps* (Paris: Gallimard, 1959); and Louis de Launay, *Descartes* (Paris: Payot, 1923). The best accounts of Cartesian science are William Shea, *The Magic of Numbers and Motion: The Scientific Career of René Descartes* (Canton, Mass.: Science History Publications, 1991); and E. J. Aiton, *The Vortex Theory of Planetary Motions* (London: Macdonald; New York: American Elsevier, 1972). A recent biography in English is Jack R. Vrooman, *René Descartes: A Biography* (New York: Putnam, 1970). The philosophical literature is vast. Some interesting recent books that have informed this discussion include Susan Bordo, *The Flight to Objectivity: Essays on Cartesianism and Culture* (Albany: State University of New York Press, 1987); and Richard Rorty, *Philosophy and the Mirror of Nature* (Princeton: Princeton University Press, 1979). For a concentrated dose of the American "Cartesian" school, see Michael Hooker, ed., *Descartes: Critical and Interpretive Essays* (Baltimore: Johns Hopkins University Press, 1978). Since so much of the literature derives from Baillet and Adam, I will generally cite only one of them unless other sources correct or add to it. Likewise, in explicating Descartes's work, I will not refer to secondary literature in any detail, except where I am indebted to particular authors for difficult points of interpretation.

2. The curriculum at La Flèche at the time Descartes attended does not survive. Adam, *Vie,* chap. 2, presented reasonable conjectures based on the *ratio studiorum* of the Jesuit schools, books in print at the time, and schoolbooks mentioned in Descartes's later papers. Although the Jesuit curriculum was fairly standardized, there is little particular information about La Flèche. Shea, *Magic of Numbers,* pp. 4–8, presented a convenient summary of the literature. Descartes's retrospective account of his education in the *Discourse on Method* has obvious polemical purposes and must be discounted; at any rate, it offered no specifics.

3. For the most spirited defense of the Jesuits as a progressive force in early modern science see J. L. Heilbron, *Electricity in the Seventeenth and Eighteenth Centuries: A Study of Early Modern Physics* (Berkeley: University of California Press, 1979), pp. 101–108, and on the Galileo affair, p. 2.

4. Adam, *Vie*, pp. 39–40, could produce no documentary evidence for Descartes's whereabouts in 1615–1616 and therefore placed him at Poitiers during the period. Baillet, *Vie*, vol. 1, p. 36, claimed he was in Paris.

5. Baillet, *Vie*, vol. 1, pp. 35–36.

6. Ibid., pp. 36–46.

7. Beeckman's notebooks have been edited by C. de Waard, *Journal tenu par Isaac Beeckman de 1604 à 1634* (The Hague: Nijhoff, 1939–1953). See also Shea, *Magic of Numbers*, for an appreciation of the relations between Descartes and Beeckman.

8. Baillet, *Vie*, vol. 1, pp. 81–86, provided the basic account of the dreams, reporting material in Descartes's letters, now lost.

9. An extensive analysis appears in J. P. Weber, "Sur la composition de la Regula IV de Descartes," *Revue philosophique de la France et l'étranger*, no. 154 (1964).

10. Baillet, *Vie*, vol. 1, p. 35.

11. Ibid., vol. 1, p. 117. De Launay, *Descartes*, supplied the figure; see also Shea, *Magic of Numbers*, pp. 94–95.

12. On Mydorge, see Pierre Speziali, "Mydorge," *Dictionary of Scientific Biography*, ed. Charles Coulston Gillispie, (New York: Scribner, 1970–1980), vol. 9, pp. 589–590.

13. The anecdote originated with Baillet, *Vie*, vol. 1, pp. 160–161. Baillet cited a manuscript letter, now lost, in which Descartes related the story.

14. He would remark in the *Discourse on Method*, "I did not find myself, thanks to God, in a condition which would oblige me to make a career of science to supplement my income." I shall quote the English translation of Paul Olscamp, *Discourse on Method, Optics, Geometry, and Meteorology* (New York: Bobbs-Merrill, 1965), p. 9; AT.VI.9.

15. Baillet, *Vie*, vol. 1, pp. 196–198.

16. *Optics*, discourses 3–6.

17. *Recueil general des questions traitees és conferences de Bureau d'adresse, sur toutes sortes de matieres, par les plus belles esprits de ce temps* (Paris: I. B. Loyson, 1658–1660), vol. 1, *Conf.* 12, "Des trois soleils."

18. This discussion of Descartes's work on the false suns and the composition of *The World* follows the introduction by M. S. Mahoney to his translation of *Le monde, ou traité de la lumière*, with a facsimile of the 1677 ed. (New York: Abaris Books, 1979), and Adam, *Vie*, pp. 165–179. Shea, *Magic of Numbers*, chap. 9, provided a similar and more detailed account.

19. Descartes to Mersenne, 8 October 1629; AT.I.22–29.

20. Descartes to Guillaume Gibieuf, 18 July 1629; AT.I.17.

21. *Discourse on Method*, p. 35; AT.VI.42.

22. Descartes to Mersenne, 22 July 1633, AT.I.268. Cf. Adam, *Vie*, pp. 165–179.

23. Descartes to Mersenne [undated, ca. April 1634]; AT.I.271.

24. Ibid.

25. Adam, *Vie*, pp. 181–185.

26. Letter to Vatier, 22 February 1638, cited in Wendy Gibson, *Women in Seventeenth-Century France* (New York: St. Martin's Press, 1989), p. 30.

27. Adam, *Vie*, pp. 197–208, provided a brief analysis; W. E. Knowles Middleton, *The History of the Theories of Rain and Other Forms of Precipitation* (London: Oldbourne, 1965), took Descartes's work as the starting point for the seventeenth and eighteenth centuries.

28. From the preface to the French translation of the *Principles,* AT.IX(pt. 2).15.

29. *Géométrie*, p. 309 of the 1637 ed., in facsimile, with facing translation by David Eugene Smith and Marcia L. Latham, published as *The Geometry of René Descartes* (New York: Dover, 1954), pp. 22–23.

30. *Meteorology.* I quote the Olscamp translation: *Discourse on Method, Optics, Geometry, and Meteorology*, p. 264; AT.VI.232.

31. Ibid.; AT.VI.233.

32. Ibid.

33. Ibid., p. 268; AT.VI.239.

34. *Discourse on Method*, Fifth part, pp. 34–35; AT.VI.40–41.

35. *Meteorology*, pp. 267–268; AT.VI.237–239.

36. Ibid., p. 268; AT.VI.238.

37. Ibid., p, 269; AT.VI.240.

38. Ibid., p. 290; AT.VI.269.

39. Ibid., pp. 287–288; AT.VI.265–266.

40. Ibid., pp. 353–354; AT.VI.355–356.

41. Ibid., p. 357; AT.VI.361.

42. Baillet, *Vie*, vol. 1, p. 275.

43. *Discourse on Method*, p. 60; AT.VI,75. The term *libraire*, which I translate as "book dealer," is more often rendered as Olscamp did, as "publisher."

44. The best accounts of the Cartesian world as set out in the *Principia* are Shea, *Magic of Numbers*, chap. 12, and Aiton, *Vortex Theory*, chap. 3.

45. *Principia*, 3.19. I shall cite part and paragraph numbers; I shall quote the translation of Elisabeth Haldane and G. R. T. Ross, *The Philosophical Works of Descartes* (Cambridge: Cambridge University Press, 1911), p. 110.

46. Ibid., 3.94–118, pp. 156–172.

47. Ibid., 4.55–56, pp. 230–231.

48. Ibid., 4.30–44, pp. 216–225.

49. Ibid., 4.77–79, pp. 241–242.

50. Ibid., 4.58, p. 233.

51. Ibid., 4.63, pp. 235–236.

52. Ibid.

53. Ibid., 4.133, p. 271.

54. See Adam's introduction to the translation, AT.IX(first part).iii–x. See also Joseph Deande, "Clerselier," *Dictionary of Scientific Biography*, vol. 3, pp. 320–321.

55. On Descartes's participation, see Baillet, *Vie*, vol. 2, pp. 325–335; Adam's preface to the translation AT.IX(second part).iii–xx; and the translator's preface to sections of the *Principles of Philosophy*, trans. Blair Reynolds (Lewiston, N.Y./Queenston, Ont.: Edwin Mellen Press, 1988).

56. The story told in Baillet's *Vie*, vol. 2, pp. 323–373, must be read in conjunction with the less enthusiastic but better documented account in Adam, *Vie*, pp. 458–473.

57. The best account of the Swedish sojourn appears in Baillet, *Vie*, vol. 2, 414–423.

58. Translated in René Descartes, *A Discourse on Method; Meditations on the First Philosophy; Principles of Philosophy*, trans. John Veitch (London: Dent; New York: Dutton, 1975), pp. 154–155; AT.IX.11–12.

59. Translated in Aiton, *Vortex Theory*, p. 43; AT.V.259.

60. The most extensive argument comes in Carolyn Merchant, *The Death of Nature: Women, Ecology, and the Scientific Revolution* (New York: Harper and Row, 1980). See also Susan Bordo, *Flight to Objectivity*.

61. For a technical account, see Aiton, *Vortex Theory*, pp. 36–41, or Shea, *Magic of Numbers*, chap. 12.

62. *Principia*, 2.52.

63. Ibid., 2.53.

CHAPTER 4

1. Antoine Baudeau de Somaize, *Le Dictionnaire des précieuses*, ed. C.-L. Livet, 2 vols. (Paris: Janet, 1856). On the *Dictionnaire*, see Carolyn Lougee, *Le Paradis des femmes: Women, Salons, and Social Stratification in Seventeenth-Century France* (Princeton: Princeton University Press, 1976), pt. 3, "The Personnel of Polite Society."

2. Somaize, *Dictionnaire*, articles on Beroé (Mlle Bourdon), vol. 1, pp. 40–41; Berolas (M. Bary), p. 47; Clorinde (Christina, queen of Sweden), pp. 49–50; Camile, seconde du nom (Mme la comtesse de Carly), p. 58; Circé (Mlle de Chetaignaires), pp. 58–60; Cleoxene (M. Conrart), p. 61; Damophile (Mme du Buisson), p. 68; Diophantise, seconde (Mlle Dupré), pp. 68–69; Galérice (Mme de Guédreville), p. 103; Galexée (Mme la baronne du Gargnier), pp. 107–108; Melite (Mme Mareschal), pp. 161–162; Maraine (Mlle Magnon), pp. 163–164; Panthée (Mlle Petite), pp. 192–193; Virginius (M. le marquis de Vilaine), p. 239.

3. Ibid., article on Circé, pp. 59–60.

4. Ibid., article on Galérice, p. 103.

5. The journal was edited with notes and introduction by Henri Brugmans as *Le Séjour de Christiaan Huygens à Paris et ses relations avec les milieux scientifiques français* (Paris: Andre, 1935); that edition was also published in vol. 22 of *Oeuvres complètes de Christiaan Huygens, publiées par la Société hollandaise des sciences*, 22 vols. (The Hague, 1880–1950) (hereafter, Huygens, *Oeuvres*). See also J. Mesnard, "Les Premières Relations parisiennes de Christiaan Huygens," in René Taton, ed., *Huygens et la France* (Paris: Vrin, 1982), pp. 33–40.

6. Huygens visited the set for *Jason* on 16 February and another set on 29 December (Brugmans, *Séjour de Huygens à Paris*, pp. 140 and 153). On March 7, he remarked, "Saw the comedy *Jason* at the Marets, and the machines of the Marquis de Sourdac. Some of the scene changes were stunning, and also the aerial combat" (ibid., p. 157).

7. Huygens attended lectures on 13 and 17 November and 20 and 21 December 1660 (ibid., pp. 130 and 138). He reported a large number of auditors in a letter to his brother Lodewijk, 18 December 1660 (Huygens, *Oeuvres*, vol. 3, pp. 209–210). Rohault's father-in-law, Claude Clerselier, noted in his preface to vol. 2 of the *edition nouvelle* of Descartes's *Lettres* (Paris, 1666–1667), "Women often take the first row" in the lectures. On Rohault, see Clerselier's preface to *Oeuvres posthumes de M Rohault* (Paris, 1682); Alexandre Saverien, *Histoire des philosophes modernes*, 6 vols. (Paris, 1768), vol. 6, pp. 1–62; Paul Mouy, *Le Développement de la physique cartésienne, 1646–1712* (Paris: Vrin, 1934), pp. 108–138; Larry Laudan's introduction to John Clarke's 1723 English translation of Jacques Rohault's *Traité* as *A System of Natural Philosophy*, 2 vols. (New York: Johnson Reprint Corp., 1969); and John Schuster, "Rohault," *Dictionary of Scientific Biography*, vol. 11, pp. 508–509.

8. On the lodestone see Huygens's journal (Brugmans, *Séjour de Huygens à Paris*, p. 138). On capillary action, see Balthazar de Monconys, *Journal des voyages* (Lyons, 1660), pt. 3, pp. 33–37; and Jean Chapelain to Huygens, 10 August 1659 (Huygens, *Oeuvres*, vol. 2, pp. 467–470).

9. Huygens's journal, 13 November 1660 (Brugmans, *Séjour de Huygens à Paris*, p. 138).

10. The brief notes in Huygens's journal and Clerselier's preface in the second volume of his *edition nouvelle* of Descartes's *Lettres* make clear Rohault's Cartesianism. The *Traité* must be used with caution in assessing the contents of the early lectures; Rohault's initial explanation in Monconys's *Journal* was altered for publication.

11. Huygens to his brother Lodewijk, 27 February 1661 (Huygens, *Oeuvres*, vol. 3, pp. 252–254).

12. Clerselier spoke on rarefaction on 2 January 1661; the discussion of the transmission of light came on 19 February; cf. Huygens's journal (Brugmans, *Séjour de Huygens à Paris*, pp. 141 and 154).

13. Guédreville spoke on 5 February; Montmor presented the other astronomical address on 1 March. Huygens attended a fifth meeting of the ladies' society on 12 March but did not record its topic. See ibid., pp. 150, 157, and 159.

14. On Montmor, see S. Delorme, "Montmor," *Dictionary of Scientific Biography*, vol. 9, pp. 497–499. The best source remains Harcourt Brown, *Scientific Organizations in Seventeenth Century France (1620–1680)* (Baltimore: Wilkins and Wilkins, 1934). See also the untitled series of articles by M. G. Bigourdan, published in the *Comptes rendus* of the Académie des sciences, vol. 164 (1917), pp. 129–134, 159–162, and 216–220, which includes material published by the society's secretary Samuel Sorbière in his *Relations d'un voyage à l'angleterre.*

15. Huygens to his brother Constantijn, 18 November 1660, and to his brother Lodewijk on the same date (Huygens, *Oeuvres*, vol. 3, pp. 178–180 and 180–182).

16. Huygens's journal (Brugmans, *Séjour de Huygens à Paris*, 9 November 1660, p. 129).

17. The incident had transpired in November or early December 1658 (Huygens, *Oeuvres*, vol. 2, p. 287).

18. Chapelain to Huygens, 12 April and 10 May 1658 (ibid., pp. 165–167 and 173–178).

19. Huygens to Chapelain, 28 March 1658 (ibid., pp. 156–162). Chapelain's request came in the letter of 12 April.

20. Huygens acceded to Chapelain's request in a letter of 12 April 1658 (ibid., p. 169); Chapelain's report came in his letter of 10 May.

21. Chapelain to Huygens, 10 May 1658.

22. Ibid.

23. Huygens published the *Systema Saturnium* privately and mailed it to interested parties on 28 July 1659 (see ibid., vol. 2, p. 453). The Latin original and facing-page French translation appear in ibid., vol. 15, pp. 226–353.

24. Chapelain to Huygens, 15 October 1658 (ibid., vol. 2, pp. 494–497).

25. *System saturnium*, p. 297. Cf. Albert van Helden, "Annulao Cingitur: The Solution to the Problem of Saturn," *Journal for the History of Astronomy* 5 (1974), pp. 155–174, especially p. 161; and Bos, "Huygens," *Dictionary of Scientific Biography*, vol. 6, p. 604.

26. The material in Huygens's notebooks from October 1659 is scattered in Huygens, *Oeuvres*, vol. 14, pp. 387–397; vol. 15, p. 379 n. 3 and p. 533; vol. 16, pp. 302,

319–320, 379–380, 387–391, 405–412; vol. 17, pp. 276–291. For a more complete development of the argument offered in this paragraph, see Geoffrey Sutton, "A Science for a Polite Society: Cartesian Natural Philosophy in Paris During the Reigns of Louis XIII and XIV" (Ph.D. dissertation, Princeton University, 1982), pp. 241–277. See also Bos, "Huygens," p. 610, and Allen Gabbey, "Huygens and Mechanics," *Studies on Christiaan Huygens* (Lisse: Swets & Zeitlinger, 1980), pp. 166–199.

27. Georges Mongrédien, "L'Influence immédiate," in *Pierre Gassendi: Sa vie et son oeuvre* (Paris: Editions Alain Michel, 1955), pp. 146–147, cited the documentary evidence that supports the claims in Jean-Leonor Le Gallois, sieur de Grimarest, *Vie de Monsieur Molière* (1705; reprint, Paris, 1930).

28. Grimarest, *Molière*, pp. 79–80. Mongrédien's comments in "L'Influence immédiate" supported this claim explicitly. Molière's teasing continued in the next scene.

29. On the *Journal*, see Harcourt Brown, "History, Science, and the *Journal des sçavans*," in his *Science and the Human Comedy* (Toronto, 1976); and Betty Tremble Morgan, *Histoire du Journal des sçavans depuis 1665 jusqu'en 1701* (Paris: Presses universitaires de France, 1929).

30. For a more extensive discussion of the scientific contents of the *Journal*, see Sutton, "Science for a Polite Society," pp. 421–427 and appendix 1, which gives a statistical breakdown of the scientific articles published in the *Journal* between 1665 and 1685.

31. *Journal des sçavans* 11 (1684), preface. All citations refer to the edition reprinted by Pierre Le Grand, Amsterdam, in 1686.

32. *Journal des sçavans* 5, no. 14 (1677), pp. 205–207.

33. Fontenelle, "Eloge de M Lemery," in *Oeuvres de Fontenelle* (Paris, 1790), vol. 6, pp. 369–382, on p. 371. Lemery published his lectures as a *Cours de chymie* (Paris, 1675). The *Cours* had even greater success than Rohault's *Traité*; more than thirty French editions and translations into six languages appeared through the mid–eighteenth century. The *Conferences* of the Bourdelot academy were for a time edited by P. Le Gallois as *Conversations de l'Académie de Monsieur l'abbé de Bourdelot* (Paris, 1672, 1673, and 1674). On the Bourdelot academy, see Brown, *Scientific Organizations,* chap. 11.

34. See Brown, *Scientific Organizations;* J. M. Hirschfield, "The *Académie royale des sciences* (1663–1683): Inauguration and Initial Problems of Organization" (Ph.D. dissertation, University of Chicago, 1957); Roger Hahn, *The Anatomy of a Scientific Institution: The Paris Academy of Sciences, 1666–1803* (Berkeley: University of California Press, 1971); Jacques Roger, "La Politique intellectuelle de Colbert et l'installation de Huygens à Paris," in Taton, ed., *Huygens et la France;* and Alice Stroup, *A Company of Scientists: Botany, Patronage, and Community at the Seventeenth-Century Parisian Royal Academy of Sciences* (Berkeley: University of California Press, 1990).

35. On Chapelain's efforts to keep Huygens in Colbert's eye, see Chapelain to Huygens, 21 May, 9 July, and 31 July 1665; Huygens to Chapelain, 21 May, 9 July, and 20 August 1665; and Carcavi to Huygens, 16 July (Huygens, *Oeuvres,* vol. 5, pp. 340–342, 357–358, 396–397, 419, and 439–440). Most of the official documents surrounding Huygens's appointment are lost, including the official letter of invitation from Pierre de Carcavi, the king's librarian, in early June 1665; see Huygens to his brother Lodewijk, 15 June (ibid., pp. 373–375). On Huygens's concerns and those of his father, see Christiaan Huygens to his brother Lodewijk, 21 and 25 July (ibid., pp. 418 and 338–390); Christiaan Huygens to Carcavi, 20 August (ibid., pp. 430–439);

Chapelain's reassurances came especially in a letter of 27 August (ibid., pp 472–73). Huygens resolved to join the *académie* on 17 September 1665 (see his letters to Colbert and Louis XIV, ibid., p. 484), but owing to delays in response, he could not leave before winter. The official letter of appointment, now lost, came with a covering letter from Chapelain dated 23 October 1665; Huygens left Holland on 21 April 1666 and was introduced to the king on 4 June. Cf., e.g., Huygens to Ph. Doublet, 4 June (ibid., vol. 6, pp. 40–42). On the apartments, see Huygens to his brother Constantijn, 22 July 1666 (ibid., pp. 68–69); and Martin Lister, *A Journey to Paris in the Year 1698* (3d London ed., 1699; reprint, Urbana: University of Illinois Press, 1967), p. 116. The Gratuity Lists for the years 1664–1683, which include Huygens's pension (specified as a pension rather than a gratuity after 1665), appear in *Lettres, instructions, et mémoires de Colbert*, ed. P. Clément, 5 vols. (Paris: Imprimerie royale, 1868), vol. 5, pp. 466–498.

36. Adrien Auzout was attached to the *académie* by the time Huygens arrived; cf. Justel to Oldenburg, 26 May 1666, published in *The Correspondence of Henry Oldenburg*, ed. A. Rupert Hall and Marie Boas Hall, 13 vols. (Madison: University of Wisconsin Press, 1965–1978), vol. 3, pp. 132–134. By the middle of June, the philosophical gossip included Carcavi, Roberval, Bernard Frenicle de Bessy, and Jean Picard in the *académie* as well; cf. Oldenburg to Boyle, 16 June 1666 (ibid., pp. 153–156), the quotes appear on pp. 154–155. In July, Jacques Buot joined them in astronomical observations. Cf. Huygens, *Oeuvres*, vol. 6, p. 3; and Bernard le Bouvier Fontenelle, *Histoire de l'Académie royale des sciences, 1666–1699*, 10 vols. (Paris, 1730), vol. 1, p. 10.

37. All the original members except Auzout and Huygens had other positions in the royal bureaucracy. Carcavi was king's librarian; Roberval was a professor at the Collège de France; Frenicle was an official in the financial bureaucracy; and Bout was a royal engineer. Their gratuities ranged from 1,000 to 1,500 livres a year. Fontenelle's official history, moreover, included among the members "a couple of good chemists and some able mechanics" (as Oldenburg described them in his letter to Boyle of 16 June 1666). These included de La Voye, Pivert, Niquet, and Couplet—none of their first names are recorded—who performed such tasks as instrument building, accompanying Huygens's clocks on sea voyages, arithmetical computations, and assistance with anatomical dissections. Cf. Fontenelle, *Histoire*, vol. 1, pp. 13, 70, and 144; vol. 2, pp. 362ff.; Auzout to Oldenburg, 27 March 1668 (*Oldenburg Correspondence*, vol. 3, pp. 174–176); Justel to Oldenburg, 4 July 1668 (ibid., vol. 4, pp. 499–500); Huygens, "Sur l'essai des horloges sur mer par Monsieur de La Voye" (*Oeuvres*, vol. 6, pp. 501–503); J.-D. Cassini, "Anecdotes de la vie de J.-D. Cassini," in Charles Wolf, *Histoire de l'Observatoire de Paris de sa fondation à 1793* (Paris: Gauthier-Villars, 1902), pp. 290 and 309; and Germain Brice, *A New Description of Paris* (trans. from French)(London, 1687), p. 66. Their compensation ranged from a few hundred to 1,000 livres.

38. On the astronomical observations see Fontenelle, *Histoire*, vol. 1., p. 10; and Huygens, *Oeuvres*, vol. 6, p. 3. Cf. Huygens to Ph. Doublet, 3 September 1666: "Here, nothing is going on" (ibid., pp. 68–69).

39. *Journal des sçavans* (1666), no. 2, pp. 202–205.

40. Ibid. (1665), no. 1, pp. 11–13.

41. Ibid. (1666), no. 2, p. 204. On the reference to Descartes, see his letter to Ferrier, 13 November 1629 (*Oeuvres de Descartes*, ed. C. Adam and P. Tannery, 13 vols.

[Paris: Cerf, 1897–1913], vol. 1, pp. 53–69). Clerselier first published it in vol. 3 of his *edition nouvelle of the Lettres* (1667). The letter had attracted attention from the time Clerselier discovered it in 1659; cf. Chapelain to Huygens, 15 October 1659 (Huygens, *Oeuvres,* vol. 2, pp. 494–497).

42. *Journal des sçavans* (1666), no. 3, pp. 215–219.

43. On the appointments in natural history, see, e.g., Justel to Oldenburg, 3 October 1666 (*Oldenburg Correspondence,* vol. 3, pp. 240–241). On Claude Perrault, see A. G. Keller, "Perrault," *Dictionary of Scientific Biography,* vol. 10, pp. 519–521; André Halleys, *Les Perrault* (Paris: Perrin, 1926); and the introductory material by Charles Perrault in his *Recueil de plusieurs machines de nouvelle invention* (Paris, 1700).

44. The first physician to the king, Marin Cureau de La Chambre (who was also a member of the Académie française), died in 1669; Samuel Du Clos assumed official supervision of a natural history of plants, but there is no evidence that he personally became involved. Also appointed to assist these gentlemen were an apothecary, Jean Marchant, and his assistant, Claude Bourdelin, who did perform interminable, unpublished chemical analyses of plants; and the surgeon Louis Gayant, who assisted in anatomical dissections. Jean Baptiste de Hamel was recruited as secretary to the *académie.*

45. On the affair of the Royal Observatory, see Wolf, *Histoire de l'Observatoire,* chap. 2; J.-D. Cassini (Cassini IV, the great-grandson of our Cassini), *Mémoires pour servir à l'histoire des sciences et à celle de l'Observatoire de Paris* (Paris: Bleuet, 1810); and J.-D. Cassini (I), "Anecdotes de la vie de J.-D. Cassini," in Wolf, *Histoire de l'Observatoire.* Contemporary sources include Claude and Charles Perrault, "Pourquoi et comment l'Observatoire a esté basty," in *Lettres de Colbert,* vol. 5, pp. 515–516; Vernon to Oldenburg, 24 April 1669 (*Oldenburg Correspondence,* vol. 5, pp. 497–498); and Brice, *A New Description of Paris,* "The Observatory Royal," pp. 64–67.

46. This official historiography of the *académie* began with Fontenelle's *Histoire.* On the organization of the mathematical and physical sessions of the *académie,* see Fontenelle, *Histoire,* vol. 1, pp. 14–15; and a document by Huygens, in his *Oeuvres,* vol. 6, pp. 95–96.

47. Fontenelle, *Histoire,* vol. 1, pp. 17 and 20.

48. Fontenelle, *Histoire,* vol. 1, pp. 52–53, describing activities of 1667. This very rare pamphlet, *Observations qui ont esté faites sur un grande Poisson . . . [et] sur un Lion dissequé dans la bibliothèque de roi* (Paris, 1667), was distributed as a gift from the *académie* and the crown; cf. *Philosophical Transactions of the Royal Society of London,* no. 28 (21 October 1667), pp. 535–537, or Justel to Oldenburg, 5 October 1667 (*Oldenburg Correspondence,* vol. 3, pp. 484–486).

49. E. J. Cole, *A History of Comparative Anatomy from Aristotle to the Eighteenth Century* (London: Macmillan, 1944), provided the most extensive scientific critique of the work. See also Joseph Schiller, "Laboratoires d'anatomie et de botanique à l'Académie des sciences au XVIIe siècle," *Revue d'histoire des science* 17 (1964), pp. 97–114. For a description of the anatomical session at the *académie,* see Fontenelle, *Histoire,* vol. 1, pp. 34–37, describing activities of 1667, and pp. 322–323, describing activities of 1682; and Vernon to Oldenburg, 23 January 1669 (*Oldenburg Correspondence,* vol. 6, pp. 5–6): "I had the opportunity to see a dissection of a horse made by Monsrs Pecquet and Gayant, as operators; Gallois, their secretary, copied; and Mons. Perrault, a very knowing doctor of physic, designed [drew]."

50. Originally published as *Description anatomique d'un chameleon, d'un lion, d'un dromedaire, d'un ours, et d'un gazelle* (Paris, 1669). I have not been able to consult the original; I shall cite the republication, "Description anatomique de trois chameleons," in vol. 3 of Fontenelle's *Histoire*. The essay as republished by Fontenelle in fact described three chameleons; the original apparently did not; see Erica Harth, *Cartesian Women* (Ithaca: Cornell University Press, 1992), pp. 99–106. Harth also reported that de Scudéry's chameleons both died shortly after their arrival, which contradicts Fontenelle's account; see the "Description de trois chameleons," p. 60; cf. Lister, *Journey to Paris*, p. 96.

51. "Description anatomique de trois chameleons," p. 35.

52. Ibid., p. 61.

53. Harth, *Cartesian Women*, pp. 99–106.

54. Fontenelle, *Histoire*, vol. 1, pp. 117–118, describing activities of 1670.

55. On the complex publishing history of the *Histoire des animaux*, see Cole, *History of Anatomy*.

56. The most famous rendition appeared as the frontispiece of the 1671 volume of the *Mémoires pour servir à l'histoire naturelle des animaux*, published in Paris. It also appeared in the less famous *Mémoires pour servir à l'histoire naturelle des plantes* in the same year. There was a separate issue of a similar engraving, which, because of its curious inscription as an *"Académie des sciences et belles-lettres,"* is thought to date from the very early years of the *académie;* a copy hangs at Oxford University. For a more sophisticated reading of the picture than is usually offered, see Erica Harth, *Ideology and Culture in Seventeenth-Century France* (Ithaca: Cornell University Press, 1983), pp. 261–278.

57. See, for example, David Maland, *Culture and Society in Seventeenth-Century France* (New York: Charles Scribner's Sons, 1970).

58. *Essais de physique, ou récueil de plusieurs traités touchant des choses naturelles,* 3 vols. (Paris, 1680). References will be to the version published in his *Oeuvres diverses de physique et de mechanique* (Leyden, 1712).

59. The extensive reviews appeared in the *Journal des sçavans* (1680), no. 14, pp. 178–185, on the essays on hardness, the spring of air, and the cause of weight; no. 16, pp. 209–214, on sound; no. 17, pp. 227–228, on ancient music; no. 19, pp. 245-250, on the mechanics of animals.

60. The brief account in Fontenelle, *Histoire*, vol. 1, p. 63, describing the discussions of 1669, is strongly biased toward the Cartesians. Excerpts from the minutes of the meetings during the second half of 1669, on which Fontenelle based his account, are published in Huygens, *Oeuvres*, vol. 19, pp. 628–645. Perrault's speech (p. 645) is not reported in detail; there is no reason to expect that the version in the *Essais de physique* was changed in any substantial way.

61. For a more detailed analysis of Perrault's theory of sound and its relations to Huygens's theory of light, see Sutton, "Science for a Polite Society," pp. 364–378.

62. See especially the review of Perrault's essay on ancient music in the *Journal des sçavans* (1680), no. 17, pp. 227–228.

63. Huygens, *Oeuvres*, vol. 19, pp. 631–640.

64. Ibid., pp. 632–633. A diagram of the rotating table appeared in ibid., vol. 16, p. 327.

65. Jacques Rohault, *A System of Natural Philosophy*, trans. John Clarke (New York: Johnson Reprint Corp., 1969), vol. 2, p. 94.

66. *Journal des sçavans* (1669), pp. 14–24.

67. See Huygens's journal, 23 April 1661 (Brugmans, *Séjour de Huygens à Paris*, p. 168). On the general knowledge that Huygens understood collision, see, e.g., Oldenburg to Spinoza, 18 December 1665 (*Oldenburg Correspondence*, vol. 2, pp. 633–635).

68. Oldenburg to Huygens, 5 November 1668 (*Oldenburg Correspondence*, vol. 5, p. 103).

69. Neither Huygens nor Wren sent the rules in the first response; indeed, each suggested to Oldenburg that the other might have a ready copy of the rules; Huygens to Oldenburg, 13 November 1668 (*Oldenburg Correspondence*, vol. 5, pp. 126–127); and Wren to Oldenburg, 13 November 1668 (ibid., p. 123). Wallis did include the rules in his initial response, but with the comment, "If I remember rightly," they were already known: Wallis to Oldenburg, 15 November 1668 (ibid., pp. 164–167).

70. Huygens never referred to the incident as more than a "slight injustice"; Huygens to Oldenburg, 30 March 1669 (Huygens, *Oeuvres*, vol. 6, pp. 390–391).

71. *Journal des sçavans* (1672), no. 2, pp. 23–28.

72. Ibid., no. 7, pp. 111–122. For an extended discussion of the "anomolous suspension," see Steven Shapin and Simon Shaffer, *The Leviathan and the Air Pump: Hobbes, Boyle, and the Experimental Life* (Princeton: Princeton University Press, 1985).

73. Auzout designed the apparatus in 1642; it does not seem that Rohault was familiar with it in 1660; cf. Huygens's remarks on the lectures cited in Notes 7 and 8 to this chapter.

74. Rohault, *A System of Natural Philosophy*, vol. 1, bk. 1, chap. 12.

75. Georges Mongrédien, *Madeleine de Scudéry et son salon* (Paris: Tallandier, 1946), pp. 125–126.

76. Cf. Samuel Menjot d'Elbenne, *Madame de La Salbière, ses pensées chrétiennes, et ses lettres à l'abbé Rancé* (Paris: Plon, 1923).

77. *Journal des sçavans* (1666), p. 203.

78. Robert Hooke, *Micrographia: or, some physiological descriptions of minute bodies made by magnifying glasses* (London, 1665).

79. Cf. Boyle to Moray [undated, ca. July 1662] (Huygens, *Oeuvres*, vol. 4, p. 220).

CHAPTER 5

1. The most extensive study of Fontenelle is Alain Niderst, *Fontenelle à la recherche de lui-même* (Paris: Nizet, 1972). See also L. Marsak, "Bernard de Fontenelle: The Idea of Science in the French Enlightenment," *Transactions of the American Philosophical Society*, n.s. vol. 49 (1959), pp. 1–64. Recent contributions to the vast literature on the idea of the plurality of worlds include S. J. Dick, *Plurality of Worlds: The Origins of the Extraterrestrial Debate from Democritus to Kant* (Cambridge: Cambridge University Press, 1982); and Stanley L. Jaki, *Planets and Planetarians: A History of Theories of the Origin of Planetary Systems* (New York: Wiley, [1978]).

2. *Entretiens sur la pluralité des mondes*, ed. Robert M. Shackleton (Oxford: Clarendon Press, 1955), pp. 63–64. Where it is suitable, I have followed an anonymous English translation, presumably following that of Aphra Behn, *Conversations on the Plurality of Worlds* (London, 1757); page references to the translation will appear as "(tr. p. 10)."

3. *Conversations,* pp. 65–74 (tr. pp. 12–29).

4. On the outmoded sources of Fontenelle's astronomical distances, see Shackleton's introduction to *Conversations,* pp. 16–19, and especially p. 186, n. 118.

5. *Conversations,* p. 113 (tr. p. 188).

6. Ibid. (tr. pp. 188–189).

7. Ibid., p. 114 (tr. p. 191).

8. Ibid.

9. Ibid., pp. 125–126 (tr. pp. 210–211).

10. Ibid., pp. 124–125 (tr. pp. 209–210).

11. Ibid., p. 128. (The English translation changes the passage to make broader claims about the genius of the European mind.)

12. Ibid., pp. 118–119 (tr. p. 199).

13. Ibid., p. 121 (tr. p. 202).

14. Ibid., p. 122 (tr. p. 204).

15. I shall cite *The Celestial Worlds Discovered* (London: Frank Cass, 1968), a reprint of the first English edition (London: Timothy Childe, 1698). The Latin version appeared under the title *Cosmotheoros.*

16. *Celestial Worlds,* p. 3.

17. "To the Reader," ibid., pp. iii–iv.

18. Ibid., pp. 1–2.

19. Ibid., p. 22.

20. Ibid., pp. 27–28.

21. Ibid., p. 57.

22. Ibid., p. 74.

23. Ibid., p. 60.

24. Ibid., p. 63.

25. Ibid., p. 86.

26. Ibid., p. 87.

27. Ibid., pp. 99–100.

28. John Locke, *Essay Concerning Human Understanding* (Oxford: Clarendon Press, 1975), p. 10.

29. The seventeenth- and eighteenth-century publication history of the *Conversations on the Plurality of Worlds* is extensively documented in Shackleton's edition.

30. The English editions appeared in 1698, 1722, and 1757; Latin in 1698 and 1699; and a French translation in 1718.

31. Fontenelle's *Histoire de l'Académie royale des sciences, 1666–1699* (Paris: 1730), 10 vols., which addressed the period before he joined the *académie,* is not dependable. His extreme self-confidence in asserting that traditions with which he was familiar had begun in the early years of the institution are most misleading. The standard accounts of the formation of the *académie* are extremely derivative from Fontenelle's early history and must be used with caution. The regular, annual publications Fontenelle composed and edited appeared as the *Histoire de l'Académie royale des sciences, avec les Mémoires de Mathématique et de Physique.* Subsequent references will be to the *Histoire* and *Mémoires.*

32. See, for example, "Sur la flux et reflux," *Histoire* (1710), pp. 4–10, and (1720), pp. 1–3; less extensive comments to the same effect came in 1712, 1713, and 1714.

33. "Observations de physique générale," *Histoire* (1715), pp. 3–4.

34. On Varignon, see Pierre Costable, "Varignon," *Dictionary of Scientific Biography*, v. 13, pp. 584–587, and Fontenelle's "Éloge de Varignon," *Histoire* (1722), pp. 136–146.

35. On Varignon's style and accomplishments, see E. J. Aiton, *The Vortex Theory of Planetary Motions* (London: Macdonald; New York: American Elsevier, 1972), pp. 125–126.

36. *Histoire* (1707), pp. 55–58. Varignon's article appeared in the *Mémoires*, pp. 12–17.

37. *Histoire* (1707), p. 58.

38. Ibid. (1710), p. 52, referring to Lemery's work on corals.

39. The work explicitly in the recreational genre is Claude-Gaspard Bachet de Méziriac, *Problemes plaisans et delectables* (Lyon, 1612 and 1624), which was not reprinted until the nineteenth century. Bachet's edition of Diaphontus also included many pleasant and delectable diversions. On Bachet, see William Schaff's article in the *Dictionary of Scientific Biography*, vol. 1, pp. 367–368, and JoAnn Morse, "The Reintroduction of Diophantus' *Algebra* in the Renaissance" (Ph.D. dissertation, Princeton University, 1981).

40. Paris editions appeared in 1694, 1696, and 1698. Posthumous French editions, with considerable additions especially in terms of the physical theory covered, appeared in 1720, 1725, 1735, 1778, and 1790. The Amsterdam edition appeared in 1698. English editions appeared in 1708, 1756, and four times in the nineteenth century. See the article by William Schaff in the *Dictionary of Scientific Biography*, vol. 10, pp. 263–265.

41. *Histoire* (1707), pp. 92–97, on p. 92.

42. "Sur les forces centrales des planets," ibid., pp. 97–103.

43. Aiton, *Vortex Theory*, pp. 155–165, provided an extensive account of Villemot's book, which I have not consulted, and pointed out the inadequacy of Fontenelle's review.

44. "Sur les forces centrales des planets," p. 101.

45. See, for example, "Sur les planets en general, et sur Saturn en particulier," *Histoire* (1704), pp. 65–72, on pp. 67ff. Fontenelle described a new method in the *Histoire* (1719), pp. 69–71; Cassini's "Méthode de déterminer la première Equation des Planets" appeared in *Mémoires* (1719), pp. 147–156.

46. On Maria Cunitz, see Londa Schiebinger, *The Mind Has No Sex?: Women in the Origins of Modern Science* (Cambridge: Harvard University Press, 1989), pp. 79–101, and Schiebinger, "Maria Winkelmann at the Berlin Academy: A Turning Point for Women in Science," *Isis* (1987), pp. 174–200.

47. See, for example, *Histoire* (1705), pp. 117–121, and (1706), pp. 95–101.

48. "Éloge de Cassini," ibid. (1712), pp. 83–104, on p. 101.

49. One summary of such work appeared in an article by the elder Deslisle on cartography in the *Mémoires* (1720), pp. 365–384. Deslise himself went to Louisiana in 1722, and a M. Bason repeated his measurements several years later; see *Histoire* (1730), pp. 104–105. See also the letters from Couplet discussed in this chapter and the voyages discussed in Chapter 7.

50. "Extrait de quelques lettres écrites de Portugal & du Brésil, par M Couplet le fils . . . ," *Mémoires* (1700), pp. 171–178.

51. Ibid., p. 178.

52. Ibid. (1726), pp. 18–20, on p. 19. Emphasis in original.

53. Ibid. (1700), pp. 101–110, Lemery, "Explication physique et chymique des feux souterraines, des tremblemens de Terre, des Outrans, des eclaires et tonnere."

54. Ibid., pp. 101–102.

55. *Histoire* (1703), pp. 47–49.

56. Ibid. (1704), pp. 37–39, on p. 39.

57. Ibid. (1708), pp. 1–3.

58. "Du souphre principe, article troisième," *Mémoires* (1705), pp. 88–96, on p. 91.

59. "Sur le phosphore du baromètre," *Histoire* (1700), pp. 5–8, on p. 8.

60. An extract of Bernoulli's letter appeared in the *Mémoires* (1700), pp. 178–190, where it was incorrectly dated 1707.

61. "Sur le phosphor du baromètre," *Histoire* (1700), p. 7.

62. "Sur le phosphor du baromètre," ibid. (1701), pp. 1–8.

63. Ibid. (1701), pp. 5–6.

64. "Sur la lumière des corps frottés," ibid. (1707), pp. 1–3, on pp. 2–3.

CHAPTER 6

1. Most modern recountings of the story rely on the rather drier version in David Brewster, *Memoirs of the Life, Writings, and Discoveries of Sir Isaac Newton* (Edinburgh, 1855), vol. 2, p. 339. Brewster's source, in turn, is John Theophilus Desaguliers, *A Course of Experimental Philosophy* (London, 1745), 2d ed., corrected, vol. 1, p. viii. Desaguliers wrote, "This I was told several times by Sir Isaac Newton himself."

2. The literature is vast, beginning in the early years of the Enlightenment. The most important source is Voltaire, *Lettres philosophiques, ou Lettres anglaises,* ed. Raymond Naves (Paris: Éditions Garnier Frères, 1964). Recent scholarship has taken as its starting point Ernst Cassirer, *The Philosophy of the Enlightenment,* trans. Fritz C. A. Koelin and James P. Pettegrove (New York: Beacon Press, 1951), the classic study. See also Peter Gay, *The Enlightenment: An Interpretation,* 2 vols. (New York: Knopf, 1966–1969).

3. For those who expect that this claim is overblown, see, for example, Sergeant-Welch Scientific Company catalog, 1992–1993, p. 498, "Ballistics car," two versions; p. 503, "Trajectory apparatus," which correspond to experiments discussed below, and pp. 476–477, "four experiments on center of gravity," all of which appear elsewhere in the works cited, and which are cited by Thomas Hankins, *Science and the Enlightenment* (New York: Cambridge University Press, 1985), pp. 46–50. The Mariotte collision apparatus described in this chapter is also readily available as both a demonstration piece and a coffee-table toy.

4. One significant exception to this neglect is Margaret Jacob, *The Cultural Meaning of the Scientific Revolution* (New York: Knopf, 1988), who offered an incisive analysis of the role of the lecturers in England and Holland. See also Hankins, *Science and the Enlightenment.* A rather different perspective on experimental practice appears in Steven Shapin and Simon Shaffer, *The Leviathan and the Air Pump: Hobbes, Boyle, and the Experimental Life* (Princeton: Princeton University Press, 1985), pp. 274–276.

5. The phrase comes from Clifford Truesdell, "A Program Toward Rediscovering the Rational Mechanics in the Age of Reason," *Archive for the History of the Exact*

Sciences 1 (1960), pp. 3–36, and Truesdell, *Essays in the History of Mechanics* (New York: Springer, 1968).

6. There is relatively little biographical material on Polinière. The material in the preface to his *Expériences de physique* (Paris, 1709) is often polemical. Posthumous editions include an "Abrégé de la vie de M Polinière"; this is the basis for most information. David Corson, "Polinière," *Dictionary of Scientific Biography,* vol. 11, pp. 67–68, offered a good summary of his life. Corson also discussed some unpublished material on the mercurial phosphor experiments in "Pierre Polinière, Francis Hauksbee, and Electroluminescence: A Case of Simultaneous Discovery," *Isis* 59 (1968), pp. 402–403.

7. Polinière, *Expériences de physique,* preface (unnumbered page, verso of page designated as signature aiiij).

8. Ibid. (unnumbered page, verso of page designated as signature avi).

9. Ibid.; the "Avertissement" of the second edition quoted three pages of Fontenelle's discussion of the "Revolution" in science.

10. The second edition reversed the order of these experiments, without any particular change in either the argument or the arrangement of the experiment.

11. Shapin and Shaffer, *The Leviathan and the Air Pump,* pp. 274–276.

12. Polinière, *Expériences de physique.* In the discussion of the pneumatic experiments I shall cite the 2d ed. The introductory material on air pumps appears in vol. 1 on pp. 121–141.

13. Ibid., experiment 27, pp. 142–143.

14. Ibid., experiment 28, pp. 146–147.

15. On the collecting instincts of the seventeenth century, see Joseph Levine, *Dr. Woodward's Shield: History, Science, and Satire in Augustan England* (Berkeley: University of California Press, 1977).

16. Polinière, *Expériences de physique,* vol. 1, experiments 31, pp. 156–157; 32, p. 157; 33, pp. 159–160; 36, pp. 171–172, and 34, pp. 161–164.

17. Ibid., experiment 40, pp. 181–184.

18. Ibid., vol. 2, p. 6.

19. Ibid., p. 8.

20. Ibid., 3d ed., vol. 2, p. 6.

21. Ibid. This explanation remained even in the third (posthumous) edition—experiment 8, pp. 64–69.

22. Ibid., 2d ed., vol. 2, p. 9.

23. Ibid., pp. 10–11.

24. Ibid., p. 12.

25. Ibid., experiment 71, pp. 356–358.

26. Among the most important sources see Karl Popper, *The Logic of Scientific Discovery* (New York: Basic Books, 1959), and Carl Hempel, *Aspects of Scientific Explanation* (New York: Free Press, 1966), and Hempel, *Philosophy of Natural Science* (New York: Prentice-Hall, 1966).

27. Hauksbee published his electrical experiments as the most prominent of various experiments in *Physico-Mechanical Experiments on Various Subjects* (London: R. Burgis, 1709).

28. The classic studies are by Robert King Merton. A convenient sample is included in his collection *The Sociology of Science* (Chicago: University of Chicago Press, 1973). See, especially, "Priorities in Scientific Discovery," originally published

in 1957; "Singletons and Multiples in Scientific Discovery," originally published in 1961; and "Resistance to the Systematic Study of Multiple Discoveries in Science," originally published in 1963.

29. The standard account of the exploration of the mercurial phosphor began with Joseph Priestley's *History and Present State of Electricity* (London: Dodsley, 1767). It has been adopted by most subsequent histories. See, for example, J. L. Heilbron, *Electricity in the Seventeenth and Eighteenth Centuries: A Study of Early Modern Physics* (Berkeley: University of California Press, 1979).

30. Hauksbee, *Physico-Mechanical Experiments.*

31. For a more extensive account of the development of this line of experimental inquiry, see Chapter 8 herein.

32. Desaguliers remains rather obscure. A. Rupert Hall, "Desaguliers," *Dictionary of Scientific Biography*, vol. 4, pp. 43–46, is the best source but must be supplemented by additional biographical material in Jacob, *Cultural Meaning of the Scientific Revolution.*

33. Jacob, *Cultural Meaning of the Scientific Revolution*, p. 171, n. 10, cited a broadside in the British library to this effect, which advertised Desaguliers's lectures in 1713. Desaguliers published a description of his lectures in 1717; see Note 42 herein.

34. A transcription of the lectures, published as J. T. Desaguliers, *Lectures of Experimental Philosophy*, "2d ed." (London, 1719), included a set of the plates; an explanation of their use appeared in the preface Desaguliers prepared after the work was printed; see the third unnumbered page. On the publishing history of the lectures, see Notes 42 and 43 herein.

35. The 1719 edition of the *Lectures of Experimental Philosophy*, which contained the plates, also included "A description of Rails Horary, being a machine to represent the motion of the Moon about the earth, and the Earth and Venus and Mercury about the Sun," on pp. 195–201.

36. The most extensive description came in Desaguliers's 1745 *Course of Experimental Philosophy*, vol. 1, pp. 448–466. By this time he had changed his attribution of the first planetarium from one constructed by J. Rails for the Earl of Orrery, from whence it got its name, to an earlier version by George Graham, which Rails had copied.

37. David S. Landes, *Revolution in Time: Clocks and the Making of the Modern World* (Cambridge: Harvard University Press, 1983), discussed the ascendancy of the British industry in the eighteenth-century in his chapter 14. In the quoted remark he was referring to an eighteenth-century British marine chronometer (ibid., fig. 20).

38. Jacob, *Cultural Meaning of the Scientific Revolution*, made a strong argument that demonstration-lectures like those considered here supplied "The Cultural Origins of the First Industrial Revolution," as she called one of her chapters.

39. The classic study is Eric Robinson and A. E. Musson, *James Watt and the Steam Revolution* (London, 1969).

40. Jacob, *Cultural Meaning of the Scientific Revolution*, placed great emphasis on Desaguliers's work. These problems were addressed only at the end of a forty-year career. See especially the preface to the second volume of Desaguliers's *Course of Experimental Philosophy*, which did not appear until 1744, the year of his death. In the preface Desaguliers apologized for the ten-year delay between the first and second volume. He said it had occurred in part because he had added material on machines, in response to recent attempted frauds perpetrated by "boasting engineers."

41. Jacob, *Cultural Meaning of the Scientific Revolution.* It is ironic that Jacob specifically contrasted the later lectures of Nollet with "the relative scientific backwardness of the University of Paris" (p. 201); she seemed totally unaware of Polinière's contribution.

42. J. T. Desaguliers, *Physico-Mechanical Lectures, or, an Account of What Is Explained and Demonstrated in the Course of Mechanical and Experimental Philosophy* (London, 1717).

43. J. T. Desaguliers, *Lectures of Experimental Philosophy,* "2d ed." (London, 1719). The transcription was prepared by Paul Dawson, who attended the lectures. Desaguliers's preface explained that the work had not been authorized and that although he had attempted to correct it, he disclaimed responsibility for errors.

44. For biographical information see A. Rupert Hall, "'sGravesande," *Dictionary of Scientific Biography,* vol. 5, pp. 509–511.

45. D. J. Struick, "Musschenbroek, Petrus van" *Dictionary of Scientific Biography,* vol. 9, pp. 594–595, included material on Petrus's brother Jan as well.

46. Willem Jacob 'sGravesande, *Physices elementa mathematica, experimentis confirmata, sive, introductio ad philosophiam Newtonianam,* 2 vols. (Leyden, 1720–1721).

47. Desaguliers, *Course of Experimental Philosophy,* 2d ed., vol. 1, pp. viii–ix. See also Petrus van Musschenbroek, *Essai de physique* (Paris, 1739), for similar sentiments.

48. Petrus van Musschenbroek, *The Elements of Natural Philosophy,* trans. John Colson (London: J. Nourse, 1744), author's preface, p. iii. See also Desaguliers, *Course of Experimental Philosophy,* 2d ed., vol. 1, p. v.

49. Musschenbroek, *Elements,* p. vi.

50. Desaguliers, *Course of Experimental Philosophy,* 2d ed., vol. 1, p. 45.

51. Among the better discussions see Carolyn [Merchant] Iltis, "The Leibnizian-Newtonian Debates: Natural Philosophy and Social Psychology," *British Journal for the History of Science* 4 (1973), pp. 343–377; and Hankins, *Science in the Enlightenment,* pp. 28–33.

52. Other future members included Alexis-Claude Clairaut, Charles Marie de La Condamine, and a later secretary of the Académie royale des sciences, Jean Paul Grandjean de Fouchy. On Nollet, see Jean Torlais, *Un physicien au siècle des lumières: L'Abbé Nollet 1700–1770* (Paris: Sipuco, 1954), pp. 18–21; Heilbron, *Electricity in the Seventeenth and Eighteenth Centuries,* p. 279, and especially Jean Itard, "Clairaut," *Dictionary of Scientific Biography,* vol. 3, p. 281.

53. Jean Antoine Nollet, *Programme ou idée générale d'un cours de physique expérimentale, avec un catalogue raisonné des instrumens qui servent aux expériences* (Paris, 1738), pp. xiv–xv.

54. Ibid., pp. xvi–xvii.

55. Nollet reported variously that he had been giving the lectures for three years or four years at the time (ibid., p. vii and p. xxviii).

56. Ibid., xviii.

57. Desaguliers, *Course of Experimental Philosophy,* 2d ed., vol. 1, preface, p. x.

58. Mme du Châtelet to Francesco Algarotti, author of the popular *Newtonians for Ladies,* 20 April 1736; in *Voltaire's Correspondence,* ed. Theodore Besterman (Geneva: Institut et Musée Voltaire, 1953–1977), vol. 5, #1024, pp. 136–140, on p. 139.

59. Cardinal François Joachim de Pierre de Bernis, reminiscing about Paris in the 1730s, 26 July 1762, in ibid., vol. 49, #9799, pp. 139–140.

60. Voltaire to Charles Augustine Feriol, comte d'Argental, 7 September 1761; in ibid., vol. 47, #9292, pp. 6–7.

61. See, for example, Willem Jacob 'sGravesande, *Mathematical Elements of Natural Philosophy Confirm'd by Experiments*, trans. Desaguliers, 4th Eng. ed. (1731), preface, p. xviii.

62. See the French edition of the *Essay de physique*—the subtitle reads "Avec une description de nouvelles sortes de Machines pneumatiques"—(Leyden, 1739), for a price list.

63. Nollet, *Programme*, pp. 116–117.

64. Ibid., pp. xiv–xv.

65. Voltaire to Bonaventure Moussinot, 5 June 1738, in Voltaire, *Correspondence*, vol. 7, #1448, pp. 194–195; see also the letter to Henry Pitot, in ibid., #1441, pp. 178–179. I have found no biographical material on Cousin.

66. Nollet repaired a camera obscura for Mme du Châtelet; see her letter to Francesco Algarotti, 20 April 1736, in ibid., vol. 5, #1024, pp. 136–140, on p. 139.

67. Voltaire to Bonaventure Moussinot, his Parisian business agent, 30 May 1737; in ibid., vol. 6, #1274, pp. 152–153, on p. 153.

68. Voltaire to Bonaventure Moussinot, 18 May 1738, in ibid., vol. 6, #1440, p. 177.

69. Voltaire to Nicolas Claude Thieriot, 27 October 1738, in ibid., vol. 7, #1567, pp. 422–423.

70. Jean Antoine Nollet, *Leçons de physique expérimentale*, 6 vols. (Paris: Guerin, 1745), vol. 1, p. xxiij.

71. Ibid.

72. Ibid., on Fontenelle, p. xxxv; on Malebranche, p. xxiij.

73. See the discussion of the second book of Newton's *Principia* in Chapter 7.

74. Nollet, *Leçons,* vol. 2, p. 201–202.

75. Ibid., p. 62.

76. Ibid., pp. 57–61.

77. Ibid., vol. 1, pp. 79–80.

78. Ibid., vol. 2, p. 86.

79. Ibid., vol. 6, p. 11.

80. Nollet, *Programme*, pp. 180–182.

CHAPTER 7

1. The best short biography is Esther Ehrman, *Mme du Châtelet* (Dover, N.H.: Berg, 1986). Ira O. Wade, *Voltaire and Madame du Châtelet: An Essay on the Intellectual Activity at Cirey* (Princeton: Princeton University Press, 1941), is the classic, if rather outdated, intellectual biography. Mme du Châtelet's correspondence is included in *Voltaire's Correspondence*, ed. Theodore Besterman (Geneva: Institut et Musée Voltaire, 1953–1977). See also René Taton, "Châtelet, Gabrielle-Émilie le Tonnier de Breteuil, Marquise du," *Dictionary of Scientific Biography*, vol. 7, pp. 215–217.

2. For one account, see Ehrman, *Mme du Châtelet*, p. 24.

3. The only full-length biography is Pierre Brunet, *Maupertuis* (Paris: Blanchard, 1929). Bentley Glass, "Maupertuis, Pierre Louis Moreau," *Dictionary of Scientific Biography*, vol. 9, pp. 186–189, concentrates overly much on questionable claims about Maupertuis's biology as a precursor to genetics.

4. Académie royale des sciences, *Mémoires* (1732), pp. 112–117.

5. Jean Itard, "Clairaut," *Dictionary of Scientific Biography*, vol. 3, pp. 281–286, is an outstanding entry. A more extensive discussion of Clairaut's theoretical accomplishments, and his disputes with d'Alembert, appears in Thomas L. Hankins, *Jean D'Alembert: Science and the Enlightenment* (Oxford: Clarendon Press, 1970), especially pp. 28–42.

6. The literature on Voltaire is immense. The authoritative biography in English is Theodore Besterman, *Voltaire* (New York: Harcourt, Brace, and World, 1969).

7. Ibid., p. 161.

8. Voltaire, *Lettres philosophiques, ou Lettres anglaises,* ed. Raymond Naves (Paris: Éditions Garnier Frères, 1964), p. 57.

9. Ibid., p. 70.

10. Ibid., pp. 80–81.

11. Ibid., p. 81.

12. Pierre Brunet, *Les Physiciens hollandais et la méthode expérimentale en France au XVIIIe siècle* (Paris: Blanchard, 1926), pp. 117–118.

13. Gabrielle Émilie du Châtelet-Lomont, *Dissertation sur la nature du feu* (Paris: Prault, 1744).

14. Ibid., p. 6.

15. Ibid., pp. 3–5.

16. Ibid., pp. 7–8.

17. Ibid., pp. 37–38.

18. Ibid., p. 23.

19. Ibid., p. 54.

20. Ibid., p. 53.

21. Voltaire to Nollet's assistant Cousin, 3 July 1738, in Voltaire, *Correspondence*, vol. 7, #1472, pp. 247–248.

22. The most important discussion of the professionalization of French scientific institutions appears in Charles Coulston Gillispie, *Science and Polity in France at the End of the Old Regime* (Princeton: Princeton University Press, 1980).

23. Mme du Châtelet to Maupertuis, 2 September 1738, quoted in Ehrman, *Mme du Châtelet*, p. 29.

24. *Histoire* (1737), pp. 90–96.

25. See Mary Terrall, "Representing the Earth's Shape: The Polemics Surrounding Maupertuis' Expedition to Lapland," *Isis* 83 (1992), pp. 218–237.

26. Émilie du Châtelet, *Institutions de physique* (Paris, 1740) p. 4.

27. E. A. Fellmann, "Koenig, Johan Samuel," *Dictionary of Scientific Biography*, vol. 7, pp. 442–444.

28. du Châtelet, *Institutions*, pp. 5–7.

29. Jean Antoine Nollet, *Leçons de physique expérimentale* (Paris: Guerin, 1745), vol. 2, p. 202.

30. See, for example, Carolyn Merchant, *The Death of Nature* (New York: Harper and Row, 1980), chap. 12.

31. 29 August 1740, trans. in Ehrman, *Mme du Châtelet*, p. 57.

32. Pierre Louis Moreau de Maupertuis, *Venus physique*, trans. as *The Earthly Venus* by Simone Brangier Boas, with an introduction by George Boas (New York: Johnson Reprint Corp., 1966), pp. 3–4.

33. Ibid., chap. 17, pp. 54–58.

34. Several responsible accounts of Maupertuis's reproductive theories are now available. See Michael H. Hoffheimer, "Maupertuis and the Eighteenth-Century Critique of Preexistence," *Journal of the History of Biology* 15 (1982), pp. 119–144, or Thomas L. Hankins, *Science and the Enlightenment* (New York: Cambridge University Press, 1985), chap. 5.

35. Maupertuis, *Earthly Venus*, p. 59.

36. Euler to Clairaut, 30 September 1747, trans. by and quoted in Hankins, *D'Alembert*, p. 32.

37. The suggestion came in a letter to Cramer, 16 June 1748, quoted at length in ibid., pp. 33–34.

38. Émilie du Châtelet, *Principes mathématiques de la philosophie naturelle* (Paris: Desaint & Saillant and Lambert, 1756).

39. Voltaire to d'Argenson, 4 September 1749, quoted in Ehrman, *Mme du Châtelet*, p. 43.

40. *Micromégas, Histoire philosophique,* included in *Oeuvres complètes de Voltaire,* 43 vols. (Paris: Garniers Frères, 1877–1885), in vol. 21, pp. 105–122. I shall follow the translation of William F. Fleming in *The Works of Voltaire,* 42 vols. (Paris: E. R. DuMont, 1901), in vol. 3, pp. 20–50, although I will sometimes alter the translation. References to the translation will appear as (tr. pp. 20–50).

41. *Micromégas*, p. 106 (tr. p. 23).

42. Ibid., p. 107 (tr. p. 22).

43. Ibid., p. 107 (tr. p. 23).

44. Ibid., p. 107 (tr. pp. 23–24).

45. Ibid., pp. 107–108 (tr. p. 24).

46. Ibid., p. 108 (tr. pp. 24–25).

47. Ibid., p. 111 (tr. p. 30).

48. Ibid., p. 111 (tr. p. 30). Castel had served as a mathematical tutor to both Maupertuis and Clairaut.

49. Ibid., p. 112 (tr. p. 32).

50. Ibid., p. 113 (tr. pp. 33–34).

51. Ibid., p. 114 (tr. pp. 36–37). Fleming translated *deux filles lappones* as "lapland servants."

52. Itard, "Clairaut," p. 281.

53. *Micromégas*, p. 11 (tr. p. 38). Fleming translated *la graine* as "rudiment."

54. Ibid., p. 120 (tr. p. 46).

55. Ibid., p. 120 (tr. p. 47).

56. Ibid., p. 121 (tr. p. 48).

57. Ibid., p. 121 (tr. p. 49).

58. Ibid.

59. Ibid., p. 122 (tr. p. 50).

CHAPTER 8

1. Willem D. Hackmann, *Electricity from Glass: The History of the Frictional Electrical Machine, 1600–1850* (Alphen aan den Rijn, The Netherlands: Sijthoff & Noordhoff, 1978), especially pp. 42–47.

2. John Heilbron, "Gray," *Dictionary of Scientific Biography*, vol. 5, pp. 515–517, mentioned Gray's assistance at Desaguliers's lectures; A. Rupert Hall reported in his

article on Desaguliers, *Dictionary of Scientific Biography*, vol. 4, pp. 43–46, that Gray also lived in Desaguliers's residence. J. L. Heilbron, *Electricity in the Seventeenth and Eighteenth Centuries: A Study of Early Modern Physics* (Berkeley: University of California Press, 1979), offers the most extensive account of Gray's career.

3. The letter was finally published by R. A. Chipman, "An Unpublished Letter of Stephen Gray on Electrical Experiments, 1707–1708," *Isis* 49 (1954), pp. 33–40.

4. The experiments are reported in Stephen Gray, "Letter to Cromwell Mortimer, Containing Several Experiments Concerning Electricity," *Philosophical Transactions of the Royal Society of London*, vol. 37 (1731), pp. 18–44. The letter is dated 8 February 1731.

5. Ibid., pp. 19–23.

6. Ibid., p. 33.

7. Ibid., pp. 23–25.

8. Ibid., pp. 31.

9. Ibid., pp. 33–40.

10. Heilbron, *Electricity in the Seventeenth and Eighteenth Centuries*, p. 251.

11. Charles François Cisternay Dufay published six articles in the *Mémoires* of the Académie royale des sciences (1733), pp. 23–35, 73–84, 233–254, 457–476, and (1734), pp. 341–361 and 503–526.

12. The most extensive discussion of Dufay's research appears in Heilbron, *Electricity in the Seventeenth and Eighteenth Centuries*, pp. 250–260 and 276–278.

13. Fontenelle's introduction prefaced all the articles published in 1733 and appeared in the *Histoire* for that year, pp. 6–13. As Heilbron pointed out (ibid., p. 276 n. 1), Fontenelle's introduction offered a rather more generic Cartesian explanation than Dufay's articles in the *Mémoires* merited; this was in character for the perpetual secretary.

14. Heilbron, *Electricity in the Seventeenth and Eighteenth Centuries*, indeed presents Dufay's theoretical discussion of electricity in a chapter entitled "Electricity in France After Dufay," a discussion that, before turning to Nollet, considers primarily the theories of Privat de Molières.

15. Jean Antoine Nollet, *Programme ou idée générale d'un cours de physique expérimentale, avec un catalogue raisonné des instrumens qui servent aux expériences* (Paris, 1738), pp. 99–104.

16. Nollet reported the sensation, for example, in "Conjectures sur les causes de l'électricité des corps," *Mémoires* (1745), pp. 107–151, on p. 110.

17. Nollet briefly noted and dismissed Dufay's suggestion of two sorts of electrical material in ibid., pp. 145–146.

18. The first clear enunciation was published in Jean Antoine Nollet, *Essai sur l'électricité des corps* (Paris: Guerin, 1746).

19. Nollet, "Conjectures sur les causes de l'électricité des corps," p. 108.

20. Nollet, *Essai sur l'électricité*. Although the book was not published until 1745, it was based on demonstrations that evolved from the work in Dufay's lab.

21. Nollet attributed the electrified kiss to Bose; see Jean Antoine Nollet, *Lettres sur l'électricité* (Paris: Guerin, 1753) vol. 1, p. 199.

22. Christine Johnson pointed out in a conversation the rhymes in Georg Matthias Bose, *Die Electricität nach ihrer Entdeckung und Fortgang mit poetischer Feder entworffen* (Wittenberg: Ben Johann Joachim Ublfelden, 1744). Bose is better known for his *Tentamina electrica* (Wittenberg, 1744).

23. Johann Heinrich Winkler, "Essai sur la nature, les effets et les causes de l'électricité," appeared in *Recueil de traités sur l'électricité traduits de l'allemand et de l'anglois* (Paris, 1748), p. 5.

24. Christian August Hausen, *Novus proectus in historia electricitatis* (Leipzig, 1743).

25. Georg Matthias Bose, *Hypothesis soni perraultiana* (Leipzig: Typographica Breitkofiana, 1734).

26. Winkler, "Essai sur la nature, les effets et les causes de l'électricité." See also, in the *Philosophical Transactions* 45 (1748), pp. 262–270.

27. From the German edition, Johann Heinrich Winkler, *Die Starke der electrischen Kraft des Wassers in glasernen Gefassen* (Leipzig: Breitkopf, 1746); the illustrations were not included in the French. Rubbers applied to tubes are described in Winkler's "Essai sur la nature, les effets et les causes de l'électricité," p. 6.

28. Nollet, "Conjectures sur les causes de l'électricité des corps," *Mémoires* (1745), pp. 107–151, on p. 127.

29. Winkler, "Essai sur la nature, les effets et les causes de l'électricité," p. 6.

30. Ibid., pp. 7–8.

31. Ibid., p. 7.

32. Heilbron, *Electricity in the Seventeenth and Eighteenth Centuries*, pp. 265–266.

33. Winkler, "Essai sur la nature, les effets et les causes de l'électricité," pp. 28–29.

34. Ibid., p. 41.

35. Ibid., pp. 48–50.

36. Winkler's exposition of his vortex theory came in ibid., pp. 76–80.

37. Ibid., pp. 90–94.

38. Jean Antoine Nollet, *Essai sur l'électricité des corps* (Paris, 1746).

39. Ibid., "Preface," p. xi.

40. Ibid., pp. 142–147.

41. Ibid., pp. 194–215.

42. Le Monnier's laboratory was described in a "Letter from Mr. Turberville Needham, Concerning Some New Electrical Experiments Lately Made at Paris," read at the Royal Society of London on 23 October 1746 and published in the *Philosophical Transactions of the Royal Society of London* 44 (1746), pp. 247–263.

43. Ibid., p. 257.

44. Ibid., p. 261.

45. Nollet, *Recherches sur les causes particuliers des phénomènes électriques* (Paris: Guerin, 1749).

46. Ibid., p. 426.

47. Ibid., p. 254.

48. Ibid., appendix, pp. 425–430, advances this theory of the Leyden jar.

49. Nollet offered several examples of phenomena offered as original by Franklin that had been published in Europe before the American took up electrical studies, including the electrified kiss; see Jean Antoine Nollet, *Lettres sur l'électricité* (Paris: Guerin, 1753), vol. I, pp. 199–201; Nollet suggested that the false claims of priority resulted from ignorance rather than plagiarism; see p. 8.

50. Benjamin Franklin, *Autobiography* (New Haven: Yale University Press, 1964), p. 243.

51. Benjamin Franklin, *Experiments and Observations on Electricity*. I shall cite I. Bernard Cohen's edition (Cambridge: Harvard University Press, 1941). The quote appears on p. 174.

52. Ibid.; the statement appears in a note added in the fourth edition, 1769, and therefore had no effect on the French reception of this work.

53. Ibid., p. 213.

54. Franklin, *Autobiography*, p. 243.

55. Nollet, *Lettres sur l'électricité*, vol. 1, p. ix, and p. 7.

56. Franklin, *Experiments and Observations*, p. 183.

57. Ibid., p. 222.

58. Nollet, *Lettres sur l'électricité*, vol. 1, p. 14.

59. Ibid., pp. 8–9.

60. Ibid., p. 18.

61. Ibid., p. 136.

62. Franklin, *Experiments and Observations*, pp. 370–371.

63. Joseph Priestley, *History and Present State of Electricity* (London: Dodsley, 1767), p. 552.

64. Geoffrey V. Sutton, "The Politics of Science in Early Napoleonic France: The Case of the Voltaic Pile," *Historical Studies in the Physical Sciences* 11 (1981), pp. 329–366.

Bibliography

[Académie française]. *Les Sentimens de l'Académie françoise sur le tragi-comedie du Cid.* Ed. Georges Collas. Paris: Picard, 1912.

————. *Les Sentiments de l'Académie française sur le Cid.* Ed. Colbert Searles. Minneapolis: University of Minnesota Press, 1916.

Adam, Antoine. *Grandeur and Illusion: French Literature and Society, 1600–1715.* Trans. Herbert Tint. New York: Basic Books, 1972.

Aiton, E. J. *The Vortex Theory of Planetary Motions.* London: Macdonald; New York: American Elsevier, 1972.

Baillet, Adrien. *La Vie de monsieur Des-Cartes.* 2 vols. Paris: Horthemels, 1691; reprint, Hildesheim: Olms, 1972.

Besterman, Theodore. *Voltaire.* New York: Harcourt, Brace, and World, 1969.

Bigourdan, M. G. Untitled series of articles, *Comptes rendus* of the Académie des sciences. Vol. 164 (1917), pp. 129–134, 159–162, and 216–220.

Bordo, Susan. *The Flight to Objectivity: Essays on Cartesianism and Culture.* Albany: State University of New York Press, 1987.

Bose, Georg Matthias. *Die Electricität nach ihrer Entdecklung und Fortgang mit poetischer Feder entworffen.* Wittenberg: Ben Johann Joachim Ublfelden, 1744.

————. *Hypothesis soni perraultiana.* Leipzig: Typographica Breitkofiana, 1734.

————. *Tentamina electrica.* Wittenberg, 1744.

Brewster, David. *Memoirs of the Life, Writings, and Discoveries of Sir Isaac Newton.* 2 vols. Edinburgh, 1855.

Brice, Germain. *A New Description of Paris.* Trans. from French. London, 1687.

Brown, Harcourt. *Scientific Organizations in Seventeenth Century France (1620–1680).* Baltimore: Wilkins and Wilkins, 1934.

Brugmans, Henri, ed. *Le Séjour de Christiaan Huygens à Paris et ses relations avec les milieux scientifiques français.* Paris: Andre, 1935.

Brunet, Pierre. *L'Introduction des théories de Newton en France au XVIIIe siècle.* Paris: Blanchard, 1931.

————. *Maupertuis.* Paris: Blanchard, 1929.

Cassini, J.-D. *Mémoires pour servir à l'histoire des sciences et à celle de l'Observatoire de Paris.* Paris: Bleuet, 1810.

Cassirer, Ernst. *The Philosophy of the Enlightenment.* Trans. Fritz C. A. Koelin and James Pettegrove. New York: Beacon Press, 1951.

Châtelet-Lomont, Gabrielle Émilie du. *Dissertation sur la nature du feu.* Paris: Prault, 1744.

————. *Institutions de physique.* Paris, 1740.

————. *Principes mathématiques de la philosophie naturelle.* Paris: Desaint & Saillant and Lambert, 1756.

Chipman, R. A. "An Unpublished Letter of Stephen Gray on Electrical Experiments, 1707–1708." *Isis* 49 (1954), pp. 33–40.

Clerselier, Claude, ed., *Oeuvres posthumes de M Rohault.* Paris, 1682.

Cohen, I. Bernard. *The Birth of a New Physics.* New York: Anchor, 1960.

Colbert, Jean Baptiste. *Lettres, instructions, et mémoires de Colbert.* Ed. P. Clément. 5 vols. Paris: Imprimerie royale, 1868.

Cole, E. J. *A History of Comparative Anatomy from Aristotle to the Eighteenth Century.* London: Macmillan, 1944.

Collas, Georges. *Jean Chapelain, 1595–1674.* Paris: Perrin, 1912.

Corneille, Pierre. *Seven Plays.* Trans. Samuel Solomon. New York: Random House, 1969.

Corson, David. "Pierre Polinière, Francis Hauksbee, and Electroluminescence: A Case of Simultaneous Discovery." *Isis* 59, (1968), pp. 402–403.

Denonain, Jean-Jacques. "Les Problems de l'honnête homme vers 1635: *Religio Medici* et les *Conferences* du Bureau d'adresse." *Etudes Anglaises* 18 (1965), pp. 235–257.

Desaguliers, John Theophilus. *A Course of Experimental Philosophy.* 2 vols. London, 1734–1744; 2d ed., corrected, London, 1745.

———. *Lectures of Experimental Philosophy.* "2d ed.," transcribed by Paul Dawson. London, 1719.

———. *Physico-Mechanical Lectures, or, an Account of What Is Explained and Demonstrated in the Course of Mechanical and Experimental Philosophy.* London, 1717.

Descartes, René. *Discourse on Method, Optics, Geometry, and Meteorology.* Trans. Paul Olscamp. New York: Bobbs-Merrill, 1965.

———. *Geométrie.* Facsimile of the 1637 edition, with facing translation by David Eugene Smith and Marcia L. Latham, published as *The Geometry of René Descartes.* New York: Dover, 1954.

———. *Lettres.* Ed. Claude Clerselier. Paris, 1657; edition nouvelle, 3 vols. bound as 2, 1666–1667.

———. *Le monde, ou traité de la lumière.* Trans. and intro. M. S. Mahoney, with a facsimile of the 1677 ed. New York: Abaris Books, 1979.

———. *Oeuvres de Descartes.* Ed. Charles Adam and Paul Tannery. 13 vols. Paris: Cerf, 1897–1913.

———. *The Philosophical Works of Descartes.* Ed. and trans. Elisabeth Haldane and G. R. T. Ross. Cambridge: Cambridge University Press, 1911.

———. *Principles of Philosophy.* Trans. Blair Reynolds. Lewiston, N.Y./Queenston, Ont.: Edwin Mellen Press, 1988.

Dick, Steven J. *Plurality of Worlds: The Origins of the Extraterrestrial Debate from Democritus to Kant.* New York: Cambridge University Press, 1982.

Ehrman, Esther. *Mme du Châtelet.* Dover, N.H.: Berg, 1986.

Fabré, Antoine. *Chapelain et nos deux premières académies.* Paris: Perrin, 1890.

———. *Les Ennemis de Chapelain.* 2 vols. Paris: Thorin et fils, 1897.

Fontenelle, Bernard le Bouvier. *Conversations on the Plurality of Worlds.* London, 1757.

———. *Entretiens sur la pluralité des mondes.* Ed. Robert M. Shackleton. Oxford: Clarendon Press, 1955.

———. *Histoire de l'Académie royale des sciences, 1666–1699.* 10 vols. Paris, 1730.

Franklin, Benjamin. *Autobiography.* New Haven: Yale University Press, 1964.
———. *Experiments and Observations on Electricity.* Ed. I. Bernard Cohen. Cambridge: Harvard University Press, 1941.
Frédérix, Pierre. *Monsieur René Descartes et son temps.* Paris: Gallimard, 1959.
Gabbey, Allen. "Huygens and Mechanics," *Studies on Christiaan Huygens.* Lisse: Swets & Zeitlinger, 1980, pp. 166–199.
Gay, Peter. *The Enlightenment: An Interpretation.* 2 vols. New York: Knopf, 1966–1969.
George, A. J. "A Seventeenth-Century Amateur of Science: Jean Chapelain," *Annals of Science* 3 (1938), pp. 217–236.
Gibson, Wendy. *Women in Seventeenth-Century France.* New York: St. Martin's Press, 1989.
Gillispie, Charles Coulston. *Science and Polity in France at the End of the Old Regime.* Princeton: Princeton University Press, 1980.
Gillispie, Charles Coulston, ed. *Dictionary of Scientific Biography.* 16 vols. New York: Scribner, 1970–1980.
Gravesande, Willem Jacob 's. *Physices elementa mathematica, experimentis confirmata, sive, introductio ad philosophiam Newtonianam.* 2 vols. Leyden, 1720–1721.
Gray, Stephen. "Letter to Cromwell Mortimer, Containing Several Experiments Concerning Electricity," *Philosophical Transactions of the Royal Society of London,* vol. 37 (1731), pp. 18–44.
Grimarest, Jean-Leonor Le Gallois, sieur de. *Vie de Monsieur Molière.* 1705. Reprint, Paris, 1930.
Hackmann, Willem D. *Electricity from Glass: The History of the Frictional Electrical Machine, 1600–1850.* Alphen aan den Rijn, The Netherlands: Sijthoff & Noordhoff, 1978.
Halleys, André, *Les Perraults.* Paris: Perrin, 1926.
Hankins, Thomas L. *Jean D'Alembert: Science and the Enlightenment.* Oxford: Clarendon Press, 1970.
———. *Science and the Enlightenment.* New York: Cambridge University Press, 1985.
Harth, Erica. *Cartesian Women.* Ithaca: Cornell University Press, 1992.
———. *Ideology and Culture in Seventeenth-Century France.* Ithaca: Cornell University Press, 1983.
Hauksbee, Francis. *Physico-Mechanical Experiments on Various Subjects.* London: R. Burgis, 1709.
Heilbron, J. L. *Electricity in the Seventeenth and Eighteenth Centuries: A Study of Early Modern Physics.* Berkeley: University of California Press, 1979.
———. *Elements of Early Modern Physics.* Berkeley: University of California Press, 1982.
Helden, Albert van. "Annulao Cingitur: The Solution to the Problem of Saturn," *Journal for the History of Astronomy* 5 (1974), pp. 155–174.
Hempel, Carl. *Aspects of Scientific Explanation.* New York: Free Press, 1966.
———. *Philosophy of Natural Science.* New York: Prentice-Hall, 1966.
Hoffheimer, Michael H. "Maupertuis and the Eighteenth-Century Critique of Preexistence," *Journal of the History of Biology* 15 (1982), pp. 119–144.
Hooke, Robert. *Micrographia: or, some physiological descriptions of minute bodies made by magnifying glasses.* London, 1665.

Hooker, Michael, ed. *Descartes: Critical and Interpretive Essays.* Baltimore: Johns Hopkins University Press, 1978.

Huygens, Christiaan. *The Celestial Worlds Discovered.* 1st English ed., London: Timothy Childe, 1698. Reprint, London: Frank Cass, 1968.

———. *Oeuvres complètes de Christiaan Huygens, publiées par la Société hollandaise des sciences.* 22 vols. The Hague, 1880–1950.

Iltis, Carolyn. See Carolyn Merchant.

Jacob, Margaret C. *The Cultural Meaning of the Scientific Revolution.* New York: Knopf, 1988.

Jaki, Stanley L. *Planets and Planetarians: A History of Theories of the Origin of Planetary Systems.* New York: Wiley, [1978].

Koyré, Alexandre. *From the Closed World to the Infinite Universe.* New York: Harper, 1958.

Kuhn, Thomas S. *The Copernican Revolution: Planetary Astronomy in the Development of Western Thought.* Cambridge: Harvard University Press, 1957.

———. *The Structure of Scientific Revolutions.* Chicago: University of Chicago Press, 1964.

Landes, David S. *Revolution in Time: Clocks and the Making of the Modern World.* Cambridge: Harvard University Press, 1983.

Launay, Louis de. *Descartes.* Paris: Payot, 1923.

Levine, Joseph. *Dr. Woodward's Shield: History, Science, and Satire in Augustan England.* Berkeley: University of California Press, 1977.

Lister, Martin. *A Journey to Paris in the Year 1698.* 3d London ed., 1699. Reprint, Urbana: University of Illinois Press, 1967.

Locke, John. *Essay Concerning Human Understanding.* Oxford: Clarendon Press, 1975.

Lodge, Lee Davis. *A Study in Corneille.* 1891. Reprint, New York: Burt Franklin, 1970.

Lougee, Carolyn. *Le Paradis des femmes: Women, Salons, and Social Stratification in Seventeenth-Century France.* Princeton: Princeton University Press, 1976.

Maland, David. *Culture and Society in Seventeenth-Century France.* New York: Charles Scribner's Sons, 1970.

Marsak, L. "Bernard de Fontenelle: The Idea of Science in the French Enlightenment." *Transactions of the American Philosophical Society,* n.s. vol. 49 (1959), pp. 1–64.

Menjot d'Elbenne, Samuel. *Madame de la Salbière, ses pensées chrétiennes, et ses lettres à l'abbé Rancé.* Paris: Plon, 1923.

Merchant, Carolyn. *The Death of Nature: Women, Ecology, and the Scientific Revolution.* New York: Harper and Row, 1980.

———. [Carolyn Iltis]. "The Leibnizian-Newtonian Debates: Natural Philosophy and Social Psychology." *British Journal for the History of Science* 4 (1973), pp. 343–377.

Middleton, W. E. Knowles. *The History of the Theories of Rain and Other Forms of Precipitation.* London: Oldbourne, 1965.

Mongrédien, Georges. *Madelaine de Scudéry et son salon.* Paris: Tallandier, 1946.

Morse, JoAnn. "The Reintroduction of Diophantus' *Algebra* in the Renaissance." Ph.D. dissertation, Princeton University, 1981.

Mouy, Paul. *Le Développement de la physique cartésienne, 1646–1712*. Paris: Vrin, 1934.

Musschenbroek, Petrus van. *The Elements of Natural Philosophy*. Trans. John Colson. London: J. Nourse, 1744.

———. *Essay de physique*. Paris, 1739.

Needham, Turberville. "Letter from Mr. Turberville Needham, Concerning Some New Electrical Experiments Lately Made at Paris." *Philosophical Transactions of the Royal Society of London* 44 (1746), pp. 247–263.

Niderst, Alain. *Fontenelle à la recherche de lui-même*. Paris: Nizet, 1972.

Nollet, Jean Antoine. *Essai sur l'électricité des corps*. Paris: Guerin, 1746.

———. *Leçons de physique expérimentale*. 6 vols. Paris: Guerin, 1745–1764.

———. *Lettres sur l'électricité*. 3 vols. Paris: Guerin, 1753–1764.

———. *Programme ou idée générale d'un cours de physique experimentale, avec un catalogue raisonné des instrumens qui servent aux expériences*. Paris, 1738.

———. *Recherches sur les causes particuliers des phénoménes électriques*. Paris: Guerin, 1749.

Oldenburg, Henry. *The Correspondence of Henry Oldenburg*. Ed. A. Rupert Hall and Marie Boas Hall. 13 vols. Madison: University of Wisconsin Press, 1965–1978.

Perrault, Charles. *Recueil de plusieurs machines de nouvelle invention*. Paris, 1700.

Perrault, Claude. *Essais de physique, ou récueil de plusieurs traités touchant des choses naturelles*. 3 vols. Paris, 1680.

———. *Oeuvres diverses de physique et de mechanique*. Leyden, 1712.

Pierre Gassendi: Sa vie et son oeuvre. Paris: Editions Alain Michel, 1955.

Pitard, René. *Le Libertinage erudit*. 2 vols. Paris: Boivin, 1943.

Polinière, Pierre. *Expériences de physique*. Paris, 1709; 2d ed., 2 vols. Paris, 1734.

Popper, Karl. *The Logic of Scientific Discovery*. New York: Basic Books, 1959.

Priestley, Joseph. The *History and Present State of Electricity*. London: Dodsley, 1767.

Recueil general des questions traitees és conferences de Bureau d'adresse, sur toutes sortes de matieres, par les plus belles esprits de ce temps. 5 vols. Paris: I. B. Loyson, 1658–1660.

Robinson, Eric, and A. E. Musson. *James Watt and the Steam Revolution*. London, 1969.

Robertson, D. Maclaren. *A History of the French Academy*. New York: G. W. Dillingham, 1910.

Rohault, Jacques. *Oeuvres posthumes de M Rohault*. Paris, 1682.

———. *A System of Natural Philosophy*. Trans. John Clarke. 2 vols. 1723; Reprint, New York: Johnson Reprint Corp., 1969.

Rorty, Richard. *Philosophy and the Mirror of Nature*. Princeton: Princeton University Press, 1979.

Saverien, Alexandre. *Histoire des philosophes modernes*. 6 vols. Paris, 1768.

Schiebinger, Londa. "Maria Winkelmann at the Berlin Academy: A Turning Point for Women in Science," *Isis* (1987), pp. 174–200.

———. *The Mind Has No Sex?: Women in the Origins of Modern Science*. Cambridge: Harvard University Press, 1989.

Schiller, Joseph. "Laboratoires d'anatomie et de botanique à l'Académie des sciences au XVIIe siècle." *Revue d'histoire des science* 17 (1964), pp. 97–114.

Shapin, Steven, and Simon Shaffer. *The Leviathan and the Air Pump: Hobbes, Boyle, and the Experimental Life.* Princeton: Princeton University Press, 1985.

Shea, William. *The Magic of Numbers and Motion: The Scientific Career of René Descartes.* Canton, Mass.: Science History Publications, 1991.

Solomon, Howard M. *Public Welfare, Science, and Propaganda in Seventeenth-Century France: The Innovation of Theophraste Renaudot.* Princeton: Princeton University Press, 1972.

Somaize, Antoine Baudeau de. *Le Dictionnaire des précieuses.* Ed. C.-L. Livet. 2 vols. Paris: Janet, 1856.

Spink, John S. *French Free-Thought from Gassendi to Voltaire.* London: Althone Press, 1960.

Stroup, Alice. *A Company of Scientists: Botany, Patronage, and Community at the Seventeenth-Century Parisian Royal Academy of Sciences.* Berkeley: University of California Press, 1990.

Sutton, Geoffrey V. "The Politics of Science in Early Napoleonic France: The Case of the Voltaic Pile," *Historical Studies in the Physical Sciences* 11 (1981), pp. 329–366.

———. "Science for a Polite Society: Cartesian Natural Philosophy in Paris During the Reigns of Louis XIII and XIV." Ph.D. dissertation, Princeton University, 1982.

Taton, René, ed. *Huygens et la France.* Paris: Vrin, 1982.

Terrall, Mary. "Representing the Earth's Shape: The Polemics Surrounding Maupertuis' Expedition to Lapland." *Isis* 83 (1992), pp. 218–237.

Torlais, Jean. *Un Physicien au siècle des lumières: L'Abbé Nollet, 1700–1770.* Paris: Sipuco, 1954.

Truesdell, Clifford. *Essays in the History of Mechanics.* New York: Springer, 1968.

———. "A Program Toward Rediscovering the Rational Mechanics in the Age of Reason." *Archive for the History of the Exact Sciences* 1 (1960), pp. 3–36.

Vincent, Leon H. *Hôtel de Rambouillet and the précieuses.* New York: Houghton, Mifflin, 1900.

Voltaire. *Voltaire's Correspondence.* Ed. Theodore Besterman. 101 vols. Geneva: Institut et Musée Voltaire, 1953–1977.

———. *Lettres philosophiques, ou Lettres anglaises.* Ed. Raymond Naves. Paris: Éditions Garnier Frères, 1964.

———. *Oeuvres complètes de Voltaire.* 43 vols. Paris: Garnier Frères, 1877–1885.

———. *The Works of Voltaire.* Trans. William F. Fleming. 42 vols. Paris: E. R. DuMont, 1901.

Vrooman, Jack R. *René Descartes: A Biography.* New York: Putnam, 1970.

Waard, C. de. *Journal tenu par Isaac Beeckman de 1604 à 1634.* The Hague: Nijhoff, 1939–1953.

Wade, Ira O. *The Intellectual Origins of the French Enlightenment.* Princeton: Princeton University Press, 1971.

———. *Voltaire and Madame du Châtelet: An Essay on the Intellectual Activity at Cirey.* Princeton: Princeton University Press, 1941.

Weber, J. P. "Sur la composition de la Regula IV de Descartes," *Revue philosophique de la France et l'étranger,* no. 154 (1964).

Westfall, Richard S. *The Construction of Modern Science: Mechanisms and Mechanics.* New York: Wiley, 1971.

Winkler, Johann Heinrich. "Essai sur la nature, les effets et les causes de l'électricité." *Recueil de traités sur l'électricité traduits de l'allemand et de l'anglois.* Paris, 1748.

———. *Die Starke der electrischen Kraft des Wassers in glasernen Gefassen.* Leipzig: Breitkopf, 1746.

Wolf, Charles. *Histoire de l'Observatoire de Paris de sa fondation à 1793.* Paris: Gauthier-Villars, 1902.

About the Book
and Author

Traditional accounts of the scientific revolution focus on such thinkers as Copernicus, Galileo, and Newton, and usually portray it as a process of steady, rational
progress. There is another side to this story, and its protagonists are more likely to be
women than men, dilettante aristocrats than highly educated natural philosophers.
The setting is not the laboratory, but rather the literary salons of seventeenth- and
eighteenth-century France, and the action takes place sometime between Europe's
last great witch hunts and the emergence of the modern world.

Science for a Polite Society is an intriguing reexamination of the social, cultural, and
intellectual context of the origins of modern science. The elite of French society accepted science largely because of their personal involvement and fascination with the
emerging "philosophy of nature." Members of salon society, especially women, were
avid readers of works of natural philosophy and active participants in experiments for
the edification of their peers. Some of these women went on to champion the new science and played a significant role in securing its acceptance by polite society.

Sutton points out that the sheer entertainment value of startling displays of electricity and chemical explosions would have played an important role in persuading
the skeptical. We can only imagine the effects of such drawing-room experiments on
an audience that lived in a world illuminated by tallow candles. For many, leaping
electrical arcs and window-rattling detonations must have been as convincing as
Newton's mathematically elegant description of the motions of the planets.

With the acceptance and triumph of the new science came a prestige that made it a
model of what rationality should be. The Enlightenment adopted the methods of scientific thought as the model for human progress. To be an "enlightened" thinker
meant believing that the application of scientific methods could reform political and
economic life, to the lasting benefit of humanity. We live with the ambiguous results
of that legacy even today, although in our own century we are perhaps more impressed by the ability of science to frighten, rather than to awe and entertain.

Geoffrey V. Sutton teaches at Macalester College.

Index

Absolutism, 143, 144, 156, 157, 161, 163–165, 186, 192, 249, 251, 252, 287

Académie française, 41, 43–51, 57, 110, 111, 119, 145, 242, 351(n31)

Académie royale des sciences
  Fontenelle and, 145, 164, 170, 278
  foundation, 119, 121–123, 141, 155, 157, 358(nn 36, 37)
  as *gloire*, 129, 130, 185, 342
  gravity discussed at, 131, 132
  Histoire des animaux, 124–126
  image in polite culture, 139, 175, 224, 256, 257
  members, 174, 181, 223, 228, 242, 244, 246, 247, 258, 267, 276, 296, 314, 343, 358(nn 36, 37), 359(nn 43, 44)
  politics in, 256, 265, 274, 282, 284
  prizes offered by, 253, 255, 266
  reorganization of 1699, 144, 164, 166, 167
  work of, 136, 178, 179, 181, 184, 185, 203, 206, 231, 234, 245, 257, 268, 280, 312, 313, 327

Air Pump. *See* Vacuum pump

Alembert. *See* d'Alembert, Jean Le Rond

Algarotti, Francesco, 257, 258

Algebra, 3, 4, 63, 94, 167, 170

Anatomy, 22, 60, 64, 123–126, 130, 140, 166, 244

Anomalous suspension, 134, 135, 289, 298, 361(n72)

Apothecaries, 22, 33, 140

Ardinghelli, Maria-Angela, 328

Aristotelian
  categories, 25, 33
  cosmology, 30

literary theory, 47, 49, 50

philosophy, 20, 24, 26, 35, 42, 52, 56, 58, 71, 89, 104, 138

school, 29, 30, 34, 66, 81, 137, 147, 281

See also Elements, Aristotelian

Aristotle, 20, 21, 25, 26, 29, 31, 35, 37, 47, 49, 50, 54, 66, 72, 137

Arnauld, Antoine, 82

Astronomy, 1, 3, 4, 9, 24, 35–37, 39, 41, 51, 109, 112, 113, 120, 121, 138, 160, 165, 166, 170–174, 181, 209, 211, 238, 239, 250, 260, 266–269, 272, 273, 283, 292, 339, 340. *See also* Comets; Copernican system; Gravity; Sun; Sunspots; Telescope; Tides

Attraction
  Aristotelian, 71
  electrical, 291–296, 299, 300, 309, 313, 321, 322
  gravitational, 236, 245, 266, 268, 270, 272, 273, 275
  magnetic, 107
  of seminal materials, 265

Auzout, Adrien, 120, 121, 135, 139, 140, 150, 358(n36)

Bachet, Claude–Gaspard, 170

Bacon, Francis, 4, 20, 250, 253, 254, 352(n44)

Bailly, Jean Sylvain, 145

Balzac, J. L. Guez de, 57

Beeckman, Isaac, 56, 58

Behn, Aphra, 361(n2)

Bernoulli, Daniel, 260, 270

Bernoulli, Jocob, 181–184, 205, 206, 255, 261, 266, 291, 339

Bérulle, Pierre de, cardinal, 58–60